THE MUSIC BUSINESS—
A LEGAL PERSPECTIVE

THE MUSIC BUSINESS— A LEGAL PERSPECTIVE

Music and Live Performances

PETER MULLER

Q
QUORUM BOOKS
Westport, Connecticut • London

Library of Congress Cataloging-in-Publication Data

Muller, Peter.
The music business—a legal perspective : music and live performances / Peter Muller.
p. cm.
Includes bibliographical references and index.
ISBN 0–89930–702–7 (alk. paper)
1. Copyright—Music—United States. 2. Music trade—Law and legislation—United States. I. Title.
KF3035.M85 1994
346.7304'82—dc20
[347.306482] 93–18523

British Library Cataloguing in Publication Data is available.

Library of Congress Catalog Card Number: 93–18523
ISBN: 0–89930–702–7

First published in 1994

Quorum Books, 88 Post Road West, Westport, CT 06881
An imprint of Greenwood Publishing Group, Inc.

Printed in the United States of America

The paper used in this book complies with the Permanent Paper Standard issued by the National Information Standards Organization (Z39.48–1984).

10 9 8 7 6 5 4 3 2 1

To
Esther
Richard, Chloe, Aur

Contents

Acknowledgments ix

Introduction xi

1. The Personal Management Agreement 1
2. The Agency Agreement 16
3. The Songwriter/Publisher Agreement 27
4. The Co-Publishing Agreement 53
5. The Administration Agreement 67
6. The Recording Agreement 78
7. The Artist/Producer Agreement 102
8. The Artist Side Letter Agreement between the Artist and the Producer 117
9. The Performing Rights Society Agreement 127
10. The Mechanical License Agreement 137
11. The Licensing Agreement 148
12. The Print Rights Agreement 169
13. The Film Producer/Composer Agreement 180
14. The Synchronization License 200
15. The Foreign License Agreement 217

16. The Tour Merchandising Agreement 233

17. The Artist Agreement for Commercials, Advertising, and Personal Appearances 257

18. The Lounge Act Agreement 273

19. The License Agreement for Mass Market Distribution of Artist's Recordings 284

20. The Tour Sponsorship Agreement 298

21. Copyright 319

Appendixes 321

Bibliography 350

Index 353

ACKNOWLEDGMENTS

The writing of *The Music Business—A Legal Perspective* was a task that involved the invaluable assistance of lawyers, law students, and the staff of several law libraries. I am grateful for their help. I would like to thank Steve Schiffman for his help in editing the manuscript, and I would particularly like to thank James Sabin and the wonderful group of professionals at Greenwood Publishing and Quorum Books who believed in the project and helped guide it to its completion.

I would especially like to express my gratitude to all the wonderful friends and clients I have made in the entertainment industry. They know who they are. Their talent, professionalism, and companionship have contributed to the many enriching times I have had as a member of this industry.

The information in this book is meant for reference only. Please consult with an attorney of your own choice prior to finalizing any agreements and contracts based on the information you have received in *The Music Business—A Legal Perspective*.

Introduction

The music business is a collection of talented performers, songwriters, producers, agents, attorneys, record company executives, publishers, and managers working in collaboration and harmony to make and distribute the very finest musical product available. Each final composition on each recording is a tribute to their efforts.

The music business is exactly what the words indicate—a blend of the art of making music and the art of selling music. It is a business where both ends, the creative and commercial, must work together if either is to succeed. While the musical composition is the melodious chord that binds together all those who contribute to the creation of a composition, it is the legal agreement which clarifies each person's obligations and responsibilities. It is that same agreement which spells out the rewards to be achieved.

The legal agreement is much more than a mere collection of words and definitions. It is a mirror of the character of the musical industry at the time of its writing. It chronicles the state of art that has been reached at particular points in time—from vinyl recordings to audiotapes to CDs. Legal contracts mark the introduction of the music video and chart its growth from a promotional medium to a commercial vehicle in its own right. The legal contract heralds the introduction of laser disks, and it acquaints musicians with the computer age through CD-ROMs and CD-Is. The legal agreement, like the musical industry itself, is prepared to evolve and embrace the future.

The Music Business—A Legal Perspective intends to introduce you to the major agreements prevalent in the recording industry. Through the agreements, you can get a glimpse of the many components that make up the creation, development, and distribution of a musical composition.

The recording industry is a worldwide business, but it is local and very personal in its creation and origin. It all starts with a melody. The music business has the room to accept all who are truly motivated to add a song and a tune to the world. I hope that *The Music Business—A Legal Perspective* will help you realize your dreams.

THE MUSIC BUSINESS—
A LEGAL PERSPECTIVE

1

The Personal Management Agreement

The personal management agreement is arguably one of the first agreements that the artist will enter in his or her professional career. The personal manager's primary function is to guide and advise the artist in the development and enhancement of his or her musical career.

It is often the personal manager who, at the outset of the artist's career, singularly believes in the artist's talent and ability to succeed as a musical performer. Relying on his or her relationships, experience, and expertise in the entertainment business, the personal manager will usually assist the artist in the following matters:

- selecting material for a recording or for a live performance,
- developing the artist's relationship with a record company,
- selecting support personnel, including accountants, lawyers, record producers, and booking or talent agents,
- expanding the artist's talents into ancillary industries, including motion pictures, television, computer software, and emerging technologies, and
- selecting additional band members.

In general, the personal manager's fundamental goal is to help the artist secure opportunities in the entertainment business and establish a successful career as an artist.

Presently, there are few licensing procedures required of a personal manager before the manager can perform the functions of the profession. It is, in many instances, a self-regulated industry, which establishes credibility on hard work, previous successes, reputation, and trust. The National Conference of Personal

Managers (NCPM) is the recognized professional association for personal managers.

Personal managers may specialize in a particular form of music. One may confine his or her expertise to classical music while another may manage a roster of rock and roll musicians, while yet another may specialize in country and western.

PARTIES

The personal manager and the artist would normally be cited as parties to the personal management agreement, including their corporate or business names and any pseudonyms or stage names. Since an artist may be identified solely by a stage name, the agreement may require that the artist include his or her social security number as a means of positive identification. The social security number acts as a personal finger print, minimizing any potential confusion in the event of any future legal claim or action.

The agreement should also include both parties' mailing addresses, to facilitate the delivery of notices and other required documents.

DUTIES

The personal management agreement is, in essence, an agreement in which the artist retains the personal manager to perform specific functions and duties.

The primary duty of the personal manager is, most often, to give the artist advice, guidance, and counsel in the development and enhancement of the artist's professional career in the entertainment industry. The artist's professional career may include his or her employment as a musician, composer, arranger, publisher, performing artist, actor, writer, and director.

The personal manager may also expand and develop the artist's career into different areas of the entertainment industry as the artist's popularity advances and flourishes and as the entertainment business extends into new and previously undiscovered avenues.

Representation in Negotiations

The personal manager, as the artist's business representative, would often be called upon to represent the artist in his or her professional negotiations, which may include advising and fixing terms that regulate the use, employment, and commercial exploitation of the artist in all aspects of the entertainment industry. The personal manager may also be asked to advise the artist's employers, including record labels, music video directors, and motion picture producers, how to utilize the artist's talents in such a manner that would best serve the artist.

Availability

Customarily, the personal manager would agree to make himself or herself available to meet and counsel the artist at all reasonable times and places, in connection with matters relating to the artist's professional career.

Additional Personnel

In most cases, the personal manager's duties would include assisting the artist in selecting, engaging, and discharging additional personnel integral to the development of the artist's career in the entertainment industry, including booking agents, business managers, publicists, accountants, attorneys, record producers, promoters, engineers, technical crew, and "roadies," or road managers.

Band Members

As an additional function, the personal manager may be asked to assist the artist in selecting band members for the artist's musical group, including back-up singers, lead guitar, bass, keyboard, and horn players.

Advertising and Promotion

The personal manager would typically be granted the right to approve, for the purpose of trade, advertising and publicity, the use, reproduction, distribution, and commercial exploitation of the artist's name, likeness, photograph, image, and voice. An additional duty of the personal manager may be to assist the artist in the selection of the material utilized in album recording or stage performances, including props, light shows, and stage designs. The personal manager may also help construct the "look" of the artist, the image that the artist intends to portray to the public.

Relationship with Record Companies

Based on the personal manager's experience and expertise in the recording industry, and his or her knowledge of show business, the personal manager's duties would typically include advising, counseling, and guiding the artist in the development of his or her relationship with record companies. The personal manager may act as liaison between the artist and the record company as well as between the artist and all applicable trade unions and guilds.

The personal manager would also help negotiate record deals, including the royalty payments the artist is to receive as compensation, and the promotional strategies the record company intends to implement, including the production of music videos and tours. As a rule, the personal manager would also assist in the promotion of the artist in time with the release of each album.

Some of the duties which the personal manager typically performs during a recording release include the placement and proper display in record retail stores of point-of-purchase promotion materials, including life-size figures of the artist. The personal manager may also be required to meet with radio station program managers and negotiate for proper radio exposure for the artist.

Music Video

The personal manager would usually negotiate with music video directors and help to script and stage music videos that would be most beneficial to the development and enhancement of the artist's career.

Business Advisor, In General

In essence, the personal manager's duties are to be the artist's business advisor and partner so that together, as a coordinated team, they can develop the artist's career most effectively.

The artist's business manager, as opposed to the personal manager, is often an accountant who typically concerns himself or herself with the artist's ongoing economic goals and tax planning.

PERSONAL MANAGER NOT AN AGENT

The personal management agreement should clarify the distinction between the duties of the personal manager and the duties most often associated with a booking or talent agent. In many states, only a booking agent licensed by that state has the capacity and legal capability to seek and procure employment for the artist. Most states deal severely with an individual, including a personal manager, who engages in procuring employment for an artist, such as booking the artist into clubs and venues without the proper license.

In the event of a lawsuit in which it is held that the personal manager overstepped his or her legal capacities and breached his or her fiduciary relationship with the artist, it is probable that the personal manager would forfeit all commissions he or she earned as a result of the unlicensed booking.

New York Law, under General Business Law sec. 171, permits occasional talent booking by the personal manager "where such business only incidentally involves the selling of employment thereof. . . . " It is important, though, for the personal manager to carefully consider the advisability of securing employment for the artist. In California, while only a licensed agent can secure employment for the artist, Labor Code sec. 1700 specifically provides that no employment agency license is needed for a personal manager to obtain a recording contract for the client.

In order to place the artist on notice regarding what functions the personal manager can and cannot perform under the legal guidelines of the state, the agreement should clarify, in precise language, that the personal manager is not an agent, has not indicated that he or she is an agent, will not perform the functions of an agent, and will not seek or procure employment for the artist. The personal manager's function, it should be stipulated, is to secure and represent the artist with the agent who, in turn, would be permitted to secure employment for the artist.

NONEXCLUSIVITY

In most cases, the personal manager would be free to represent other artists in the music and recording field, even though those third-party artists have talents which are similar to those of the artist and therefore may conflict with those of the artist. In addition, the personal manager would usually not be required to spend all of his or her professional time exclusively in the furtherance of the artist's musical career.

EXCLUSIVITY

The artist would typically be represented exclusively by the personal manager and would normally obligate himself or herself to utilize his or her best efforts to perform those functions necessary to best perform the obligations accepted when entering the personal management agreement.

ARTIST TO SEEK ADVICE OF PERSONAL MANAGER

The artist would, as a rule, stipulate that he or she would seek advice, counsel, and guidance from the personal manager alone and would not engage the services of any other manager or representative to perform similar services and functions as the personal manager. In addition, the artist would usually assert that he or she would not perform the personal manager's functions and would therefore not negotiate, accept, or agree to any agreement concerning his or her career in the entertainment business without first securing the personal manager's written consent.

DELEGATION OF DUTIES

While the services rendered by the artist are unique and nontransferable, the personal manager would typically argue that his or her services should not be considered unique. The personal manager may therefore demand the right to delegate some or all of his or her duties and responsibilities to a third party.

The artist would normally argue that he or she entered the agreement with the personal manager based on the following:

- the personal manager's performances in the past,
- the personal manager's accumulated respect in the musical industry, and
- the personal manager's expertise and knowledge.

Since the personal manager is, in essence, the key reason behind the artist's acceptance of the personal management agreement, the artist may protest the personal manager's decision to delegate his or her obligations to a third party.

ASSIGNMENT

The personal manager may negotiate for the right to assign the agreement to another personal management company. While the artist may disapprove of such an assignment initially, he or she might consent to the assignment on one of the following conditions:

- the personal manager become a part of the third-party management company and be responsible for the management of the artist's career,
- the personal manager assign the agreement to a management company of similar stature in the music industry, or
- the personal manager assign the agreement to a company owned in whole or in part by the personal manager.

The party with the stronger bargaining position would usually prevail in the negotiations involving the right of assignment.

ATTORNEY-IN-FACT

A provision in the agreement which should be considered carefully is the one granting the personal manager the power of attorney to negotiate, execute, and approve all types of agreements and financial arrangements on behalf of the artist in regard to the artist's career in the entertainment industry. This provision may be drafted as narrowly, or as broadly, as negotiated by the parties.

The personal manager would typically negotiate for a broad power, arguing that it would be in the best interests of the artist that the personal manager perform all such business functions without losing time or subjugating the artist to the details of the business deal.

The personal manager may request the irrevocable right to be the artist's lawful attorney-in-fact, with the right to make, execute, and deliver all contracts and agreements in the artist's name. In addition, the personal manager may claim the right to receive all claims, money, revenues, and earnings which may be due and owing the artist. The personal manager may be permitted the right to execute and deliver releases, to defend, settle, compromise, litigate, or submit to arbitration any and all actions, suits, claims, and demands in a manner that he or she alone deems advisable. The artist would usually be required to refrain from performing those functions granted to the personal manager by the power of attorney unless the personal manager agrees to share those rights in a signed writing.

The artist would usually prefer that the rights granted to the personal manager by the power of attorney be limited to specific functions, such as making and executing live performance agreements only if the artist is more than an agreed number of miles from the venue.

COMPENSATION

The compensation the personal manager would be entitled to receive in exchange for his or her services and functions under the agreement are typically based upon a percentage of the artist's earnings in the entertainment business. Generally, the percentage would be between 15 and 25 percent of the artist's gross revenues, though it may differ, based on negotiations between the parties.

In most cases, the personal manager would receive his or her compensation directly from the artist or would retain his or her compensation from the artist's gross revenues and receipts.

If so agreed, the personal manager would be entitled to a commission based on all income derived and relating to the artist's professional career in the entertainment business. In order to define with exactitude the derivation of such compensation, the agreement should clarify what is meant by the "entertainment industry."

Definition of "Entertainment Industry"

Typically, the entertainment industry would include recordings, video, radio, books and other literary material, computer software, CD-ROM, CD-I, digital and laser technology, communications satellite, merchandising, virtual reality, endorsements, music publishing, motion picture, television, cable, legitimate theatre, advertising, and any and all other similar fields now known or to be devised at any time in the future.

Compensation Based on "Gross Revenues"

The compensation earned by the personal manager would generally be based on the gross revenues accrued to, or received by, the artist during the following periods of time:

- the term of the agreement,
- all extensions or modifications of the agreement,
- following the termination of the agreement resulting from all services performed by the artist during the term of the agreement, and

- all agreements substantially negotiated during the term of the agreement and fulfilled by the artist subsequent to the termination of the agreement.

Commissions Following Termination of Agreement

Those contracts, negotiations, and agreements which, following the expiration of the personal management agreement, may be commissioned by the personal manager under the terms of the personal management agreement customarily include but are often not limited to the following:

a) All recording agreements executed or substantially negotiated during the term of the agreement, generating royalties from their sale, license, or commercial exploitation.

b) All songwriting and publishing activities executed or substantially negotiated during the term of the agreement, including mechanical royalties, generating revenues from their commercial exploitation.

c) All television, cable, or motion picture activity performed or substantially performed during the term of the agreement, generating royalties or fees from their sale, license, or commercial exploitation.

d) All agreements regarding videocassette, videodisk, and other forms of media intended for home use, executed or substantially negotiated during the term of the agreement, generating royalties or fees from their commercial exploitation.

e) All merchandising rights executed or substantially negotiated during the term of the agreement, generating royalties or fees from their commercial exploitation.

f) All computer software rights, including CD-ROM and CD-I, executed or substantially negotiated during the term of the agreement, generating royalties or fees from their commercial exploitation.

Definition of "Gross Revenues"

The definition of ''gross revenues'' is central to the agreement. It should be defined clearly so that there is no question as to its scope. ''Gross revenues'' usually is defined as any and all forms of income, earnings, monies, and sums derived from the artist's professional career, without any deductions whatsoever, including but not limited to total compensation, salaries, fees, royalties, residuals, repeat or rerun fees, gifts, bonuses, shares of stock, shares of profit, percentages, real property, personal property, endorsement fees and products, and advances against royalties or any other type, kind, or manner of income or revenue which is reasonably related to the artist's career.

Often, the agreement would stipulate that all expenses, costs, and disbursements incurred in connection with the artist's professional career would be deducted prior to the calculation of the personal manager's compensation under the terms of the agreement.

Deductions from "Gross Revenues"

The personal management agreement may provide for certain definitive deductions from the definition of "gross revenues." The specific deductions are usually a matter of negotiation between the personal manager and the artist.

The deductions may include the following:

a) Recording Costs. In the event the costs of producing a recording are advanced by the record company and are considered an advance against royalty, the artist may argue that such advance should not be commissioned by the personal manager since those costs are usually paid directly to a third party, including record producers and recording studios.

b) Tour Support. If the record company agrees to advance monies to the artist as a means of offsetting expenses related to a tour, those monies may not be subject to the personal manager's compensation.

c) Video Budget. With the popularity of music videos as promotional tools utilized by the record company to commercially exploit the artist's album, the record company may advance the costs of producing such a music video. Those costs are typically not commissioned by the personal manager.

INCORPORATION

The artist may form a corporation during the term of the personal management agreement whose purpose would be to exploit the artist's talents in the entertainment business. The agreement should consider such an eventuality and stipulate that the newly formed corporation would be obligated to enter into a management agreement with the personal manager identical in every respect to this agreement, including the payment to the personal manager of a commission equal in percentage to the commission received under the terms of the agreement.

Tax Requirements Regarding Corporations

The agreement should evaluate the unique tax requirements of the newly formed corporation and consider whether or not the corporate taxes and related expenses should be deducted from the definition of "gross revenues" prior to the personal manager's receiving his or her commission.

Shares of Stock Regarding Corporations

In addition, the agreement should stipulate whether the personal manager would be entitled to receive shares of stock of the artist's corporation equal to the personal manager's percentage of the artist's gross revenues earned as the personal manager's commission.

ADDITIONAL ARTISTS

In the event the artist engages additional artists to perform with him or her as part of a musical band, and such band does perform, record, and engage in the musical business as a musical band, the personal manager may require that the additional members of the musical band enter into management agreements with the personal manager containing the same terms and provisions as contained in the personal management agreement with the artist.

PAYMENT OF FEES RELATED TO ARTIST'S PROFESSIONAL CAREER

The personal manager and the artist may agree that the artist would be solely responsible for the payment of all fees reasonably related to his or her career. Those fees may include booking agency fees, union dues, publicity fees, fees related to promoting and advertising the artist, road managers, back-up musicians and singers, studio rentals, equipment fees, artist-related entertainment, and any and all other costs incurred as a result of the artist's professional career.

If any of those fees are paid in advance by the personal manager, the agreement may stipulate that the artist would be obligated to reimburse those fees promptly upon receipt of a statement from the personal manager or that the personal manager may withhold those fees from the artist's earnings.

General Overhead

General overhead and day-to-day business expenses are standard in any business, including the entertainment business. The personal management agreement may stipulate that all expenses incurred by the personal manager relating to the artist's career are to be paid by the artist. Those expenses typically include long-distance phone calls, telefaxes, mailings and messenger service, legal fees, accounting fees, bookkeeping fees, travel and living expenses when outside of the personal manager's normal place of business, and any and all other general overhead expenses incurred by the personal manager on behalf of the artist.

TERM

The term, or length, of the agreement, is customarily a negotiated provision in the agreement. It would usually be defined as a period of years, commencing on the date of the signing of the agreement.

The agreement may stipulate that following the termination of the initial term, the personal manager would be granted the option of extending the agreement for an additional term of years. The agreement may stipulate that upon rendering to the artist written notice, within a fixed number of weeks prior to the termination of the prior term, of its intention to exercise the option, the option would become effective.

The artist would probably argue for the achievement by the personal manager of a certain performance plateau prior to the manager's being granted the right to exercise the option to extend the agreement for an additional term. Those performance plateaus may include the following:

a) the formalization and execution of a record agreement with a major label,
b) the solicitation of bona fide record or endorsement deals which, even if refused by the artist, were with business entities ready, willing, and able to enter such deals, or
c) the attainment by the artist of agreed gross revenue earnings in the fiscal year prior to the exercise of the option.

BOOKS AND RECORDS

The artist would generally demand that the personal manager maintain accurate books and records pertaining to the subject matter of the agreement—the revenues earned by the artist during the term of the personal management agreement. The personal manager may be required, by the artist, to submit an accounting on a regular basis, perhaps quarterly, semiannually or annually.

Right to Inspect Books

Intending to plot the flow of revenue earned from his or her career, the artist will often negotiate for the right to inspect such books and records following the delivery to the personal manager of a written notice detailing the artist's intention to do so. The personal manager may require that the books and records be inspected by a certified public accountant in the place where the books and records are normally held, during normal business hours, within an agreed time period following the submission of each accounting.

Final Accounting

The personal management agreement may provide that, upon its termination or cessation, a final accounting must be rendered to the artist. The final accounting would generally be accompanied by the payment of the balance, if any, of any and all payments payable to the artist and personal manager pursuant to the agreement.

NO CHANGE OR AMENDMENT

The agreement typically stipulates that it would be considered complete and accurate as written and that changes, amendments, or modifications would not be permitted by either party unless both parties agree to such revisions and signify their approval in a signed writing.

BREACH BY MANAGER

In the event of a breach of any of the warranties or representations made in the agreement by the personal manager, the artist would often be granted the right to inform the personal manager of such breach or default in a written notice. Following the receipt of such notice, the personal manager may be alotted a fixed period of time in which to cure the breach or default prior to the agreement terminating, thereby becoming null and void.

UNIQUENESS

The artist would generally acknowledge that his or her talents are unique and therefore irreplaceable. The personal manager could then argue that any breach by the artist would be considered material and may cause him or her unavoidable damage for which he or she may not be adequately compensated by monetary judgments alone. In the event of such material breach by the artist, the personal manager may request, and may be entitled to seek, injunctive relief in addition to monetary damages.

NO PARTNERSHIP OR JOINT VENTURE

The agreement may stipulate that the artist and personal manager have entered a business relationship which is not a partnership or joint venture. The parties would therefore not be liable, under the laws of partnership, for the actions of the other. They may add that they are acting as independent contractors.

STATE OF JURISDICTION

The personal management agreement should stipulate which state of the union will be the one governing all actions and litigations arising between the parties resulting from the agreement. Typically, the state where both parties conduct their business is the state of choice. In the event the parties live in different states, often it is the state where the stronger party resides that is the state of choice.

Another consideration often reviewed when negotiating this provision is the laws governing potential bookings of employment by the personal manager. While New York State permits "incidental booking," California is typically more harsh on personal managers who exceed their legal bounds.

UNENFORCEABILITY OF A PART OF THE AGREEMENT

Since certain provisions may be found to be unenforceable or illegal by a court of law, the personal management agreement may provide that such an occurrence would not render the whole agreement unenforceable. This provision may uphold the legality of the agreement even if laws evolve and change, or if an illegal and unenforceable provision is erroneously added to the agreement.

LIFE INSURANCE

Arguing that much of the personal manager's business revolves around the career of the artist, which, naturally, depends on the artist's health and existence as a performer, the personal manager may request the right to obtain life insurance on the life of the artist with the personal manager named as the sole beneficiary. If the artist agrees, all costs and expenses regarding such policy are generally maintained by the personal manager. The artist would typically agree to make himself or herself available for all required physical examinations and would complete any and all documents required to effectuate the life insurance policy.

RIGHT TO ENTER AGREEMENT

The artist would usually be required to warrant and represent to the personal manager that he or she has the exclusive permission and authority to license the rights stipulated in the contract and by so doing will not infringe on any rights of any other person or entity. Furthermore, the artist would normally represent that he or she is not under any disability or prohibition preventing the artist from performing his or her representations, warranties, and obligations under the terms of the agreement.

Not Subjecting Personal Manager to Liability

By entering the agreement, the artist would usually be prepared to warrant and represent that the personal manager would not be subject to any claim, action, or liability, nor will any provision in this agreement result in the violation or breach of any statutory or common law or rights of any party, including without limitation, contractual rights, trademarks, copyrights, and rights of publicity and privacy.

NO GRANTS TO OTHERS

The artist would usually further warrant and represent that he or she has not granted, and will not grant, any right, title, or interest to any other person or entity effective during the validity of this agreement which would conflict with or be in limitation of any of the rights granted. Furthermore, the artist would typically be prohibited from entering any third-party agreement, effective during the term of this agreement, with any other party with respect to competing aspects of this exclusive agreement.

INDEMNIFICATION

In most cases, the artist would be required to indemnify and hold the personal manager harmless from any damages, costs, expenses, or fees (including legal and court fees) incurred by the personal manager as a result of any claim, action, or suit instituted by or against the personal manager resulting from a breach of any warranty or representation made by the artist.

BANKRUPTCY

If the personal manager becomes insolvent or files a petition in bankruptcy, or if a petition in bankruptcy is filed against the manager, or if the manager makes an assignment for the benefit of creditors or makes any arrangement pursuant to any bankruptcy law, or if a receiver is appointed, this agreement may be automatically terminated by the artist, if so agreed by the parties.

FORCE MAJEURE

Since most entertainment contracts are created to ensure the fulfillment of a specific performance, it is important to provide a provision which considers the occurrence of events external to the control of the owner which make the performance impossible or impractical.

The *force majeure* provision covers such unforeseen events and acts to avoid a material breach. If at any time during the validity of the personal management agreement by reason of any act of God, fire, earthquake, flood, explosion, strike, labor disturbance, civil commotion, act of government, its agencies or officers, any order, regulation, ruling, or action of any labor union or association of artists, musicians, composers, or employees affecting the artist or personal manager, their subsidiaries or affiliates or the industry in which it is or they are engaged or any shortage of or failure or delays in the delivery of materials, supplies, labor, or equipment, or any other cause or causes beyond the control of the parties of this agreement, the performance of the artist's or personal manager's obligations under this agreement is delayed, hampered, interrupted, or interfered with or otherwise becomes impossible or impracticable, and if such condition exists for an agreed period of time, then either party may upon notice to the other terminate this agreement.

NOTICES

The agreement would generally stipulate that all notices related to the agreement must be in writing and delivered by certified or registered mail, return receipt requested, or by verifiable mail (Federal Express, UPS, DHL) to the addresses of the parties listed in the agreement.

The agreement may also clarify that a copy of all notices to or from the personal manager should be sent to:

PERSONAL MANAGER
Address: ____________________

ARTIST
Address: ____________________

Generally, properly addressed notices delivered or sent as provided under this contract shall be deemed given when postmarked.

VOIDABLE PROVISION

If any provision of this agreement should be held void, voidable, invalid, or inoperative, the parties may stipulate that no other provision of the agreement would be affected as a result of such action. Accordingly, the remaining provisions of this agreement would remain in full force and effect as though such void, voidable, invalid, or inoperative provision had not been contained in this agreement.

However, notwithstanding the foregoing, in the event any provision held void, voidable, invalid, or inoperative would impair the personal manager's right to receive his or her compensation under this agreement, then the manager may demand that such a provision be deemed a material provision. In that case, the agreement may be terminated without prejudice to either side.

SIGNATURES

By affixing their signatures to the agreement, the parties customarily signify their understanding and acceptance of its provisions and representations.

2

THE AGENCY AGREEMENT

The talent, or booking, agent usually works in collaboration with the artist's personal manager, record company, and attorney, serving a vital role in the development and enhancement of the artist's career. The agent, drawing upon his or her expertise, connections, and experience in the music business, presents the artist to, among others, club owners, promoters, and producers, for the purpose of securing bookings for the artist into clubs, arenas, concert halls, and other performance venues.

The agent may be asked to negotiate the employment agreement for the artist. Therefore, the agent should be familiar with the present rate of compensation for a performer of the artist's stature. The agent should also be aware of what the club owner, promoter, or producer would be willing to pay for the artist's services.

The agent is customarily licensed by the state within which he performs his services and must meet the basic requirements of that state if he intends to continue offering his services to the artist.

PARTIES

As in most agreements, the agency agreement details the names and addresses of the agent and the artist, including all corporate names and pseudonyms.

SCOPE OF AGREEMENT

The artist would usually agree to employ the agent as his or her sole talent agent in the musical industry. Similarly, the agent would formally accept employment as the artist's exclusive talent agent and representative with respect to the artist's services, appearances, and endeavors as a musician, agreeing to perform all functions and duties normally associated with an agent in the music industry.

TERRITORY

The territory granted to the agent in which to perform his or her services should be clearly defined to allay any possibility for confusion or doubt. It may be as broad as "the world," or it may be limited to a specific country, such as the United States of America and territories. The territory may even be more limited, confining the bounds of the agreement to a particular city, such as New York City; a state, such as New York State; or a portion of the country, such as the New England states.

DUTIES OF AGENT

The duty the agent accepts by signing the agency agreement is, specifically, to secure employment for the artist by "booking" the artist into various clubs, arenas, halls, rooms, and venues within the territory granted by the agency agreement. The agent typically performs his or her function by obtaining offers of employment and by soliciting the artist's services for employment in the musical field. Typically, the agent would agree to use reasonable efforts to accomplish his or her duties.

Negotiation

Once employment for the artist is secured by the agent, the attorney or personal manager may negotiate the terms of the employment contract with the assistance and advice of the agent. On many occasions, the agent may negotiate the agreement in its entirety, generally submitting its provisions to the artist or the artist's representative for approval.

Advice

While the agent would often render advice in conjunction with the counsel of the artist's personal manager and attorney, the agent would usually limit his or her suggestions to the artist's employment schedule specifically related to live performances.

PROMOTION OF ARTIST'S NAME

In order to facilitate the availability of employment opportunities for the artist, the agent may, upon consultation with the artist's personal manager, be granted the right to promote and publicize the artist's name, likeness, unique sound, and talents to those performance venues he or she considers probable places of employment for the artist as a live performer.

BUSINESS CORRESPONDENCE

With the approval of the artist, the agent may engage in business correspondence on the behalf of the artist relating to his or her performance activities. Typically, the artist would limit the agent's rights of correspondence to upcoming tours and performances and to those matters specifically relating to engagements of employment for live performances.

The artist may demand that the agent's correspondence rights be limited to negotiation and suggestion. If so agreed, the agent would usually not be granted the power of attorney to sign for the artist, nor to obligate the artist to a particular performance at a particular venue and for a particular fee.

COOPERATION

It is likely that, in the furtherance of the agent's primary interest of securing employment for the artist within the agent's assigned territory, the agent would agree to cooperate fully with the artist and the artist's management with regard to all matters relating to live performances, including dates, venues, fees, and the artist's personal needs.

AGENT'S OFFICE

In order to ensure consistency on the agent's part, the artist may demand that the agent maintain an office, staff, and facilities considered, by industry standards, to be reasonably adequate for the successful accomplishment of the agent's duties toward the artist. This may include provisions requiring the agent to possess a state-of-the-art computer software package, faxes, and ample staff to assure the artist professional attention.

PRIOR APPROVAL BY ARTIST

Most agency agreements stipulate that the agent would not accept any performance dates on behalf of the artist without the artist's prior approval, in writing. Typically, the agreement would provide that the artist not unreasonably withhold his or her approval.

APPLICABLE LAWS

It is usually the responsibility of the agent to ensure the artist that the agent will fully comply with all applicable laws, rules, and regulations of any and all governmental authorities, whether local, state, or federal, governing employment agencies. Furthermore, the agent will usually be obligated to secure all appropriate licenses, as may be required in order to render his or her services within his or her jurisdiction.

Typically, local, state and federal law require strict compliance by the agent regarding the acquisition and retention of appropriate licenses. The failure by the agent to secure the license required to perform his or her services has often resulted, when such an issue is argued in court, in the agent's forfeiting all, or a portion, of his or her past and future commissions.

UNIONS

The union usually associated with directing and guiding the careers of performers in the musical industry is the American Federation of Musicians (AF of M). Its standard agreement, like most union agreements, is typically ratified by its union membership after a period of collective bargaining and extensive negotiations.

Most business representatives negotiating for the artist should be familiar with the AF of M. agreement. Membership in the AF of M is open to those who perform an instrument as well as to those performers who are singers and vocalists. Copyists, arrangers, and orchestrators are also included in the membership. Therefore, most rock and roll, "cover," big band, wedding, and special occasion musical artists would typically be eligible for AF of M membership. The American Federation of Television and Radio Artists (AFTRA) also includes in its membership some segments of the musical community, since it is open to vocalists, actors, announcers, narrators, and sound effects engineers. Since the AF of M is more closely associated with the musical profession, this study will consider some of the provisions included in the union's standard agreement.

It is advisable for the artist to review the benefits of union or guild membership since, upon joining, he or she becomes eligible for all the benefits and protections stipulated in the union or guild charter and collective-bargaining agreements.

EXCLUSIVITY

Under most agreements, the artist agrees to be represented exclusively by the agent and would not, except with the written consent of the agent, engage any other person, firm, or corporation to perform the services which are delegated to the agent. Certainly, if the agent's strength is specific to a particular field of the music industry, such as hotel lounges, the agent may be granted a limited exclusivity.

RIGHTS OF THE AGENT

Unlike the relationship of the artist to the agent, which is often exclusive, the agent would normally be permitted to render his or her services to other musical performers and may engage in other businesses and ventures. However, depending on the bargaining strength of the artist, this provision may contain certain restrictions imposed on the agent. The artist may propose, for example, that the agent be limited to representing a single act, or an agreed number of acts, in the artist's specialized music genre—such as heavy metal, rap or big band. This limitation is usually not agreeable to the agent.

PROMPT NOTICE

The agent would usually request that he or she be given prompt and immediate notice by the artist of all communications, written or oral, received by or on behalf of the artist relating to the live appearances and performances of the artist. All such correspondences should be imparted to the agent in order to minimize the possibility of confusion and the overlapping of bookings. In addition, keeping the agent apprised of all such communication adheres to the intent of the exclusive agency agreement, which grants the agent the exclusive right to book a performing engagement. That authority limits the artist's ability to perform professionally, or offer to do so, other than through the services of the named agent.

PUBLICITY

In order to gain the maximum visibility for the artist, the agent may request the right to use, or to permit others to use, the artist's name, sound, and likeness in advertising or publicity relating to the artist's services and appearances. Usually, the agent would be obligated to coordinate all such advertising and promotion strategies with the artist and his or her management team.

Furthermore, the agent would normally be granted the right to publicize the fact that he or she is the exclusive booking agent and representative of the artist. This may enhance the agent's position in the marketplace if the artist is a well-established and highly desirable musical performer.

EXPENSES

While the agent is, as a rule, responsible for his day-to-day operating expenses, including the maintenance of his office and the payment of the salaries of his employees, the artist may agree to pay certain agency expenses specifically dealing with the artist's career, such as long-distance phone calls and travel-related expenses (airfare and hotel accommodations). Typically, the artist would limit such expenses to an agreed-upon amount. All expenses that exceed the permissible amount would usually require the artist's written authorization.

BREACH BY ARTIST

In the event of a breach by the artist, the artist may insist that the agent's sole right and remedy be limited to the receipt from the artist of the fee commissions due and owing, as agreed in the agency agreement. The agent, under this provision, would usually not be granted the right to seek injunctive or additional civil penalties against the artist.

COMPENSATION OF THE AGENT

The agency agreement typically provides a compensation, usually in the form of a commission, to be paid to the agent in exchange for the performance of his or her services under the provisions of the agreement. The agent's commissions would usually be payable on all monies and other considerations earned and received by the artist resulting from the bookings and contracts negotiated by the agent and entered into by the artist during the term of this agreement. The commissions due the agent may also be warranted on all earnings received during any and all subsequent modifications, extensions, renewals, or substitutions, regardless of when the artist receives his or her payment, even if the compensation is received following the termination of the agency agreement.

Generally, the agent would be entitled to receive his or her commission if, as, and when the artist earns his or her compensation from the promoter or performance venue. In most cases, the agent's commission would be based on the artist's gross income.

No Commission Due Agent in Excess of Negotiated Fee

The agency agreement should provide, in clear and concise language, that the agent would not be entitled to retain any sums in excess of the negotiated compensation.

Earnings from Other Sources

If the agent does receive a fee or consideration from any sources other than from the artist, directly or indirectly, on account of, as a result of, or in connection with furnishing the services of the artist, then the agent would usually be required to report such related income to the artist, and the additional amount may be deducted from the commissions payable by the artist to the agent.

Bookings Made Prior to Agency Agreement

Should both parties agree, the provision may also maintain that the agent would be entitled to receive his or her agreed commission on all bookings actually made prior to the signing of the agency agreement, but performed during the lifetime of the agreement and serviced by the agent. In the event such prior bookings are commissioned to a third-party agent, the agent may negotiate for a reduction of the third-party agent's fee and accept a reduction of his or her own fee, thereby assuring the artist that he or she would receive the artist's standard compensation.

Schedule of Payment

The commissions owed the agent are customarily due and payable no later than an agreed period of time following the receipt of the compensation by the artist or by any of the artist's representatives. In the event the artist is not paid for his or her work, no commission may be due the agent unless such nonpayment occurs as a result of a fault or wrongdoing on the artist's part.

AF of M Collective-Bargaining Provisions

Most AF of M sanctioned contracts stipulate that in no event would the payment of commissions result in the retention by the artist for any engagement or performance of an amount less than the applicable and approved minimum scale of the AF of M or of any other union organization having jurisdiction over such engagement. The artist should therefore be assured that if he or she earns less than the AF of M minimum compensation, after deducting the agency commissions, the agent may be required to rebate to the artist ample funds necessary to equal the minimum requirements.

Nonpayment of Agent's Compensation

Under the provisions of the AF of M collective-bargaining agreement, the agent would typically have a remedy available in the event of nonpayment. The agent may bring the issue of nonpayment to an arbitration board, conducted under the auspices of the AF of M's International Executive Board. The board may be granted the authority to award damages to the agent, the sum to be based on the actual expenses incurred as the direct result of the cancellation of an engagement, when such cancellation was demonstratively the fault of an AF of M member.

GROSS INCOME

Because of the significance, in terms of earned income, of the definition of the phrase "gross income," it is highly recommended that the words be defined in clear and unambiguous language, leaving no room for inexactitude by any of the future interpreters of the agency agreement. A typical definition of "gross income" is as follows: any and all amounts received by the artist for each engagement less taxes and all expenses incurred in collecting amounts due for any engagement, including costs of arbitration, litigation, and attorney's fees. It must be clarified that the definition of "gross earnings" could be decided by and between the parties.

ADVANCE AGAINST FUTURE EARNINGS

The agent may negotiate for an advance payment in anticipation of future earnings by the artist. If the agent has exhibited much success in the past in securing successful play dates for the artist, the artist may agree to such an advance payment. In most cases, the advance payment would be a flat fee payable in one lump sum, usually upon the signing of the agency agreement, or in several installments over the life of the agreement.

ACCOUNTING

Under the terms of an AF of M contract, and standard for most agency agreements, the artist would normally be permitted to request an accounting from the agent on a periodic basis, generally within fixed intervals during each term, within a fixed period of time following the termination of each term, and within an agreed period of time following the termination or expiration of the agency contract.

Such an accounting usually includes a detailed statement itemizing the gross amounts received by the artist for all engagements secured by the agent during the period for which an accounting is requested. That income would typically be the sum upon which the agent's commissions are based. The accounting should clarify the amount the agent actually would be entitled to receive in commissions.

Under the terms of the AF of M collective-bargaining agreement, a provision may be included requiring, upon request, a copy of such statement to be furnished promptly to the Office of the President of the AF of M.

TERM

The agency agreement should stipulate in precise language the term, or duration, of the validity of the contract.

TERMINATION

In the event that the artist is unemployed for a fixed number of consecutive weeks at any time during the term of this contract, the artist may have bargained for the right to terminate the agency agreement without liability or prejudice.

Notice of the intention to terminate this agreement should be sent to the parties by certified mail, return receipt requested, or by private mail service with verifiable receipt of mailing, such as Federal Express or UPS. Failure to give proper notice could constitute a waiver of the right to terminate this agreement. Under the rules of the AF of M collective-bargaining agreement, a copy of the termination notice should also be sent to the union offices.

It should be noted that the termination provision may state that the artist's unreasonable refusal to accept and perform a bona fide engagement would not, by itself, either deprive the agent of his or her right to, or give the artist the right to, terminate the agreement as provided in its provisions, unless specifically agreed upon by the parties.

AF OF M MEMBERSHIP

Under the provisions of the AF of M collective-bargaining agreement, the agent may be required to stipulate that he or she is, or will become, a party to the AF of M booking agent agreement, which is then in full force and effect. If the event the AF of M booking agent agreement lapses or is renegotiated, the rights of the parties would usually be governed by the terms and conditions of the succeeding booking agent agreement, which would be incorporated into the agency agreement by reference.

INCORPORATION OF AF OF M BYLAWS

Under the provisions of the AF of M collective-bargaining agreement, the AF of M bylaws are meant to be incorporated into and made part of the agency agreement. The parties would be required to acknowledge their responsibility to be fully acquainted, now and for the duration of the agency agreement, with the contents of the AF of M bylaws, rules, and regulations.

ARBITRATION

In the event of disputes, the agent and artist may agree to submit all arguments to arbitration, rather than litigation. If they so choose, the agreement may provide that every claim, dispute, controversy, or difference arising out of, dealing with, relating to, or affecting the interpretation or application of the agency agreement, or the violation or breach, or the threatened violation or breach resulting from the agency agreement, should be submitted to, heard, and determined by a recognized arbitration association, such as the American Arbitration Association (AAA) or, if signatories to the AF of M, by the International Executive Board of the AF of M in accordance with the rules of such board. The determination of the AAA or the board is usually considered conclusive, final, and binding on the parties.

SOLE AGENCY AGREEMENT

It is likely that the parties would stipulate that no other agreement concerning or conflicting with the elements of this agency agreement is in existence.

RIGHTS TO ENTER AGREEMENT

Both parties would usually be required to warrant that they have the right to enter the agency agreement without infringing on the rights of any other person or business entity, including copyrights and rights of privacy.

NO PARTNERSHIP OR JOINT VENTURE

The agency agreement may also stipulate that the agent and artist have not entered a joint venture or partnership. Each would specify that it is working as an independent contractor in regard to the agency agreement, thereby protecting itself in most instances from shared liabilities.

VALIDITY OF THE PROVISIONS IN THE AGREEMENT

Since the agency agreement is comprised of a collection of clauses and provisions, some of which may be deemed unenforceable by a court of law, the agreement may stipulate that if any single clause is adjudged unenforceable, and that clause is not a material breach of the contract as a whole, that clause may be deleted and such deletion would neither nullify nor invalidate the whole agreement, but only the provision in question. The remaining provisions would therefore remain in full effect.

STATE OF JURISDICTION

The agreement generally stipulates which state would have priority in the interpretation of the definition of a particular clause or provision.

FORCE MAJEURE

The *force majeure* provision concerns itself with unforeseen events external to the control of the parties which make the performance of the provisions of the agency agreement impossible or impractical and which, therefore, may require the termination of the agreement, without liability or prejudice to either party.

ASSIGNMENT

The artist would usually not agree to an assignment of the agent's rights in the agency agreement unless the artist consents, in writing, to the transfer. The artist may approve an assignment if it meets the following conditions:

- the third-party agency is owned, in whole or in part, by the agent, and
- the third-party agency possesses equal or better expertise, experience, and knowledge

of the agency business than the agent. Such stature may be premised on the third party's prior business history, reputation, and past earnings.

APPROVAL BY AF OF M

In accordance with the provisions of the AF of M collective-bargaining agreement, an executed copy of the agency agreement should be submitted to the AF of M for its written approval.

SIGNATURE

By their signatures, the agent and the artist indicate that they understand the provisions of the agency agreement and approve its contents.

3

The Songwriter/Publisher Agreement

The songwriter creates the very product on which the industry is based, the words and music. In accordance with the 1976 Copyright Act, the ownership of the copyright of that musical composition vests in the songwriter at the moment of its creation if it is fixed in a tangible instrument of expression.

After composing or writing a composition, the songwriter would ordinarily go about the business of marketing that musical composition through its commercial sale, license, or distribution. Very often, the songwriter transfers the copyright ownership of his or her created works to a publisher who, having the contacts with those parties that could successfully exploit the composition, including musical performers, television and motion picture producers, sheet music publishers, nonbroadcast public performances, airplanes, cruise ships and other modes of exploitation, will typically warrant to use his or her best efforts to generate income from that composition through its commercial distribution. The publisher may also administer all ancillary rights of the song and thereby negotiate all agreements, local and foreign, regarding that particular song.

Consequently, pursuing the songwriter's goal of getting his or her composition published and into the mainstream of commerce, the songwriter would usually enter into an agreement with a publisher experienced in the music industry. It is therefore imperative that the songwriter enter the songwriter/publisher agreement understanding the legal and economic interests of both parties.

PARTIES

The songwriter/publisher agreement is typically entered into between the songwriter and the publisher. If the songwriter performs under a pseudonym, it is generally advised that both names be cited in the agreement.

TRANSFER OF RIGHTS

The songwriter would often transfer, assign, and license the copyright of a particular composition to the publisher. The rights would usually include all the musical and nonmusical rights that bind themselves to the composition, including the title of the song, the lyrics to the song, the characters contained in the song, as well as the copyright, or legal ownership, to the song.

RIGHTS TO SELL AND LICENSE THE COMPOSITION

The publisher would typically demand the right to print, sell, and distribute the copyrighted compositions, in bound and unbound editions, as an individual composition or in a collection with other compositions by the same songwriter or by other songwriters.

NAME(S) OF COMPOSITIONS

The name of the composition should be clarified in this agreement since the rights being transferred are specific to that particular composition. If the songwriter is not convinced that the present title will in fact, be the final one, any ambiguity as to the title of the composition could be alleviated by adding that the name of the song of composition is ''tentatively entitled________.'' It should be noted, however, that a title of a composition cannot generally be copyrighted or protected. It is the composition itself that is being protected.

Copyright Registration Number

In the event that the composition is already copyrighted, it is important that the songwriter/publisher agreement list clearly and concisely the copyright registration number of the composition. The publisher may demand a photocopy of the copyright registration for his or her records. The copyright registration number filed with the Register of Copyright in Washington, D.C., is the composition's identifying fingerprint. It is unique, on file, and is public information.

SALE OR LICENSE PRICE

In many cases, marketing is the key to successful promotion of any song or composition. The publisher may therefore negotiate to retain as much flexibility as possible over the manner in which the song is sold, licensed, or commercially exploited. Depending on the bargaining power of the publisher in relation to the songwriter, the publisher may also negotiate to retain the sole right and authority to set and establish the price to sell or license the composition, as well as to stipulate the terms and conditions of the sale or license agreement.

SALE BELOW MARKET VALUE

The songwriter may demand that the composition not be dumped or sold at below market value prices. Such an action may damage the reputation of the songwriter and make it more difficult to retain his or her market value for future compositions. The publisher would usually negotiate for the need to retain the right to sell the composition at below market value, under certain pre-approved circumstances, asserting a need to be able to deal freely in response to changing market conditions.

TERRITORY

Depending on the stature of the songwriter in the musical industry as well as his or her nationality, the songwriter may wish to retain exploitation rights for certain territories. However, given the practicability of this shrinking globe in terms of commerce, it is highly probable that the publisher will negotiate for, and ultimately be given the right to, the worldwide exploitation rights for the composition. From the publisher's vantage point, such a widespread grant of territory would enable him or her to better market that composition and remain economically viable in a global marketplace.

If the songwriter is hesitant to grant worldwide geographic rights to the publisher, he or she may negotiate the grant of specific territorial rights. The songwriter may grant rights to territories based upon a common linkage, such as a common language or culture (all English-speaking countries, including the United States, Canada, and Great Britain, or all Spanish-speaking countries including Spain, South and Latin America), or based on a particular geographic location, such as the Benelux countries or all of Southeast Asia, or to a specific country, such as the United States, Germany, or Japan.

TRANSLATION

The songwriter/publisher agreement typically addresses the issue of the ownership of the rights to translate and rephrase the lyrics of the composition. While the composition's music and arrangement remain basically the same worldwide, a faulty translation of its lyrics may be critical to the composition's acceptance by the public. A composition's translation may be less poetic than the original, or the translated lyrics may not convey the same message as the original text. Therefore, the songwriter would usually require that the agreement clarify which party retains creative control over the translation and the translator. Most often, the artist would request that all such creative decisions remain in his or her control. The publisher would usually balk at granting the songwriter such widespread authority over the lyrics, insisting that less than accurate translations may be required in some instances, in order to better merchandise the composition.

In addition, the agreement should specify whether the composition is to be released in its original version or as the translation. The songwriter would typically prefer that the composition remain in its original version, but may appreciate the publisher's argument that, at times, translations help sell the composition in the diverse territories of the world.

OWNERSHIP OF RIGHTS

The agreement would, as a rule, stipulate that the publisher has, by entering the agreement with the songwriter, secured all copyrights in the composition for the duration of the term of the agreement in the agreed territory.

Registration of Rights

The publisher would probably negotiate for the right to register all claims to the copyright in the composition, as well as the right to register all documents, including the assignment of copyright. All such rights affect the ownership of the rights in the composition with the United States Copyright Office. The purpose is to specifically place on notice the public declaration that the publisher has secured the copyright in the composition.

Renewal of Copyright

Furthermore, the publisher may have the right, if agreed, to renew the copyright in the composition if the term of the agreement extends beyond the term of the copyright, and to secure the registration of claims to that copyright in the publisher's name in accordance with the copyright laws of the appropriate territory, such as the United States and all other laws or treaties that apply, worldwide.

It should be stipulated that if the publisher has acquired the right of copyright renewal, the publisher alone would be required to take all the necessary steps to renew the copyright and provide for any and all remedies in the event that he or she, by neglect, fraud, or otherwise, causes the composition to fall into public domain for any reason whatsoever.

ADDITIONAL RIGHTS GRANTED THE PUBLISHER

If the publisher has been granted the exclusive right to sell, publish, license, and exploit in general the composition, he may demand additional rights to ensure that he will be in a position to exploit his rights to his fullest capacity. Several additional rights may include the right to

- reproduce copies of the composition,
- have the composition licensed to record companies,
- create derivative works based on the composition,

- create dramatic and musical works based on the composition,
- perform the composition in public by all means, now know or to be devised in the future,
- loan, rent, sell, and lease copies of the composition, and
- acquire all additional rights to the composition, now known or to be devised in the future.

RETENTION OF CERTAIN INCOME

The publisher would generally be granted the right to receive and retain his or her agreed-upon compensation derived from the exploitation of the composition, less the payment of the agreed royalties to the songwriter. It should be noted that public performance royalties are typically paid directly to the songwriter and to the publisher by the performing rights societies.

NAME AND LIKENESS

The publisher would usually negotiate for the right, within agreed parameters, to utilize the name and likeness of the songwriter, as well as all biographical material about the songwriter, for use in connection with, and for the purpose of, advertising or promoting the composition.

If the songwriter has sufficient bargaining strength, he or she may have retained the right to review the biographical material and approve the use of his or her name and likeness by the publisher in its marketing strategy. If the songwriter has secured such a right, he or she may demand that prior to the use of a photograph, sketch, or other image or facsimile in the promotion of the songwriter's composition, his or her written approval be secured. The publisher may grant the songwriter such creative power, but would typically demand that the songwriter not unreasonably withhold his or her permission.

PERFORMING RIGHTS SOCIETIES

Typically, the parties would stipulate that the composition should be licensed with one of the major performing rights societies. Presently, the leading performing rights societies in the United States are the American Society of Composers, Authors and Performers (ASCAP), Broadcast Music Inc. (BMI), and Society of European Stage Authors and Composers (SESAC).

Since the public performance societies would usually collect and distribute fees earned from the public performance of the composition, the publisher would usually clarify in the songwriter/publisher agreement that if the public performance societies collect and distribute all such fees, then he or she would not be required to collect and pay the songwriter public performance fees.

COMPENSATION

The songwriter would typically be entitled to compensation from the publisher for those rights granted the publisher in this agreement, in exchange for according to the publisher the rights enumerated in the agreement. Since the songwriter can receive compensation from various means of exploitation, it would be imperative that the compensation provision be explained in detail.

The compensation the songwriter receives is most often in the form of a royalty. The songwriter would usually receive his or her royalty for the term of the copyright and for the duration of time that the publisher retains his or her rights in the composition. The songwriter is generally entitled to receive a royalty from the exploitation of the composition in the following media:

a) Piano or vocal copy. Generally the songwriter is entitled to an agreed price per regular sheet music edition or copy sold and not returned to the vendor.

b) Retail Selling Price of the Recording of the Composition. The songwriter is typically entitled to a net percentage of the retail selling price (or, if so agreed, the wholesale price). Net selling price would typically mean the retail price less deductions, including trade discounts, sales taxes, and other taxes, of each unit sold containing the composition, paid for and not returned in the territories negotiated in the songwriter/publisher agreement.

c) If the composition is included in a folio or songbook of musical material, the songwriter may be entitled to a percentage of the retail selling price on the net sales (copies sold, paid for and not returned) of such publication.

d) Mechanical Rights. The songwriter would typically receive a guaranteed percentage of all the monies which the publisher receives from the exploitation of the mechanical rights in the composition. These rights include income generated by a sale of recordings, including audiotapes, DAT, and CDs. The mechanical royalty is established by the Copyright Royalty Tribunal, under the auspices of copyright law, though the rate can be negotiated separately.

e) Synchronization and Related Rights. The songwriter would usually receive an agreed percentage of the earnings derived from the exploitation of the motion picture, television, video, and other applicable broadcast synchronization rights (the synchronization of sound to visual images) in the composition.

f) Foreign (outside North America) Sales and Licenses. The songwriter may be entitled to receive a percentage of the earnings received as a result of the exploitation of the composition outside the United States. The publisher may utilize the services of an affiliate, representative, or sublicensee to exploit the composition in the foreign territories. The songwriter/publisher agreement should clarify the use of such foreign entities and should list their names. Since a substantial percentage of a composition's revenues may be derived from the foreign exploitation of the composition, the songwriter may wish to ensure that the foreign affiliate or representative of the publisher has a successful history in exploiting similar musical compositions.

g) Composite Book. The songwriter would usually be entitled to receive a fee for each composite book or magazine which contains his or her composition.

FEES COLLECTED BY AGENCY

Typically, the commissions charged by agencies who often collect mechanical royalties, such as the Harry Fox Agency, would be deducted prior to the songwriter's receiving his or her fees. Whether the commissions are to be deducted from the songwriter's share or from the entire license payment depends on the agreement between the songwriter and the publisher.

BEST EFFORTS

The songwriter may demand that the agreement include a provision stipulating that the publisher use his or her best efforts in fulfilling the songwriter's objectives of the exploitation of the composition in the agreed territory. In furtherance of this provision, the publisher may be required to state that he or she will exploit the songwriter's compositions by all means granted in the agreement, to the ends contemplated by the agreement.

While a publisher would rarely make any guarantees of sale or royalty payments, other than a guaranteed advance against future royalties, the use of the term "best efforts" would indicate that the publisher would earnestly try his or her best to promote and market the works involved.

EXCLUSIONS FROM THE PAYMENT OF ROYALTIES BY PUBLISHER TO SONGWRITER

If by mutual agreement, the publisher does not receive a portion of his or her compensation from the exploitation of the composition, the songwriter may likewise not be entitled to a proportionate allotment of his or her royalty.

Donation of Composition

In the event the composition is donated to a charitable cause with the understanding that the publisher would not receive any compensation from the use of the composition but that all earnings received from the exploitation of that composition would be retained by the accredited not-for-profit organization, it would most likely be stipulated by the parties that the songwriter would likewise not be compensated.

The agreement should clarify whether the publisher has bargained for the unilateral right to make such donations, or whether the songwriter retains the right to decide whether or not such charitable, nonrevenue-bearing contributions could be made. In addition, this agreement should stipulate in clear and concise language, so as to bar any confusion at a later date, whether the expenses incurred as a result of such a charitable contribution, including transfers and shipping, will be the responsibility of the publisher, the songwriter, or both. Even if the parties agree that the publisher may offer the compositions to charities, in most situations the publisher would give notice to the songwriter of the publisher's intention to make such an offer.

Returns

Typically, all returns and unpaid units are not included in the calculations of the songwriter's royalties.

Complimentary Copies

The publisher would usually not be required to pay a royalty to the songwriter on complimentary copies of the composition which are distributed, without charge, to radio and television stations, cable networks, artists, and orchestras as means of promoting the composition. Again, such a policy should be negotiated and agreed upon by the parties. Typically, the publisher would contend that he or she had been granted the right to freely distribute the complimentary copies of the compositions, stressing that marketing the composition in such a manner is a proven and effective way of promoting a composition. Furthermore, the issuance of complementary copies is considered normal business practice in the industry. It is advisable, though, that the artist be aware of such a provision since complimentary copies are usually not royalty bearing.

Limitations on Complimentary Distribution

Since the songwriter's livelihood depends, to a large part, on the commercial exploitation of the composition, he or she may request the right to limit the number of complimentary or professional copies the publisher has the right to distribute gratuitously. The songwriter may also request the right to mutually decide with the publisher whether the composition may be donated, without compensation, for charitable purposes.

ADVANCE AGAINST ROYALTIES

In addition to the receipt of royalties from the exploitation of his or her work, the songwriter may negotiate for an advance against future royalties, such advance to be paid to the songwriter upon his or her signing the songwriter/publisher agreement.

The ability to negotiate for an advance, and the size of the advance, generally depend on the bargaining strength of the songwriter. A songwriter with a string of hits obviously wields a larger negotiating stick than a first-time songwriter. While most first-time songwriters usually do not earn income equal to the amount advanced, the advance against future royalties may be credited to future compositions of the songwriter. On the other hand, the publisher may write off the unrecouped advance as the cost of doing business.

Recoupable Sums

The publisher would typically require that all monies advanced to the songwriter be recoupable by the publisher from any and all earnings received by the songwriter, including royalties and advances against future earnings paid to the songwriter by a recording company or a performing artist. Such sums are usually recoupable prior to the songwriter's receipt of his or her revenues. The songwriter may therefore negotiate for a nonrecoupable advance against future royalties. The stronger the songwriter's bargaining position, the more chance he or she has in gaining this point.

RESERVE

The publisher may request the right to withhold from all royalties earned by the songwriter as a result of the exploitation of the composition an agreed upon sum of money as a reserve. That money would be utilized in the event returns or rebates are required or as an offset for any collection fees due and owing, or to be due, the publisher. In most cases, the amount requested to be retained in reserve, if any, would ultimately depend on the industry clout of the songwriter in relation to the publisher.

BONUS

A successful songwriter with a history and reputation as a hit maker is a prized asset which most publishers value. Such "hot properties" build up a publisher's roster of songwriters and artists. Moreover, the addition of successful songwriters to a publisher's inventory generally increases the value of the publisher's catalogue enhances the possibility of the publisher's generating a substantial income from the exploitation of that songwriter's composition, and attracts other popular songwriters to the publisher's company.

In order to entice the successful songwriter to his or her publishing company, the publisher may offer the songwriter a signing bonus, in addition to the advance against royalties and the percentage earned by the songwriter as his or her royalties earned from the exploitation of the composition, in general. The amount of the bonus would usually be in proportion to the success of the songwriter. The bonus is typically paid to the songwriter upon his or her signing the songwriter/publisher agreement, though it may be paid according to an agreed schedule.

It should be noted that a bonus may be paid in a form of compensation other than cash. The songwriter may receive a bonus in the form of stock equity, options to purchase stock, and personal or real property. Such bonus payments are generally negotiated on a case-by-case basis.

In the final analysis, the granting of a bonus is generally for those rare artists whose income is expected to produce substantial sums of money for, and to add to the reputation of, the publisher.

COLLECTION OF FEES

A portion of the songwriter's livelihood usually depends on the ability of the publisher to market and exploit the songwriter's composition and the ability of the publisher to collect the fees earned as a direct result of that exploitation. In selecting a publisher, the songwriter should evaluate the publisher's capabilities and strengths in all the above fields of endeavor.

It is imperative that the songwriter question the publisher's prior history in the musical industry, reviewing whether the publisher adequately represents his or her existing clients, whether the publisher has been adequately compensated for the exploitation of the compositions in his or her catalogue, and of equal importance to the songwriter, whether the publisher has collected the fees earned as a result of the exploitation of his or her catalogue.

The collection of fees due the publisher, and thereby due the songwriter as a result of his or her royalty agreement, requires a firm understanding of the standard accounting procedures utilized in the music industry to calculate license fees and royalties.

ADMINISTRATION FEES

The publisher may demand a fee for administering and collecting the songwriter's royalties. The fee is typically a percentage of the net (or gross, if so negotiated) receipts earned as a result of the exploitation of the composition. It is important to note that this fee is usually distinct from, and may be in addition to, the percentage that the publisher will normally retain for himself or herself as compensation for the exploitation of the compositions under the rights granted in the songwriter/publisher agreement.

ROYALTY PAYMENTS

The songwriter may have agreed to receive certain royalty payments in exchange for granting to the publisher the rights to exploit the composition.

Under the provisions of the royalty arrangement, the songwriter would typically receive an established and specific royalty, or percentage of the revenues derived from the exploitation of the compositions granted under this agreement, paid according to a fixed schedule. Those sums due the songwriter are usually revenues earned by the publisher for contracts entered or substantially negotiated during the term of the songwriter/publisher agreement.

PAYMENT SCHEDULE

The publisher and songwriter would usually stipulate a timetable, or schedule, for payments due to the songwriter. The payment schedule may, for example, be monthly, bimonthly, quarterly, or semiannually.

Agreement of Royalty Paid Songwriter

When negotiating this provision, the publisher may insist on the insertion of a clause providing that, absent a written letter of protest by the songwriter delivered, according to the notice provision of this agreement within a specific number of days following the receipt of an accounting and/or payment, the songwriter would accept that the amount so credited, or sent, connotes the full and proper amount due the songwriter. By accepting the accounting, both parties would therefore agree to the payment schedule. It is clear that the parties should determine precisely the period of time within which the artist would be allowed to challenge the accounting.

The royalty payment provision should be negotiated with exactitude and clarity in an effort to ensure that there exists no possibility of confusion or doubt as to the intent of the parties. Without such precision, the songwriter may find himself or herself in a position of relinquishing his or her right to contest the accounting by instituting a cause of action in a court of law or, if so agreed, by arbitration.

PAYMENT IN THE EVENT OF SONGWRITER'S DEATH

The songwriter/publisher agreement would generally stipulate that in the event the songwriter dies and royalty payments are due, the publisher would make such payments to the person or business entity legally entitled to receive such payments for the duration of the copyright period. The person or entity entitled to receive such payment typically includes the songwriter's estate, administrators, representatives, heirs, or assignees.

CREATIVE CONTROL

Creative control over the composition is often a hotly negotiated term in the agreement and usually remains in the arms of the party with the stronger bargaining position, or industry clout. A songwriter would typically demand control over the creative elements of the composition, yet until the songwriter acquires some prominence in the music industry, he or she is often prey to the publisher's demands.

AGREEMENT TO CHANGES IN THE COMPOSITION

It is a practice in the music industry to create new versions of existing compositions in addition to translations. Those version may include adaptations, or additional editing, of the original composition. The publisher may demand the right, in his or her sole discretion, to initiate such re-creations of the original composition. Until the songwriter gains substantial bargaining position, the publisher would usually wield the more prevailing influence over what goes in and what is omitted from this agreement regarding such changes to the original composition.

For example, the publisher may require that the songwriter agree, in the songwriter/publisher agreement, to grant to the publisher total control over the composition in regard to any changes, edits, and new arrangement the publisher alone would deem appropriate. The publisher may require changes or edits such as

- the addition of lyrics to the music,
- the addition of music to the lyrics,
- a change of title,
- a change of lyrics,
- the editing of lyrics or music,
- the translation of some words into another language, and/or
- new arrangements to the compositions.

The publisher may also demand the right to the copyright of any such revised version of the original composition in the publisher's name.

It is probable that the songwriter would argue energetically against allowing the publisher such a broad range of control over the musical compositions. But if the songwriter must agree to the publisher's demands, he or she would usually negotiate for the right to include a provision that specifies that while the publisher has been granted the right to change and edit portions of the composition, those changes should be made in consultation with the songwriter. If there is no mutual agreement as to the changes in question, the agreement may require that the publisher forgo all such changes or reevaluate the changes until a consensus could be reached between the parties.

Additional Songwriters

The publisher may also bargain for the prerogative to assign additional songwriters the task of rewriting or re-creating the original composition. It is likely that the original songwriter would contest such a broad grant to the publisher and may only agree to the publisher's demands if the songwriter is accorded the right to consult with the publisher regarding any new songwriters to be attached to the original composition.

The songwriter's royalties could be affected in the event additional writers are added to the composition since the publisher may negotiate for the right to allocate to the additional writers a share of the songwriter's royalties. In that case, the songwriter would normally demand that the publisher agree to limit the amount allotted to the additional songwriters to an agreed percentage of the original songwriter's royalties.

SEVERAL WRITERS

Compositions may be written by more than a single writer. In such a case, the songwriter/publishing agreement should stipulate clearly the share of the royalties (and advances against royalties, if applicable) due each songwriter. Moreover, the agreement should indicate which person, if any, would receive top, or priority, billing when the composition is promoted and advertised in print, radio, broadcast, and news segments. If the contribution is equal among the writers, that fact should be reflected in the agreement. If one party contributed more than the other, that fact too should be reflected.

Payments Schedule to Co-Writers

The agreement should clearly specify the payment schedule for the co-writers. It should consider, for example, whether the publisher is required to make a single payment to the songwriters, who will then divide the royalties among themselves, or whether the publisher should be responsible to pay to each writer his or her individual compensation. Typically, if the songwriters are a collaborative team and have established a corporation or partnership among themselves, they would insist that the publisher make a single payment to such business entity, which would then disperse the funds among its shareholders or partners—the songwriters. If the songwriters are independent of each other, and have formed a joint venture, they may negotiate that the publisher make separate payments to each.

Co-Writers' Share of Royalty

If it is the responsibility of the publisher to send to each songwriter his or her appropriate share of the royalties, the percentage of royalty due each co-writer should be clearly stipulated in the songwriter/publisher agreement. Such a schedule may be clarified by a simple chart:

Songwriter 1 ________ Share of Royalty ________%

Songwriter 2 ________ Share of Royalty ________%

ASSIGNMENT

Since each party to the songwriter/publisher agreement has agreed to enter the agreement based on the particular talents of the other—the songwriter for his or her unique creative songwriting talents, and the publisher for his or her unique strength and experience as a music publisher—the agreement would usually state that neither the songwriter nor the publisher would be granted the right to assign the agreement without the prior written consent of the other party. As a specific exception, the publisher may argue for the right to assign this agreement to any wholly owned subsidiary, or to any person, firm, or corporation owning or acquiring a substantial portion of the publisher's stock or assets. Typically, the songwriter would need to be assured that the assignee of the publisher be a bona fide professional and expert in the area of music publishing. Before granting such an exception to the assignment clause, the songwriter would usually negotiate for the right to approve the publisher's assignee, arguing that he or she entered the agreement with the publisher based on that specific publisher's experience, reputation, skills, and knowledge. Furthermore, the songwriter would most likely require that the assignment by the publisher be granted only to a publisher in the music industry with an equal or better reputation than the original publisher. While the third party publisher may prefer to renegotiate all the contracts entered into by the original publisher, the songwriter would probably insist that, notwithstanding the assignment, he or she should not be required to renegotiate the royalty payment agreed upon under the provisions of the original agreement.

Songwriter's Right to Assign

It is likely that the publisher would demand that the songwriter be prohibited from assigning the agreement to a third party songwriter. The publisher would surely contend that he or she has entered the songwriter/publisher agreement with a specific songwriter, believing in the value and worth of that individual songwriter's compositions. Each songwriter has a unique creative touch that sets him or her apart from any other songwriter, and most of the time, another songwriter will simply not be a justifiable substitute for the original songwriter.

ORIGINAL WORK

The songwriter would typically be required to represent and warrant that he or she is the original creator of the composition, that the composition is original and does not infringe on the rights of any other writer.

LEGAL AUTHORITY TO ENTER AGREEMENT

The songwriter would generally stipulate that he or she has the legal authority to grant the rights accorded in the agreement and that the rights conferred are free of any claims, liens, encumbrances, or other obligations. In addition, the songwriter would usually maintain that based on his or her legal ownership of the composition, he or she has the unencumbered authority to enter into, and abide by the provision of, the songwriter/publisher agreement.

NO FUTURE CLAIM OF COPYRIGHT OWNERSHIP

The songwriter may, moreover, be required by the publisher to represent that if the agreement calls for him or her to assign the copyright in the composition to the publisher, he or she will not register any future claims of copyright in the composition and will no longer claim the exclusive right to the composition.

NO PRIOR PUBLISHING OF THE COMPOSITION

The songwriter would usually be required to warrant to the publisher that the composition has not been printed in any manner or form, nor has it been recorded or distributed publicly as a phonorecord, analog or digital tape, or CD. In the event the composition has been publicly distributed, the publisher may require that the songwriter list in detail the date and location of such distribution.

INDEMNIFICATION

Indemnification is the process whereby one party agrees to hold the other party free and harmless from any claims, loss, damages, suit, or liability, often including lawyer's fees and court costs, arising out of, or incurred as a result of, a breach of any of the warranties, representations, or covenants made by the indemnifying party. An indemnification provision typically applies to the songwriter and publisher's breach of warrant, as well as to any claim brought or made by or against each party arising out of the other party's breach of any of its representations, warranties, or obligations made pursuant to this agreement or through the negligence or intentional acts of its officers, directors, employees, or representatives.

Prompt Notice

If so agreed, the parties of the songwriter/publisher agreement, would give each other prompt written notice of any action, claim, or suit initiated by or against one, or both, of the parties. In return, the party so noticed would, if so established in the agreement, be granted the opportunity, at its option, to participate in the defense of the alleged claim, utilizing counsel of its own choice at its sole cost and expense.

Withholding of Payments Due Songwriter

In the event a claim or dispute does arise which may call into action the agreed indemnity based on the songwriter's breach of warranty or representation, the publisher may demand the right to withhold payments due the songwriter stemming from the songwriter/publisher agreement. Such an offset of forthcoming royalties the songwriter may argue, should be an amount no greater than the amount required to cover the claim. The songwriter may be granted the ability to post a bond acceptable (in form and amount) to the publisher with respect to any such claim or liability.

Publisher's Right to Dispose of Lawsuit

Depending on whether the agreement permits the publisher to retain sole discretion in regard to all lawsuits concerning the composition, the contract typically allows the publisher the right to dispose of any defense and to settle any claim in the manner he or she alone determines to be in the best interest of both the songwriter and publisher.

NEGOTIATING WITH RECORD LABELS

The songwriter would typically endorse the publisher's right to negotiate with record companies with the aim to record, license, and promote the composition on terms that the publisher would deem proper and within industry standards. What would be considered proper and standard are typically those terms reasonably defined as acceptable by custom and practice in the music business at the time of the recording deal for an artist of the stature of the songwriter.

Publisher and Record Company Owned by a Single Parent Company

In the event the publishing company is a subsidiary of a multifaceted music corporation which includes the record company engaged in negotiations for the rights to record the songwriter's compositions, the songwriter would typically require that the deal points agreed upon with the record company be no less favorable to the songwriter than those deal points that could have been agreed upon with a nonaffiliate record company.

RECORDING SESSIONS

The publisher may agree to supply the songwriter with studio facilities in which to record the composition for the purpose of making a demonstration tape (''demo''). A demo is typically a rendition of the composition acceptable to the musical industry, utilized primarily for the purpose of marketing the composition to recording studios, motion picture or television producers, or to other entities which may acquire the license of or may purchase the rights to the composition. The publisher may argue that since the production of the demo is intended to make the composition marketable, and, thereby will generate an income for the songwriter, the songwriter should not be entitled to any compensation for the utilization of the composition in the production of the demo.

Recording Costs for the Demo

In many cases, the publisher would advance the costs required to produce a demo of a quality acceptable in the music industry. He or she may then require that such funds advanced be recouped from any royalties or advances otherwise payable to the songwriter, earned from the exploitation of the composition. The songwriter would probably argue that such costs should not be recouped by the publisher. They should be considered costs of doing business and, therefore, risk money normally expended by the publisher. If the composition is commercially exploited, the songwriter could argue, both the publisher and the songwriter benefit. As a further argument, the songwriter may contend that the demo tape typically remains the exclusive property of the publisher. Therefore, he or she should not be required to bear the full cost of its production. Usually, though, the party with the stronger bargaining position prevails.

ACCOUNTING OF BOOKS AND RECORDS

Since the songwriter is entitled to receive royalty payments based on the sales of the composition under the terms of the agreement, he or she customarily requires that the publisher maintain accurate books and records of all accounts governing the transactions relating to the licensing or sale of the composition during the term of the agreement.

The publisher generally would pay or, if agreed to in advance, would credit the songwriter all royalties due him or her, providing there are royalties forthcoming, within an agreed period following the date on which the publisher receives payment in connection with the sale or license of the composition. Both parties may prefer to provide, in the agreement, an interim or informal accounting each month, thereby assuring both parties an uncluttered and regular schedule within which to account for all monies due and owing under the terms of the agreement.

Accounting Following Expiration of the Songwriter/Publisher Agreement

Typically, the agreement would require the publisher to furnish to the songwriter a complete and final accounting of gross receipts derived from the sale of the items within a reasonable period of time following the expiration of the contract. This final accounting typically includes the following:

- a statement of all gross receipts derived from the sale or exploitation of the composition,
- the number of units containing the composition sold,
- the gross sales prices of each such unit less applicable taxes, and
- the calculation of the songwriter's royalty.

This provision would generally require that the final accounting be accompanied by the payment of the balance, if any, of any and all royalties due and payable to the songwriter pursuant to the contract.

RIGHT TO AUDIT BOOKS

In an effort to ensure the accuracy of the royalty payments, the songwriter, or his or her duly authorized representative (typically a certified public accountant), would negotiate for the right to audit the books and records of the publisher related to the compositions. The right would typically be granted subject to certain limitations, including the following:

- the audit should take place no later than an agreed time period following the date of the accounting;
- the audit should be conducted at the songwriter's sole expense;
- the audit should be limited to the subject matter of this agreement;
- reasonable notice should be given to the publisher prior to the grant of the right to audit;
- the audit should be conducted during normal business hours;
- the audit should be performed at the place where the books and records are normally held; and
- the audit should not unreasonably interfere with the publisher's ongoing business activities.

Discovered Inconsistency

In the event the songwriter detects an accounting inconsistency during an audit conducted in accordance with the provisions of this agreement, and it is discovered that the publisher has underpaid the songwriter, the publisher may be granted the opportunity, if agreed to by the songwriter, to pay to the songwriter such disputed amount plus an agreed interest, accrued from the date the underpayment occurred. It is also likely that the songwriter would insist that the publisher, if such an error is uncovered, would be responsible to reimburse the songwriter for the costs of the audit.

In the event the failure is not cured, or remedied, within the agreed time period, the songwriter may insist on the right to terminate the agreement without liability or further obligation. The effect of the termination of the agreement would generally render the selling, licensing, or commercial exploitation of any manner or sort actionable. The infringing publisher would therefore be subject to liability and to all additional remedies as provided by law.

Timely Objection to an Accounting Statement

In an effort to minimize long-standing disputes, the songwriter/publisher agreement may provide that all accountings and statements rendered by the publisher would be binding upon the songwriter and would therefore not be subject to question for any reason unless specific objection is made by the songwriter by written notice to the publisher stating the basis of the objection. Furthermore, the publisher may require that such objection be made within an agreed time period following the songwriter's receipt of the accounting statement. Under this provision, if the agreed time limit has expired following a scheduled accounting, the songwriter would have forfeited his or her right to maintain any action.

Without barring the songwriter's right to protest an accounting statement, the publisher may negotiate a time-barring provision. Such a provision would stipulate that, should the songwriter wish to initiate legal action following the proper and timely rendering of notice, the songwriter would have an agreed end-fixed time period within which to file such a suit, claim or proceeding against the publisher in a court of competent jurisdiction.

UNIQUE SERVICES

The songwriter's services would generally be considered unique, exceptional, and extraordinary, and may therefore be categorized as personal services. Consequently, the services of the songwriter could be considered irreplaceable. Therefore, in the event the songwriter breaches any of the provisions, conditions, or terms of the songwriter/publisher agreement, the publisher may negotiate for the right to initiate an action demanding injunctive relief in addition to all other rights and remedies allowed by law.

WAIVER OF SONGWRITER'S BREACH

Even though the publisher may waive or disregard a single breach or default by the songwriter, the parties may stipulate that such a waiver should not be considered a waiver of any other breaches or defaults by the songwriter. The songwriter, therefore, would be obligated to adhere to the balance of the agreement and to his or her obligations thereunder.

DELIVERY OF THE COMPOSITION

Typically, the publisher would require that the songwriter deliver to the publisher all documents required to confirm and protect any of the rights granted to the publisher by the songwriter/publisher agreement. Those documents required by the publisher to be delivered by the songwriter, upon the execution of the songwriter/publisher agreement, often include a lead sheet, a recording of the composition, and the copyright registration if the song has already been registered with the Library of Congress. It should be noted that the delivery of the agreed-upon items should be by a prescribed date and by a verifiable method of delivery.

Execution of Further Documents

If negotiated, the songwriter would be required to fully execute any documents of transfer required by the publisher, including an assignment of copyright in the composition by the songwriter to the publisher, and then deliver those documents to the publisher in accordance with the provisions of this agreement.

BINDING AGREEMENT

The songwriter/publisher agreement would typically state that the agreement would be binding upon all the parties to the agreement, specifically the songwriter and the publisher, as well as their legal representatives.

ENTIRE UNDERSTANDING

The agreement as written would, as a rule, be considered the entire agreement between the parties and could not be terminated, amended, or changed except in a writing signed by both parties to the songwriter/publisher agreement.

BINDING LAWS

Since the laws governing contracts may differ in the various states of the United States, it is generally advisable that the songwriter/publisher agreement stipulate which state law would be applicable and binding in regard to the agreement. Generally, the state where both parties reside would be acceptable to both parties. In the event the parties reside in different states, the party with the stronger bargaining position, that is, the party with more economic power, generally retains the winning position in selecting the state of jurisdiction. The parties would usually agree that any lawsuit or proceeding initiated by one party against the other in connection with this contract would be brought in that state and that the agreement's validity, construction, interpretation, and legal effect would be governed by the laws of that state.

NOTICES

Most agreements stipulate that all notices, statements, and payments required under the terms of the songwriter/publisher agreement should be in writing and, together with all payments provided under this contract, sent by United States mail, postage prepaid, or by certified mail, registered mail, mail delivered with return receipt requested, or a verifiable overnight delivery service (for example, Federal Express or UPS), to the address set forth in the agreement or such other address as may be designated in writing by the parties. The agreement may also provide for certain third parties, such as each party's attorney or designated representative, to receive a copy of all notices. The actual date of notice is usually calculated as the date of the post mark, if the notice is properly addressed and delivered or sent as provided under this agreement.

BREACH

The agreement may stipulate that in the event of a breach of any of the conditions of the agreement, the breaching party would be granted an agreed amount of time within which to cure, or remedy, such breach.

EXCLUSIVE RIGHT

The publisher would usually demand that the songwriter warrant and represent to the publisher that the songwriter has the exclusive right and authority to grant the rights granted in the agreement and is therefore under no disability, restriction, or prohibition, whether contractual or otherwise, with respect to his or her right under this agreement and to perform his or her agreed obligations.

NO VIOLATION OF RIGHTS OF OTHER PARTIES

The songwriter would typically warrant and represent that by granting the publisher the rights in the composition, the publisher would not be infringing on, in violation of, or in breach of, any statutory or common law or rights of any other entity or party. The agreement would generally list examples of possible infringements. Those include contractual rights, trademarks, copyrights, and rights of publicity and privacy.

GRANT OF SIMILAR RIGHTS TO THIRD PARTIES

In order to ensure the publisher's primacy of position regarding the rights granted the publisher by the songwriter, the publisher may insist on including a provision that would limit the songwriter's abilities in respect to granting similar rights to other people or legal entities. As such, the agreement may provide that the songwriter has not granted, and will not grant at any time during the term of the songwriter/publisher agreement, any right, title, or interest in the composition to any other person or entity, if such a granting would result in a possible conflict with, or be in limitation of, any of the rights granted the publisher under this contract.

The publisher may also include a provision in the songwriter/publisher agreement prohibiting the songwriter from entering into any other agreement, effective during the term of this agreement, with any other party with respect to competing aspects of this exclusive contract. The songwriter, to counterbalance the publisher's demand, may insist that the publisher acknowledge that he or she has no rights in the composition except as otherwise expressed within the text of this agreement, and except as so provided, the songwriter reserves all rights.

INFRINGEMENT

The protection of the rights of copyright, trademark, and service mark, inherent in each composition, and which party to the agreement bears the ultimate responsibility to insure that protection, is an issue which should be resolved, in clear and concise language in the songwriter/publisher agreement.

Responsibility to Register

It is imperative to the protection of all the rights intrinsic to the composition that there exists a valid copyright, trademark, or service mark. The agreement should therefore stipulate which party will initiate and maintain valid registrations. In many cases, it is the songwriter who, at his or her sole expense, would bear the responsibility to register and maintain, or cause to be registered and maintained, all appropriate copyrights, trademarks, and/or service marks in any of the compositions.

The obligation to register and maintain all the appropriate copyrights and marks in the composition is typically required to be repeated in all territories granted the publisher by the songwriter.

The songwriter, however, would probably insist that his or her responsibility be limited in the event that the actual copyright is assigned to the publisher. Following such an assignment, the songwriter would typically insist that the obligation to ensure the protection of the intellectual property rights inherent to the song be shifted to the publisher. That responsibility would include the maintenance of all copyrights and the registration of all additional marks.

Best Efforts

It is likely that both the songwriter and the publisher would pledge that, in the final analysis, both would use their best efforts to protect the rights of either parties with respect to the marketing and exploitation of the composition. In general, this would include, without limitation, both parties acknowledging the importance of a composition's rights and their commitment to use their best efforts to discover, prevent, and prohibit the illegal license and sale of lyrics, melodies, and orchestrations of the composition by unlicensed third parties. Again, the songwriter would generally insist that his or her responsibility be limited if the publisher insists upon, and is granted, full ownership of the copyright.

Notification of Infringement

Both the publisher and the songwriter would usually consent to promptly notify the other in the event an infringement or other unauthorized exploitation of the composition or licensed subject matter by any third party is discovered.

Response to Infringement

In many agreements, both the songwriter and the publisher are accorded the right, but not the obligation, to take whatever steps, at their own expense, they deem necessary to prevent any further infringement or unauthorized exploitation of the composition or licensed subject matter. If separate legal action is commenced, it is typical that such legal action be filed in the name of the initiating party.

In the event that the second party to this agreement elects to join with the initiating party in pursuing such action or proceeding, then the agreement could provide that all legal costs should be divided equitably. Those costs typically include, but are not limited to, all legal and court costs and fees incurred in connection with the lawsuit. In the case of a shared lawsuit, the rewards earned from such a lawsuit, including all awards, would be divided equitably.

TERMINATION

The termination, or cessation of the validity of the songwriter/publisher agreement, may occur if either the songwriter or the publisher breaches any of the material terms and conditions of the agreement. If such a breach does occur, then the party claiming such breach would generally be obligated, if it chooses to proceed, to serve upon the party alleged to be in breach of the contract a written notice of its intention to terminate this agreement. The party alleged to be in breach may be granted, if agreed upon by the parties, a fixed time period within which to remedy the breach.

If the breaching party, be it the publisher or the songwriter, fails to cure the breach, that is, fails to take actions that will cause it to remedy the violation so as not to be in breach of the agreement, then upon the expiration of the agreed time period, the agreement could be automatically terminated. The termination could be, if so established, without prejudice to any other rights which either party may otherwise have against the other.

Insolvency

If either party becomes insolvent, or files a petition in bankruptcy, or if a petition in bankruptcy is filed against either party, or if either party makes an assignment for the benefit of creditors or makes any arrangement pursuant to any bankruptcy law, or if a receiver is appointed, both parties may specify in this agreement that the songwriter/publisher agreement be automatically terminated.

ENTIRE UNDERSTANDING

The parties would usually stipulate that the songwriter/publisher agreement, as written, sets forth and represents the entire understanding of the parties relating to the subject matter of this agreement.

NO MODIFICATION

The agreement should also stipulate that no modification, amendment, waiver, termination, or discharge of this agreement, or any of the terms or provisions included in this agreement, would be binding upon either of the parties unless that modification, amendment, waiver, termination, or discharge is confirmed by a written instrument, signed by both parties.

WAIVER

In addition, the agreement would typically state that no waiver by either party of any term or provision of the songwriter/publisher agreement, or of any default under the terms of this agreement, would affect that party's rights thereafter to enforce such term or provision or to exercise any available right or remedy in the event of any other default, whether or not similar.

VOIDABLE PROVISION

If any provision of this agreement should be found to be void, voidable, invalid, or inoperative, then the parties may agree that no other provision of this agreement would be affected as a result of such action, and accordingly, the remaining provisions of this agreement would remain in full force and effect as though such void, voidable, invalid, or inoperative provision had not been contained in the songwriter/publisher agreement.

However, both the publisher and the songwriter may insist on including a provision that reflects a modification on the voidable provision. In the event any provision that is found void, voidable, invalid, or inoperative actually impairs the songwriter's right to receive his or her royalties under this agreement or impairs the publisher's right to manufacture, distribute, and sell the licensed items authorized under this agreement, then such a provision could be deemed a material provision, and the agreement would therefore be considered terminated without prejudice to either side.

NO JOINT VENTURE OR PARTNERSHIP

As a means of limiting each party's liabilities, the songwriter and the publisher may agree to include a provision that provides that the agreement does not create a partnership or joint venture between them. Therefore, neither party to the agreement would have the right to obligate or bind the other in any manner whatsoever nor hold itself out contrary to the terms of this paragraph. In addition, neither party would become liable for any representation, act, or omission of the other contrary to the provisions stipulated in this agreement.

IN THE EVENT OF A PROCEEDING

In the event of any action, suit, or proceeding arising from or based upon this agreement brought by either party against the other, the prevailing party may be entitled, if agreed by the parties, to recover from the other its reasonable attorney's fees in connection with enforcement of this contract in addition to the costs of such action, suit, or proceeding.

CUMULATIVE RIGHTS

The songwriter/publisher agreement may state that except as otherwise provided in this agreement, all rights and remedies stipulated would be cumulative, and none of them would be in limitation of any other right or remedy.

ATTORNEY-IN-FACT

Three words which bear an inordinate amount of power and should be granted by one party to the other only after excessive counsel and thought are "attorney-in-fact." By tendering the power of attorney-in-fact, the granting party may have given the other party the right to sign agreements, contracts, checks and payments in the first party's name, and even to bind the first party to the signed document. The grant of attorney-in-fact can be as broad or as narrow as parties to the grant recognize. While the attorney-in-fact has a fiduciary obligation to the grantor of the right to act in the best interests of the grantor, it is imperative that the grantor consider the grant of the right carefully and limit that grant to specific acts and situations.

The publisher may request that the songwriter authorize the publisher as the songwriter's attorney-in-fact, thereby granting to the publisher the authority and right to execute all documents deemed relevant for the purpose of confirming and exercising the rights granted in the songwriter/publisher agreement, including the authority both to register and to name the publisher as the owner and holder of the copyright in the composition. The songwriter would probably seek to limit those rights to only those acts deemed vital to the furtherance and enhancement of the songwriter's professional career.

FORCE MAJEURE

Since most entertainment contracts are created to ensure the fulfillment of a specific performance, it is important to provide a clause which specifies what the requirements are on both parties if events external to the control of the publisher make the performance impossible or impractical. The *force majeure* provision concerns itself with such unforeseen events which will typically require the cessation of the performance obligation. The practical effect of the *force majeure* clause is to avoid a breach of the contract and to provide for a cure. This, customarily, would provide for the resumption of the obligation as soon as the event which triggered the clause is declared gone.

The intent behind the *force majeure* clause is to accommodate the unforeseen difficulties imposed upon the publisher by forces outside of his or her control. Those outside forces may include the following: act of God, fire, earthquake, flood, explosion, strike, labor disturbance, civil commotion, act of government by its agencies or officers, any order, regulation, ruling, or action of any labor union or association of songwriters, musicians, composers, or employees affecting the songwriter or publisher, its subsidiaries or affiliates, or the industry in which it is or they are engaged, any shortage of or failure or delays in the delivery of materials, supplies, labor, or equipment, or any other cause or causes beyond the control of the parties of this contract.

The *force majeure* clause usually provides that if the unforeseen problem continues for an agreed period of time, then either party, the songwriter or the publisher, would have the unilateral right to terminate this contract. The parties may also confirm that such termination would not be declared a breach of contract, relieving the terminating party from any liability.

SIGNATURE

The songwriter/publisher agreement customarily concludes with both parties signing the agreement, indicating their understanding and acceptance of the provisions.

4

THE CO-PUBLISHING AGREEMENT

Music publishers control a substantial revenue source by commercially exploiting, typically by license, musical compositions. In many instances a songwriter co-publishes the controlled compositions with a publisher.

The publisher's primary obligation is to market the musical composition through various means, including broadcast (TV, radio, cable), nonbroadcast (hotels, inflight, discos, restaurants), mechanical royalties (audiotapes and CDs), sheet music, synchronization of music to film or tape (movies and video), special permission (greeting cards, toys, lyrics in books), dramatic rights (live theatre, opera), juke boxes, and foreign rights. It is therefore imperative that the original copyright owner, typically the songwriter, evaluate the expertise, experience, and industry clout of the publisher prior to entering the co-publishing agreement.

PARTIES

The co-publishing agreement will customarily note the names of the parties to the agreement, usually the publisher and the original copyright owner, including any pseudonyms and corporate names used in the normal course of the named parties' businesses. This paragraph clearly indicates who are the parties to the agreement and to whom its provisions apply.

INTENTIONS

The agreement should state clearly the objectives of the parties in entering the contractual relationship. The co-publishing agreement would typically affirm that both parties to the agreement, the publisher and the original owner of the copyrighted composition, intend to jointly own all the rights, titles, interests, and obligations in and to the copyright of, and attached to, the compositions covered by the scope of the co-publishing agreement.

COMPOSITIONS

The driving force of the co-publishing agreement is the musical work itself, the copyrighted composition. The agreement should clarify clearly and unambiguously the following points:

- the name of the composition,
- the songwriter, and
- the copyright notice.

Very often such clarification is best done with a simple chart.

Composition	*Songwriter*	*Copyright Notice*

RESPECTIVE SHARES

The owner and the publisher would usually agree to their respective shares of the earned revenues derived from the commercial exploitation of the composition. In an effort to alleviate costly negotiations or litigation in the future as the parties argue over their earnings, the co-publishing agreement typically stipulates each party's respective share in clear and unambiguous language.

Owner ______________________ *Respective Share* ____% of 100%

Publisher ______________________ *Respective Share* ____% of 100%

TERRITORY

In order to clarify the countries or territories within which the rights granted in the agreement apply, the parties should agree upon the territorial extent of the grant. Such provision may state that the territory assigned is a single country, such as the United States or France; a group of countries, such as the English-speaking countries; a geographic region such as South America; or, in some cases, worldwide. Very often, the co-publishing agreement grants worldwide rights with the understanding that the powers and rights granted in this agreement may be assigned to a foreign subpublisher.

REGISTRATION OF COPYRIGHT

Since the co-publishing agreement specifically relates to the ownership of the copyright in and to the composition, the agreement would ordinarily state that the parties intend to register claims to copyright the composition with the Register of Copyrights of the United States of America. The publisher will usually demand that the copyright be registered in the names of both the publisher and the owner and that they be registered as co-owners of the copyright.

ASSIGNMENT OF COPYRIGHT

The agreement may also state that if the copyright in and to the composition has previously been registered in the name of the owner, the owner would be required to deliver to the publisher an assignment of the rights granted, in a legally acceptable form. As a means of securing the publisher's co-ownership in the composition against any future claims by the owner or by any other party, the assignment should be recorded with the Copyright Office by the publisher.

ADMINISTRATION

There are several different types of co-publishing/administration agreements commonly utilized that clarify the rights of the co-publishers in the exploitation, or exploitation in the marketplace, of a co-owned composition.

a) The Exclusive Administration Agreement. In this agreement, one publisher typically retains the exclusive right to administer all rights in and to the musical composition. The co-publisher not administering the composition is customarily entitled to receive his or her share in the income.
b) The Joint Administration Agreement. Under this agreement, each co-publisher retains the right to administer the musical composition and to grant nonexclusive licenses for the composition.
c) The Limited Joint Administration Agreement. Under this grant, each co-publisher is granted the right to grant licenses for his or her interest alone in and to the composition.

It is not uncommon for the parties to the co-publishing agreement to agree to "the Exclusive Administration Agreement," granting the publisher the right to administer the rights that are attached to and inherent in the composition. By securing the sole rights to administer the composition, the publisher could argue, he or she would be in a better position to commercially exploit the composition and manage the rights and obligations inherent in the copyright, including the right to renew and extend the copyright upon its expiration.

RENEWAL OF COPYRIGHT

If the parties so agree, the co-publishing agreement may provide the co-publishers, in this case the original copyright owner (often the songwriter) and the publisher, with the joint responsibility to renew and extend the copyright in and to the copyrighted compositions at the time of its expiration. In most cases, though, the publisher would be accorded the responsibility and obligation to renew or extend the copyright to the composition. The publisher would then normally be held accountable and liable for any failure on his or her part in renewing or extending the copyright.

BUSINESS JUDGMENT

An additional obligation borne by the publisher upon being granted the sole right to commercially exploit and administer the copyright, is the responsibility to use his or her best business judgment in the accomplishment of the objectives of the parties to the agreement. Most basically, the objective of both parties is the successful generation of revenues from the commercial territory-wide exploitation of the composition.

MECHANICAL REPRODUCTIONS

The agreement would typically provide the publisher with the right to issue licenses granting permission to commercially exploit mechanical and electronic reproduction of the composition on phonorecords, prerecorded digital and analog audiotapes, CDs, CD-ROMs, and on any other method of mechanical and electrical reproduction, now known or to be devised at any time in the future.

The publisher may grant to a collection agency, such as the Harry Fox Agency, the right to license for commercial use on all recordings the musical composition, to collect all mechanical fees, to audit the records of companies, and to sue to enforce delinquent accounts.

PUBLIC PERFORMANCE

It is usually agreed by the parties that the co-publishing agreement would allow the publisher the right to commercially exploit the composition through the grant of public performance rights of the composition. The publisher would generally be given the right to license such public performance rights in all media normally conveyed under such rights by granting a performing rights society, customarily ASCAP, BMI, or SESAC, the right to license the public performance of the composition. The performing rights society would then usually be authorized to collect the revenues earned from the public performance of the composition. The performing rights society, in turn, would typically be required to pay to the publisher the agreed-upon sum due and owing the publisher as a result of the exploitation of the composition by the grant to the performing rights society.

MOTION PICTURES

The commercial exploitation of the composition through the means of motion pictures (as a motion picture soundtrack, for example) is an added source of revenues for the owner and publisher. In furtherance of the publisher's rights conveyed under the terms of the co-publishing agreement, he or she would typically be granted the right to issue the appropriate license for the recording of the composition with motion pictures and television productions (including free and pay TV) and with any and all other audiovisual devices now known or to be devised at any time in the future, including but not limited to videocassettes and laser discs. The grant would generally include the right to make copies of such recordings and the right to export those copies throughout the territories provided in the agreement.

PRINT

Another means of commercially exploiting the composition is through the print medium. Therefore, the publisher would usually negotiate for and would often be granted the right to print and commercially exploit by sale, license, or rental, the printed composition throughout the territory granted in the agreement, in forms normally associated with printed compositions now known or to be devised at any time in the future. The rights granted normally include, but are not limited to, sheet music, song books, albums, arrangements, and traditional educational formats.

TRANSLATION

The right to translate the lyrics to the composition into other languages would generally be extended to the publisher. The grant may limit the right of translation to a selective group of languages, such as French, Spanish, and Portuguese. On the other hand, the grant may broadly encompass all languages.

ORCHESTRAL ARRANGEMENTS

The publisher may also be granted the right to make band, orchestral, choral, and any and all other musical arrangements of the composition.

NAME AND LIKENESS

Recognizing that the owner's public persona may assist in the commercial exploitation of the composition, the publisher would typically request the right to utilize the owner's name (generally this grant is limited to the owner's stage name or pseudonym, if that name is used by the owner professionally), likeness, and photographs as a means of promoting and advertising the composition in relation to its commercial exploitation. In addition, the publisher would often negotiate for the right to publicize the owner's biographical material in any acceptable promotional manner or form in relation to the commercial exploitation of the composition. The owner may agree to grant such right only on the condition that he or she be allowed the right to approve the final rendering of the biographical and photographic material being distributed.

COLLECTION

As administrator of the composition, the publisher would generally be the party obligated to receive and collect all earnings, revenues, and receipts derived from the commercial exploitation of the composition throughout the territory granted by the co-publishing agreement.

OWNER'S COMPENSATION

In accordance with the provision agreed upon in the co-publishing agreement, the owner would usually be entitled to receive his or her share of the net (of gross) income received by the publisher, such income to be earned from the commercial exploitation of the composition. Typically, the owner and the publisher share equally in the earnings, revenues, and receipts. This provision should detail the compensation agreed upon in clear and unequivocal language, alleviating the possibility of disagreements and ambiguities in the future, as revenues are earned and distributed among the parties.

Net Income

The term ''net income'' is a term of art which must be clearly defined in the agreement in order to ensure an unambiguous understanding of its definition. ''Net income'' as used in the entertainment industry is usually defined as broadly as the final layer of income remaining after any and all expenses, taxes, salaries, overhead, additional net and gross participation agreement, bonuses, incentives, dues, and all additional payments, are paid in full, or as narrowly as the income remaining after payment of the publisher's actual expenses and compensation.

In this agreement, the term ''net income'' often means all gross earnings and receipts earned by the publisher from the commercial exploitation of the composition, less certain specific payments which may include the following:

a) the administration fee of an agreed percentage of the gross (or net) earnings and receipts,

b) royalties and any and all additional payments due the songwriters of the composition by the publisher,

c) those fees which are charged by agencies utilized by the publisher to collect and administer the mechanical license granted in the composition,

d) any and all fees and expenses actually expended by the publisher in regard to the composition. Those expenses may include the copyright registration fees, promotion expenses, costs to produce demonstration tapes, costs of transcribing lead sheets, and advertising fees,

e) all attorney fees which are actually expended, in respect to the composition, specifically excluding the costs of the co-publishing agreement, and

f) all costs expended by the publisher relating to the printing, arranging, and editing of editions of the composition.

PAYMENTS TO SONGWRITER (IF DIFFERENT FROM THE OWNER)

It should be clarified in the co-publishing agreement, if so negotiated, that the owner would be solely responsible for all payments due and owing the songwriter, if the songwriter is different from the owner, in accordance with the songwriter agreement entered by and between the owner and the songwriter. The parties may wish to attach the songwriter/owner agreement to this co-publishing agreement as an exhibit, thereby clearly demonstrating the owner's responsibilities and obligations.

WARRANTIES

The warranties and representations contained in the agreement are those promises made by the parties that guarantee the statements and provisions made, and relied upon by the other party to the agreement, are true and accurate. They are the foundation of veracity upon which an agreement is bound.

PARTIES OWN THEIR RESPECTIVE SHARES

The publisher and the owner would typically warrant and represent that each owns his or her respective share of the rights inherent in the composition.

FULL RIGHT TO ENTER AGREEMENT

In addition, the owner and the publisher would customarily warrant and represent that each has the full right and authority to enter the co-publishing agreement, and by doing so, neither infringes on the rights or privileges of any other party or entity. This provision ensures each party that neither has signed away its rights in any undisclosed agreement. The parties would, as a rule, further warrant that the rights they are conferring in the agreement are free and clear of any claims, demands, or encumbrances.

INFRINGEMENT

This provision addresses the issue of infringement of copyright, trademark, and service mark. It should specify which party bears the responsibility to defend such suits if they should arise. Infringement lawsuits are usually commenced by or against the parties to this agreement if there exists a violation of a valid copyright, trademark, or service mark.

Protection of Rights

The rights granted by the co-publishing agreement must be protected in order to ensure that the composition will be capitalized to its maximum potential. In furtherance of this goal, both parties would typically agree to use their best efforts to protect the rights granted to both the owner and the publisher in and to the composition, including without limitation, to use their best efforts to discover, prevent, and prohibit the illegal exploitation of the composition by unlicensed third parties.

Both publisher and owner would usually agree to promptly notify the other of such an infringement or other unauthorized exploitation of the composition by any third party. Both parties may then have the right, but not the obligation, to take whatever steps, at their own expense, they deem necessary to prevent any further such infringement or unauthorized exploitation including but not limited to the commencement of any legal and/or equitable action provided, however, that such action would be in their name alone.

In the event that one party initiates any action or proceeding in connection with the foregoing and the other party elects to join in the lawsuit, then the joining party would usually agree to contribute and pay an equitable portion of any and all costs and expenses of such lawsuit, including but not limited to legal and court costs. All monies then recovered on account of any such action or proceeding would usually be shared equitably among the parties, after deduction of any and all reasonable costs and expenses incurred by the respective parties in prosecuting such action.

ACCURATE BOOKS

The publisher would typically be obligated to keep and maintain accurate books of account governing all transactions relating to the the co-publishing agreement.

REVIEW OF ACCOUNTING BOOKS

The compensation derived as a result of the co-publishing agreement is customarily royalty based. Apart from an advance against future royalties, if such an advance is agreed upon, the receipt of each party's compensation relies on an exact accounting of all earnings and revenues derived from the commercial exploitation of the composition.

In most cases, the publisher would receive all such earnings and revenues derived from the commercial exploitation of the composition and would thereafter be responsible to deliver to the owner an exact accounting and statement in a timely manner. The agreement should state, unequivocally and unambiguously, that a detailed accounting is to be made by the publisher to the owner on an agreed schedule, perhaps quarterly or semiannually, together with the payment of all accrued royalties and fees due and owing the owner. The agreement may also stipulate that an experienced accounting firm, agreeable to both parties, would be retained to audit the accounting from time to time throughout the term of the co-publishing agreement.

PERIOD TO CHALLENGE THE BOOKS

In the event the owner wishes to question the validity and accuracy of the statements presented, the agreement should stipulate a time period, perhaps within one year after receipt of the statement in question, during which he or she may contest the accuracy of the statement. Typically, the publisher would demand that the owner deliver written notice of his or her intention to examine the publisher's books and records. Additionally, the publisher may require that the books and records be inspected by a certified public accountant at the place where the books and records are normally stored. The publisher may further request that the owner utilize his or her right to inspect the publisher's books and records according to an agreed schedule, such as a semiannual or annual inspection.

PAYMENTS OF ROYALTIES

Since the revenues earned from the exploitation of the composition represent the owner's income, the owner may negotiate that his or her earnings be paid no later than a fixed number of business days following the date on which the publisher receives payment of gross receipts in connection with the exploitation of the composition.

DEFERMENT OF PAYMENTS

Depending on the complexity of the deal, both parties may prefer to provide in the agreement an interim or informal accounting which may be rendered on a monthly schedule.

ACCOUNTING UPON TERMINATION OF AGREEMENT

It is common, due to fluctuations in the marketplace, that all payments due and owing the owner in accordance with the provisions of the co-publishing agreement may not be paid in full upon the termination of the agreement. Payment could possibly be received from vendors and licensees months following the agreement's termination due to the third party's accounting and payment schedules. The owner should therefore negotiate that the publisher be obligated to furnish to the owner a complete and final accounting of gross receipts derived from the sale of the composition within a reasonable period of time following the expiration of the agreement.

Final Accounting

This report often includes detailed data, including a statement of all gross receipts derived from the sale of the composition indicating the number of compositions sold, the gross sales prices of each such item less applicable taxes, and the calculation of each party's royalty due and owing. The final accounting is typically accompanied by the payment of the balance, if any, of any and all royalties payable to the owner pursuant to the agreement.

PAYMENTS DUE ON ACCOUNT OF ERRORS

If an audit conducted by the owner, in accordance with the provisions of this co-publishing agreement, accurately reveals an inconsistency in the books and records, uncovering the fact that the publisher has made an underpayment to the owner in regard to the royalty payment, the publisher may be granted a period of time within which he or she must pay that amount plus an agreed interest. The interest would typically commence on the date the error causing the discovered underpayment occurred.

Depending on the strength of the parties, the agreement may provide for a provision indicating that if a discrepancy in the accounting is discovered, and such discrepancy is due to fraud or fabrication, the party in error would be required to reimburse the other party for the costs of the accounting audit, in addition to the payment of the full amount outstanding, including interest.

OBJECTING TO DATA IN BOOKS

The publisher would usually negotiate for a clause providing that all accountings and statements rendered to the owner should be considered binding upon the owner and would not be subject to objection for any reason unless the specific objection is made by the owner by written notice to the publisher stating the basis of the objection.

Sunset Provision for Objection

The objection clause may include a sunset provision stipulating that if the agreed-upon time limit has expired subsequent to the final accounting, the owner would no longer possess the right to maintain any action, claim, or proceeding against the publisher in any forum or tribunal with respect to any accounting or statement due under the co-publishing agreement.

TIME LIMITS TO ACTUALLY FILE A LAWSUIT

If the owner chooses to maintain legal action and, in accordance with the provisions of this agreement, gives notice of his or her intent, the publisher would typically demand that the owner be limited to an agreed time period following the date such accounting or statement is rendered within which to file such a suit or claim or proceeding against the publisher in a court of competent jurisdiction.

NO DISABILITY

Both parties to this contract would usually warrant and represent that they are under no disability, restriction, or prohibition, whether contractual or otherwise, with respect to their rights to execute this contract, to grant the rights listed in this contract, and to perform the obligations stated in this agreement.

OWN ACCOMPANYING WORK

Since the delivery of the composition may be tendered with artwork, a video, or any other form of accompanying work, the publisher would, as a rule, require that the owner warrant and represent that none of the accompanying work furnished, or to be furnished, by the owner for use by the publisher pursuant to the terms of this agreement would or could result in the violation or breach of any statutory or common law or rights of any third party. Those rights usually include, without limitation, contractual rights, trademarks, copyrights, and rights of publicity and privacy.

CONFLICTS OF INTEREST

To ensure a clear chain of ownership in the composition, the publisher would usually require that the owner warrant and represent that he or she has not granted, and will not grant, any right, title, or interest to any other person or entity effective during the validity of this contract which would conflict with, or be in limitation of, any of the rights granted the publisher under this contract. Furthermore, the agreement could insist that the owner not enter into any other agreement effective during the term of this co-publishing agreement with any other party with respect to competing aspects of this exclusive contractual agreement.

WITHHOLDING OF FUNDS DUE

In order to ensure receipt of the monies due the publisher for cause based on claims of violation of any of the owner's warranties and representations, the publisher may negotiate for the right to withhold all or a portion of the compensation due the owner under the provisions of the co-publishing agreement. Such a request should be specifically detailed as to the following:

If the publisher is awarded a money judgment in settlement of the claim, or in judgment of a claim, the agreement may provide that such recovery will be divided among the parties in accordance with their respective share in the co-publishing agreement, after deducting all expenses relating to the claim, including attorney fees and court disbursements.

NET DAMAGE AWARDS

If a court action is initiated against the publisher and a judgment or settlement is found against the publisher in regard to the composition as a result of a breach of the owner's warranties, then the publisher may demand that he or she be granted the right to deduct all costs incurred in his or her defense from any future royalties earned by the owner. The owner may wish to limit his or her obligations to those legal costs incurred by the publisher only as a result of the owner's breach of a material provision of the co-publishing agreement or as a result of the owner's negligence or fraud. Typically, the party with the better bargaining position will secure the provision according to its needs.

SALE OR ASSIGNMENT OF OWNER'S SHARES IN THE CO-PUBLISHING AGREEMENT

The publisher may demand a right of first refusal if a change in ownership of the composition is contemplated by the owner. If agreed to by the parties, the owner would not be permitted to sell or assign his or her rights and interest in the composition without first offering the opportunity to the publisher to purchase those rights at the same price and on the same conditions as those offered to the prospective, bona fide third-party purchaser. In the event the owner would make such a sale or assignment without first offering the same opportunity to the publisher, the co-publishing agreement may stipulate that such sale or assignment would be considered null and void.

The owner, if he or she is in accord with this provision, may demand that the co-publishing agreement state that in the event the publisher refuses the owner's offer to purchase his or her share in the composition, the owner would be free to pursue such sale license or assignment with other third parties.

TERM

The agreement should spell out the length of time within which the co-publishing agreement is effective and operational. Generally, the length of the co-publishing agreement extends for the term of the copyright of the composition, including any and all modifications and extensions to the copyright.

DOCUMENTS

It is typical for the parties to stipulate that they will execute any and all documents necessary to validate and make effective the provisions and conditions agreed upon in this co-publishing agreement. Some of those documents may be attached to, and made part of, the co-publishing agreement as exhibits, riders, or attachments, while others would normally be delivered to the requesting party within an agreed upon time period for its records. They may include letters of direction from mechanical license agents, performance rights societies, foreign performance rights societies, and assignment of copyright.

Since these documents and letters are central to the authority granted the parties by the co-publishing agreement, the publisher may demand that if such documents and letters of direction are not delivered in the agreed timely manner, the publisher would have the right, as the owner's attorney-in-fact, to execute any and all necessary documents and letters needed to effectuate the intent of the agreement.

REVERSION

While confident in the abilities of the publisher, the owner may elect to maintain a degree of control over the means by which he or she earns a living, specifically, the revenues earned from the commercial exploitation of the musical composition. The owner may agree to the terms of the co-publishing agreement conditioned upon certain performance plateaus expected to be reached by the publisher. In the event the publisher does not succeed in commercially exploiting the composition to the minimum level of success established among both parties during the term provided, then the owner would be guaranteed the right to terminate the co-publishing agreement, following written notice of his or her intention to do so without liability or indebtedness.

CURE OF REVERSION

The publisher may demand the right to cure such failure within a fixed period of time following its occurrence.

NO PARTNERSHIP OR JOINT VENTURE

While the owner and the publisher have entered a co-publishing agreement granting each an established percentage of the respective shares in the composition, the agreement may stipulate that they have not entered a joint venture or partnership. Each would, in that case, be working as an independent contractor in regard to the co-publishing agreement, thereby protecting the other from shared liabilities and collective risk.

VALIDITY OF THE PROVISIONS IN THE AGREEMENT

All agreements comprise a collection of clauses and provisions, some of which may be deemed invalid or unenforceable by a court of law. The co-publishing agreement may provide that if any single clause is adjudged invalid but yet not be considered a material breach of the contract as a whole, the deletion of that clause would not nullify and invalidate the whole contract, but only the clause in question. The remaining provisions would therefore remain in full effect.

NOTICES

The co-publishing agreement would typically state that all notices, in order to be considered valid, should be sent to the receiving party in writing, by registered or certified mail, return receipt requested or by express mail. This method of delivery is intended to ensure proper validation of the date of mailing.

STATE OF JURISDICTION

The agreement generally stipulates which state would bear primary jurisdiction in the event of litigation. The state most often established is the state wherein the parties maintain their businesses. In the event that the parties reside in separate states, it is often the party with the stronger bargaining position that will prevail in the battle of jurisdictions.

FORCE MAJEURE

Since most entertainment contracts are created to ensure the fulfillment of a specific performance, it is important to provide a provision considering the validity of the agreement if events external to the control of the owner make the performance impossible or impractical. The *force majeure* provision accommodates such unforeseen difficulties imposed on the owner or publisher by outside forces. It may include a termination provision that is mutually beneficial, which will have the effect of avoiding an indefinite suspension of the agreement.

SIGNATURES

All agreements, including the co-publishing agreement, require the signatures of the parties in order to be considered, understood, and accepted.

5

THE ADMINISTRATION AGREEMENT

The owner of the composition may choose to establish a publishing company, thereby retaining all the rights, privileges, and remunerative rewards normally retained by a publisher. The rights generally include the following:

- ownership of the copyright on the composition,
- the right to issue licenses with respect to mechanical reproductions of the composition,
- the right of public performance and of licensing such right to public performance societies,
- the right to issue synchronization licenses for the recording of the composition in and with motion pictures and television,
- the right to license the production of audiovisual devices, including videocassettes and videodiscs, and
- the right to print the composition in the form of sheet music, arrangements, song book, and albums.

By serving as publisher of his or her composition, the owner would generally retain all the royalties (including the songwriter's share and the publisher's share) earned as a result of the commercial exploitation of the composition. If the owner does opt to self-publish his or her composition, it is likely that the owner would retain the services of an established and experienced administrator for the purpose of administering the rights in and to the composition, collecting royalties, and supervising the filing and maintenance of all copyrights and other marks attached to the composition.

PARTIES

The administration agreement would typically list the names and addresses of the owner of the copyrighted composition and of the administrator as the principle parties to the agreement.

DUTIES

The agreement would probably stipulate that the administrator has been retained by the composition owner as the sole administrator of the musical compositions owned or controlled by the owner, as well as all other compositions which the owner may add, from time to time, to the administration agreement.

LIST OF COMPOSITIONS

In order to delineate the compositions which are subject to the terms of the administration agreement, and to preclude any possibility of misunderstanding or ambiguity, the agreement should detail clearly the names, owners, and copyright notices of the compositions. Often, the list is drafted in a chart as follows:

Title of Composition	*Owner*	*Copyright Notice*

TERRITORY

The administrator is typically granted the right to administer the composition over a specified territory, mutually agreed by the parties. The territory can be limited to a particular country, to a group of countries, or it may be as expansive as a worldwide grant.

RIGHTS

The agreement would usually grant to the administrator the following rights, among others:

a) the right to administer and exploit the composition in the agreed territory,

b) the right to print and publish the composition,

c) the right to sell and license the use of the composition,

d) the right to grant licenses for mechanical reproduction of the composition,

e) the right to grant licenses for the public performance of the composition, and

f) the right to grant licenses for the synchronization of the composition with motion pictures and television.

RIGHTS TO PROSECUTE

In order to protect the interests he or she has been granted by the administration agreement, the administrator may demand the right to prosecute and defend, as well as to settle, suits, claims, and actions, regarding the composition.

Right to Protect Copyright

In addition, the administrator would probably demand the right to take any and all legal actions required in an effort to protect the copyright in the composition, including preventing and restraining the infringement of the copyright.

All monies recovered as a result of such suits or actions would customarily be divided between the administrator and the owner in proportion to each party's respective shares in and to the composition, after deducting all costs and expenses expended by the administrator in regard to such suits or actions. In the event the suits or actions were decided against the administrator and the owner, and monetary settlements are due and owing, the administrator may negotiate for the right to deduct all such payments from the royalty share due and owing the owner as a result of the exploitation of the composition by the administrator unless it can be shown that the loss was due solely to the actions of the administrator and not the owner.

TERM

The rights granted in the administration agreement may be accorded for a limited number of years or for an extended time. The owner could grant the administrator the rights inherent in the agreement for a term equal to the length of the copyright, including all extensions and renewals thereof, or for a fixed number of years, with the option to extend the agreement for an additional time period. In either instance, the grant of rights will most probably not exceed the length of the copyright.

All negotiated extensions to the term of the agreement may be qualified by the administrator's achievement of certain performance plateaus within the prior term. The administrator may be required to secure an agreed minimum in gross revenues, for instance, in order for the option to renew the agreement for an additional term to become operable.

ASSIGNMENT

The administrator would usually request the right to assign the administration agreement to a company performing similar administrative functions. If the composition owner agrees to such a provision, he or she would probably demand the prerogative to place limits upon the right of assignment by demanding final approval over any proposed assignment. The owner would probably require that the assignee of an administrator be of similar qualifications, reputation, and ability as the administrator.

Key Person

If the composition owner agreed to enter the administration agreement with the administrator based on the administrator's personal reputation and qualifications, then the owner may demand permission to limit the right of assignment to a company that remains wholly owned or partially owned by the administrator, and only if the administrator is retained as key person, that is, as the owner's principle administrator for the duration of the term.

RIGHT TO COLLECT RECEIPTS

One of the administrator's main functions, after commercially exploiting the composition, is to collect all fees and earnings earned as a result of such exploitation. The agreement would generally illustrate that responsibility, by stating that the administrator would be granted the right and capacity to collect all gross or net earnings derived from the commercial exploitation of the composition, using whatever legal and contractual means available.

Gross Earnings

If the owner is contracted to receive, from the exploitation of the composition, earnings based on "gross earnings," the administration agreement should clearly define "gross earnings," since the manner in which it is defined may impact directly on the amount of revenues earned by the owner. The phrase may be defined as all revenues, earnings, income, and sums, earned in any manner, form or format, derived from the commercial exploitation of the composition, without any deductions whatsoever. This would typically include, but not be limited to, earnings resulting from salaries, bonuses, royalties, shares of personal and real property, and shares in a public or private company.

Net Earnings

If the administrator is to pay the owner an agreed percentage of the "net earnings" derived from the exploitation of the composition, the expression "net earnings" should also be clearly defined. Typically, "net earnings" would mean all the gross revenues, as defined in the agreement, derived from the commercial exploitation of the composition (including the owner's and publisher's shares), less certain deductions which should be clearly delineated in the agreement.

Those deductions typically include, but are not limited to, the following:

a) collection fees actually charged and received by agencies granted the right to collect mechanical fees,

b) attorney's and accounting fees, if applicable, paid by the administrator for any contracts, agreements, or projections in regard to the composition,

c) the costs of printing, arranging, and editing editions of the composition, if paid by the administrator,

d) any and all administration expenses, including such costs of commercially exploiting the composition as all registration fees, advertising expenses, promotion expenses, and the costs of the production of demonstration ("demo") tapes, if they are recoupable,

e) an administration fee, which is typically calculated as an agreed percentage of the gross earnings (as defined in the agreement) derived from the commercial exploitation of the composition, after deducting any agreed-upon fees, and

f) any and all royalties due and owing the composer(s) of the composition, if different from the owner. If those royalties are usually paid by the administrator, the administrator would normally be bound by the contract entered into by and between the owner and composer, outlining the composer's remunerations.

Attachment of Agreements

The administrator may demand that all agreements entered into by the owner regarding sources of income, including, among others, those agreements with record companies, public performance societies, mechanical license agency agreements, and merchandise license agreements, be attached, and made part of, the administration agreement. Those agreements would normally define the manner in which the owner is to receive his or her compensation.

PAYMENT TO OWNER

Following the receipt of all gross or net earnings derived from the commercial exploitation of the composition, the administrator would, as a rule, be contractually obligated to pay to the owner the latter's compensation, after deducting those sums retained by the administrator to compensate the administrator for his or her services, as established in this administration agreement.

LIMITATIONS

The administrator may wish to limit his or her obligation regarding prepayment of remunerations to any songwriters or composers, if they are different from the owner.

If the administrator does agree to make all such payments, the administrator would customarily request copies of all such contractual arrangements entered into by and between the owner and the songwriters or composers. Following the receipt of all such documents, the administrator would then pay the songwriters or composers their respective shares from the revenues earned, according to an agreed schedule of payment. One such schedule may be as follows:

When a sum equal to the amounts due and owing the songwriters or composers is collected, the administrator would be obligated to pay all fees from the owner's share, to the third-party composers or songwriters.

Indemnification Regarding Payments Due Others

The administrator may request that the owner indemnify, and hold the administrator harmless, from any and all claims, liabilities, or damages stemming from the payment of monies due the songwriters or composers based on the owner's agreement with those third parties.

PERFORMING RIGHTS SOCIETY AND COLLECTION AGENCY

The administrator would most likely specify in this agreement the names and obligations of the performing rights society authorized to receive all revenues derived from the public performance of the composition (e.g., ASCAP, BMI, or SESAC), and the collection agency authorized to receive the mechanical rights for the composition (e.g., the Harry Fox Agency), that are to be utilized by the owner in the commercial exploitation of the composition.

ACCOUNTING

The parties would ordinarily agree on a schedule of royalty payments accompanied by accountings of the royalties payable under the provisions of the administration agreement. The accounting may be on a quarterly, semiannual, or annual schedule, or on any other schedule mutually satisfactory.

The royalty statements are usually subject to review, as to their validity, by the composition owner. The parties may agree to a time limit within which the owner would be granted the right to contest the statement.

Maintaining Books and Records

The administrator would usually be required to warrant that he or she will maintain accurate books and records regarding the subject matter of the administration agreement.

Right to Inspect Books

If the owner negotiates the right to inspect the books and records maintained by the administrator, the administrator may demand that such inspection be performed only after advance written notice is submitted to the administrator, notifying the administrator of the owner's demand. The administrator would also probably request that the inspection be executed by a certified public accountant during normal business hours and in the place where the books and records are normally kept. Furthermore, the administrator may demand that such inspection be held no more than an agreed number of times during each fiscal year and that all payments for such inspection be the sole responsibility of the owner.

Inconsistency

In the event of a discovered inconsistency or underpayment to the owner in regard to the royalty due and owing, he or she may demand that the administrator be liable to pay such inconsistency immediately upon the discovery of such a disparity. The agreement may also stipulate that the administrator would be obligated to pay, as a penalty, an agreed interest, which would be calculated commencing the date the error causing such underpayment occurred. In addition, the agreement may provide that, in the event of such a discovered inconsistency, the party in error will pay or reimburse the other party for the costs of the accounting audit.

Final Accounting

The administration agreement would customarily require the administrator to furnish to the owner a complete and final accounting of gross receipts derived from the general exploitation of the compositions covered by the agreement. The final accounting would be required to be rendered to the composition owner within an agreed period of time following the termination, or cessation, of the administration agreement.

The final statement should include detailed data, such as a statement of all receipts derived from the exploitation of the compositions. Typically, the final accounting will be accompanied by the payment of the balance, if any, of any and all royalties payable to the owner pursuant to the agreement.

NONEXCLUSIVITY

It is not uncommon for an administrator to represent several copyright owners. The administration agreement would usually indicate that fact in a clear statement, elucidating the owner's understanding that the administrator has retained the right to administer third-party compositions.

DOCUMENTS

In order to effectuate the terms, conditions, and intent of the agreement, each party would normally agree to supply to the other all documents, letters of intent, and appropriate assignments of rights. The documents would usually include the following:

a) letters from performing rights societies, including ASCAP, BMI, and SESAC, verifying their agreement with the copyright owner regarding the collection of fees from the public performance of the composition,

b) letters from collection agencies, such as the Harry Fox Agency, verifying their commission to collect fees generated from the exploitation of the mechanical license,

c) copies of any and all agreements by which the owner acquired the copyright to the composition, if any, and

d) copyright certificates and assignments of copyright, if required.

POWER OF ATTORNEY

The agreement may stipulate that if the required documents are not delivered within an agreed time period, then the other party would be granted the right to sign any and all documents, in the name of the defaulting party, necessary and required to effectuate the terms, conditions, and intent of the agreement. The owner would usually demand that this power of attorney provision be defined narrowly and should be limited only to the specific documents required by the parties in regard to the administration agreement.

EXCLUSIVE RIGHT

The owner would usually warrant that he or she has the exclusive power and authority to grant the rights detailed in the administration agreement, and by doing so he or she will not violate or breach any statutory or common law or rights of any other party or entity, including without limitation, contractual rights, trademarks, copyrights, and rights of publicity and privacy.

NO RESTRICTION

Both parties would usually warrant and represent that they are not under any disability, restriction, or prohibition, whether contractual or otherwise, with respect to their rights to execute this agreement, to grant the rights enumerated in this agreement, and to perform the obligations stated in this agreement.

NO ADDITIONAL GRANT

The owner would customarily be obligated to stipulate that he or she has not granted, and will not grant, any right, title, or interest to any other person or entity effective during the validity of this agreement which would conflict with or be in limitation of any of the rights granted under this agreement. In addition, the administrator usually requires that the owner state that he or she will not enter into any other agreement effective during the term of this agreement with any other party with respect to competing aspects of this exclusive contract.

LIMITATION OF RIGHTS GRANTED

The owner would usually stipulate that no rights in the compositions would be granted to the administrator except as otherwise expressed within the text of this agreement, and except as so provided, the owner reserves all rights in the compositions not being granted.

NO MISUSE

In order to protect his or her property value in the composition, the owner may require that the administrator stipulate that the administrator will not harm, misuse, or bring into disrepute any of the compositions covered by the administration agreement, and furthermore, that the administrator will not create any expenses chargeable to the owner without the prior written approval of the owner.

INDEMNIFICATION

The owner and the administrator would usually agree to indemnify, defend, protect, save, and hold each other harmless from and against any and all actions, claims, suits, losses, judgments, penalties, liabilities, damages, costs, and expenses (including reasonable attorney's fees and court costs) of whatever kind and nature imposed, incurred, brought, or made by or against each party arising out of the other party's breach of any of its representations, warranties, or obligations made pursuant to this agreement or through the negligence or intentional acts of its officers, directors, employees, or representatives.

In addition, the parties typically agree to give each other prompt written notice of any such action, claim, or suit, and the party so noticed would usually negotiate to retain the opportunity, at its sole option, to participate in the defense of the alleged claim, through counsel of its own choice at its sole cost and expense. In the event the administrator suffers a loss resulting from any such claim, the administrator would usually require that he or she be accorded the right to withhold royalties and sums payable to the owner in an amount equal to such loss.

TERMINATION

If either party of this contract breaches any of the material terms and conditions of this agreement, the party claiming such breach may have retained the right to serve upon the party alleged to be in breach a written notice of its intention to terminate this agreement. The party alleged to be in breach may have, if so established, a fixed period of time within which to remedy the breach. If the party alleged to be in breach fails to cure or remedy the alleged breach, then upon the expiration of the agreed time period, the agreement would automatically be terminated without prejudice to any other rights which either party may otherwise have against the other.

Insolvency

If the administrator becomes insolvent or files a petition in bankruptcy, or if a petition in bankruptcy is filed against it, or if it makes an assignment for the benefit of creditors or makes any arrangement pursuant to any bankruptcy law, or if a receiver is appointed, the owner may demand that this agreement be automatically terminated without liability or further obligation.

FORCE MAJEURE

If at any time during the term of the agreement, by reason of any act of God, fire, earthquake, flood, explosion, strike, labor disturbance, civil commotion, act of government, its agencies or officers, any order, regulation, ruling, or action of any labor union or association of artists, musicians, composers, or employees affecting the owner or administrator, its subsidiaries or affiliates or the industry in which it is or they are engaged or any shortage of or failure or delays in the delivery of materials, supplies, labor, or equipment, or any other cause or causes beyond the control of the parties of this agreement, the performance of the parties' obligations under this contract is delayed, hampered, interrupted or interfered with, or otherwise becomes impossible or impracticable, and if such condition exists for an agreed time period, then either party may upon notice to the other terminate this agreement, without prejudice or liability.

NOTICES

All notices and statements provided for under this agreement would typically be required to be in writing and, together with all payments provided under this contract, sent by United States mail, certified or registered mail, return receipt requested, by messenger, or by other means of verifiable mail, including Federal Express or UPS. All notices would customarily be sent to the addresses listed in the agreement, or to different addresses, if such new address is designated in a signed writing. The addresses may be detailed as follows:

ADMINISTRATOR
Address: ____________________

OWNER
Address: ____________________

ENTIRE AGREEMENT

The parties would usually agree that the administration agreement as written sets forth the entire understanding of the parties relating to the subject matter of this agreement and that no modification, amendment, waiver, termination, or discharge of this agreement or any of the terms or provisions included in this agreement will be binding upon either of the parties unless confirmed by a written instrument signed by the parties.

NO WAIVER

The parties would usually agree that no waiver by either party of any provision of this agreement or of any default under this contract would affect that party's rights thereafter to enforce that provision or to exercise any right or remedy in the event of any other default, whether or not similar.

NOT A PARTNERSHIP OR JOINT VENTURE

While technically the parties are in business together in respect to the compositions covered by the administration agreement, the agreement may specify that the parties are neither partners nor joint venturers. They would typically maintain that they are independent contractors joined in a business relationship, but without the legal obligations inherent in partnerships or joint ventures.

INVALID CLAUSE

In order to ensure that the whole agreement would not be invalidated based on the unenforceability, illegality, or invalidity of a single provision, clause, sentence, or paragraph, the parties may stipulate that any finding of invalidity would not affect the remainder of the agreement, which would therefore remain in full force and effect.

STATE OF JURISDICTION

The agreement should stipulate which state would have jurisdiction in the event of a claim or lawsuit. Typically, the state where both parties have established their business is the state of choice.

SIGNATURES

By affixing their signatures to the agreement, the parties customarily signify their understanding and acceptance of its terms, provisions, and conditions.

6

The Recording Agreement

The recording agreement is at the very heart of the artist's professional career. It is the contract which outlines the manner in which the artist commercially distributes his or her musical compositions through records, cassettes, disks, audiotapes, CDs, advanced digital technology, and any other form of recording reproduction manufactured and sold primarily for home and/or trade use. In addition, the recording agreement often provides for the synchronization of the artist's music with visual images on videotapes, including short and long form music videos.

It is important that the artist be aware of the record company's strengths, financial capabilities, distribution capacities, and artist selection process in order to maximize his or her chances for success in the highly competitive business of musical entertainment. Some recording companies are smaller, boutique labels which distribute their own recordings; others have entered distribution agreements with major recording/distribution companies; and others are the major companies, having the capacity to record and release a musical artist in-house.

Smaller boutique labels typically have ample funding and capacity to sign only a limited number of new artists per year and have limited funds set aside for the promotion and advertisement of the artist's recording. Other recording companies may have a larger distribution base but specialize in limited styles of music, such as gospel, rap, or dance. The larger, better established recording companies are usually more diverse in their artist roster, and often have the capacity to invest more heavily in the production of the artist's album and in the promotion and advertising necessary to "break," or release, the album nationwide.

ARTIST AND REPERTOIRE

Typically, the artist and repertoire (A&R) department of a record company discovers, selects, and nurtures the artists that are signed to a contractual agreement with the label. It is their "ears," their capacity to recognize an artist's talent, that is the A&R executive's curriculum vitae for securing and maintaining his or her position as the discoverer of new talent. They tend to listen for a sound that has wide appeal, that will remain fresh album after album, and that possesses a distinctive yet recognizable quality. The winning combination often represents a commercially successful artist/record company relationship that is highly profitable for all parties connected with the artist and the record company.

PARTIES

Once the record company and the artist agree on the terms of the agreement, the parties to the agreement are named. Typically, the record company is listed by its corporate name, address, and state of incorporation. The artist is often listed by his or her given name, stage name, or pseudonym, if applicable. The artist also lists his or her address. Including the addresses of the named parties is central to all agreements. It establishes a means of identification as well as indicating the addresses to be used in the event notices are sent to either party.

LISTED MEMBERS OF THE BAND

If the recording agreement is with a musical band, then all members of the band are usually named in the agreement, individually and as members of the musical band.

TERRITORY

The territory negotiated in this agreement may be as expansive or as limited as agreed among the parties. Typically, if the record company is an international company, with offices in several countries, the territory granted is worldwide. If the label is local, the territory granted may be limited to the United States, Canada, and their possessions.

TERM

The artist is customarily signed to a recording agreement that extends for a particular term or designated period of time. The initial term is usually a period deemed appropriate in which the artist can fulfill his or her commitment, often one or several master recording(s) to be distributed as a single or a series of singles and a sufficient number of master recordings, or sides, to constitute one or several long-playing album(s) to be released as one or several analog or digital audiotapes, or CDs, as well as any other means and forms of distribution utilized by the record company.

OPTION TO EXTEND AGREEMENT

Often, the artist grants to the record company the option to extend the agreement for a fixed number of years during which time the artist would usually be obligated to record a specific number of master recordings and albums or records.

OPTION ON SAME TERMS AS ORIGINAL

The record company would usually require that the options be granted on the same conditions as those in operation during the initial term, through the length, or term, of each option. The performance requirement and the rate of compensation may vary from the term of the initial period. In order to exercise its right to the option, or to any number of option periods granted by the agreement, the record company would usually be required to send to the artist written notice, within an agreed time during the prior term, of its intention to exercise such option, which would typically begin immediately upon the termination of the prior option period without a gap of time.

MODES OF DISTRIBUTION

It should be noted that the recording industry has several means of distributing the recorded master to the public. Typically, they are the diminishing vinyl LP, the analog and digital audiotape, and the laser compact disk (CD). Additional means of distribution may be in use presently and may be discovered and used in the future. Rather than listing all means of distribution, the agreement will typically use a single phrase defining all common methods of distribution as well as all additional methods of distribution, now known or to be devised and utilized in the future.

MASTER RECORDING

Master recordings usually refers to any original recording, whether recorded on magnetic tape or on any other substance or material generally used to record master recordings by the recording industry, for phonograph records, analog or digital tapes, CDs or any other form of record or album.

THE COMPOSITION

The composition usually means music with or without lyrics, in the form of an instrumental or as a composition consisting of music and vocal qualities, embodied on a master recording.

LONG-PLAYING VS. SINGLE

A long-playing album, or record, typically means the collection of master recordings equal to a long-playing album. A single typically connotes a master recording containing one or two cuts. With the advent and popularity of longer compositions, such as dance cuts, a single may constitute a single, extended play, cut.

MINIMUM ALBUM OBLIGATION

The recording agreement will typically enumerate the number of singles, albums, records, and music videos the record company is obligated to deliver, and on which the artist is obligated to perform, during each year of the term of the agreement. The recording agreement may limit the record company's obligation to a single release as a means of testing the artist's acceptability with the public, followed by a long-playing album of the artist's compositions, or it may be an extensive agreement, obliging both the artist and the record company to record an agreed number of long-playing albums for the term of the recording agreement.

LIMITED OBLIGATION DURING INITIAL PERIOD

The record company may wish to limit its obligation until the artist's popularity is assured, while the artist may negotiate for a longer term agreement, assuring him or her a number of long-playing albums during the term of the agreement.

ARTIST'S DUTIES

The artist would typically be called upon to perform specific and agreed-upon duties during the term of the recording agreement. Those duties may be concrete, as recording an agreed number of long-playing albums, or ambiguous, as in the best efforts clause.

AGREE TO PERFORM

Generally, the record company would require that the artist perform and, if appropriate, write and compose master recordings of new, original, and not previously recorded compositions. There may also be included a provision granting the artist the right to record his or her own recordings in a "best of," or "collection," album.

If the artist is to perform cover songs, that is, songs previously performed and popularized by another artist, that fact should be specified clearly in the recording agreement as a safeguard against a claim of nonoriginality by the recording label.

APPROVAL OF RECORDING STUDIO

The record company would usually insist upon final approval of the recording studios utilized by the artist for the performance of his or her duties and obligations under the terms of the recording agreement. In addition, the record company may demand the right to have a representative of the record company present at the recording sessions, to ensure that the record company's rights are preserved and that a quality master tape, capable of being released to the general public, will be recorded.

APPROVAL OF COMPOSITION

The record company may request the right to approve the musical compositions performed by the artist and to oversee the quality of each recording, in an effort to ensure that the quality of each recording would be considered satisfactory for the manufacture and sale of recordings.

In the event the record company considers any master recording by the artist to be below its level of acceptability, the record company would typically demand the right to require that the artist rerecord such musical composition until the composition reaches the level the company considers satisfactory for commercial distribution. The artist may maintain that he or she alone be granted the right to approve the quality of the final composition since it is his or her career which hinges on the quality of the sound and the choice of recording, but the party with the stronger bargaining position, usually the record company, would probably emerge the victor in this argument.

NO SHOW BY TALENT

Should the artist fail to appear at previously scheduled recording sessions, resulting in the company's failing to fulfill its minimum recording commitment as agreed in the recording agreement, the record company would usually bargain for either of the following:

- the right to reduce its obligation to the artist by the number of master recordings that were not recorded because of the artist's failure to attend the recording sessions, or
- the right to extend the term of the recording agreement for a period of time ample to record the required recording commitments.

Reimbursement for No Shows

Moreover, the record company would usually argue for the right to seek reimbursement from the artist for any expenses and costs it incurred as a result of the recording sessions missed. The record company would typically demand the right to charge such expenses against the artist's future royalties.

BEYOND MINIMUM RECORDING COMMITMENT

If the artist fulfilled his or her minimum recording commitment according to the recording agreement, and proceeded to record more than the agreed minimum, the record company may negotiate for the right to apply those master recordings against the minimum recording obligations and requirements of the following term.

PREEXISTING MASTER RECORDINGS

The artist may own a selection of master recordings recorded prior to the recording agreement entered with the record company. If those recordings are of a quality and nature the record company would find acceptable for commercial release, the record company may negotiate for the right to record those recordings on the artist's album and charge those recordings against the record company's minimum obligation as established in the recording agreement.

MUSIC VIDEO

With the advent of the popularity of music video (which have been popularized on such cable television networks as MTV and VH-1) and the utilization, in general, of music videos as a means of promoting and advertising the artist's album or records, the recording agreement may guarantee the artist that the company would produce, or have a third-party producer produce, an agreed number of music videos based on one or several musical compositions recorded on the album to be released by the record company.

Payment of Production Costs

The record company may agree to pay, as an advance against future receipts, the costs of the production of such music video(s), agreeing with the artist on a budget for such production. The record company would, as a rule, negotiate the right to charge such costs against all royalties due and owing the artist from the commercial exploitation of the album or record recorded under the terms of the recording agreement, while the artist may argue that the costs incurred by the record company in the production of the music video should be considered the cost of doing business and should therefore not be deducted from his or her royalties. Typically, those production costs are deducted from an artist's future earnings.

Mutual Approval

Generally, the record company would seek mutual approval, with the artist, regarding the musical compositions, or cuts, selected to be produced as a music video. In addition, the record company may demand approval on all creative expressions regarding the subject matter on the music video itself.

RECORD COMPANY'S RIGHTS

The record company would typically insist on retaining as its property, free of any claims or actions from the artist and the artist's heirs or representatives, all master recordings recorded by the artist during the term of the recording agreement as well as all the performances embodied on those recordings.

RIGHT TO OWNERSHIP OF MASTER RECORDINGS

In furtherance of its right, the record company may negotiate to acquire the right of ownership in the master recording while the artist would usually argue, as forcefully and effectively as the company, that he or she should be granted such ownership. In many cases, the record company emerges the victor in the battle of ownership of the master recordings.

TRANSFER OF COPYRIGHT

In the event the musical composition is deemed to be the property of the record company, and the artist holds a copyright in that musical composition, the recording agreement may require that a transfer of such copyright from the artist to the record company be put in place. The artist, as further testament of such transfer, may be obligated to sign a written transfer and assignment of such copyright in the musical composition from the artist to the record company.

Right to Renew Copyright

In furtherance of its rights, if secured, the record company would usually negotiate for the right to renew and extend all such copyrights.

RIGHT TO MANUFACTURE AND DISTRIBUTE

As a means to commercially exploit the artist's compositions, the record company would usually secure the right in the recording agreement to manufacture, produce, sell, distribute, lease, license, and commercially exploit in general all master recordings through all reasonable means of distribution, in any and all means and manners of use, on any means of recording device (including records, analog and digital tapes, CDs, and any and all other means of distributing recordings now known or to be devised in the future), under conditions and terms considered acceptable by the record company.

RIGHT TO ADVERTISE

In addition, the record company would typically bargain for the right to advertise and publicize the master recordings in its efforts to commercially exploit, by all established means, the master recordings.

RIGHT TO PUBLISH

In furtherance of the rights granted the record company, the record company would, as a rule, acquire the right to publish, and grant the right to others to publish, the artist's professional name, his or her photograph or likeness, biographical information, and other pertinent material, in connection with advertising and promotion of the artist and the master recordings during the general course of trade in regard to the commercial exploitation of the master recordings by all means agreed upon in the recording agreement.

AVAILABILITY FOR SHOOTING

Consequently, the record company would usually insist that the artist make himself or herself reasonably available for all photography and video recording sessions required to effectuate the terms of this agreement.

PUBLIC PERFORMANCE

The record company typically retains the right to perform the master recordings publicly and to allow others to perform the master recordings publicly, by means of radio, television, cable, satellite transmission, and any other means or methods of public performance, now known or to be devised in the future.

RESTRICTIONS ON ARTIST

The record company, by entering the recording agreement with the artist, generally commits to developing and expanding the artist's musical career by investing in and exploiting the artist's musical compositions and persona. Intending to protect that investment, the record company may place some restrictions on the artist regarding his or her activities during, and even following, the term of the recording agreement.

Exclusivity

The recording agreement may limit the artist's ability to perform or record any of the compositions recorded during the term of the agreement by stipulating that the artist not record, or license any other party to record, the compositions that are recorded under the provisions of this agreement, and that the artist not permit another business entity to utilize his or her identity and persona, in connection with any recording recorded by the artist during the term of the recording agreement, for an agreed time period. The time period typically agreed upon by the parties usually extends for:

- the term of the recording agreement, including all modifications and extensions,
- an agreed time following the date that the composition was actually recorded, or
- an established period of time following the termination of the recording agreement.

IN CASE OF BREACH OF EXCLUSIVITY

In the event the artist breaches the warranty of exclusivity, or agrees to the use of his or her identification by a third party, in connection with a recording originally recorded during the term of the recording agreement, the record company may argue for and be granted the right to limit, or actually cease, paying the artist royalties which otherwise would be due and owing the artist under the terms of the recording agreement for the exploitation of those master recordings which contain the artist's compositions in question.

COMPENSATION

The income the artist receives from the record company is typically the bottom line issue of the recording agreement. It is the reason for entering the agreement, and it is often negotiated down to a fraction of percentage points, since each percentage point based on the gross or net sales of an album or recording can represent a sizable amount of revenue for both the artist and the record company. The royalty the record company agrees to pay to the artist would normally be due and owing if the artist complies with the provisions of the recording agreement.

BASIS OF ROYALTY PAYMENTS

The royalty may be based on the retail list price, or net sales, of each recording containing the musical compositions recorded during the term of the recording agreement on records or albums manufactured, from the sides or cuts, released and distributed by the record company in the negotiated territory, or it may be based on the wholesale price, which is generally the price to the distributor or record retailer, after deducting an agreed percentage.

ROYALTIES BASED ON DISTRIBUTION METHODS

With the popularity of CDs and audiotapes unseating the long-playing vinyl record as the selection of preference by the consuming population, the record company may stipulate disparate royalty rates based upon the sales of the varying methods of recording. The royalty due and owing the artist, for example, may be lower for those records and albums sold as CDs than for those sold as audiotapes. The record company may wish to retain a larger slice of the earnings and revenues pie, often basing its contention on the amount of research and development needed to develop and exploit the newer technologies.

Flat Payment Irrespective of Distribution Mode

The artist may argue that he or she should receive the same royalties, no matter the format embodying the recordings or the means of distribution. This point, such as so many others, should be negotiated vigorously, but the party with the stronger bargaining position is often the winner.

RETURNED RECORDS AND ROYALTY PAYMENTS

The record company would usually stipulate that it should not be responsible to pay to the artist a royalty for all records or albums actually returned to the company unsold. Records and albums may be returned if the retail establishment has return or exchange privileges, if the units have been defective, or if there were errors in billings and/or shipments.

Royalty Held in Reserve

The record company typically negotiates for the option to retain, and hold in reserve, a fixed portion of the artist's royalty, in consideration of the potential returns and credit. The artist may agree to such a holdback but may wish to reduce the actual amount to be held back in reserve by the record company.

LIMITATION OF RETURNED RECORDS

The artist regularly negotiates for the right to limit the number of returns and to inspect the record company's books and records as a means of verification of the number of returns stated by the record company. The artist should not shy from asking for such an inspection provision, since it is typically the only means which he or she has available to control his or her income flow.

ROYALTY THRESHOLDS

Domestic Sales

The artist may negotiate for an escalation in the royalty rate, basing such an increase on the number of domestic sales of the record. If the parties so agree, the recording agreement may stipulate that the artist would be entitled to receive an agreed percentage for all sales up to an agreed number of units sold and a further increase in the royalty rate for all sales surpassing an additional agreed number of units sold. The required number of domestic units obliged to be sold in order to stimulate and put into effect each agreed bonus, should be negotiated and agreed upon by the parties at the outset of the recording artist/record company relationship. This bonus is often intended as an incentive to the artist, increasing his or her returns based on the popularity of the records.

Foreign Sales

The record company may insist that the artist accept a lower royalty rate from earnings based on sales of the artist's albums and records of any format manufactured and sold outside the United States by the record company or by a third party under license with the record company. In defense of its claim requesting a reduction in the royalty rate due the artist, the record company may cite its added administrative costs and fluctuating exchange rates as the primary reasons for its appeal. Whichever formula is agreed among the parties, the royalty owed the artist would usually be paid only after the record company receives its payment from all foreign sources.

FOREIGN SALES AND CURRENCY CALCULATIONS

Customarily, the record company negotiates for the right to compute the sales for all records and albums sold outside the United States in the currency of the country where the recordings are manufactured, where then recordings are sold or, if it so chooses, in U.S. dollars. In most cases, the record company would also require that the artist be paid at the comparable rate of exchange utilized by the record company.

CURRENCY CONTROL OBSTACLES

In the event the record company receives its compensation in the currency of the country of sale or license of the records and albums, and the rules and regulations of that country require that such currency remain blocked within the boundaries of that country, then the record company would generally be permitted to deposit the royalties earned, and therefore due the artist under the terms of the recording agreement, in an approved banking and financial institution within the border of that country. By proper notice, the record company would then be required to notify the artist that it has made such a deposit.

VARIOUS ROYALTY RATES

The rate of royalty payments due and owing the artist may change with the various forms of recordings in use, or with the manner in which the artist's recordings are distributed and exploited commercially.

A Selection of Artist's Musical Compositions

For those records and albums which do not consist entirely of all the artist's master recordings, the recording agreement may specify that the artist be entitled to receive a royalty based on the number of the artist's master recordings on the record in comparison to the total number of master recordings contained on the record, payable on a pro-rated basis.

Third-Party Distributors

In the event records containing the artist's master recordings are sold to third-party distributors at a discounted price lower than the regular wholesale price, the artist's royalty would typically be reduced in proportion to the discount or may be reduced by an agreed figure.

Record Clubs

Record clubs and other similar sales clubs have become popular in the United States as a means of selling records. The record company would usually assert that all royalties earned by the artist from record club sales should be based on the income actually received by the record company. The record company may argue that royalty rates should therefore be negotiated at a different percentage rate, usually lower, than the negotiated rate configured on retail sales of the composition. The record company may contend, as a means of substantiating its request, that record clubs often discount their product in various forms, and it is therefore more difficult to maintain the club's advertised selling price. For example, record clubs typically offer free bonus selections in addition to its normal discounted offerings.

Bonus Records

Depending on the bargaining strength of the parties, the record company may stipulate that royalties and payments of any sort will not be due and owing the artist for all records and albums distributed as free or bonus records by the record club.

Merchandising Plans

The record company would generally retain the right to sell and distribute the records and albums under various merchandising and promotional plans it considers viable, in its business judgment, as a means of commercial exploitation. If records and albums are promoted at a lower than average wholesale price, then, the record company would argue, the artist should receive a royalty based on the lower price. The artist may negotiate for the right to approve all such merchandising and promotional plans, since they directly affect the income he or she receives from the commercial exploitation of the master recordings.

Free Promotional Records

Often, the record company distributes free of charge, or sells at a nominal charge, records for the purpose of promoting or advertising the records and the artist. Those records may be given to disc jockeys, radio stations, television or cable stations, discotheques or college stations, among others. It is likely that the artist would not be entitled to receive a royalty based on those promotional items. In fact, if the parties approve, the record company may be authorized to deduct the fair value of those promotional copies as a business expense to be offset against profits, and consequently royalties, payable to the artist.

Scrap

For records sold as scrap, the artist would probably be entitled to receive only a greatly reduced royalty, or in some cases, no royalty at all. Typically, records are deemed as scrap when they are distributed in bulk to jobbers or wholesale outlet retailers, irrespective of titles, and are thereafter, sold at nominal prices, often with the album cover defaced in some way to indicate their status as scrap records.

Compilation Records

As a means of introducing the artist or the artist's compositions to the public, the record company may elect to compile a selection of compositions performed by various performers, including the artist, and sell, license or distribute that record at a reduced, promotional price. In such a case, the artist would usually receive a pro-rated share of the royalty on the sale of the compilation record, with a royalty rate configured on the lower retail price of the record or album. If those albums or records are distributed free of charge, then the artist would usually not be entitled to receive any royalty at all.

Flat-Fee Sublicense

The record company may choose to license the master recordings to a third-party distributor on a one-time, flat-fee basis. The artist would generally be entitled to a percentage of the flat fee received by the record company. In such a situation, the flat fee owed to the artist or copyright owner could be paid by either the third-party licensee or by the record company. The flow of income from any third-party distributor should be in the recording agreement, since most negotiations and subsequent agreements between established third-party licensees and the record company typically do not involve the artist's participation.

Various Means of Distribution

The recording agreement should also enumerate the various forms of distribution available to the record company and the differing royalty rates due and owing the artist under those separate agreements. The master recordings may be distributed to transportation facilities, retail facilities, or to third-party distributors who license music for distribution to commercial establishments as background music. The records may also be distributed to armed forces, ships at sea, airplanes, as well as to educational and not-for-profit institutions. The various means of distribution are usually calculated at different royalty schedules and should be established with charity and exactness in the recording agreement.

ACCOUNTING

It is common business practice for the record company to submit an accounting and statement to the artist at regular intervals, agreed upon by the parties in the recording agreement, containing a record of the sales in the prior accounting period, together with payment of accrued royalties earned during the prior accounting period.

Periodic Accounting

The accounting period may be quarterly, semiannually, or on any other schedule agreed upon by the parties.

Time within Which to Contest

The record company would usually demand that the recording agreement contain a provision stipulating that if the artist intends to lodge a protest in regards to the accounting and statement, he or she must file a formal notice of protest within a fixed period of time following his or her receipt of the accounting and statement. Failure by the artist to file a protest in a timely and proper manner would serve as constructive notice to all parties that the accounting and statement, as submitted, are to be considered acceptable, exact and valid.

Objection Found in Books

In the event the artist does file an objection to the accounting and statement in a timely and proper manner, the recording agreement may provide that the artist would possess the right to inspect the books and records maintained by the record company specifically regarding the recording agreement between the artist and the record company. Usually, the record company would negotiate strongly to restrict such inspection to a certified public accountant selected by the artist. In addition, the record company would usually insist that the artist be granted the right to inspect the books and records only after giving the record company written notice of his or her intention to make such inspection. Furthermore, the inspection would probably have to take place at the place where the books and records are normally held during normal business hours.

ADVANCE AGAINST ROYALTIES

The record company may agree to pay to the artist, as compensation for his or her services under the provisions of the recording agreement, an advance against future royalties. The advance may be nonrefundable if the artist's past sales performance warrants such a generous offer. If, on the other hand, the artist is launching a career and his or her past sales performances have been rather shaky, the advance may be charged against the royalties the artist would be entitled to receive from the commercial exploitation of his or her master recordings.

SIGNING BONUS

As a means of inducing a highly desirable artist to sign a recording agreement with the record company, the record company may agree to pay to the artist a signing bonus—a sum of money, upon the signing of the agreement. The bonus is usually considered a nonrefundable, flat-fee payment that serves as an incentive to the artist to enter the agreement with the record company.

The signing bonus is typically proposed if the artist is in negotiations with various record companies vying for his or her services, or if the artist has proven that he or she can generate a high volume of sales. Prior sales performances by the artist or a proven loyal following are usually standards by which the record company makes its decision on whether to pay the artist a signing bonus, and if it will pay, how much.

PAYMENT OF PRODUCTION COSTS

The artist would usually insist that the record company pay, either as a recoupable advance against future royalties or as a nonrecoupable cost of production, the recording costs expended by the artist in the production of the master recordings recorded for manufacture, sale, license distribution, and exploitation by the record company. It is typical that the artist and record company would mutually agree upon a recording budget that would insure the artist ample funds to produce a commercially viable recording.

Definition of Recording Costs

In an effort to clarify with exactness the costs to be advanced by the recording company as "recording costs," the agreement should spell out its definition in clear and unambiguous language. "Recording costs" usually means all costs utilized in respect to the production of the master recordings of the artist and the artist's compositions.

Elements of Costs

The recording costs would generally include the costs of equipment, back-up musicians, composers, arrangers, orchestrators, copyists, vocalists, mixing, mastering, engineering, travel, producing, dubbing, transportation of equipment and personnel, studio rental, tape, and any and all other costs normally utilized in the recording of a master recording.

Excess Recording Costs

In the event the recording costs exceed the agreed recording advance, the record company may insist that the artist be solely responsible for all such excess costs. Typically, the record company would have the right to deduct all such excess recording costs from any royalties due and owing the artist under the terms of the recording agreement.

PUBLICITY

In an effort to promote the sale of albums or records, the record company would probably insist that the artist be required to appear for poster and cover photographs as well as other promotional art. Furthermore, the artist may be obligated to make himself or herself available for interviews with the various media and to be reasonably available for all additional promotional services. The artist would usually agree to all such promotional obligations, so long as they do not interfere with his or her professional recording activities, if the promotional schedule is reasonable, and if all expenses are paid by the record company.

MECHANICAL ROYALTIES

The record company will typically be responsible for the payment of mechanical royalties to all copyright owners of the compositions performed by the artist on the records or albums released under the terms of the recording agreement by the record company. The artist may be required to assist the record company in obtaining the required mechanical licenses from the proper copyright owners if the owner is a person or business entity other than the artist.

WARRANTIES AND REPRESENTATIONS

Both the artist and the record company would usually insist that the other make certain warranties and representations in regard to each party's right to enter the recording agreement and in respect to the musical compositions utilized on the master recordings.

NO PREEXISTING RESTRICTIONS

Typically, the record company would require that the artist confirm that there are no encumbrances, liens or restrictions of any sort, with respect to the musical compositions which the artist will record and perform during the term of the recording agreement. Furthermore, the record company will usually demand that the artist stipulate that he or she is not a signatory to, or bound by, any contract or agreement which would serve to limit or hinder his or her ability to perform his or her obligations and duties in accordance with the provisions of the recording agreement.

LACK OF INFRINGING BEHAVIOR

In addition, the artist would usually warrant that by entering the recording agreement, he or she is not infringing on the rights, including copyright and rights of publicity, of any other party or business entity.

RIGHT OF PUBLICITY

In most recording agreements, the artist would customarily stipulate that he or she has the right and capacity to utilize his or her professional name in the furtherance of his or her professional career. By doing so, he or she would not hinder any right granted to a third party or business entity.

In the furtherance of the rights granted in the recording agreement, the record company would usually clarify that it has bargained for the right to utilize, and allow others to utilize, the artist's professional name in connection with the commercial exploitation of the recordings made under the provisions of the agreement.

REQUIREMENT TO INDEMNIFY

In order to protect itself from any breaches of warranties and representations made by the artist of which the record company may not be aware, the record company may insist that the artist indemnify and hold the record company harmless from any loss, fees, monies, or payments stemming from any claim or action resulting from or by a breach of any of the warranties or representations made by the artist in the recording agreement. In the event an action or claim is initiated by or against the record company, the record company would probably demand the privilege, as a matter of right, to withhold a certain sum of money normally due and owing the artist under the terms of the compensation provisions of the recording agreement, as a reserve against any possible loss it may sustain.

EXTENSION OF TERM

In the event an act outside the control of the record company occurs, which serves to inhibit the record company's ability to perform its functions for a particular period of time (for example, if by some external occurrence, such as a union strike or natural disaster, the record company is hindered from manufacturing, distributing, and exploiting the records and albums in accordance with the terms of the recording agreement), the recording agreement may provide that the record company has the right to extend the term of the agreement for a period of time equal to the length of such delay.

Delays of Performance

The reasons for such delay may include fire, labor disagreements, shortage of materials, acts of war, natural catastrophe, and other events normally outside the control of the record company.

EXTENSION OF TERM IN EVENT OF BREACH

If the artist breaches the terms of the recording agreement and cures or remedies such breach within an agreed period of time, the record company may have negotiated for the right to extend the term of the recording agreement for the period of time equal to the period during which the artist remained in breach of the recording agreement.

LIMIT ON OUTSIDE RECORDINGS

Under typical situations, the record company would prefer to maximize its investment in the artist by limiting the artist's exposure and commercial enterprises to those under the direct control of the record company or its representatives. In that regard, the recording agreement may stipulate, if the record company wins this deal point, that the artist would not be granted the right to be recorded, and would therefore not knowingly permit himself or herself to be recorded, either in a live performance or in a recording studio, without taking all reasonable steps to assure that such recording, if done, would not be manufactured, sold, and exploited commercially through any means of distribution, including records, radio, television, cable, and satellite transmission.

PREAPPROVAL BEFORE LIVE PERFORMANCES

The recording agreement may further stipulate that if the artist does agree to record a musical composition for exposure on radio, television, cable, or satellite transmission, he or she should secure the written approval of the record company prior to any such recording.

RESTRICTIONS ON USE OF APPEARANCE

Under some circumstances, the record company may agree to such recordings or performances, under the condition that the recording and records of all such live performances made under these limited circumstances would not be utilized for distribution over the normal distribution channels exploited worldwide by the record company, and the record company would be compensated for the issuance of the license to record the artist by the third party. The record company would, in most cases, require approval of all contracts and agreements entered into by the artist and all third parties in such cases.

EXCLUSIVE RECORDING ARTIST

The provisions of the recording agreement generally state that the record company has bargained for the exclusive right to record, manufacture, distribute, and commercially exploit the artist and the product of the artist's work. The artist may be required, if agreed, to use his or her best efforts to be billed with the credit, in all promotion and advertising, as ''Artist, A Record Company Exclusive Recording Artist.''

UNIONS

Most recording agreements contain a provision stipulating that the artist would remain, or become if not already, a member of the applicable unions and trade guilds covering members of the musical professions, typically the American Federation of Musicians. The recording agreement may specify that the record company would be responsible to pay all dues and fees, including pension and welfare, required of all members, if the artist and record company so agree.

RECORD COMPANY OBLIGATIONS FOLLOWING TERMINATION

In an effort to limit its liability in the event of nonperformance of its obligations under the provisions of the recording agreement during the term of the agreement, the record company may assert the right to notify the artist, in a signed writing within an agreed number of days following the termination of the contract year, of its desire to fulfill its minimum recording requirement for that contract year by either of the following:

- commencing its recording obligation within an agreed number of days following the submission of the written notice, or
- paying the artist the union minimum scale for the recording of the agreed minimum number of master recordings required by the recording agreement.

DELIVERY OF RECORDED COMPOSITIONS

The record company often plans a promotion campaign well in advance of the delivery of the completed master. It usually takes into consideration the time of release of the album or record, customarily basing its release schedule on marketing data accumulated through its in-house, or retained, marketing specialists.

SCHEDULE OF DELIVERY

A delay may be detrimental to the commercial success of a particular recording and may cost the record company a substantial amount of money invested in promotion and advertising, as well as lost income from the sales that were delayed based on the late delivery of the master recording. In order to control its release schedule, the recording agreement would normally outline a schedule of delivery of completed master recordings from the artist to the record company. The schedule usually considers the time required to record, mix, and master the final master recording. The recording agreement would also typically add that the minimum recording obligation is to be delivered to the record company within an agreed number of months following the commencement of the contract year.

CURE FOR LACK OF PERFORMANCE

If the artist fails to deliver the minimum contractual obligation to the record company in a timely manner as prescribed in the recording agreement, and if such failure is not based on a breach by the record company, the record company would usually bargain for the right to extend the contract year by the number of days, weeks, or months equal to the time period of the artist's failure of delivery. In addition, the record company may insist that all options and renewal dates be extended by an equal amount of time, thereby lengthening the contract term by the period of the delay.

PRODUCER

The artist may prefer to select a producer of his or her own choice, but the record company would probably require that it participate in, and approve of, the selection. As a compromise, the parties may agree to select a producer that is satisfactory to both. The agreement usually binds both parties to a time limit, typically a fixed number of days following the commencement of the recording agreement, within which to select a producer.

Extension of Terms to Find Appropriate Producer

In the event a producer acceptable to both parties cannot be designated within the agreed time period, the record company may argue that the term of the recording agreement should be extended by a period of time equal to the delay. This provision, apart from maintaining equity in the agreement, could also serve to prevent unnecessary and unreasonable delay on the part of the artist.

Compensation of Producer

The record company would probably argue that the compensation due the independent producer should be paid by the artist from the recording fund negotiated between the record company and the artist. If no such fund is negotiated, the producer's compensation may still be the artist's obligation and responsibility, though the artist would certainly negotiate that all producer's fees should be a commitment borne solely by the record company.

In-House Producers

In the event the producer hired to produce the artist's recording is an employee of the record company and receives his or her compensation from the record company, the record company would most likely insist that it deduct the producer's compensation from the royalty fees received by the artist as compensation for his or her services under the terms of the recording agreement.

SUCCESSORS

Most recording agreements contain a provision insuring that its obligations and considerations would inure for the benefit of the heirs, successors, administrators, and assigns of all the parties to the agreement.

ASSIGNMENT

By the Artist

Claiming that the artist's talents are unique and irreplaceable, the record company would typically deny the artist the privilege of assigning his or her rights under the terms of the recording agreement to another artist or to members of the artist's musical group, though it may amend the provision by agreeing to an assignment only if the record company is granted the right of approval.

By the Record Company

The artist would probably limit the record company's right of assignment unless the assignment is to a third party record company of equal stature, position and entertainment industry clout as the original record company.

APPLICABLE LAW

The recording agreement would customarily stipulate that its authority be governed by the laws of a mutually agreed state. Such state may be the state of the record company's incorporation, the artist's state of residence, or another mutually agreed state. Often, the party with the stronger bargaining power will select the state of jurisdiction, based on the proximity to its place of business or on the laws of that state in regard to contracts between individuals and corporations.

PROMPT WRITTEN NOTICE OF PENDING LITIGATION

The parties to this agreement may be required to give each other prompt written notice of any action, claim, or suit. The party so noticed would typically be granted the opportunity, at its option, to participate in the defense of the alleged claim, utilizing counsel of its own choice and at its sole cost and expense.

TERMINATION

If either party of the recording agreement breaches any of its material terms and conditions, the party claiming such breach would generally have the right, if he or she so elects, to serve upon the party alleged to be in breach of the recording agreement a written notice of his or her intention to terminate this agreement, and the party alleged to be in breach would thereupon have a period of time within which to remedy the charged breach. If the party alleged to be in breach fails to cure or remedy the alleged breach within the agreed time period, then the agreement, if so specified, would be automatically terminated. The termination is generally without prejudice to any other rights which either party may otherwise have against the other.

An Example of a Material Breach

In the event the artist's right to receive his or her royalties under this agreement is impaired as a result of a breach of warranty by the record company, such an occurrence could be deemed a material provision, nullifying the agreement under the terms of the termination provision.

FINANCIAL INSTABILITY

If the record company is facing financial problems which probably would result in bankruptcy, or if it does indeed become insolvent or actually does file a petition in bankruptcy, or if a petition in bankruptcy is filed against the record company, or if the record company makes an assignment for the benefit of creditors or makes any arrangement pursuant to any bankruptcy law, or if a receiver is appointed, the artist should have the right to terminate the recording agreement.

NOTICES

All notices and statements provided for under this agreement should be in writing and, together with all required payments, sent by United States mail, postage prepaid, or sent by certified or registered mail, return receipt requested, or by other means of express mail delivery which offer a receipt, including but not limited to Federal Express, UPS, and Express Mail, to the address set forth in this agreement or such other address as may be designated in writing by the parties.

The agreement may list the addresses of the parties in a simple chart, as follows:

ARTIST
Address: ____________________

RECORD COMPANY
Address: ____________________

Typically, properly addressed notices delivered or sent as provided under this agreement would be deemed given when postmarked or delivered.

REAFFIRMING OF TERMS OF AGREEMENT

This provision usually reaffirms that the agreement as written sets forth the entire understanding of the parties in regard to its subject matter. Furthermore, no modification, amendment, waiver, termination, or discharge of this agreement or any of the terms or provisions included in this agreement would therefore be considered binding upon either of the parties unless confirmed by a written instrument signed by the parties.

LIMITATION OF WAIVER OF CLAUSES

Usually, no waiver by either party of any term or provision of this agreement or of any default under this agreement would affect that party's rights thereafter to enforce that term or provision or to exercise any right or remedy in the event of any other default, whether or not similar to the initial default.

EXCLUSIONARY CLAUSE

The parties would usually agree that if any provision of the recording agreement should be determined void, voidable, invalid, or inoperative, no other provision of the agreement should be affected as a result of that provision's invalidity or unenforceability. Accordingly, the remaining provisions of this agreement would be considered valid and in full force and effect as though that void, voidable, invalid, or inoperative provision had not been contained in the agreement.

AFFIRMATION CONCERNING LEGAL RELATIONSHIP OF PARTIES

In an effort to protect both parties, the artist and the record company would usually agree that regardless of the contractual relationship created as a result of their entering *the* recording agreement, nothing in the agreement constitutes the establishment of a partnership or joint venture between them. Neither party, therefore, would have the right to obligate or bind the other in any manner whatsoever outside the framework of the agreement, nor could either party hold itself out contrary to the terms of this paragraph. Furthermore, neither party would become liable for any representation, act, or omission of the other contrary to the provisions stipulated in this agreement.

RECOVERY OF REASONABLE ATTORNEY COSTS AND FEES

In the event of any action, suit, or proceeding arising from or based upon this agreement brought by either party against the other, the prevailing party may have the right, if so established in the agreement, to recover from the other its reasonable attorney's fees in connection with enforcement of this agreement in addition to the costs of such action, suit, or proceeding.

SIGNATURES

The parties to the recording agreement will typically signify, by their signatures, their understanding and acceptance of its provisions and conditions.

7

THE ARTIST/PRODUCER AGREEMENT

The artist may enter an agreement with an independent producer, engaging the producer to produce and engineer a master recording of the artist's musical composition. The producer would often be selected based on his or her prior history of successful efforts as well as his or her ability to produce, mix, and engineer a recording intended for commercial release or, in some cases, a demonstration tape (a "demo").

The production agreement discussed in this study concerns itself with an artist who has engaged the services of a record producer that has been approved by the record company to produce professional quality master recordings for distribution on a forthcoming album or record.

PARTIES

The artist/producer production agreement customarily notes the names of the producer and his or her production company as well as the name of the artist, including any stage name or pseudonym he or she uses in the course of his or her entertainment business.

DUTIES

Performance of Services Required

The producer would usually be expected to perform all services required to successfully accomplish his or her primary objective: the production of the master recordings agreed upon in the artist/producer agreement.

The agreement usually lists in detail the musical compositions to be produced by name, copyright owner, and copyright filing number. If the musical compositions are previously unrecorded, the agreement would typically stipulate that fact.

Availability of Producer

The producer would usually be obligated to be available, on a nonexclusive basis, to produce one or a series of master recordings containing the musical performances of the artist. It is common for the producer to request that reasonable written notice be given to him or her prior to each recording session.

Form of Master Recording

The master recording would generally be, in its final version, a fully edited and fully mixed stereo tape or any other means for recording acceptable by the musical industry and approved by the record company, whether in existence at the present time or to be invented and utilized in the future.

Number of Master Recordings

It is likely that the agreement would state with specificity the number of master recordings required of the producer. It may also express the approximate length of each recording. A dance recording is typically longer than a pop version of a similar recording, and the agreement should clarify the distinction.

The artist/producer agreement may also designate whether the producer would be required to produce differing versions of the same composition. The agreement should then clarify whether each such version is considered a new master recording or simply a different version of a single master recording.

Delivery of Session Tapes

The problem of unendorsed or pirated recordings of an artist's recording sessions should be controlled by an agreement between the parties to restrict the use of the session tapes outside of their original intent. To that end, the artist/producer agreement could insist that the producer would be obligated to deliver to the artist or record company any and all original session tapes in the producer's possession, whether on tape, acetate, or on any other means of recording tape utilized by the producer. The artist and record company would, in this manner, attempt to limit the likelihood for a pirated tape from entering the stream of commerce prior to, or even during, the general distribution of the artist's album or record. In the market, a pirated tape could potentially, reduce the earnings and revenues derived from the general commercial exploitation of the artist's record or album, and in addition, may damage the artist's reputation for excellence and quality work if the pirated tape is of a lesser quality than the album released by the record company.

No Further Obligations by Producer

Once the master recording is delivered to the artist, the artist may insist, and the producer would generally agree, that the producer would no longer possess the right to cut, edit, remix, remaster, or resequence the master recording, nor to alter the master recording in any manner, without receiving prior written permission of the artist or the record company.

Right to Re-edit Session Tape by Record Company

The record company may have negotiated for the right to make all alterations as required of the musical composition in order to release the master recording as a dance recording, as a single, or under any other musical format, or for any other reason which it alone may decide. If such is the case, the record company would usually present to the producer written notice of its intention to re-edit, remix, remaster, resequence or alter the master recording in a manner it alone decides along with the artist's written approval, if required by contract, for such creative editing. The record company would then typically grant the producer a reasonable amount of time in which to re-edit, recut, remix, remaster, resequence, or alter the master recording.

DELIVERY OF MASTER TAPE TO RECORD COMPANY

The record company has usually conceived of, and set into motion, a marketing plan for the manufacture and release of the album. Intending to accommodate that schedule, the record company, which typically has negotiated for the exclusive right to distribute the master recording for an agreed term and in an agreed territory, would generally require that the artist and producer complete the production of the master recording by an approved date and deliver it to the record company prior to the expiration of an established and fixed time period. In order to effectively control the production of the master tape, the production agreement may also stipulate the date on which the producer would be required to commence the production of the master recordings.

TERM

The length of the production agreement is typically limited by the date stipulated in the artist/record company recording agreement.

RECORDING STUDIO

In an effort to maintain a level of control over the quality of the recording studio, the recording equipment and the expertise of the studio personnel, the artist or record company could insist on designating the recording studio of its choice as the studio to be utilized for the production of the master recording. In the case where the producer has built an established relationship with a recording studio, where he or she is familiar with the recording equipment and technicians, the producer may be granted permission to select the recording studio and the equipment to be utilized in the performance of his or her services. The artist or record company, though, may insist on approving the recording studio, the technicians utilized by the producer, including the mixer and sound engineer, the equipment being used by the producer, including multitrack analog and/or digital sound recording systems, and the materials being used, such as recording tape.

SELECTION OF THE RECORDINGS

The artist would usually select the musical compositions to be produced, including the lyrics and style of music. In the event the record company has secured the right to approve the selection of musical compositions to be included in the record or album, the artist's choice of composition would typically be subject to the record company's approval.

Delivery of Satisfactory Recordings

The producer would customarily be required to deliver to the artist master recordings that are satisfactory in all respects for the manufacture and distribution of commercial quality records, tapes, and CDs. Satisfactory quality would usually be judged as a level of quality consistent with the standard commonly utilized for distribution of similar recordings in the musical industry at the time the artist's recording is being mastered and released.

UNIONS

Generally, the producer would be obligated to be a signatory in good standing of all unions and guilds required of an individual performing the producer's services and would be required to pay all union and guild fees. In addition, the producer would generally be obligated to stipulate that the master recordings would be produced in accordance with all the appropriate by-laws, rules, and regulations of all applicable and appropriate unions and guilds.

TEST PRESSINGS

Constantly aware of the importance of quality in the recording to be distributed, the artist and the record company would usually insist that the producer oversee and approve all test pressings of the master recording, evaluating it, and judging it against industry standards for its overall quality. The producer would typically accept this responsibility since he or she is ultimately responsible for the level of quality of the master recording. As mentioned previously, the test pressings typically remain the property of the artist or record company and are not intended for general, commercial release.

OWNERSHIP OF THE MASTER RECORDINGS

The artist/producer agreement would frequently stipulate, in clear and unambiguous words, that the master recordings, as well as the lyrics, music, and performances contained on the master recordings, remain the sole and exclusive property of the artist or the record company. If the artist had negotiated the right of ownership of the compositions, he or she would customarily have also retained the right to the exclusive copyright of the musical composition and of the master recordings produced under the terms of the production agreement as the owner and author of the musical compositions and master recordings. The artist, therefore, would usually have the right to renew, extend, and modify the copyrights.

Subject to all other agreements entered into by and between the artist and all other third parties, specifically the record company, the artist typically possesses the right to perform the master recordings publicly.

If the record company has negotiated for the rights of ownership in and to the master recordings, then all rights inherent in such ownership would vest in the record company.

RIGHT TO MANUFACTURE

In order to establish the limitation on the producer's rights in and to the master recordings, the artist/production agreement would normally stipulate, if so agreed among the parties, that the record company, or any of the subdistributors or other entities assigned the right to distribute the master recording by the record company, would have the exclusive right to manufacture the master recordings produced by the producer under the terms of the artist/producer agreement. The agreement may go on to state that the record company, or any of the subdistributors or other entities assigned the right to distribute the master recording by the record company, would also have the unencumbered right to sell, license, distribute and produce, advertise, publicize, lease, or use in any other way, manner, or form the master recordings, and to release derivatives of any or all of the master recordings on any medium now in use or to be devised in the future, under any name, trademark, or label, throughout the territory granted it in the recording agreement.

Notice of Copyright

A notice of copyright should be prominently displayed on all publicly distributed recordings. The symbol (p) is customarily exhibited on the recording, followed by the year the recording was first published and the name of the owner of the copyright. An example of the proper notice copyright is as follows: (p) 19 __, ABCD Inc.

The copyright notice on copies of literary, dramatic, and other visually perceptible work is (c), followed by the year the work was first published and the name of the copyright owner: (c) 19 __, ABCD Inc.

Additions to the Composition

The artist would usually insist that the artist/producer agreement clarify that all additions, suggestions, and creative embellishments made by the producer to the musical composition and master recording are, and will remain, the property of the artist. Furthermore, the artist may require that the producer declare that he or she would not possess, and would not demand at any time in the future, any rights or privileges inherent to those embellishments.

ASSIGNMENT OF COPYRIGHT

In the event the artist and the record company have agreed, and have so stipulated in the recording agreement between them, that the artist would assign and transfer the copyright in the master recordings to the record company, it is highly unlikely that anything in the artist/producer agreement would be included that would have the capacity or power to impede such a transfer or assignment.

PRODUCER'S NAME AND LIKENESS

The producer would generally grant to the artist the right to use the producer's name, photograph, likeness, and biographical material for the purpose of promoting and advertising the master recordings produced under the provisions of the artist/producer agreement. In furtherance of this provision, the producer would usually be obligated to make himself or herself available for photography sessions and research meetings at a time and at a place convenient to all parties.

CREDIT

Credits are a producer's calling card, a visible symbol of his or her work product and stature within the music industry. The producer would generally negotiate vigorously for the right to receive prominent credit as producer on all individual recordings or, if applicable, as the producer of the album or record on the label of all distributed records or albums, including singles, long-playing albums, audiotapes, and CDs, on the jackets of all discs and tapes, on all trade advertisements, and on all commercial advertisements and promotional campaigns. This provision may require that the record company, including its subdistributors or other entities to which the right to distribute the master recordings was assigned or granted, use its best efforts to ensure that the credit provision as negotiated in the production agreement is honored.

Inadvertent Breach

The record company may argue, though, that if the credit provisions negotiated in the artist/producer agreement are inadvertently deleted, then the record company would use its best efforts to remedy such mistake but would not be liable for any claims, actions, or damages resulting from such inadvertent deletion, nor would such inadvertence be considered a breach of the production agreement, or any agreement, entered into between the parties.

APPROVAL OF ALBUM COVER LINES

On rare occasions, depending on the clout and prominence of the producer within the entertainment community, the producer may negotiate for the right to approve all album cover line notes regarding the producer's career and contributions to the album. If so negotiated, the record company would usually deliver to the producer a sample of the album cover lines for approval. It is likely that the producer would be granted an agreed period of time within which to approve of such cover lines or to make any changes which he or she deems appropriate.

COMPENSATION

The producer may receive his or her compensation in various forms, including flat fees and royalties. In addition, the producer may have negotiated to receive advance compensation against future royalties.

Flat Fee

A flat fee is typically a one-time payment of a fixed and agreed sum, which may be paid in a single lump sum or on an agreed payment schedule, such as:

- weekly installments payable during the term of the agreement, or
- partial payment upon the signing of the artist/producer agreement and final payment upon the delivery of a satisfactory master recording.

Advance against Future Royalties

If the producer has negotiated to receive, as his or her compensation, a royalty based on net or gross earnings of the distributed recording, it is probable that the producer will negotiate to receive an advance payment against future royalty earnings. The advance would, as a rule, be recoupable from royalties payable to the producer under terms agreed upon between the producer and the record company or artist. Usually, the advance against future royalties is considered to be nonrefundable unless the producer materially breaches the agreement and, if so agreed in the production agreement, fails to cure, or remedy, the breach within the stipulated time period.

The producer usually receives his or her advance payment upon the signing of the artist/production agreement, though the advance may be divided into several payments commencing with the signing of the agreement and concluding at the time the approved master recording is delivered.

Royalty Rate

The royalty rate payable to the producer as compensation for his or her services under the terms of the artist/producer agreement should be detailed precisely. Often, the producer receives as his or her royalty payment a portion of the royalty due and owing the artist under the provisions established in the record company/recording artist agreement. If the artist has consented to pay the producer a share of his or her royalty as the producer's compensation, then the producer may stipulate that the artist/production agreement clarify that the artist be responsible to ensure that the producer receive the stipulated royalty fee. Normally, the producer would insist that artist be obligated to direct the record company, in a signed writing, to make the guaranteed royalty payments directly to the producer at the established schedule of payment.

If so agreed, the royalty due the producer would typically be based on similar conditions and provisions as agreed in the record company/recording artist agreement. Therefore, the producer would probably be paid a royalty derived from the gross or net sales of recordings, including audiotapes and CDs, sold through normal retail channels in the United States and in any and all foreign territories. The producer may also negotiate that he or she be entitled to receive a royalty based on the earnings generated from the sale of the master recordings released on CD-ROMs, music videos, soundtracks, merchandising, commercials, among other mediums, whether released in the United States or outside the United States, whether distributed through the means of retail stores, record clubs, infomercials, or under any other merchandising strategy now in use or to be used at any time in the future.

Increase in Royalty Rate

The producer would typically negotiate for an increase in the royalty rate of compensation due and owing him or her, basing such an increase on the achievement of certain performance sales levels for the master recording. If the artist has agreed to such an escalation in royalty rate in his or her agreement with the record company, then the artist/producer's agreement may reflect that agreement and stipulate that the producer's royalties are to be calculated and paid according to the same schedule and manner as royalties payable to the artist. Under those circumstances, though, the producer would usually be subject to the same limitations on royalties due and owing the artist. For example, the records distributed free of charge as promotional and advertising giveaways would therefore not be considered when calculating royalty (to the producer) figures if a similar provision is included in the artist/record company agreement.

Incorporation of Artist/Record Company Agreement

Since the recording agreement entered into by and between the record company and the artist is an integral part of the producer's agreement, the producer may request that the record company/recording artist agreement be incorporated as part of the artist/producer agreement, annexing it as an exhibit or rider to the artist/producer agreement.

Pro-Rated Fees

The artist and producer would usually stipulate that if album-length audiotapes or CDs are commercially released containing only one or several of the master recordings produced by the producer, then the producer's royalty fee would be pro rated on the basis of the number of master recordings produced by the producer which are on the release as compared to the total number of recordings on that release.

ARTIST'S BREACH

In the event the obligations to be performed under the provisions of the artist/producer agreement are not concluded as a result of a breach by the artist, the producer would usually argue vigorously, and would probably achieve as a deal point, that he or she continue to receive the agreed compensation without being penalized for the artist's default.

RECORDING COSTS

The costs for recording the master recordings are generally paid by either the artist or the record company, relieving the producer from any responsibility or liability in connection with the routine expenditures of the production of the master recordings. The costs of the recordings are typically budgeted and agreed upon in advance in the artist/record company agreement.

The artist and the record company may insist, though, that if the costs incurred in the production of the master recording exceed the agreed recording costs as a result of a fault, or stemming from unwarranted neglect on the part of the producer, then all such excess charges and fees should be the producer's responsibility. The artist or the record company would probably retain the right to charge all such excess fees against the producer's royalty fees due under the terms of the artist/producer agreement, or to deduct all such excess fees from any flat-fee payments due and owing the producer.

LIMITATION OF PRODUCER'S ROYALTIES

The artist would usually argue that the producer's right to receive his or her royalty fee be restrained until all the costs incurred by the record company for the production of the master recording are recouped in full. The producer would usually demand that his or her right to receive royalty fees be identical in nature to those of the artist in the artist/record company agreement.

DELIVERY OF STATEMENTS

The producer would typically request that all statements and accountings regarding the subject matter of the artist/producer agreement be sent to his or her attention in accordance with an agreed schedule and in compliance with the notice provision of this agreement. The schedule for delivery of all statement and accounting are usually similar to the one detailed in the record company/recording artist agreement. If any payments are due and owing the producer in accordance with his or her compensation schedule, then that payment would typically accompany the statement, if so agreed by the parties.

BOOKS AND RECORDS

The artist and the record company would usually be obligated to maintain accurate and correct books and records regarding the master recordings produced by the producer under the terms of the artist/producer agreement if the producer's compensation is calculated as a royalty based on gross or net sales of recordings.

Right to Contest Statements

Upon the producer's receipt of the statements and accountings in accordance with the schedule fixed in the agreement, the producer would usually have an agreed period of time, if so negotiated, within which to contest and challenge those tabulations.

Right to Inspect Books and Records

The producer would usually negotiate for the right to inspect the books and records after giving the artist and record company written notice of his or her intention to do so. The record company and artist would typically agree to the producer's request for an audit, if the audit is to be conducted by a certified public accountant at the place where the company books and records are normally kept, during normal business hours and at the producer's sole cost and expense.

NOTICES

The artist/producer agreement would usually stipulate that all notices required to be sent among and between the parties should be sent by certified or registered mail, return receipt requested, or by an express mail service, such as Federal Express or UPS. The notices are normally required to be sent to the addresses listed in the agreement, or to different addresses if the demand for a change of address is made in writing and sent by the requesting party to the other party in the manner and form established in the agreement.

RIGHT TO ENTER AGREEMENT

The artist/producer agreement, like most other agreements, relies on the validity of the warranties made by the parties for its justification. As such, the agreement would usually require that each party attest that it possesses the unencumbered right and authority to grant the rights accorded in the agreement. Furthermore, each party would customarily warrant and represent that it is not under any disability, restriction, or prohibition, whether contractual or otherwise, with respect to its rights to execute this agreement, to grant the rights listed in this agreement, and to perform the obligations stated in this agreement.

NO VIOLATION

The artist will usually be required to warrant and represent that none of the lyrics, music, or other creative work utilized by the artist in the production of the master recordings produced by the producer in accordance with the provisions of the artist/producer agreement, nor the exploitation of the composition as authorized under this agreement, would result in the violation or breach of any statutory or common law or rights of any party, including without limitation, contractual rights, trademarks, copyrights, and rights of publicity and privacy.

NO ADDITIONAL GRANT

The agreement should also provide that the artist has not granted and will not grant any right, title, or interest to any other person or entity effective during the validity of this agreement which would conflict with or be in limitation of any of the rights granted the producer under this agreement. In addition, the artist would normally stipulate that he or she will not enter into any other agreement effective during the term of this agreement with any other party with respect to competing aspects of this exclusive contract.

NO ATTACK OF ARTIST'S RIGHTS

The artist would probably insist that the producer warrant that he or she will not attack or contest the rights, titles, or ownership of the artist in and to the lyrics, music, or any other aspect of the musical compositions being produced and recorded in accordance with the terms of the artist/producer agreement, including the rights of copyright and trademark. Furthermore, the artist would usually demand that the producer warrant that he or she will not harm, misuse, or bring into disrepute the lyrics, music, or any other aspect of the musical compositions being produced and recorded in accordance with the terms of the artist/producer agreement. The artist would also require that the producer warrant that he or she would not create any expenses chargeable to the artist without the prior written approval of the artist.

INDEMNIFICATION

The artist/producer agreement would usually stipulate that both parties would indemnify, defend, protect, save, and hold each other harmless from and against any and all actions, claims, suits, losses, judgments, penalties, liabilities, damages, costs, and expenses (including reasonable attorney's fees and court costs) of whatever kind and nature imposed, incurred, asserted, brought, or made by or against either party arising out of the other party's breach of any of its representations, warranties, or obligations made pursuant to this agreement or through the negligence or intentional acts of its officers, directors, employees, or representatives. In addition, the parties would usually agree to give each other prompt written notice of any such action, claim, or suit.

TERMINATION

If either party of this agreement breaches any of the material terms and conditions of this agreement, the party claiming such breach will generally have the right, if so agreed, to serve upon the party alleged to be in breach a written notice of its intention to terminate this agreement. The party alleged to be in breach will then usually be granted a fixed period of time within which to remedy the breach. Failure to remedy the breach will probably result in the agreement's being automatically terminated without prejudice to any other rights which either party may otherwise have against the other.

Insolvency

If the producer becomes insolvent or files a petition in bankruptcy, or if a petition in bankruptcy is filed against the producer, or if the producer makes an assignment for the benefit of creditors or makes any arrangement pursuant to any bankruptcy law, or if a receiver is appointed, this agreement may be automatically terminated by the artist or the record company if the parties so agree.

NO WAIVER

Generally, the parties would agree that no waiver by either party of any provision of this agreement or of any default under this agreement would affect any of that party's rights thereafter to enforce that provision or to exercise any right or remedy in the event of any other default, whether or not similar.

NO PARTNERSHIP

The parties would usually emphasize that nothing in the artist/producer agreement should be construed to constitute a partnership or a joint venture between them. Therefore, neither party would have the right to obligate or bind the other in any manner or form nor hold itself out contrary to the terms of this agreement. Furthermore, the parties would probably affirm that neither party would be liable for any representation, act, or omission of the other which is contrary to the provisions stipulated in this agreement.

STATE OF JURISDICTION

As in most contracts, the parties to the artist/producer agreement would agree to a particular state which would have jurisdiction over the provisions and application of this agreement.

EXPENSES

The producer may request that all expenses he or she incurs in regard to the production of the master recordings, including airfare and living accommodations if the recording studio is more than an agreed number of miles from the producer's residence, as well as general overhead (long-distance phone calls, messengers, cost of tape, etc.), should be paid by the artist or record company immediately upon receipt of a documented statement by the producer.

RIGHT TO ASSIGN

The producer is usually selected for his or her particular and unique expertise, knowledge, and creative abilities. Since those traits are often not interchangeable, the artist may attempt to limit the producer's right to assign the production agreement to only those producers who have been approved, in a signed writing, by the artist and record company, if mutual approval is required by the record company/recording artist agreement.

MODIFICATION

The parties would usually agree not to alter, amend, or change the provisions in the production agreement, unless they agree to such amendment, change, and alteration in a writing containing both their signatures.

UNENFORCEABILITY

In the event a provision in the agreement is deemed by a competent court of law to be unenforceable, then the artist/producer agreement may stipulate that only that unenforceable provision would be considered null and void, while the remainder of the agreement would remain valid and operative. Of course, the courts may deem that the challenged provision is in fact, a material ingredient of the contract. Subsequently, if a material clause is affected, the entire contract could be deemed null and void.

The producer may insist that in the event any provision held unenforceable would impair the producer's right to receive his or her royalties under the provisions of this agreement, then such a provision should be deemed material which could require that the agreement be terminated without impairing the producer's right to receive his or her compensation.

FORCE MAJEURE

If events external to the control of the producer make the performance of his or her obligations impossible or impractical, the *force majeure* provision typically serves to avoid a breach of the contract and provide for a cure. As a rule, the agreement would provide for the resumption of the producer's obligation as soon as the event which triggered the clause is declared concluded.

AGREEMENT TO INURE TO BENEFIT OF ADDITIONAL PARTIES

The parties would usually agree to the standard provision that the artist/producer agreement, including all its provisions, would inure to the benefit of certain additional parties including the assigns, successors, administrators, representatives, heirs, and estates of the parties to this agreement.

SIGNATURES

The parties would customarily be required to sign the agreement, signifying their understanding and acceptance of its terms, obligations, responsibilities, and provisions.

8

The Artist Side Letter Agreement between the Artist and the Producer

The enterprising record producer may initiate a record deal between himself or herself and a record company by entering a recording contract with an artist, producing a record, then selling or licensing that record to a record company for compensation, usually consisting of an advance payment recoupable against future royalties and agreed royalty payments.

In order to ensure the record company that the producer has willingly contracted with the artist, and that the record company's obligations and responsibilities to the artist would not duplicate those of the producer, the producer may request that the artist enter into a side letter agreement which encompasses the artist's commitment to the producer.

The side letter is also regularly used as an inducement to the record company, assuring it that the artist has indeed entered into the recording commitment with the producer who has secured the right to license the master recording to the record company.

The seasoned artist would routinely seek the right to review the recording agreement entered into, by and between the producer and the record company. Simultaneous with the right to review the record company agreement would be the artist's request to approve its provisions and conditions prior to entering the side letter agreement.

PARTIES

The side letter is typically drafted in the form of a business letter between the producer and the artist.

STATEMENT OF THE GRANT

Defining the relationship between the parties, the side letter would usually stipulate that the artist has entered into a recording contract with the producer. Customarily, the recording contract is attached to the side letter in an exhibit or rider, and made part of the side letter.

Services of Artist and Producer

The producer would ordinarily indicate in the side letter that his or her primary responsibility would be to produce one or several master recordings. The artist's responsibility would be to record to his or her best ability, one or several master recordings, the number of which to be decided upon in this side letter.

Artist Aware of Producer's Intent

If the side letter is intended to induce the record company to enter into an agreement with the record producer regarding the artist's musical compositions and recordings, the artist would customarily stipulate that he or she has been notified of the producer's intent to enter an agreement with the record company to convey and deliver to it some or all of the master recordings made and produced by the producer of the artist's musical compositions during the term of the agreement entered into, by and between the producer and artist. The side letter should also provide that the artist is in approval of the agreement between the producer and record company and, with the intent of inducing the record company to enter the agreement, will agree to all the stipulations included in the side letter and in the recording agreement.

PRODUCER'S RIGHT

The artist would usually confirm and guarantee in the side letter that the producer has the right to enter into the agreement with the record company in order to confirm the producer's right to produce, and the artist's desire that the producer produce, the master recordings that are the subject matter of this letter.

TERM

Typically, the side letter would state that the right granted to the producer would continue, and remain valid, for the term of the recording agreement and until all the commitments and obligations under the recording agreement have been fully executed.

PRODUCER'S WARRANTIES REGARDING ARTIST

The artist would usually state to the satisfaction of the record company that all the warranties, representations and commitments which the producer made in the recording agreement regarding the artist are true, correct, and actual.

ARTIST'S PERFORMANCE GUARANTEE

The artist would typically warrant and represent that he or she will perform, to the best of his or her ability, all the obligations and responsibilities required of the artist by, and guaranteed by the producer in, the recording agreement.

Artist's Obligations

The obligations and responsibilities of the artist usually include the following:

- recording the musical compositions which have been approved by the producer and the artist and, if so agreed, the record company,
- approving the recording studio selected by the producer, and
- adhering to a recording schedule with an agreed commencement date.

Recording Budget

In most cases, the recording budget has been preapproved, and all expenses required for the production of the master recordings have been considered and justified.

Creative Elements

In addition, it is likely that the creative elements have been established and bound by contract, including the back-up musicians and technical team of engineers and mixers. In essence, the letter would verify that the full mechanism required to produce, in a timely and reasonable manner, the agreed master recordings has been approved by the producer, the record company and the artist.

INCLUSION OF EXHIBITS

Since the artist/producer agreement and the record company agreement are integral parts of the side letter agreement, being referred to on several occasions, both agreements would usually be attached to, and made part of, the side letter as exhibits or riders. Typically, the record company would insist on reviewing the artist/producer agreement to determine whether it meets all the needs and requirements of the record company. The artist may also negotiate for the privilege of reviewing the record company agreement in order to examine and approve its provisions.

CESSATION OF ARTIST/PRODUCER AGREEMENT

The record company is usually prepared to invest its marketing and distribution expertise for the purpose of exploiting, in all the markets to which it has aquired the right, the master recordings of the artist's musical composition, produced by the producer. Often, it has invested time, energy and financial commitment toward that end. In order to protect the record company's investment, the artist would usually be required to stipulate his or her continued commitment to the musical project. Typically, the artist would be obliged to declare that if the contractual relationship with the producer ceases and terminates, and the artist by that action is no longer committed to fulfilling his or her services in accordance with the artist/producer agreement, or if the producer fails, neglects, or refuses for any reason to perform his or her services under the artist/producer agreement, the artist would nonetheless fulfill his or her recording commitments with the record company.

As a rule, the record company would also insist that the artist commit himself or herself to personally undertake and assume all the obligations and responsibilities established in the agreement entered into between the producer and the record company. By that commitment, the artist would be ensuring the record company that it would be guaranteed all the benefits it would have enjoyed had the producer continued his or her recording commitment, including the delivery of the agreed number of master recordings of a quality suitable for commercial distribution, in a timely manner.

The artist would typically agree to the record company's demands, but may make a few demands of his or her own. As a condition to accepting the record company's requirement, the artist could insist that, considering he or she would be obligated to deliver the contracted master recordings to the record company according to the schedule agreed upon in prior agreements with the producer, he or she should be entitled to receive the full value of the artist/producer agreement, including all advances, royalties, expenses, and other remunerations and compensations negotiated for and guaranteed. It is likely that the record company would agree to compensate the artist according to the terms of the artist/producer agreement unless it feels it can renegotiate the terms of the agreement, specifically regarding the artist's compensation, without sacrificing the quality required in the master recording to assure the recording viability in the marketplace.

If the record company and artist choose, the recording commitment by the artist could be invalidated without prejudice or liability to the artist if that recording commitment is nullified, voided, and invalidated in a writing signed by the record company and the artist.

NAME AND LIKENESS

The artist would normally stipulate in the side letter, that both the producer and the record company would be accorded the right to use the artist's name, likeness, photograph, and any and all other identifiable images for the purposes of advertising and promotion in regard to the master recordings produced under the terms of the artist/producer agreement and distributed by the record company.

Artist Approval

The artist may request that he or she be granted the right to approve all identifiable images utilized by the producer and the record company, but it is likely that the producer and record company would retain those rights, unencumbered by the artist's approval, unless the artist is a performer of some note and industry clout.

EXCLUSIVE RECORDING ARTIST

As an inducement to the record company and to the producer, the artist may be required to designate himself or herself as the "exclusive recording artist" for the record company, as well as the producer's "exclusive recording artist" on all advertising, promotional, and biographical material. Under the terms of this provision, if the artist appears, courtesy of the record company or the producer, on a third-party record company's recording, or if the artist makes public appearances at live performances, the artist would, in most cases, be designated as the record company's exclusive recording artist on all programs, jackets, album covers, and any and all additional advertising and promotional material.

EXCLUSIVITY

Guaranteeing his or her exclusive arrangement with the producer and the record company, the artist would usually warrant that during the term of the record company/producer agreement, the artist would not perform his or her musical compositions for any other producer for the purpose of producing master recordings. The exclusivity binds the artist to the producer, prohibiting him or her to enter a recording agreement with any other entity or person without the producer's written consent.

The record company and producer may demand, and the artist may pledge that following the expiration of the record company/producer agreement, he or she will not record or produce, with the intention of producing master recordings, any master recordings contained on the master recordings submitted to the record company under the terms of the record company/producer agreement for either of the following:

a) an agreed number of years following the termination of the record company/producer agreement, or

b) an agreed number of years following the last recording of the master recording in question.

ARTIST'S GUARANTEE

The artist would usually be required to empower the record company with the right to initiate all pertinent legal actions and proceedings, in order to enforce any and all of his or her guarantees, including the timely delivery of the agreed master recordings, under the record company/producer and the artist/producer agreements. The artist may further guarantee, in clear and concise language to allay any possibility of ambiguity or confusion, that he or she would perform any and all of the services required of him or her under the terms of the record company/producer agreement, including any agreed modifications made to that original agreement.

PAYMENT OF ROYALTIES

The side letter would usually stipulate, if so established in the artist/producer agreement, that the producer would be solely liable to the artist for the payment of all agreed advances, royalties, expenses, recording costs, and any and all other fees in connection with the production, recording, manufacturing, distribution, and commercial exploitation of the master recordings throughout the territory agreed in the record company/producer agreement.

The established compensation and payment schedule would usually be outlined in detail in the artist/producer agreement which, as indicated elsewhere in this chapter, is customarily attached to the side letter as an exhibit or rider. This provision would usually be subject to the producer's fulfilling his or her obligations and responsibilities under the terms of the record company/artist agreement.

ACCOUNTING

Since the artist's livelihood depends to a large part on his or her receipt of royalties from the producer, the artist would usually demand, and the side letter would so state, that the producer is obliged to render to the artist regular accountings of gross receipts due the artist under the terms of the artist/producer and producer/record company agreements. The accounting, customarily accompanied by the artist's payment, would usually be delivered according to an agreed-upon schedule, which may be quarterly, semiannually, or annually.

Accurate Books

The artist would typically insist that the producer keep and maintain accurate books of account regarding all transactions relating to the artist's compensation under the provision of the artist/producer, and producer/record company agreement. Typically, the artist would request the right to inspect the books and records of the producer with respect to the subject matter of the side letter. The producer would usually agree under the condition that the artist give reasonable notice of his or her intent to inspect the books and records. Furthermore, the producer may require that the inspection take place during normal business hours and at the place where the books and records are normally held.

Discovered Inconsistency

In the event of a discovered inconsistency by the artist, the artist could insist, if so negotiated, that the producer pay that amount plus a fixed rate of interest as a penalty. The artist may have also negotiated the proviso that the party found to be in error pay or reimburse the other party for the costs of the accounting audit.

Time within which to Contest

As a means of placing the artist's right to contest the accounting within a reasonable time frame, the producer may insist that all accountings and statements rendered to the artist would be binding upon the artist and would not be subject to objection for any reason unless specific objection is made by written notice to the producer stating the basis of the objection within an agreed time period following the artist's receipt of the accounting.

RIGHT TO ENTER SIDE LETTER

Typically, the artist would be required to warrant and represent that he or she has the exclusive right and authority to enter the side letter agreement and that by doing so, he or she would not violate or breach any statutory or common law or other rights of any party, including without limitation, contractual rights, trademarks, copyrights, and rights of publicity and privacy.

NO DISABILITY

Both parties would usually agree that neither is under any disabilities, restrictions, or prohibitions, whether contractual or otherwise, with respect to executing or performing the obligations stated in this side letter agreement.

NO GRANT TO OTHERS

The producer would probably insist that the artist warrant that he or she has not granted, and will not grant, any right, title, or interest to any other person or entity effective during the validity of this side letter which would conflict with or be in limitation of any of the rights granted.

INDEMNIFICATION

The artist and the producer would usually agree to indemnify, defend, protect, save, and hold each other harmless from and against any and all actions, claims, suits, losses, judgments, penalties, liabilities, damages, costs, and expenses (including reasonable attorney's fees) of whatever kind and nature imposed, incurred, asserted, brought, or made by or against either party arising out of the other party's breach of any of its representations, warranties, or obligations made pursuant to this agreement or through the negligence or intentional acts of its officers, directors, employees, or representatives. They may also agree to deliver to each other prompt written notice of any such action, claim, or suit.

TERMINATION

If either party to this side letter breaches any of its material terms and conditions, the party claiming such breach would generally have the right to serve upon the party alleged to be in breach a written notice of its intention to terminate this side letter, and the party alleged to be in breach would then have an agreed period within which to remedy the breach. Failure to remedy the breach could result if so negotiated, in the side letter's being automatically terminated.

ASSIGNMENT

The side letter's capacity to reflect the objectives of the producer and the artist usually depends on the specific expertise and talents both parties bring to the arrangement. Therefore, it is likely that both parties would stipulate that neither would assign the side letter to a third party without the prior written consent of the other party. The producer may negotiate for the right to assign this side letter to any wholly owned subsidiary, or to any person, firm, or corporation owning or acquiring a substantial portion of the producer's stock or assets, provided said subsidiary, person, firm, or corporation is a bona fide professional and expert in the musical producing field and the producer will continue his or her services and obligations, as agreed to in the artist/producer and producer/record company agreements. Rarely, would the artist object to such an assignment of the producer's interests.

NOTICES

Both parties would probably stipulate that all notices and statements provided for under the provision of the side letter should be in writing and, together with all payments due and owing, sent by United States mail, certified or registered mail, return receipt requested, or by verifiable express mailing, such as Federal Express or UPS. All notices should be sent to the addresses listed in this side letter or to any other address that is designated in writing by either of the parties.

ENTIRE UNDERSTANDING

The parties would usually indicate that this side letter represents the full understanding of the parties and that no modification, amendment, waiver, termination, or discharge of this side letter or any of the terms or provisions included in it will be binding upon either of the parties unless confirmed by a written instrument signed by the parties.

VOID PROVISION

In most cases, the parties would agree that if any provision of the side letter is held void, voidable, invalid, or inoperative by a competent court of law, no other provision would be affected as a result of such action, and accordingly, the remaining provisions would remain in full force and effect as though such void, voidable, invalid, or inoperative provision had not been contained in the side letter. The artist would probably insist on adding a clause that would provide him or her the assurance that if any provision held void, voidable, invalid, or inoperative would impair his or her right to receive his or her royalties, then the side letter would be deemed to be terminated.

NO PARTNERSHIP

The parties would probably stipulate that nothing in this side letter constitutes a partnership or a joint venture between the parties, and therefore neither party would have the right to obligate or bind the other in any manner whatsoever, and neither party would become liable for any representation, act, or omission of the other contrary to the provisions stipulated.

STATE OF JURISDICTION

A clause in the side letter would usually designate the state whose laws retain the final authority in regard to the interpretation of the provisions of the side letter.

ATTORNEY-IN-FACT

The producer would probably negotiate for the privilege of acting as the artist's attorney-in-fact with the right to make, execute, and deliver all contracts and agreements in the artist's name, specific to the side letter. If the artist agrees to such a provision the artist may be required to refrain from performing those functions granted to the producer by the power of attorney unless the record producer agrees otherwise in a signed writing.

The grant of the rights of attorney-in-fact to the producer should be considered carefully by the artist. The clause itself may be drafted as narrowly or as broadly as negotiated by the parties. The producer would usually negotiate for broad powers, arguing that since he or she is bound to the record company by the producer/record company agreement, he or she would be in a better position to expedite and oversee all matters concerning the provisions expressed in the side letter. The producer may assert that the ability to act as the artist's attorney-in-fact would facilitate his or her duties. The artist, though, would typically prefer power of attorney, if granted at all, be limited to specific, clearly defined functions.

NO PREJUDICE

The artist would probably require that the producer agree not to take any action during the effectiveness of the side letter that will prejudice the artist's rights.

FORCE MAJEURE

If events external to the control of the producer make the performance impossible or impractical, the agreement may provide for an avoidance of a breach and provide for a cure. It may also call for the resumption of the obligation incumbent on both parties as soon as the event which triggered the impossibility is declared terminated.

SIGNATURES

By the signatures both parties place on the side letter, they customarily signify their approval and understanding of its provisions and conditions.

9

The Performing Rights Society Agreement

Copyright owners of musical compositions, usually the publishers or songwriters, are entitled to license the nondramatic public performance rights of their compositions. The owners, through the efforts of the public performance societies, receive earnings generated from the nondramatic public performance of the copyrighted compositions by the following means:

- live performances in such locations as hotels, nightclubs, schools, discotheques, and public arenas,
- background music services, such as heard in retail stores and other public locations, and
- the media, including television, cable, and radio.

The performing rights societies—the American Society of Composers, Authors and Publishers (ASCAP), Broadcast Music, Inc. (BMI), and the Society of European Stage, Authors and Composers (SESAC)—customarily acquire the rights to license the compositions for nondramatic public performance from the songwriters and publishers in exchange for a fee. The societies then grant licenses to use those compositions in those locations under their auspices. The performing rights societies typically issue a blanket license or a program license to radio and television broadcasters, as well as to live venues (including concert halls, colleges, discotheques, hotels, and public arenas) for the use of its catalogue, and to collect, in exchange for granting the license, a fee. If a source license is issued, the broadcaster or user of the licensed compositions may negotiate directly with the publisher or copyright owner.

After revenues are earned and collected by the performing rights societies from the users of the musical licenses, the performing rights societies customarily distribute directly to the songwriters and publishers their respective shares.

The performing rights societies are often furnished daily or regularly scheduled, logs of the music performed from major cable, networks, and radio stations in addition to logs from public performance venues. In addition, the public performance societies typically select a random group of representative radio stations or television broadcast stations, request the logs of the music played by those stations, and calculate the value of such composition to the songwriter and publisher. The performing rights societies may also collect programs from the concert and symphonic halls and log the performance of compositions for their computations.

Songwriters usually join one of the performing rights societies. They often join the society they feel can best commercially exploit their compositions and, once exploited, can best collect the royalties they have earned as payment for the composition's public performance. Publishers, on the other hand, normally join all the societies since a songwriter member of one society customarily has his or her composition published by a publisher who is a member of the same society.

Since most performers typically earn a large segment of their revenues from licensed performances of their music, it is highly advisable that the artist familiarize himself or herself with the performing rights societies services and agreements. Public performance societies generally license nondramatic performances of compositions, rather than the "grand rights," which are usually defined as the performance of musical compositions in a dramatic context, including live performances of ballet, opera, and musical theatre.

PARTIES

The public performance agreement entered into between the performing rights society and the songwriter and/or publisher typically states clearly the names of all parties to the agreement, including any pseudonyms or stage names, and the exact date the agreement becomes effective.

TERM

The length and duration of the performing rights society agreement will customarily be determined and agreed upon by the parties to the agreement. The society may secure the right to exercise an option to review the agreement for one or several, additional terms, following the expiration of the initial term.

TERRITORY

The agreement would usually clarify the territory over which the society has retained the rights of public performance. Those rights may be limited to a particular country or may be as broad as the world. If the society demands world rights to the composition, that grant would typically be subject to the society's agreements then in effect with foreign country performance rights societies.

RIGHTS GRANTED

The songwriter and/or the publisher, the owners of the copyrighted composition, typically grant to the performing rights society for the agreed-upon term of months or years, and in the agreed territory, the exclusive right to license the public performances of the compositions owned by the owners.

Public Performance

The definition of "public performance" generally means vocal and/or instrumental renditions or representations by means of radio and television (including pay or fee television) and by means of nondramatic live performance such as live performances in select venues including public arenas, colleges, concert halls, discotheques, and nightclubs.

Grant of Compositions

The public performance agreement should clarify the exact composition which is being granting by the owner to the society. It should further stipulate that such rights would typically commence as soon as the composition is written, composed, acquired, owned, published, or copyrighted by the owner.

The owner would, as a rule, grant rights in those copyrighted compositions of which

a) the owner is the sole owner of the copyrighted compositions,

b) the owner is the composer or publisher, or has acquired or owns, either alone or in collaboration with another,

c) the owner presently has rights, titles, and interests,

d) the owner may write, compose, acquire, own, publish, or copyright during the term of the performing rights society agreement, either alone or in collaboration with another, or

e) the owner may acquire the right, title, and interest in, during the term of the performing rights society agreement.

CLEARANCE SHEETS

The society would ordinarily require that the owner furnish it with clearance sheets which attest to the owner's copyright ownership in the composition, including the names of the co-owners and publishers, as well as the assurance that performing rights in the composition have not been granted to or reserved by another performing rights society.

ENFORCING THE COPYRIGHT

The performing rights society entering the agreement with the owner would usually demand, and the owner would generally grant to the society, the right to pursue all rights and remedies required to enforce the copyright in the compositions, whether the copyright is registered in the name of the owner or in the name of the society, in order to protect the rights granted to the society.

FRAGMENTS OF SONGS AND ARRANGEMENTS

It is generally understood that by entering the public performance agreement, the owner is granting to the performing rights society the right of the public performance of the separate numbers, songs, arrangements, selections, or melodies which may comprise a part of a musical play or of a dramatic-musical performance. The owner typically does not grant to the society the right of performance of musical plays or dramatic-musical performances in their entirety on the legitimate stage.

CLUBS, HOTELS, ETC.

The performing rights agreement customarily grants to the performing rights society the right to exploit the compositions in certain specific venues, including clubs, hotels, performance arenas, colleges, discotheques and retail establishments. Usually, the society grants a blanket license for the venue, if the venue is in the business of regularly offering music to its customers. The society would normally base its license fee on the following considerations:

- the seating capacity of the venue,
- whether there is an admission charge,
- the amount of the admission charge,
- the weekly music budget for live performances, and
- the number of hours per week musical entertainment is provided to a paying audience.

If the venue offers musical entertainment on an irregular schedule, the performing rights society may attempt to collect its fees from the promoter or producer.

RADIO

The owner usually assigns to the society the right to exploit the public performance the copyrighted compositions by means of radio broadcasting. The performing rights society would generally offer the broadcaster a blanket license or a program license.

TELEVISION

The owner would also be prepared to grant the right of the public performance of the compositions by means of television broadcast. Usually included in this grant are the grants to license the composition on pay cable, including such stations as Music Television (MTV) and Home Box Office (HBO). The society normally offers the television broadcaster a blanket license or a program license to perform selections from its catalogue.

Restrictions on Grants of Rights of Public Performance by Means of Television Broadcast

The owner generally excludes several rights from the right of public performance by means of television broadcasting. The owner may not grant to the society the right to license the public performance of opera, musical comedies, plays, or similar "dramatic performances," in whole or in part. Furthermore, re-creations of performances from the owner's operas, musical comedies, or plays are usually also not granted, so long as the re-creations resemble the original work.

"Dramatic performances" may be defined, in the performing rights society agreement, as those performances of a musical composition in which a definite and recognizable plot exists and is depicted by ascertained action. The musical compositions are generally intertwined with the plot and serve the purpose of moving the plot forward. The mere use of dialogue as an introduction of a performance of a composition is generally not considered to be a dramatic performance.

MOTION PICTURES IN FOREIGN TERRITORIES

The owner would probably assign to the society the right to collect license fees from the commercial exploitation of performance of the copyrighted compositions in motion pictures exhibited in public cinemas or theatres in many foreign territories (outside the United States).

LIMITATIONS

The owner of the compositions may feel, at times, that the public performances of several or all of his or her compositions could potentially damage the exploitation of those compositions by other means of presentation, including motion pictures, operas, or musical comedies. As such, the owner may negotiate for the right to limit and restrict the exploitation, by public performance, of those specific compositions for an agreed time period. In addition, the owner may request that certain compositions be restricted for a period of time, pending the resolution of a suit or claim that the composition in question infringes on the right of another and that the society may not, in actuality, have the right to the public performance of the composition.

The society may agree to the owner's demands on the following conditions:

- the owner proves that unless those compositions are in fact restricted he or she would suffer economic or professional loss and
- the owner demonstrates that the restrictions the owner aims to have imposed on one or several of his or her compositions have not been suggested merely for the sake of altering or regulating fees.

EXCLUSION FROM AGREEMENT

The performing rights society may demand the right to exclude at its option the following compositions:

- those which appear similar to an existing composition and may therefore constitute copyright infringement,
- those which may be considered offensive, in bad taste, or against public morals,
- those which may not be suitable for public performance, or
- those which may be or are based on compositions in the public domain.

BEST EFFORTS

Since the rights granted the performance society represent a substantial source of income for the owner, he or she would typically demand that the society use its best efforts in fulfilling the objectives of the society, specifically those of exploiting the compositions to their maximum potential and collecting all fees earned from such exploitation in a timely manner.

USE OF ROYALTIES

Furthermore, the owner may demand that a provision within the performing rights agreement stipulate that the society utilize all royalties, profits, and advantages which derive from the exploitation of the owner's compositions by means of the public performance rights granted in the agreement, to the ends granted to the society by its charter.

ENFORCEMENT OF THE RIGHTS OF PUBLIC PERFORMANCE

Typically, the owner of the copyrighted compositions would grant to the society the right to enforce the rights of public performance from infringement. The permission granted by this provision generally includes the right to litigate all claims of infringement and to collect the damages arising from that infringement. Furthermore, in defense of the rights granted under this agreement, the society would generally be granted the authorization to join in suits initiated by or against the owner, in regard to the copyrighted compositions.

ATTORNEY-IN-FACT

The granting of the right, by one party to the other, for the latter to act in the name of the former, is a privilege which should considered and evaluated carefully before being bestowed. Such right can be as sweeping or as limited as defined by the parties and should reflect the intent of both parties.

In the performance rights agreement, the owner may grant the right to the society to act as his or her attorney-in-fact for the specific purpose of performing all acts, and of executing, acknowledging, and delivering any and all documents, instruments, papers, and pleadings that are necessary in order to restrain the infringement of the rights of the public performance of the compositions or to collect damages arising from the settlement of a claim arising from such infringement. Furthermore, the society may request that the owner grant to the society additional documents and powers of attorney that would be necessary in order to exercise and enforce its rights as granted by the performing rights agreement. The owner would typically restrict the scope of the power of attorney accorded the society to certain specifically detailed acts. The more defined the acts in question, the less chance of the society overstepping its authority.

METHOD OF PAYMENT OF ROYALTIES

The society will typically emphasize in the agreement that it is comprised of songwriters and publishers, that the sums it receives as royalties from the licensees and distributes among members of the society will be divided among the songwriters and publishers, and disbursed among each group as determined by the committees controlling such distribution.

ESTIMATED NUMBER OF PERFORMANCES

Since it is highly difficult for the society to ascertain with one hundred percent accuracy the exact number of times the owner's work has been performed on a broadcast venue during a particular payment cycle, the society will usually disclose that its calculations are based on an estimation of the number of performances of the artist's compositions, utilizing its current system of computation.

CO-OWNERS

In the event the composition was composed by co-owners, the performing rights society may stipulate that the fees it pays to each owner would be equal to his or her pro rata share, determined by the number of co-owners. If the co-owners have instructed the society, in a signed writing, of their desire that their shares be divided according to a different payment percentage, the society would usually agree to abide by the written and signed instructions.

FOREIGN REVENUES

The society would usually stipulate that upon receiving earned revenues from the foreign exploitation of the compositions, it would distribute to the owner his or her share, less the standard deduction it applies as reasonable handling charges.

CLASSIFICATION OF OWNER

In order to eliminate the possibility of confusion, the performing rights agreement would frequently classify the owner according to his or her professional classification, that is, as either a songwriter or a publisher. The parties to the agreement also are likely to stipulate that the owner would be entitled to receive his or her remunerations in accordance with the rules established by the society committee controlling his or her classification. On occasion, the owner may request permission to amend or change his or her classification. To reflect that possibility, the agreement should contain a clause providing that upon the owner filing his or her request for a change in status, an appeal process would be initiated within a reasonable period of time after the initial filing, to decide the issue. Typically, if the owner should be granted the appeal, the society would demand that the decision of the appeal board be final and binding upon both the society and the owner.

STATEMENTS

The society would usually agree to submit to the owner statements according to an agreed schedule, detailing the number of performances during the preceding payment cycle. The statements would typically be accompanied by the payment due and owing the owner.

COMPETING SOCIETY

In the event the performing rights society secures reasonable information indicating that the owner is receiving payments for the composition from a competing performing rights society, the society would usually argue that this agreement should be terminated immediately and all payments halted until the society receives conclusive evidence that the owner is not receiving dual payments from the exploitation of a single composition.

FORCE MAJEURE

Since most entertainment contracts are created to ensure the fulfillment of a specific performance, where time is of the essence, it is important to provide a clause which considers the validity of the agreement if events external to the control of the society make the performance impossible or impractical. The *force majeure* provision addresses such unforeseen events which may, if so agreed by the parties, require the tolling of the performance obligation. The practical effect of the *force majeure* clause is to avoid a breach of the contract and to provide for a cure. The clause would also provide for the resumption of the party's obligation as soon as the event which triggered the execution of the *force majeure* clause is declared gone.

The intent behind the *force majeure* clause is to accommodate the unforeseen difficulties imposed on the society and owner by outside forces. If the event triggering the application of the *force majeure* provision remains in effect for an agreed period of time, then this clause may allow for the termination of the agreement, thereby avoiding an indefinite suspension of the agreement.

NO PARTNERSHIP OR JOINT VENTURE

While the parties entering this agreement typically grant each other specific rights, the agreement would usually clarify that they have not entered a joint venture or partnership. This provision intends to protect the parties from shared liabilities.

VALIDITY OF THE PROVISION IN THE AGREEMENT

The agreement would usually indicate that if any single provision is adjudged invalid, the subsequent deletion of that provision would not nullify and invalidate the whole contract. The only provision invalidated would be the single provision in question, while the remaining provisions would remain in full effect.

NOTICES

Both the owner and the society would usually require, as an assurance against subterfuge, that all notices and statements provided for under this contract be in writing and, together with all payments provided under this contract, shall be sent by United States mail, postage prepaid, or by certified or registered mail, return receipt requested, or by other forms of mail that maintain records and receipts, including Federal Express, UPS, and DHL, to the address set forth in the performing rights society agreement or to any other address as may be designated in writing by the parties.

The agreement could list the addresses as follows:

OWNER
Address: ____________________

SOCIETY
Address: ____________________

Properly addressed notices delivered or sent as provided under this agreement would usually be deemed given when postmarked.

ENTIRE UNDERSTANDING

A provision would usually be included to indicate that the agreement, as set forth, contains the entire understanding of the parties relating to the subject matter of this agreement. No modification, amendment, waiver, termination, or discharge of this agreement or any of the terms or provisions included in this agreement would be binding upon either of the parties unless confirmed by a written instrument signed by the parties.

NO WAIVER

In most cases, the agreement would also include a provision asserting that no waiver by either the owner or the society of any term or provision of this agreement, or of any default under this agreement, would affect that party's rights thereafter to enforce the term or provision in question or to exercise any right or remedy in the event of any other default, whether or not similar.

ASSIGNMENT

In an effort to protect the exploitation of the owner from third parties, the performing rights society may not agree to the owner's assigning his or her performance royalties to a third party.

STATE OF JURISDICTION

The agreement would typically stipulate which state would bear the ultimate jurisdiction in the event of litigation. The state most often agreed upon is the state where both parties maintain their businesses. In the event that the parties reside in separate states, it is often the party with the stronger bargaining position that will prevail in the battle of jurisdictions.

SIGNATURES

By signing their names to the agreement, the parties signify their understanding of and agreement to the provisions, terms, and conditions of the contract.

10

The Mechanical License Agreement

The owner of the copyright of a musical composition, in many cases the publisher or songwriter, has the right to license that composition through various means in order to commercially exploit it. One prevalent method of marketing that composition is through its rendition on a recording intended to be commercially distributed to the public for private use.

Mechanical royalties are those royalties paid to the copyright owner, usually the publisher or songwriter, by a record company based on the sale or other distribution of recordings that contain the composition. The Copyright Act of the United States has created guidelines, clearly stated compulsory provisions, by which the owner of the copyright is mandated to license the composition. The Copyright Act has established a statutory rate for each composition recorded which is set by the Copyright Royalty Tribunal (CRT). The ''Statutory Rate'' is generally the standard guide by which the amount charged for each composition recorded, and the manner of payment to the copyright owner, will be fixed. The fixed statutory rates may be changed by the CRT in order to reflect industry needs. It must be stressed, though, that the record company and copyright owner are free to determine a negotiated mechanical license different from the one formalized by the CRT.

Most copyright owners retain the services of specialized agencies to collect the fees due and owing them from the commercial exploitation of the mechanical royalty. Typically, the agency granted the right to collect such fees, such as the Harry Fox Agency, will charge a collection commission in exchange for its services and will enter into an agreement with the user of the composition, outlining the terms of the agency agreement.

PARTIES

The mechanical license agreement entered into between the collecting agent and the record company, the user of the composition, states clearly the names of all parties to the agreement, including any pseudonyms or corporate names.

TITLE

Since the mechanical license is specific to the copyrighted composition and to the particular recordings of the copyrighted composition as performed by various artists, clarity is paramount in the description of the title of the composition. Without ambiguity, the agreement should state:

TITLE: ____________________

The agreement should equally specify the songwriter, or songwriters, of the copyrighted composition and the copyright owner, if different from the songwriter. The agreement should also list the copyright registration number.

SONGWRITER: ____________________

COPYRIGHT OWNER: ____________________

COPYRIGHT REGISTRATION NUMBER: ____________________

DUTIES

The agency would typically state that it has been retained by the owner of the copyrighted composition, in most cases the publisher or songwriter, in negotiation with the user of the composition, in most cases the record company, with regard to the collection of fees based on the commercial exploitation of the mechanical or compulsory license.

The agency typically performs the following functions:

- issues mechanical licenses on behalf of publishers to the composition users, the record companies,
- collects mechanical royalties,
- distributes those royalties to the publishers after deducting its fixed commission,
- conducts audits of the books and records of record companies on behalf of the publishers,
- licenses movie, television, and video synchronization rights,
- licenses television commercial synchronization rights, and
- collects foreign income on the account of the publishers.

INTENT OF USER

The user of the composition would typically indicate that it desires and intends to obtain a mechanical license to make, manufacture, and distribute commercially recordings of the copyrighted composition referred to in the agreement.

RIGHTS GRANTED

Following the distribution of the recording to the public under a grant of authority by the copyright owner, the user of the composition, upon obtaining the mechanical license, would thereafter be accorded all the rights which are granted the user of the copyrighted composition. The user of the composition, the compulsory licensee, would typically be bound, and would usually agree to be and remain, for the term of the agreement, in full compliance with all the obligations imposed upon it by the provision of the Copyright Act.

It should be understood by all parties that under the provisions of the Copyright Act, after a composition has been commercially distributed and released to the public on a recording or album with the knowledge and consent of the copyright owner, then any and all other artists and record companies have the right to record, distribute, and release the composition to the general public so long as the user complies strictly with the requirements of the compulsory license provisions.

TERRITORY

The agreement should state clearly the territory over which the agency has authority. Since the mechanical and compulsory license is governed by the Copyright Act of the United States, the agency agreement would typically stipulate that the agreement would be limited to the United States, including its territories and possessions.

COMPENSATION

The user would generally be obligated to pay to the agency, as collection agency for the copyright owner, the agreed fees for the recordings made, manufactured, and distributed publicly. It may be stipulated that the fee would be the statutory rate that is in effect at the time the recording is made and manufactured unless the parties negotiate a different rate.

The parties to the agreement, including the publisher of the composition, the user of the composition, and the agency in its capacity, may agree to alter the fee, using the statutory rate as a starting point in their negotiations. The agreed fee will generally be stipulated in a clearly annotated chart.

ARTIST: ____________________

FEE: ____________________

The collection agency would normally charge a commission in exchange for its services.

Use of Composition in Medley

In the event the composition is to be utilized in a medley, the copyright owner may agree to a different royalty rate. The alternate rate should be clearly fixed in the agreement by a chart or other means of illustration.

SPECIFIC COMPOSITION

The mechanical license granted to the user is strictly limited to the particular recording of the copyrighted composition agreed in the agreement. The agreement should specify the name of the artist recording the composition and the particular recording, using detailed and exact means of identification, including a recording number, if available.

The mechanical license agreement would generally not alter, affect, or amend other agreements entered into between the recording artist, the composition copyright owner, and the record company in respect to the recording of the copyrighted work, unless agreed to by all the parties.

DATE OF RELEASE

The parties to the agreement would usually clarify the date that the particular recording considered by the agreement would be released.

DATE OF RELEASE: ____________________

PAYMENT SCHEDULE

The mechanical license agreement would typically stipulate the fee payment schedule and may require that the user account and pay the agreed fees to the agency, on behalf of the copyright owner, within an agreed period of time following each payment date, which may be monthly, quarterly, semiannually, or annually.

FAILURE TO ACCOUNT AND PAY

In the event the user does not account to the agency and fails to pay the fees due and owing in accordance with the agreement, the copyright owner, either individually or through its agent, would generally give the user written notice of the failure. In the event the failure is not cured, or remedied, within an agreed period of time, the copyright owner may exercise the right to terminate the mechanical license without relinquishing any of its rights regarding the compensation due and owing, including the implementation of any and all legal remedies.

The effect of the termination of the grant of license may render the making, manufacturing, and distributing of the recording for which the agreed royalties have not been paid, actionable as an act of copyright infringement under the Copyright Act. The infringer may therefore subject himself or herself to liability and to all the remedies as provided in the act.

NOTICE OF INTENTION TO OBTAIN A MECHANICAL LICENSE

Though the Copyright Act requires all users to file a notice of intention to obtain a mechanical license prior to the actual manufacture and distribution of the subject recording, the agency may grant the user, if the user complies with all the provisions agreed upon between all the parties concerned, including the copyright owner, agency, and user, a waiver from the requirement.

ACCOUNTING

In accordance to a determination among the parties, the contract may specify that the user render to the agency, and the agency to the copyright owner, an accounting in writing of all gross receipts earned. Furthermore, the user may be obliged to all additional pertinent and relevant data necessary to compute fees payable to the agency, and from the agent to the copyright owner. In accordance with the Copyright Act, the user must strictly comply with the notice, payment, and accounting provisions of the act. Failure to do so may constitute copyright infringement.

BOOKS AND RECORDS

The agency would customarily agree to keep and maintain accurate books of account governing all transactions relating to the subject matter of the mechanical license agreement.

Right to Inspect Books and Records

The copyright owner would usually demand the right to inspect and audit the books and records of the agency with respect to the subject matter of the agreement. Typically, the agency would agree to such inspection if reasonable notice is received requesting the audit and if the audit is conducted during business hours at the place where the books and records are normally kept. The agency would also insist that the copyright owner bear all costs and expenses in relation to such an audit.

Time within which to Audit

The agency would usually require that the copyright owner initiate its demand to audit the agency's books within an agreed time period following the owner's receipt of the agent's statement. Failure to request such an audit within the fixed time period would usually signify the copyright owner's agreement with the statement received and ban an audit at a later date unless a finding of fraud is discovered. Failure to request a timely audit may also deny the copyright owner the right to maintain any action, claim, or proceeding against the agency in any forum or tribunal with respect to the questionable accounting statement.

Discovered Inconsistency

If an audit conducted by the copyright owner, in accordance with the provisions of the mechanical license agreement, accurately reveals or discovers that the agent has made an underpayment to the owner in terms of the fees, the agency may be required to pay that amount plus an agreed amount of interest, usually calculated from the date the error causing such underpayment occurred.

Legal Action

Should the copyright owner wish to initiate legal action and deliver proper notice of his or her intent of doing so within the time provision of this agreement, the agreement may stipulate that the owner would have a specific period of time within which to file such a suit, claim or proceeding against the agency in a court of competent jurisdiction after the date such accounting or statement is rendered.

RIGHT TO ENTER AGREEMENT

The parties to the mechanical license agreement would typically be required to warrant that they are under no disability, restriction, or prohibition, whether contractual or otherwise, with respect to their rights to execute this agreement, to grant the rights listed in this agreement, and to perform the obligations stated in this agreement.

RIGHT TO GRANT SPECIFIC RIGHTS

The copyright owner would usually warrant that he or she has the exclusive right and authority to grant the rights granted to the agent in the mechanical license agreement.

NO BREACH OF COPYRIGHT

In addition, the copyright owner would, as a rule, warrant that he or she has not granted and will not grant any right, title, or interest to any other person or entity effective during the term of this agreement which would conflict with, or be in limitation of, any of the rights granted under this agreement. He or she would further warrant that any action taken by the agency as a result of entering this agreement would not result in the violation or breach of any statutory or common law or rights of any party, including without limitation, contractual rights, trademarks, copyrights, and rights of publicity and privacy.

NO FURTHER AGREEMENT

The copyright owner would also represent, in accordance with the agency's request, that it will not enter into any competing mechanical license agency agreement with regard to the compositions addressed in this agreement with any competing collection agency within the parameters of the antitrust laws, nor will the copyright owner issue its own licenses and conduct its own audits in regard to the compositions, during the term of this agreement.

LIMITED RIGHTS GRANTED

The copyright owner would usually clarify that the only rights granted the agency are those rights specified in the agency agreement. The owner would therefore reserve all additional rights in the composition.

NO MISUSE

The copyright owner may require that the agency stipulate that the agency would not intentionally harm, misuse, or bring into disrepute the agreed upon compositions.

NO CHARGEABLE EXPENSES

In an effort to curb his or her cost of operations, the copyright owner may require that the agency stipulate that the agency would not create any expenses chargeable to the owner without the prior written approval of the owner.

INDEMNIFICATION

The parties to the agreement would usually stipulate that each agrees to indemnify, defend, protect, save, and hold the other harmless from and against any and all actions, claims, suits, losses, judgments, penalties, liabilities, damages, costs, and expenses (including reasonable attorney's fees and court costs) of whatever kind and nature imposed on, incurred by, asserted, brought, or made by or against that party arising out of the other party's breach of any of its representations, warranties, or obligations made pursuant to this agreement or through the negligence or intentional acts of its officers, directors, employees, or representatives.

Written Notice

The mechanical license agreement may also require, in accordance with the demands of the parties, that each give the other prompt written notice of any such action, claim, or suit. The party so noticed would usually be granted the opportunity, at its option, to participate in the defense of the alleged claim, through counsel of its own choice at its sole cost and expense.

REGISTRATION OF COPYRIGHT

It is generally the obligation of the owner of the composition in question, at his or her sole expense, to register and maintain, or cause to be registered and maintained, appropriate copyright(s), trademark(s), and/or service mark(s) for the composition.

If the user's utilization of the composition requires additional copyrights, trademarks, or service marks, the obligation to register and maintain, or cause to be registered and maintained, appropriate copyrights, trademarks, and/or service marks for the new composition could be the obligation of the user if so agreed by and between the user and the copyright owner, at the user's sole expense.

TERMINATION

If either party breaches any of the material terms and conditions of this agreement, the party claiming such breach would generally have the right to serve upon the party alleged to be in breach a written notice of its intention to terminate this agreement. The party alleged to be in breach would usually be granted a mutually agreed time period within which to remedy said breach. If the party alleged to be in breach fails to cure or remedy the alleged breach within the established time period, then the mechanical license agreement could be automatically terminated, if so agreed, usually without prejudice to any other rights which either party may otherwise have against the other.

Insolvency of Agency

If the agency becomes insolvent or files a petition in bankruptcy, or if a petition in bankruptcy is filed against the agency, or if the agency makes an assignment for the benefit of creditors or makes any arrangement pursuant to any bankruptcy law, or if a receiver is appointed, the parties may agree that the mechanical license agreement would be automatically terminated by the copyright owner at his or her sole election.

FORCE MAJEURE

If at any time during the validity of the mechanical license agreement, by reason of any act of God, fire, earthquake, flood, explosion, strike, labor disturbance, civil commotion, act of government, its agencies or officers, any order, regulation, ruling, or action of any labor union or association of artists, musicians, composers, or employees affecting the copyright owner or agency, its subsidiaries or affiliates or the industry in which it is or they are engaged or any shortage of or failure or delays in the delivery of materials, supplies, labor or equipment, or any other cause or causes beyond the control of the parties of this agreement, the performance of either party's obligations under this agreement is delayed, hampered, interrupted or interfered with, or otherwise becomes impossible or impracticable for an agreed period of time, then either party may upon notice to the other terminate this agreement.

ASSIGNMENT

On most occasions, the copyright owner has entered the mechanical license agreement with the agency based on the agency's reputation, experience, and expertise in the music industry. The owner would, therefore, most likely demand that the agency not be granted the right to assign this agreement without the prior written consent of the owner. The copyright owner may agree, though, to the agency's assigning the agreement to the agency's wholly owned subsidiary, or to any person, firm, or corporation owning or acquiring a substantial portion of the agency's stock or assets, provided said subsidiary, person, firm, or corporation is a bona fide professional and expert in the area covered by the mechanical license agreement.

NOTICES

All notices and statements provided for under the mechanical license agreement would usually be required to be in writing and, together with all payments provided under the agreement, should be sent by United States mail, postage prepaid, or sent by certified or registered mail, return receipt requested, or by other means of verifiable mailing.

The agreement usually lists the addresses where the notices and statements are to be sent.

COPYRIGHT OWNER
Address: ____________________

AGENCY
Address: ____________________

Properly addressed notices delivered or sent as provided under this contract are usually deemed as given when postmarked.

NO MODIFICATION

Generally, both parties would agree that no modification, amendment, waiver, termination, or discharge of this agreement, or any of the terms or provisions included in this contract, would be binding upon either of the parties unless confirmed by a written instrument signed by the parties.

WAIVER

The parties may also agree that no waiver by either party of any term or provision of this agreement or of any default under this agreement would affect that party's rights thereafter to enforce that term or provision or to exercise any right or remedy in the event of any other default, whether or not similar.

VOIDABLE PROVISION

If any provision of this agreement should be held void, voidable, invalid, or inoperative, both parties could agree that no other provision would be affected as a result of such action. Accordingly, the remaining provisions of this agreement would remain in full force and effect as though the void, voidable, invalid, or inoperative provision had not been contained in this agreement.

The copyright owner would probably demand that if any provision held void, voidable, invalid, or inoperative would impair the owner's right to receive his or her payments under this agreement, then that provision would be deemed a material provision, and the agreement would be considered to be terminated without prejudice to either side.

NO PARTNERSHIP

To limit each party's liabilities, the agreement may stipulate that nothing in the agreement should be understood to constitute a partnership or a joint venture between the copyright owner and the agency. Neither party to the agreement would therefore have the right to obligate or bind the other in any manner whatsoever, and neither party would become liable for any representation, act, or omission of the other party contrary to the provisions stipulated in this agreement.

STATE OF JURISDICTION

The parties will usually agree which state would have jurisdiction in the event of a dispute regarding the interpretation, validity, and construction of agreements and in regard to the venue where such a dispute can be contested.

NO ACTION TO PREJUDICE THE COPYRIGHT OWNER

The copyright owner would usually insist that the agency agree not to take any action during the effectiveness of the agreement that may serve to prejudice or misrepresent the rights of the owner.

BREACH OF CONTRACT

Should either of the parties breach the aforementioned warranties or misrepresent itself, then, if the parties so agree, the agreement would be considered null and void. Usually, a breach is defined as a failure, refusal, or neglect to comply with any of the contract's material obligations. The parties may agree to include the right of the breaching party to cure, solve, or mitigate the breach within an agreed period of time.

SIGNATURES

By signing their names, the parties generally signify their understanding of and agreement to the provisions, terms, and conditions contained in the mechanical license agreement.

11

The Licensing Agreement

A thriving business has evolved around the licensing of products utilizing the name, likeness, photograph, and sound of performing artists. The licensed products range from such items as badges, lunch boxes, and stickers to sweatshirts, hats, and T-shirts. In fact, any item that can carry the image or bear the sound of the artist is potentially a licensed product.

The licensing business often represents a substantial source of income to the artist, ancillary to the revenue earned from the marketing of his or her musical compositions and recordings. The licensed products typically carry a likeness, sound, or image of the artist. Most artists would choose to maintain a certain level of control over the image that is portrayed to the public by the licensed goods, insuring that the licensed item best exemplify his or her style of music and public image. It is imperative, therefore, that the licensing agreement be evaluated critically before being agreed upon and signed by the parties.

PARTIES

The agreement customarily begins by naming the parties, including their stage names or pseudonyms, and addresses. The addresses given are frequently utilized by the parties in the event notices and legal correspondences are sent between them.

RIGHTS GRANTED

The licensing agreement should spell out in clear and concise language the rights granted by the artist to the licensee under the terms of the agreement. The grant of the license can be limited to a specific item, such as a license to portray the image of the artist on T-shirts or coffee mugs, or can be extensive, such as a grant to license the image of the artist on all apparel products now produced or to be produced in the future.

EXCLUSIVITY VERSUS NONEXCLUSIVITY

By granting the licensee the right to exclusively exploit the licensed product, the artist is normally eliminating all possible alternative licensing agents for the term granted in the license agreement. The artist may therefore negotiate for the right to issue the licensee a nonexclusive licensing agreement. The artist may feel that a nonexclusive agreement could increase his or her potential to exploit commercially all licensed products arising out of his or her image, likeness or sound. The licensee, on the other hand, may claim that since his or her investment in the licensed product would be substantial, in terms of money and time, he or she should be granted the exclusive right to license all products depicting the artist's image, likeness and sound. An exclusive, rather than a nonexclusive arrangement, the licensee could contend, would put him or her in a better position to successfully promote and sell the licensed product. The license agreement should, therefore, specify whether the arrangement between the artist and the licensee is exclusive or nonexclusive.

NAME, LIKENESS, AND LOGO

The parties would usually agree that the licensee has been granted the license to commercially utilize the name, likeness, character, logo, visual representation, and sound of the artist, including those images and representations utilized on posters and record jackets, in connection with any and all retail and mail order sales, artist tours as well as any and all other means of distribution, now utilized or to be utilized at any time in the future, in which the licensee has been granted permission to commercially exploit the licensed products.

QUALITY CONTROL

Intending to ensure that he or she would retain control over the appearance and quality of the finished product, the artist may negotiate for certain quality control demands. The licensee would usually be wary about granting complete quality control to the artist unless the licensee would be forced to surrender to the demands of a well-established and highly recoginized artist. Under most circumstances, the licensee would expect the final say in all decisions regarding the quality of the products manufactured, citing his or her experience in the licensing business, though he or she may agree to confer upon the artist reasonable and limited consultation rights.

LICENSED PRODUCTS

The items to be licensed generally include all, or some, of the following (the list is not intended to be inclusive):

T-shirts, sweatshirts, hats, jerseys, head bands, tour programs, badges, belts, buttons, bumper stickers, calendars, decals, emblems, jackets, keychains, mugs, patches, photographs, pins, postcards, spiral notebooks, stickers, and posters.

In order to alleviate any possibility for confusion or ambiguity, the items licensed should be listed in an attached exhibit or schedule. Additions or deletions from the master list usually require written approval by the parties to the agreement. This agreement is typically strictly construed, limiting the manufacture and production to those items stipulated on the agreement.

LICENSEE'S DUTY

The licensee, upon entering the license agreement with the artist, would typically agree to perform specific duties connected with the manufacture, distribution, and commercial exploitation of the licensed product. Those duties, being an integral part of the agreement, customarily are specified individually. The failure by the licensee to perform his or her duties may be considered a material breach of the agreement.

MANUFACTURE AND DISTRIBUTE

The primary duty granted the licensee is the commitment to manufacture, distribute, and commercially exploit, in all manners agreed upon in the agreement, the licensed product.

PRIOR WRITTEN APPROVAL FOR EXPENSES

The artist may demand that the licensee obtain the written approval of the artist prior to generating expenses that would be chargeable to the artist. In this manner the artist could oversee expenditures outside his or her immediate control.

NO INFRINGEMENT OF ARTIST'S COPYRIGHT

The licensee would usually be required to stipulate that he or she will not infringe on the copyright or trademark owned by the artist and will not at any time in the future initiate a suit, claim, or action contesting those rights.

BEST EFFORTS

In addition, the licensee would usually guarantee to the artist that the licensee plans to utilize his or her best efforts to protect his or her right to manufacture, distribute, and commercially exploit the licensed products. The licensee should ensure that he or she will undertake all precautions to prevent counterfeiting or piracy. In the event the licensee gains knowledge of any infringements or threatened infringements of the licensed products, he or she could be required to notify the artist of such an infringement. The licensee may be obligated, if so agreed in this agreement, to commence legal action to prevent the cited infringement.

LEGAL RECOURSE

The legal action available to the licensee to defend against the infringement of the artist's copyright and the licensee's rights secured by this agreement may include injunctions, temporary restraining orders, and seizures. In the event any sums, monies, or judgments are recovered as a result of the legal action, the licensee and the artist would usually receive their agreed share of the award, following the deduction of all legal expenses incurred in the action.

ARTIST APPROVAL

The licensed product ordinarily carries the name, likeness, image, or sound of the artist and often reflects on the image the artist intends to portray to the public. The artist has typically spent much of his or her career developing that image, carrying it through from album to album, from live performance to live performance. It is, therefore, an integral part of the persona that comprises an integral part of the the artist's success. The artist would probably in defense of his or her public image, negotiate for the right to approve the likeness, portrayal, and sound manufactured and distributed by the licensee, prior to its commercial exploitation.

The licensee, citing his or her financial expenditure in the purchase of the rights granted in this agreement, as well as in the cost of developing and manufacturing the products to be distributed, would typically negotiate certain limitations on the artist's right of approval.

Usually, a comprise could be worked out between the parties. One such compromise would grant the artist approval of the artistic renditions of his or her likeness or portrayal, prior to the manufacture of a prototype or sample. The licensee would retain all artistic approvals following the manufacture of the prototype or sample.

Providing of Samples

The more bargaining power exercised by the artist, the more clout he or she would have when negotiating this provision. The successful artist, in order to maintain a high level of control over the image portrayed on the licensed product, would frequently stipulate that the licensee submit to the artist, at the licensee's sole cost and expense, a sample of the licensed product. The artist would then express his or her approval or disapproval as to the licensed product's quality and style. The artist would probably insist that the licensed product could not be manufactured and produced without first obtaining the artist's written approval.

Additional Material

In addition to the licensed product itself, the artist may demand the right to approve the textual and pictorial material that relates directly to the licensed products, such as promotional displays, packaging, and advertising material.

Unreasonable Withholding of Approval

The licensee would probably argue, most vigorously, that the artist's approval should not be unreasonably withheld if actually, the artist has been granted the right of textual, pictorial, creative, or quality approval. In furtherance of this provision, the license agreement may set forth a time period within which the artist must respond with his or her disapproval, after which the licensed product or the additional material would be deemed satisfactory and approved.

MONITORING OF PRODUCTION

If the artist has amassed substantial clout within the entertainment industry, he or she may demand the right to oversee all agreements entered into by the licensee for product licensing, manufacture, and distribution of the licensed products, stipulating that without his or her absolute approval, any such agreement would be null and void. Under these absolute conditions, the artist would usually stipulate that once he or she approves any license product agreement entered into by the licensee, that agreement may not be changed or amended without his or her prior written approval.

PREMIUMS

The artist would typically require the licensee to obtain the artist's written approval prior to using the licensed products as premiums or giveaways. Utilizing such command over the licensed products, the artist would be exerting maximum control over the flow of royalty payments due him or her under the license agreement, since in most instances royalties are not calculated on premiums or giveaways. And in most cases, unless he or she so approves, the artist would not appreciate seeing his or her income reduced by the liberal use of promotions and giveaways.

ENDORSEMENTS AND PROMOTIONS

The placement of the licensed product in an undesirable or unflattering setting may impact negatively on the image the artist has so rigorously nurtured. In an effort to maintain control over the image that the artist has developed, and will continue to develop throughout his or her career, the artist may demand written approval prior to permitting the licensee the right to utilize the licensed product as a commercial tie-in, endorsement, or promotion in an advertisement, motion picture, or television broadcast.

SUBLICENSE AGREEMENT

The licensee may be restrained from entering a sublicense agreement or from assigning the license agreement to another entity prior to obtaining the written approval of the artist. By controlling the assignment, the artist typically endeavers to ensure that the sublicensee possess a level of expertise, knowledge, and stature within the industry equal to or greater than that of the licensee.

It should be carefully noted that in most situations, there exists a difference between sublicensing a licensed product to a sublicensee distributor and contracting to a manufacturer the right to produce the licensed product. Typically, the latter is not considered a form of sublicensing. Generally, if a sublicensee has been granted the right to act as sublicensee, he or she would be required to agree to all the obligations, conditions, and provisions of the primary licensee, while those involved in the actual manufacturing of the product do so under a contract and typically bear no proprietary rights whatsoever in the licensed product.

STANDARD OF QUALITY

The artist may require that the licensee guarantee to manufacture the licensed products to a standard of quality, style, and appearance that would be considered high or exceptional by industry standards. In the event the manufactured licensed product falls below the agreed standard, the artist could require that the licensed product be withdrawn from the market and replaced with an approved manufactured product. This is especially true when the artist is a well-known entity and possesses valuable goodwill, which he or she intends to maintain and protect. The artist may negotiate for the right to veto the sourcing of the materials in his or her effort to ensure adequate assurances of the required high degree of quality.

CUTTING CORNERS

The issue of utilizing untested facilities to save on labor costs may pose a problem. While labor is often cheaper, the quality may be compromised. The artist would probably elect to maintain approval rights over the manufacturer, arguing that quality, not labor cost, be the deciding factor in the licensee's decision in the selection of the manufacturer.

PAYMENT OF ARTIST'S ROYALTY

The licensing agreement may stipulate if so agreed by the parties that the payment due the artist under the product license agreement entered into by the licensee and any third party should be paid directly to the artist from the licensee. In the alternative, the artist may consent to the provision directing all payments due him or her under the agreement to be paid to the licensee directly, who will then be solely responsible for making timely payments to the artist. In the latter case, the artist would probably demand assurances that the licensee would be strictly liable to make all required payments. One method to assure proper and timely payment would be to establish a trust relationship between the artist, and the licensee, thereby creating a fiduciary relationship, between them of the highest degree, while another may be the establishment of an assignment coupled with an interest.

TERRITORY

The grant of the right to license the artist's name, likeness, and image can be as limited as a single country such as the United States and possessions, or as broad as the world. The artist's decision is usually based on the strength of the licensee in the various territories and on the licensee's past experiences. If the licensee is successful and if the licensee has developed a global marketplace for the items he or she licenses, the licensee may be in a stronger bargaining position to negotiate successfully for a worldwide territory.

TERM

The term, or length, of the agreement is generally one of years and should be agreed upon to the mutual satisfaction of the parties.

UPON THE EXPIRATION OF THE TERM

The artist would typically negotiate that he or she should have the right to receive his or her compensation, as agreed in this agreement, for all products marketed under license agreements negotiated, entered and actually commenced during the term of the license agreement, even if the earnings were received after the termination and/or expiration of the agreement. In addition, the artist may negotiate that should subsequent sales be made as a result of the work product of the existing licensee, the profits should be accrued to the artist following the termination and/or expiration of the license agreement. This is especially true under certain conditions, including the following:

a) where a backlog in the distribution chain exists. By the time orders are received and paid for, the licensing agreement may have been terminated or expired.

b) if an agreement was finalized, but not commenced, during the final period of the term. The inclusion of this provision may motivate the licensee to negotiate just as earnestly for the artist on the last day of the license agreement as on the first day.

c) delay in payments by the vendors to the licensee.

DISPOSAL OF STOCK

The licensee would generally demand the right to dispose of all stock of the licensed product in the licensee's possession upon the termination and/or expiration of the license agreement. In most cases, the licensee would be obligated to pay to the artist all royalties, whether adjusted or not, due under the license agreement for the excess inventory. The parties should stipulate an agreed period of time within which the licensee would have the opportunity to exercise the rights to dispose of all excess inventory. The artist would probably demand that the licensee sell the licensed product during this sell-off period at an established distribution schedule, and for an agreed price, so as not to flood the marketplace with the licensed products. The artist would, by this action, attempt to maintain the value of the license upon its reversion to the artist.

In addition, the artist may insist that all sales promotion and advertising during the postagreement period should be of the style, quality, and standards that typified the promotion and advertising strategy utilized by the licensee during the period of the agreement's validity.

MINIMUM PAYMENT TO ARTIST

The licensing of the artist's name, likeness, and image usually represents a substantial income source for the artist in addition to the sales and licensing of his or her musical compositions. He or she may demand, as compensation in exchange for granting the rights granted in the agreement, the following:

- an advance payment,
- a royalty based on the gross (or net) sales of the licensed products, and
- a guaranteed yearly minimum payment.

Advanced Sum

In most cases, the advance payment is designed as an irrevocable guarantee from the licensee to pay the artist a nonrefundable advance of an agreed-upon payment. The licensee would usually argue that though the advance is nonrefundable, it is recoupable from future sales of the musical compositions. The artist would typically argue just as vigorously that the advance should be considered solely a good faith nonrefundable payment. It is usually the party with the stronger bargaining strength who prevails in these discussions.

Lump-Sum Payments and Installment Payments

There are typically several methods available to the licensee of making the advance payment. The advance may be paid in a one-time, lump-sum payment, or it may be paid according to an agreed schedule of installment payments. The payment schedule may include a payment upon the signing of the license agreement, and additional payments on agreed dates conditioned upon the artist's performing his or her agreed functions, such as a live performance tour promoting the licensed goods.

Since the advance is generally in the form of guaranteed payments, or a series of installment payments, based on projected earned revenues, the licensee may negotiate that a provision stipulating that the royalties earned by the artist will reduce on a dollar-for-dollar basis the obligation by the licensee to pay the artist the scheduled advance against future royalties as yet unreceived be included in the agreement.

Advance Royalty Payments

If, on the other hand, the artist has bargained to receive his or her full and complete advance prior to the accumulation of royalties earned as a result of the commercial exploitation of the license agreed upon in this agreement, the licensee may demand to receive all or an agreed part of all retail royalties, touring royalties, and licensing royalties until such time as the licensee has recouped, in full, the advance payment to the artist. This provision should be detailed as to the schedule of payment, for the benefit of both parties.

ROYALTIES

The agreement should state in clear and unambiguous language that the artist would receive, as compensation from the sale of the product licensed under the terms of the license agreement, a royalty equal to an agreed percentage of all gross (or net) sales revenue.

INTERNATIONAL SALES

The licensee may contend that the artist should receive a slightly lower royalty for sales of the composition outside the United States, contending that the added administration costs for such foreign licensing transactions diminish the licensee's gross margins and inhibit his or her potential to earn a profit under the terms of the agreement. In the event both parties agree to a separate royalty rate for earnings attained from foreign sales of the composition, the agreed percentage and payment schedule should be included in the agreement.

Currency Conversions

An added problem attached to foreign sales is that of currency conversion. In an effort to tackle such a situation, the parties should consider on which basis the calculation of foreign currency into U.S. dollars would be figured. Absent such an agreement or understanding, both parties would be prisoners of the exchange rates, never certain of the exchange rates at the time of the accounting, never being able to calculate with specificity the revenues earned by the foreign exploitation of the licensed product.

The parties may also agree to an increase in the royalty rate in the event gross (or net) revenues earned from the sales of the licensed items surpass an agreed sum.

GROSS REVENUES

The term "gross revenues" should be defined clearly and unambiguously in the agreement since entertainment contracts typically define net and gross revenues on a contract-by-contract basis. The definition may be as follows: any and all sums, monies, and earnings derived from the commercial exploitation of the licensed goods, in any forum or venue (including but not limited to retail, tours, mail order, wholesale), received in any form, format, or manner, without any deductions whatsoever, except sales and applicable federal, state, city, and municipal taxes and applicable tariffs.

LICENSEE'S EXPENSES

Typically, the licensee is singularly responsible for any and all expenses he or she disburses in the execution of his or her rights under the license agreement. The expenses may include any and all sales promotions, sales shows, mailings, telephone, travel, office overhead, and advertising costs. However, the licensee could argue, while such expenses are the responsibility of the vendor or licensee, they directly relate to the manufacture and distribution of the licensed product and should therefore be deducted from the fundamental royalty base. Again, the victor is usually the party with the stronger bargaining position.

ARTIST GUARANTEES

When agreeing to enter the license agreement with the artist, the licensee would typically require that the artist use its best efforts to assist in the advertising and promotion of the licensed products. One of the most visible and successful manners in which the licensed products could be promoted is during a personal appearance performance tour where the licensed products are sold in conjunction with the tour.

Live Performances

The licensee may clarify that he or she has agreed to enter the license agreement based on the commitment of the artist to engage in one or several live personal appearance performance tours of an agreed number of performances in front of an agreed minimum audience (as calculated by the number of seats in each venue) per engagement. The parties may agree that if the audience response during the agreed tour dates is less than anticipated, the advance against future royalties paid, or to be paid, to the artist should be reduced by an agreed percentage.

Wearing of Licensed Product

The licensee may also require that the artist wear the licensed products, if doing so would not conflict with the artists image or customary wardrobe, at all public performances and appearances.

KEY PERSONS

It is not uncommon among artistic groups, that one or several of the members are more popular than the others and have engendered more positive identification by a wider range of audience than the other members of the group. The licensee, when agreeing to enter the license agreement, would have usually been induced to enter the agreement by the presence of the better known and more popular band member, the key person in the artistic group and may demand that the license agreement provide that the agreement would remain in full force and effect only if the key person remain part of the artistic group.

Loss of Key Artistic Group Member

In the event the key artistic group member no longer remains an exclusive member of the artistic group, having quit for any reason whatsoever, the licensee would probably negotiate for the right to terminate the agreement without incurring any liability or loss. Alternatively, the licensee may demand the right to renegotiate the terms of the agreement. In the event the licensee does terminate the agreement, following the exit of the key person, the licensee would probably demand that all paid but unrecouped advances be returned to the licensee on an agreeable schedule.

PUBLIC APPEARANCES

The licensee may require that the artist make a minimum number of public appearances in addition to the scheduled live personal appearance performance tour.

ACCOUNTING—CONCERT TOUR LICENSE

An accounting provision usually varies according to the type and form of licensing that has been contracted. For example, in the case of licensing of products relating to concert tours, the artist may require that the licensee render to the artist, nightly at the close of each concert engagement, an informal accounting of gross receipts derived from the sale of the licensed product in connection with the performance by the talent as well as a statement of the number and type of licensed product sold.

Representative Witnessing Accounting

The provision may authorize the artist's representative to be present with the licensee when the daily accounting occurs. If the licensee agrees to this provision, it would usually require that the artist's representative not interfere with the licensee's operations.

Weekly Versus Daily Accounting

Depending on the complexity of the concert tour, both parties may prefer to provide for an interim or informal accounting, for example, weekly or monthly rather than daily.

Final Accounting

The license agreement usually mandates that the final accounting be accompanied by the payment of the balance, if any, of any and all royalties payable to the talent pursuant to the contract.

ACCURATE BOOKS

The artist, in an effort to maintain an accurate accounting of his or her revenues earned as a result of this license agreement, would usually require that the licensee maintain accurate books of the accounts governing all the transactions entered into regarding the licensed products. Under this clause, the artist would usually retain the right, at the artist's sole expense, to audit the books and records of the licensee with respect to the sale of the products contracted under this agreement.

Reasonable Notice to Audit

Reasonable notice given to the licensee is usually demanded, in order for this audit to take place. Furthermore, the licensee would typically require that the audit be conducted during regular business hours and at the place where the books and records are normally held, so as not to unreasonably interfere with the licensee's day-to-day business of operations.

DISCOVERED INCONSISTENCY

If an audit conducted by the artist in accordance with the provisions of this clause accurately reveals an underpayment on the part of the licensee, the artist may demand that the licensee pay the outstanding balance in addition to an agreed amount of interest. The interest would usually commence on the date the underpayment commenced.

Reimbursement of Costs of Audit

Depending on the strength of the parties, the agreement may provide that if a discrepancy of more than an agreed percentage is discovered, the licensee would be required to reimburse the artist for the costs of the audit.

WAIVER OF OBJECTIONS TO ACCOUNTING

In an effort to control the possibility of any long-standing disputes, the license agreement may provide that all accountings and statements rendered by the licensee would be binding upon the artist and would not be subject to objection for any reason unless specific objection is made by the artist to the licensee by written notice stating the basis of the objection. The licensee would probably request that such an objection be made within an agreed time period, perhaps within six months or one year from the date of the artist's receipt of a statement.

Sunset Provision within Which to Make Objection

By agreeing to this sunset provision, the artist has typically agreed not to initiate or commence any action, claim, or proceeding against the licensee in any forum or tribunal with respect to any accounting or statement due under this agreement past the agreed date.

TIME LIMIT TO FILE CAUSE OF ACTION

The agreement could also contain a provision requiring that, should the artist wish to take legal action and execute proper notice of his or her intent to do so within the time provision of this agreement, the artist would have an agreed time period within which to file such a suit, claim, or proceeding against the licensee in a court of competent jurisdiction.

EXCLUSIVE RIGHT TO ENTER AGREEMENT

The artist would usually be required to warrant and represent to the licensee that the artist has the exclusive right and authority to grant to the licensee the rights granted in the license agreement.

NO DISABILITY

Both parties would normally warrant and represent that they are under no disability, restriction, or prohibition, whether contractual or otherwise, with respect to their individual rights to execute the license agreement, to grant the rights in the agreement, and to perform the obligations stated in this agreement.

OWNERSHIP OF COPYRIGHT

The artist would usually be required by the licensee to warrant and represent that the artist owns the copyrights of all the accompanying materials, such as the artist's name, likeness, image and related artwork, furnished by the artist for use by the licensee pursuant to the terms of the agreement, and the use of the materials would not result in the violation or breach of any statutory or common law or rights of any party, including without limitation, contractual rights, trademarks, copyrights, and rights of publicity and privacy.

EXCLUSIVITY OF CONTRACT

In an effort to ensure the value of the license received, the licensee would normally require that the artist warrant and represent that he or she has not granted and will not grant at any time during the term of the license agreement any right, title, or interest to any other person or entity which would conflict with, or be in limitation of, any of the rights granted under this contract. In addition, the artist would typically agree not to enter into any separate agreement effective during the term of this agreement with any other party with respect to the manufacture, distribution, sale, or advertisement in the agreed territory.

BEST EFFORTS TO CURTAIL UNAUTHORIZED SALES

The licensee would typically be required to warrant that he or she will not authorize any use, direct or indirect, of the licensed product in any areas outside the agreed territory, nor will the licensee knowingly sell items considered in this agreement to those persons or entities who intend, or are likely, to resell them in any manner other than as set forth in this agreement. By complying with this provision, the licensee customarily further agrees to prevent the dumping of the licensed product into certain discount stores and retail outlets which have historically lowered the value of licensed products.

EXPENSES

The artist would also demand that the licensee not create any expenses chargeable to the artist without the prior written approval of the artist.

INDEMNIFICATION

In order to protect themselves from the costs of lawsuits and disputes, the parties may agree to indemnify, defend, protect, save, and hold each other harmless from and against any and all actions, claims, suits, losses, judgments, penalties, liabilities, damages, costs, and expenses (including, without limitation, reasonable attorney's fees and court costs) of whatever kind and nature incurred, asserted, brought, or made by or against either party arising out of the other party's breach of any of its representations, warranties, or obligations made pursuant to this agreement or through the negligence or intentional acts of its officers, directors, employees, or representatives.

PROTECTING GOODWILL OF TRADEMARK OR SERVICE MARK

The artist would usually insist that the licensee not harm, misuse, or bring into disrepute the licensed product.

PRODUCT LIABILITY INSURANCE

Consumer laws and product liability claims may arise as a result of faulty merchandise being sold or marketed. The artist would probably demand that prior to the sale of any licensed product items, the licensee will, at his or her own expense, obtain and maintain during the life of the license agreement a products liability insurance policy from a recognized insurance company qualified to do business in the state where the licensee maintains his or her base of operations.

The artist may further demand that the licensee name the artist as an insured party and provide a policy that would serve as adequate protection in the event that such a suit, claim, or action is initiated against the artist. As proof of the compliance of the licensee with the artist's request, the artist may demand a copy of the insurance policy.

Notice in the Event of Cancellation

In order to protect himself or herself from potential liability as a result of a lapsed insurance policy, the artist would probably demand that he or she be presented with reasonable notice by both the insurance company and the licensee in the event the of the cancellation or expiration of the policy.

SELL-OFF

The artist may wish to clarify the duties and obligations to be incurred by each party in regard to the licensed products remaining and unsold following the termination of the license agreement. Typically, the licensee would negotiate for the right, usually on a nonexclusive basis, to dispose of all remaining licensed products during a fixed time period. The remaining products would probably have to be sold in the usual manner and through the licensee's normal channels rather than being marketed as distressed goods. The artist may demand that during this sell-off period, he or she be given a full and complete written inventory of the remaining products and, following the sell-off period, his or her percentage of the earnings, in accordance with the royalty rate agreed among the parties.

Sale of Goods at Less Than Market Price

If the licensed product is to be sold by the licensee, due to market conditions, at a price lower than an agreed sum, the artist may negotiate for the right of first refusal to purchase the excess inventory at the offered price, provided that the artist exercise his or her option to purchase the excess inventory within an agreed time period. Typically, the artist's payment to the licensee for the remaining licensed products would not be deemed gross receipts from which a royalty would be due the artist.

OBLIGATIONS TOWARD PROPER COPYRIGHT

The parties should clarify which of them would bear the responsibility and obligation to register and maintain, or cause to be registered and maintained, appropriate copyright(s), trademark(s), and/or service mark(s) for the licensed product in those territories where the agreement is applicable.

BEST EFFORTS TO PROTECT COPYRIGHT

In addition, both the artist and the licensee could agree to to use their best efforts to protect the rights of each party in and to the licensed product, including without limitation using their best efforts to discover, prevent, and prohibit the illegal sale of counterfeit items.

Obligation to Give Notice of Infringement

Both the licensee and the artist would customarily be bound, by a provision in the license agreement, to promptly notify the other of an infringement or any other unauthorized exploitation of the licensed product by any unlicensed third party. As an added right, but not necessarily an obligation, the parties may have negotiated for the ability to take whatever steps each deems necessary to prevent any further infringement or unauthorized exploitation, including but not limited to the commencement of any legal and/or equitable action.

Option of Joining Lawsuits

In the event that the licensee does choose to initiate any action or proceeding in connection with an infringement of copyright and if the artist elects to join with the licensee in pursuing such action or proceeding, then the artist would probably be required, if so negotiated, to contribute to the costs and expenses, including but not limited to legal and court costs and fees, incurred in connection with the lawsuit. The parties would usually agree to divide the monetary reward, after deduction of any and all reasonable costs and expenses incurred by the parties in prosecuting such action, equitably among themselves.

TERMINATION

Following the date of termination, the licensee would usually be forbidden to manufacture additional quantities of the licensed products, though exceptions may be made if a certain fixed number of units are required to be shipped in order to fulfill an unfilled or partially filled order.

PHYSICAL INVENTORY

Typically, the artist would negotiate for the right to demand and perform a physical inventory of the licensed products, following the submission to the licensee of proper notice.

MATERIAL BREACH

If either party breaches any of the material terms and conditions of this agreement, the party claiming such breach may have if so negotiated, the right to serve upon the party alleged to be in breach a written notice of its intention to terminate this agreement. The party alleged to be in breach would, thereafter, have an agreed grace period within which to remedy the breach. If the party alleged to be in breach fails to cure or remedy the alleged breach within the agreed period, then, if agreed upon, the agreement would be automatically terminated.

Termination without Prejudice

Typically, the termination would be considered to be without prejudice to any other rights either party may otherwise have against the other.

IN THE EVENT OF BANKRUPTCY

If either party becomes insolvent or files a petition in bankruptcy, or if a petition in bankruptcy is filed against either party, or if either party makes an assignment for the benefit of creditors or makes any arrangement pursuant to any bankruptcy law, or if a receiver is appointed, this agreement could be automatically terminated by the other party at its election, if the parties agree that this provision be included in the license agreement.

FORCE MAJEURE

If at any time during the validity of the license agreement, by reason of any act of God, fire, earthquake, flood, explosion, strike, labor disturbance, civil commotion, act of government, its agencies or officers, any order, regulation, ruling, or action of any labor union or association of artists, musicians, composers, or employees affecting the artist or licensee, its subsidiaries or affiliates, or the industry in which it is or they are engaged, or any shortage of or failure or delays in the delivery of materials, supplies, labor, or equipment, or any other cause or causes beyond the control of the parties of this contract, the performance of the artist's or the licensee's obligations under this contract may be delayed, hampered, interrupted, or interfered with, or otherwise become impossible or impracticable, and if such condition exists for an agreed period of time, then either party may, upon notice to the other, terminate this agreement without liability, prejudice, or financial loss.

ASSIGNMENT

Since the talents of both parties are unique and extraordinary, the license agreement may stipulate that neither the talent nor the licensee would be granted permission to assign this agreement without the prior written consent of the other party. The licensee may bargain for an exception to this provision, by requesting the right to assign this agreement to any wholly owned subsidiary, or to any person, firm, or corporation owning or acquiring a substantial portion of the licensee's stock or assets, provided the acquiring subsidiary, person, firm, or corporation is a bona fide licensee for artists of the artist's stature.

NOTICES

All notices and statements provided for under this agreement are typically required to be in writing and, together with all payments provided under this agreement, sent by certified or registered mail, return receipt requested, or by other means of verifiable mailing, including express mail, to the address set forth in this agreement or to any other address as may be designated in writing. The addresses could be detailed as follows:

ARTIST
Address: ____________________
LICENSEE
Address: ____________________

UNAUTHORIZED CHANGES IN CONTRACT

The parties usually agree that the agreement as written sets forth the entire understanding of the parties relating to the subject matter of the license agreement. No modification, amendment, waiver, change, or discharge of this agreement, or any of the terms or provisions included in the agreement, would be binding upon either of the parties unless it is confirmed by a written instrument signed by the parties.

ENFORCEMENT OF AGREEMENT'S PROVISIONS

The parties would typically acknowledge that no waiver by either party of any term or provision of this agreement or of any default under this agreement would affect that party's rights thereafter to enforce that term or provision or to exercise any right or remedy in the event of any other default, whether or not similar.

VOIDABLE PROVISIONS

If any provision of this licensing agreement should be held to be void, voidable, invalid, or inoperative, no other provision of this agreement would be affected as a result of such action, if the parties so agree. Therefore, the remaining provisions of this agreement would remain in full force and effect as though such void, voidable, invalid, or inoperative provision had not been included in this agreement.

However, notwithstanding the foregoing, in the event any provision held void, voidable, invalid, or inoperative would impair the artist's right to receive his or her royalties under this agreement or would impair the licensee's right to manufacture and distribute any licensed product authorized under this agreement, then that provision could be deemed a material provision, and the agreement may be deemed terminated without prejudice to either side.

JOINT VENTURE

In order to protect each party from liability resulting from the other party's actions, the parties would probably agree that nothing in the license agreement could be construed to constitute a partnership or a joint venture between them. Neither party to the contract would therefore have the right to obligate or bind the other in any manner whatsoever. Furthermore, neither party would become liable for any representation, act, or omission of the other contrary to the provisions stipulated in this agreement.

REMEDIES TO BE CUMULATIVE

Except as otherwise provided in this agreement, all rights and remedies stipulated in this contract could be cumulative, if so agreed by both the artist and the licensee, and none of them would be in limitation of any other right or remedy.

STATE OF JURISDICTION

The parties would normally agree on which state in the United States would have the legal capacity to exercise jurisdiction in the event of litigation. Typically, the state where both parties conduct their business is the state of choice. In the event the parties reside in separate states, the party with the stronger bargaining position usually prevails, while the weaker party would end up bearing the additional expense and discomfort of litigating in a distant location.

ARTIST'S EXPENSES

The licensee may request that the artist provide the licensee with artwork, designs, logos, photographs, caricatures, voice recordings, videotapes, motion pictures, and any other material requested by the licensee in conjunction with the license agreement. The licensee may agree to pay a part, or all, of the expenses incurred by the artist to duplicate the artwork furnished to the licensee.

Ownership of Product

The artist may insist that all artwork supplied by the artist to be used in relationship to the licensed product remain the property of the artist.

FREE GOODS

As an incentive to the artist, the licensee may agree to supply him or her with an agreed number of free samples of the licensed product immediately following its manufacture. In addition, the licensee may agree to supply the artist with additional samples of the licensed product at cost.

OWNERSHIP OF GOODWILL

In the promotion and advertising campaign surrounding the marketing of the licensed product, an intangible asset known as goodwill may be generated that could prove to be of great benefit to the artist in his or her future career development. The licensee would typically be required to stipulate that all such goodwill is the property of, and would forever remain the property of, the artist. The artist would probably contend in support of his or her request, that the licensed product is associated directly with the artist himself or herself and supersedes the actual product itself.

SIGNATURES

The parties would typically signify their understanding of the agreement and their acceptance of the provisions contained therein by signing the agreement.

12

The Print Rights Agreement

Striving to maximize the earned revenues to be derived from a musical composition, the songwriter and/or music publisher would typically seek to commercially exploit the composition in the marketplace, entertaining licensing offers from various distribution sources.

A musical composition is composed of a collection of rights that attach themselves to the creation and, in most circumstances, may be sold, licensed, or leased at the will and discretion of the copyright owner. Apart from the recording agreements and mechanical and public performance licenses, the musical composition owner may offer, to suitable licensees for commercial exploitation, the print license.

PARTIES

The print agreement is usually entered into, by and between the composition owner of the musical composition, generally the songwriter or the publisher, and the licensee. Their corporate names and addresses should be included in this provision.

As in most agreements, clarity is a requirement that will best serve all the parties to an agreement in the case of any dispute or misunderstanding. In an effort to establish with contractual certainty the identity, history, and strengths of either party, both will usually stipulate their occupations. The composition owner would generally state that he or she is, has been, and intends to remain in the business of music publishing, if a publisher, or in the business of songwriting, if a songwriter, while the licensee will often affirm that he or she is in the business of printing, publishing, and distributing, through sale, license, or lease, musical compositions.

TERRITORY

A licensee may license the musical compositions for a particular country, such as the United States or France, for a limited territory, such as the European Common Market countries, or for a broad territory, such as the world. Generally, the licensee's market strength will be considered in the grant of territory.

GRANT OF RIGHT

The heart of the print agreement is the rights granted by the composition owner to the licensee. Those rights should be stipulated in detail and usually consider the present and future strength of the composition owner as well as the licensee's ability to exploit that composition owner's work in the print marketplace.

Right to Publish

The composition owner would usually grant to the licensee the exclusive right to print, publish, and distribute, either through sale, license, or lease, the musical compositions that are enumerated in the print agreement. The licensee would often negotiate for the right to exploit the licensed musical compositions by print in all forms and formats, including folios, sheet music, songbooks, and any and all other forms and formats of printed publications, now known or to be devised in the future. The right bargained for by the licensee would generally include the licensee's right to print, publish, and distribute any and all agreed-upon publications containing the licensed compositions alone or in combination with third-party musical material and compositions in a ''mixed'' folio or other publication.

If the licensed compositions are to be coupled with compositions and materials of third-party artists in mixed publications, the licensee may require the right to combine the names, likenesses, and biographical material of the third-party artists with those of the composition owner.

EXCLUSIVITY

It is likely that the composition owner would grant to the licensee the exclusive right to exploit the musical composition, within the agreed territories and during the agreed term, on an exclusive basis. It is therefore important that the composition owner be knowledgeable of the reputation, experience, and knowledge of the licensee in the industry that is the subject matter of this agreement, the business of printing, publishing, distributing, licensing, and selling printed manuscripts of compositions.

NAME AND LIKENESS

In the entertainment industry, the name and likeness of the composition owner may help stimulate sales of printed materials and compositions. Aware of the strength inherent in the composition owner's name, the licensee would usually demand, and be granted, the right to commercially exploit the composition owner's name, likeness, and biographical information in connection with the advertising and promotion of the licensed compositions.

Approval

As a control over the dissemination of the material, the composition owner would usually retain the right to approve the biographical material, as well as the photographs and other images of the composition owner, to be distributed in this regard by the licensee. In addition, the composition owner would typically demand that the licensee utilize only photographic material either submitted by the composition owner or photographed by approved photographers.

If the licensee agreed to the composition owner's demands, it is likely that the licensee would request that the composition owner grant his or her approval of any and all biographical and photographic material within an agreed number of days, wary that any unreasonable delay may impede the licensee from performing his or her services under the provisions of the print agreement, thereby causing the licensee a potential loss of income. Furthermore, the composition owner would usually be required to provide the licensee with photographs, transparencies, audiovisual cassettes, biographical material, and any and all other materials agreed, to be used in connection with the promotion and advertising of the published materials licensed under the provisions of the print agreement. All such materials would usually be required to be delivered to the licensee in a timely and reasonable manner, so that they can be utilized most effectively by the licensee.

TERM

The term, or length, of the print agreement is a provision that may be negotiated in several manners:

a) fixed term of years—the print agreement may specify that the agreed term is for an agreed number of years.

b) fixed term with option—as an alternative to the fixed term alone, the parties may agree to extend, the term of the print agreement for one or several option periods. The options are generally exercised by written notice, submitted by one party to the other, in advance of the termination of the prior term.

   i) as an inducement for the licensee, the composition owner may stipulate that an option could only be exercised if, by the licensee's efforts, a minimum amount of revenues was generated in connection with the print agreement. Each option period would usually be evaluated in its own right, and the earnings and revenues would, as a rule, not be cumulative or averaged.

COMPOSITIONS

The musical compositions that are made a part of the print agreement should be listed in clear and unambiguous language in an effort to curtail, in advance, any possibility of dispute or misunderstanding. This objective is often best accomplished by listing each licensed composition on a chart as follows:

Name of Composition	*Composition Owner(s)*	*Copyright Index Number*

Since the licensed compositions may undergo various arrangements or orchestrations, the print agreement should specify that the agreement will include the listed musical compositions, including any and all arrangements, compositions, title changes, and translations, in the agreed territory, during the negotiated term.

RIGHT TO ENTER AGREEMENT

Any agreement is built on the promises and guarantees that the parties make to each other. The print agreement would typically require that the composition owner warrant, represent, and guarantee the he or she owns or controls all the rights granted in this agreement and that he or she has the right to enter the print agreement without infringing on any of the rights, including copyrights, of any other person or entity. Furthermore, the composition owner would usually be required to guarantee that nothing contained in the print agreement would be construed to constitute an invasion of another person's or entity's rights of privacy, nor will adhering to the provisions of the print agreement constitute unfair competition in any manner, with any other person or entity.

NO ADDITIONAL GRANTS

The composition owner would, in most cases, be required to warrant that he or she has not granted, and will not grant, any right, title, or interest to any other person or entity effective during the term of this agreement which would conflict with, or be in limitation of, any of the rights granted under this contract. In addition, the licensee may demand that the composition owner warrant that he or she would not enter into any other agreement, effective during the term of this agreement, with any other party with respect to competing aspects of this exclusive agreement.

LIMITED GRANT TO LICENSEE

The composition owner would usually clarify that the only rights granted to the licensee in his or her works, are those rights specifically expressed in the text of this agreement. The composition owner would customarily reserve all other rights in and to the compositions.

NO MISUSE

In order to protect the value of his or her work, the composition owner would usually demand that the licensee stipulate that the licensee would not intentionally harm, misuse, or bring into disrepute the compositions which are the subject matter of this agreement.

NO UNNECESSARY EXPENSES

Furthermore, the licensee would typically be required by the composition owner to stipulate that he or she would not create any expenses chargeable to the composition owner without the prior written approval of the composition owner.

COMPENSATION

The fuel of the print agreement is the compensation to be earned by the composition owner in exchange for granting the enumerated rights to the licensee. In most cases, the composition owner would receive his or her compensation from the commercial exploitation of the licensed musical compositions from one or several sources, including the following:

a) An agreed percentage of a net (or gross) retail selling price of any and all publications containing the licensed musical compositions alone, sold and not returned.

b) If the licensed musical compositions are compiled with third-party musical compositions in any of the licensee's publications, including folios and songbooks, then the composition owner will usually be entitled to his or her proportionate share of the net (or gross) retail price for all copies of the publication sold and not returned.

c) An agreed percentage of the net (or gross) retail price for each issue of a "personality" publications published by the licensee. Typically, "personality" publications contain the composition owner's musical compositions, photographs, additional likenesses, and biographical material.

d) For each copy sold as an orchestration or arrangement, including marching band and instructional arrangements, the composition owner would typically be entitled to receive a percentage of the net (or gross) retail selling price.

e) An agreed sum for each copy of sheet music sold, based on an agreed minimum net (or gross) selling price per copy. In the event the net (or gross) selling price is higher or lower than the suggested net selling price, then the sum due and owing the composition owner may change proportionally.

Free Copies

The licensee would usually negotiate for the right to reduce from the sums due and owing the composition owner earned as a result of the commercial exploitation in the print media of the licensed compositions, all published material issued free of charge as promotional and/or advertising material, as returned copies not paid for and as charitable donations. Attempting to control the over-extending of such free copies, the composition owner may either limit the number of free copies to an agreed amount per fiscal year, or demand the right to approve, in writing, all giveaways.

Advance against Future Receipts

As an incentive to make and finalize the print agreement, the composition owner may request, and receive, if he or she has acquired a degree of clout in the recording industry, an advance against future receipts from the licensee. The actual sum of the agreed-upon advance would generally be based upon the bargaining strength of the composition owner, the composition owner's prior successes, and his or her continued popularity.

The advance is typically paid upon the signing of the print agreement and is often nonrefundable. It may therefore be considered a nonrecoupable advance. Generally, the composition owner would negotiate adding a clause to this provision indicating that the licensee would have no legal recourse to recover the advance payment in the event such sums are not earned and recouped from the commercial exploitation of the licensed composition. The latter provision often acts as a stimulus to the licensee to commercially exploit the licensed composition to its maximum potential, as a means of earning back the paid and nonrecoupable advance.

STATEMENT AND ACCOUNTING

The composition owner and the licensee should agree on a regular schedule for the delivery of the statement and accounting. The schedule may be quarterly, semiannually, yearly, or according to any other schedule agreed upon by the parties. Usually, the composition owner would bargain for an agreed period of time following the receipt of the statement and accounting within which to contest the validity and authenticity of the statement. If the statement is not contested or questioned in a timely and reasonable manner, then the statement would usually be considered to be valid and accurate.

Detailed Data

The statement should include detailed data pertaining to the sale of printed matter indicating the number and description of each item sold, the gross sales prices of each such item less applicable taxes, and the calculation of the composition owner's royalty.

PAYMENT TO SONGWRITER

All payment due and owing the songwriter (if different from the composition owner) from the commercial exploitation of the licensed compositions by the licensee may be the responsibility and obligation of the composition owner, if so agreed in the composition owner/songwriter agreement. If he or she did accept the responsibility of making all payments to the songwriter, then, in the print agreement, the composition owner would ordinarily stipulate that he or she acknowledges that the songwriter's payments are his or her responsibility alone and the composition owner will therefore forever keep the licensee free from any such obligation, even under threat of claim, action, or litigation by the songwriter.

Indemnification of Licensee from Songwriter's Claims

The composition owner may agree to the licensee's demand to indemnify the licensee in the event any claim or action does arise, stemming from his or her failure to make any payments due and owing the songwriter.

BOOKS AND RECORDS

The licensee would generally be obligated, and would usually agree, to keep and maintain accurate books and records of all transactions involving the subject matter of the print agreement. In order to maintain control over the compensation due him or her under the provisions of the print agreement, the composition owner would normally request the right to inspect the books and records. It is common for the licensee to grant those rights, contingent upon the composition owner's giving the licensee reasonable written notice.

The composition owner would usually be required to make the inspection during normal business hours, in the place where the books and records are routinely kept, and under the supervision of a certified public accountant. The licensee may also insist that the composition owner bear the costs of such inspection.

COPYRIGHT

The right to exploit the licensed musical composition and to assign or transfer that right to others is traditionally held by the copyright owner. Proper notice is generally required in order for the copyright owner to maintain his or her control over the copyrighted musical composition. The notice of copyright must contain certain elements in order to be considered ample notice: the word ''copyright,'' the abbreviation "copr.," or the symbol (c); the year of publication; and the name of the copyright owner.

The composition owner would usually require that the licensee print on each and every printed publication under the control of the licensee in connection with the print agreement, a copyright notice that complies with the Copyright Law of the United States of America and with the applicable copyright laws and regulations of licensed territories, if different from those of the United States. The notice should be located in such a manner and location as to give reasonable notice of the copyright owner's claim of copyright.

TERMINATION

In the event one of the parties materially breaches the provisions of the print agreement, the other party would usually be required to give the breaching party written notice of such breach. The agreement typically grants the breaching party a fixed and agreed period of time within which to cure, or remedy, the breach, after which the print agreement would usually be terminated without prejudice, liability, or penalty,

Bankruptcy

If the licensee becomes insolvent or files a petition in bankruptcy, or if a petition in bankruptcy is filed against the licensee, or if the licensee makes an assignment for the benefit of creditors or makes any arrangement pursuant to any bankruptcy law, or if a receiver is appointed, this agreement may be automatically terminated by the the composition owner if so agreed among the parties.

FORCE MAJEURE

If at any time during the term of this contract by reason of any act of God, fire, earthquake, flood, explosion, strike, labor disturbance, civil commotion, act of government, its agencies or officers, any order, regulation, ruling, or action of any labor union or association of artists, musicians, composers, or employees affecting the composition owner, the licensee, its subsidiaries or affiliates or the industry in which it is or they are engaged, or any shortage of or failure or delays in the delivery of materials, supplies, labor, or equipment, or any other cause or causes beyond the control of the parties, the performance of the composition owner's or the licensee's obligations under this contract is delayed, hampered, interrupted or interfered with, or otherwise becomes impossible or impracticable, and if such condition exists for an agreed period of time, then either party may, upon notice to the other, terminate this agreement. Any advances given to the composition owner may be returned, if so agreed, on a pro rata basis taking into considerion the length of the delay and the term of the agreement.

FOLLOWING TERMINATION

Possessing inventory of published material, including songbooks, folios, and sheet music, the licensee would usually negotiate for the right to sell, license, and to dispose of, in general, all the printed material containing the licensed musical compositions, throughout the licensed territory, within an agreed schedule following the termination of the agreement. The schedule may call for the disposition of the licensed material either:

(a) a fixed number of months following the termination of the print agreement, or

(b) within a reasonable period of time established by both parties until all such printed material are properly disposed of.

Under either alternative, the composition owner would usually require that the licensee be prohibited from dumping, or disposing of at below market price, any of the printed material containing the licensed musical compositions, without first obtaining the written permission of the composition owner.

NOTICES

All notices required to be sent between the parties are generally considered to have been received if sent by registered or certified mail, return receipt requested, by hand delivery, or by any means of express delivery which is accompanied by a receipt of mailing, including Federal Express and UPS. In addition, the notices should be sent to the addresses contained in the print agreement.

COMPOSITION OWNER
Address: ______________________

LICENSEE
Address: ______________________

INDEMNIFICATION

Typically, the parties will agree to indemnify, defend, protect, save, and hold each other harmless from and against any and all actions, claims, suits, losses, judgments, penalties, liabilities, damages, costs, and expenses (including reasonable attorney's fees) of whatever kind and nature imposed on, incurred by, or asserted, brought, or made by or against each party arising out of the other party's breach of any of its representations, warranties, or obligations made pursuant to this agreement or through the negligence or intentional acts of its officers, directors, employees, or representatives. The parties would usually agree to give each other prompt written notice of any such action, claim, or suit.

STATE OF JURISDICTION

The print agreement usually stipulates the state having jurisdiction in the event a dispute arises among the parties. It is usually the state within which the stronger of the parties conducts his or her business or which contains laws more favorable to him or her.

ENTIRE AGREEMENT

The parties would usually agree that the print agreement as drafted constitutes the entire agreement and should not be altered, changed, or amended except in a writing signed by the parties.

BENEFIT OF OTHERS

In an attempt to preserve the validity of the print agreement over time, the parties would usually agree that the print agreement should inure to their benefit and to the benefit of their heirs, representatives, executors, and administrators.

ASSIGNMENT

The right of the licensee to assign the print agreement may be controlled by the stipulation that either

(a) the print agreement be assigned only to a licensee of equal or superior standing in the music printing industry, or

(b) that any assignment by the licensee have prior written approval by the composition owner. In this manner, the composition owner would hope to maintain the level of licensee who would be best able to exploit commercially the licensed compositions in the agreed territory.

UNENFORCEABILITY

If any provision of this agreement would be found unenforceable or void as a matter of law, the parties may agree that no other provision would be affected as a result of such a finding, and accordingly, the remaining provisions of this agreement would remain in full force and effect as though such unenforceable or voided provision had not been contained in this contract unless such unenforceable or voided provision serves to impair the composition owner's right to receive his or her royalties under this agreement. In that case, an unenforceable provision could be deemed material, thereby rendering the agreement terminated without prejudice to the composition owner.

NO PARTNERSHIP

The parties would usually agree that by entering this agreement, they are not establishing a partnership or joint venture among themselves. Neither would, therefore, have the capacity to obligate or bind the other in any manner whatsoever. Furthermore, neither would become liable for any representation, act, or omission of the other held to be contrary to the provisions stipulated in this agreement.

SIGNATURES

The parties would customarily add their signatures to the print agreement, signifying their understanding of and accord with its provisions.

13

The Film Producer/Composer Agreement

The motion picture soundtrack has become a staple of the music industry, allowing many musical composers the opportunity to write and arrange music directly for a feature-length film. The composer requires the ability to coordinate the musical components to the visual actions, blending sound with sight to form a comfortable fit. In most cases, the music should not overpower the action but should have a distinctive element that has the capacity to be exploited and marketed in its own right.

The film producer/composer agreement should consider the nature of the motion picture industry, the means of distribution and exploitation available, the rights inherent to the musical composition and how those rights relate to synchronizing the music to the audiovisual components of a film.

PARTIES

The film producer and the composer would generally be listed as the principal parties to the film producer/composer agreement.

THE MOTION PICTURE

In order to minimize any possibility of ambiguity or confusion as to the motion picture specified in the film producer/composer agreement, and in the process lessening the potential for dispute and litigation in the future, the agreement should stipulate the name of the motion picture. If the title is tentative, or not firmly established, the agreement should reflect that with the words ''tentatively entitled,'' or ''presently titled.''

TERM

The term, or length, of the film producer/composer agreement would usually be calculated from a fixed start date until a reasonable time agreed by both parties within which the composer would be required to complete, to the satisfaction of the producer and all other persons who have the right of approval over the musical soundtrack, his or her creative services as enumerated in the provisions of the agreement. The composer should negotiate, aware of his or her own schedule, that in no event should his or her services extend beyond the agreed date.

Scheduling

The musical soundtrack is an integral component of the motion picture. It is typically composed, orchestrated, mixed, produced, and mastered on a schedule which is organized according to a plan permitting the motion picture to be released commercially in concert with a pre-arranged distribution cycle. Often, an elaborate and costly marketing, promotion, and advertising plan is unveiled by the producer and distributor in preparation for a motion picture's general release. A delay in that release schedule could prove to be an expensive mistake. In addition, movie theatres are usually booked well in advance of the release date of the motion picture, often cutting short a prior movie's theatrical release schedule in order to accommodate the motion picture's scheduled release. It is therefore imperative that each element of the motion picture production should be completed in a timely manner and in accordance with a prearranged schedule, in order to meet the economic requirements stipulated by the motion picture producers, distributors and exhibitors.

SATISFACTION OF PERFORMANCE

The composer would typically be required to fully perform his or her services, as agreed in the film producer/composer agreement, to the satisfaction of the producer. The services to be performed to the producer's approval by the composer are at the core of this agreement and include his or her creative work product, as composer, writer, arranger, orchestrator, and/or musical producer.

OPTIONS

The film producer/composer agreement may contain a provision granting the producer an option for the composer's services in the future for a sequel or series based on the original motion picture. The compensation for the composer's services for such future productions may be stipulated in the film producer/composer agreement, or may be left open for negotiation upon the execution and performance of the option.

Anticipated Work Based on Possible Option

Even though the option may not be fully effective until notice has been made, the option provision may allow the producer, at his or her own expense during the period of the option, to engage in the preproduction and production of a movie anticipating the utilizing of the composer's musical works.

Limiting Composer during Option Period

During the option period, the producer may request that the composer be enjoined from negotiating with a third party regarding any motion picture productions, unless such negotiations would not conflict with the option rights granted to the producer.

Option Alleviates a Potential Problem

If the producer is trying to obtain financing or other means of support for a sequel and it is learned that a competing production team is negotiating for the same music and lyrics by the composer, the producer's credibility within the entertainment community may be compromised, thereby potentially damaging his or her possibility of finalizing the financing and production of the motion picture. Granting the producer an option on the composer's future work, specifically related to the motion picture which is the subject matter of this agreement, intends to alleviate such an uncomfortable predicament.

Breach of Option

In the event of a breach of any of the conditions granting an option of the composer's future work to the producer, the producer may permit the composer a period of time within which to cure the defect, thereby allowing the option to continue. In the alternative, the producer, may opt to nullify and void, in its entirety, the option agreement. In the latter case, the funds advanced to the composer may be returned to the producer if so stipulated. The composer may also be liable to the producer for monetary damages.

COMPENSATION

The compensation the musical score composer would be entitled to receive in consideration for the work to be performed is usually paid in one of three manners:

a) as a flat fee, payable on a schedule agreed upon by the parties, or

b) as an advance against future royalties earned from the exploitation of the musical score of the motion picture in the territories granted, and thereafter as a royalty earned from such exploitation, generally in the form of record albums featuring the soundtrack of the movie, or

c) as a royalty alone, without the payment of an advance.

SCHEDULE OF COMPENSATION

If the composer is to be paid on a flat-fee basis, the schedule of compensation due the composer may be as follows: a portion upon the commencement of the composer's services and the remaining portion upon the composer's satisfactory completion of his or her services in accordance with the provisions of the agreement.

ADDITIONAL MUSICAL PROFESSIONALS

At times, the composer may retain the services of certain third party professionals he or she feels are essential to the successful production of the score, including an orchestrator and arranger. If the producer agrees, the producer would pay the salaries for the additional professionals without deducting those expenditures from the composer's compensation.

In most cases, the producer would emphasize that the composer should not be permitted to retain the services of the additional professionals without first securing the written approval of the producer. If such approval is not acquired, the producer would probably underscore, then the composer may, at the producer's discretion, be responsible for all payments due and owing the additional musical professionals.

UNIONS OR GUILDS

The film producer/composer agreement typically specifies, in clear and unambiguous language, that all compensation to be paid to the composer under the provisions of the agreement fall within the acceptable provisions and guidelines of appropriate unions or guilds, including the AF of M or AFTRA.

It is also indicated in most agreements that the composer is, or will become prior to his or her exercise of the provisions agreed upon in the film producer/composer agreement, and will remain throughout the term of this agreement, a member in good standing of the musicians union, typically the AF of M. The producer would usually emphasize the importance of this provision, insisting that it be performed, thereby insulating himself or herself from any potential union job actions or sanctions.

COMPENSATION FOR MECHANICAL RIGHTS

The agreement may also stipulate that the composer would be entitled to receive a percentage of any and all net (or gross) sums received from the commercial exploitation of the musical compositions by means of licensing the mechanical rights, motion picture and television synchronization rights, apart from those motion picture and television rights initially granted in the original motion picture containing the musical score.

JOINT PAYMENTS

If the musical composition was created by two or more individuals, a musical composer and a lyricist, for example, the film producer/composer agreement should specify that, as a rule, the sums due and owing the composer and lyricist would be shared equally among them, unless they agree, in writing, to share such compensation according to a different percentage.

RECEIPT OF FULL AND FINAL PAYMENTS

The film producer and the composer would usually stipulate that no additional payments, other than those agreed in the original film producer/composer agreement entered into between the producer and the composer, would be due and owing the composer for the inclusion of the musical composition in the motion picture for which the musical composition was originally written, arranged, orchestrated, scored, and produced.

NO OBLIGATION TO PRODUCE

Aware of the idiosyncrasies and uncertainties of the motion picture industry, the producer would typically point out that, though he or she intends to use his or her best efforts to produce a motion picture utilizing the composer's work product, the producer would not be under any obligation or requirement to produce the proposed motion picture. If a motion picture is not produced, the producer would usually demand that he or she should not face any liability or fault.

No Obligation to Record

The film producer will usually further stress that he or she is not obligated to record, publish, or commercially exploit, in any manner or form whatsoever, the musical compositions written, scored, and produced under the provisions of the film producer/composer agreement.

RIGHT TO NEGOTIATE AGREEMENT

The producer usually negotiates an agreement with a record company, granting the record company the right to distribute and commercially exploit the musical score from the motion picture by producing a recording of the soundtrack and marketing it through the normal channels of distribution. The term "recording" should be defined to include a long-playing album, an analog or digital audiotape, a CD, or any and all other means of recording, now known or devised in the future.

ROYALTY BASED ON SELLING PRICE

The composer, if so negotiated, could be entitled to receive, as compensation for his or her services, a royalty equal to an agreed percentage of the suggested retail price of the soundtrack recording.

RESPONSIBILITY TO PAY

The film producer/composer agreement may specify that the record company would be solely responsible to pay any and all royalty payments, earned from the exploitation of the soundtrack album due and owing the composer, to the composer directly. In that case, the producer would insist that the agreement free him or her from any responsibility or liability for any such payments, even if the record company fails to make any payments due and owing the composer under the recording agreement.

If, on the other hand, the record company makes all royalty payments to the producer, then the producer would be obliged to assume all responsibilities to make all payments due and owing the composer under the terms of the recording agreement and the film producer/composer agreement.

FUTURE RELEASES OF MUSICAL COMPOSITIONS RECORDED ON THE SOUNDTRACK RECORDING

The producer and/or the record company may require that the composer agree not to authorize a recording of, or to record, the musical compositions recorded on the soundtrack recording of the motion picture for an agreed period of time following the release of the soundtrack recording of the motion picture.

SOUNDTRACK ALBUMS THE PROPERTY OF THE PRODUCER

The composer would frequently be expected to pledge that the soundtrack recording of the motion picture would be, and would remain for the agreed term, the property of the producer. Furthermore, the composer would usually stipulate in the agreement that the producer would, for the agreed term, retain the unencumbered and unlimited right to manufacture, distribute, and commercially exploit by any method or medium now known or to be devised in the future, including long-playing albums, audiotapes, and CDs, the soundtrack recording containing the composition performed and/or composed by the composer. The producer may also negotiate for the right to sell, transfer, license, and exploit in general the soundtrack recording, under any name, trademark, or logo, throughout the world.

PUBLISHED CREDITS ON ALBUM COVER

The composer would typically be granted a credit on the soundtrack recording album cover, and in any and all other written information presented in conjunction with the soundtrack recording, as composer of those master recordings performed and composed by the composer. The wording may be as follows: "Music written by ________," or "Original Motion Picture Soundtrack by ________."

STATEMENT AND ACCOUNTING

The parties to the film producer/composer agreement would usually stipulate that the composer is entitled to receive a statement and accounting of any and all monies due him or her, as compensation for his or her services under the agreement. In the event the statements are to be submitted by a publishing or record company, that provision should be included in the agreement entered into by and between the film producer and the publishing and recording companies. If the delivery of those statements and accountings are the sole responsibility of the producer, then the producer would generally be obligated to submit the statements and accountings to the composer according to a schedule agreed upon between the producer and the composer in the film producer/composer agreement.

BOOKS AND RECORDS

The producer would customarily be required to maintain accurate books and records regarding the subject matter of the film producer/composer agreement. The composer should not hesitate to negotiate for the right to inspect the books and records in order to establish that the accountings and statements presented to him or her are accurate and correct. The books and records are an accounting of the composer's revenues and earnings, and should be questioned if considered inaccurate or faulty in any manner.

PERIOD OF TIME WITHIN WHICH TO PROTEST

Generally, the composer would be granted a fixed period of time in which to contest the statement, after which the statement would usually be considered valid and acceptable.

PERMITTED INSPECTION OF ACCOUNTING BOOKS

The producer would generally agree to such inspection by the composer, if the composer renders to the producer ample written notice. The producer would usually allow the inspection of the books and records by a certified public accountant, at the place where the books and records are normally stored during normal business hours. In addition, the costs required to inspect the books and records would typically be the sole responsibility of the composer.

SCREEN CREDITS

The credit the composer receives on the motion picture is an integral aspect of the composer's career. It is a significant demonstration of his or her position in the entertainment community, a highly visible business card that is open for all members of the entertainment community to see. The composer's credit would generally be accorded him or her if all the services required of the composer are completed in a timely and satisfactory manner, and if the music score of the completed motion picture contains musical compositions which have been substantially and principally performed and/or composed by the composer.

Placement of Credit

The composer may request a credit on either a separate or shared card, of a size and position mutually agreed between the producer and the composer. The credit may read as follows: "Original Music by ________," or "Music by ________," or "Original Motion Picture Soundtrack by ________." The producer would usually designate that he or she would be the final arbiter in regards to the type of screen credit alotted, and as to whether the composer's screen credit should be placed on both the opening and closing titles.

PUBLICITY CREDIT

The composer may request credit on all advertising, trailers, publicity, and any and all means of marketing the motion picture. The producer may negotiate for the right to limit the composer's credits to the actual motion picture, unless the composer's contribution to the motion picture would be considered a positive marketing tool that would aid in the advertising and promotion of the motion picture to a wide and varied audience.

Nonmaterial Breach If Error Occurs

The producer would generally insist on the inclusion of a provision stipulating that if the credits agreed upon are inadvertently deleted from the motion picture or from any medium agreed upon in the film producer/composer agreement, the producer would be given a reasonable opportunity within which to cure such a breach without incurring any damages or liabilities. The composer would therefore ordinarily be forbidden from seeking, and would not be entitled to receive, injunctive or equitable relief for such noncompliance with the provisions of the credit requirements. The composer may agree, but may argue for the right to maintain an action at law for provable damages in the event a cure is not initiated in a timely manner. One possible cure is that the producer insure that all motion picture prints, released and distributed following the discovery of the deletion contain the composers credit in its agreed position and size.

DUTIES OF COMPOSER

Most film producer/composer agreements clarify the understanding that the composer has been employed for the purpose of writing, composing, and arranging the master recording for a musical score, or soundtrack, for a particular motion picture. In addition, the composer may be required to orchestrate his or her composition and to conduct an orchestra for the purpose of recording the composition as a master recording.

ABILITY TO SEEK THIRD-PARTY ASSISTANCE

While the producer may grant the right to the composer to engage, with the producer's approval, the services of certain third parties to assist in the composition and orchestration of the musical score, the producer may retain the right to hire any and all additional musical personnel as he or she alone sees fit, including additional composers, arrangers, orchestrators, copyists, or conductors, without infringing on any of the composer's rights or obligations.

LIMITATION OF SERVICES

If the producer has engaged the services of a third party songwriter, the film producer and the composer may stipulate in their agreement that the composer's services under the provisions of the agreement would be limited to composing the music without being required to write the lyrics of the motion picture soundtrack. The composer's compensation typically reflects the difference in his or her services, responsibilities, and obligations.

Obligation to Comply with Producer's Reasonable Requests

The composer would usually be obligated to comply with all the producer's reasonable requirements and directions regarding the composition and orhestration of the musical score for the motion picture. The composer, under the conditions of this provision, would typically be required to cede his or her creative tastes to those of the producer.

LIMITS OF COMPOSER'S OBLIGATIONS

The composer would often specify that he or she would not be obligated to write any additions, modifications, or changes to the motion picture screenplay.

RIGHT TO CHANGE AND ALTER

Since the producer is generally the final arbiter of the "look and feel" of the motion picture, the producer would usually be granted the right to edit, change, and alter the musical composition performed and/or conducted by the composer, as well as the production numbers, without infringing on any of the rights of the composer, including the moral rights, or *droit moral*, of the composer. While moral rights are rights recognized in several nations around the world, including France, those rights, in general are presently not recognized in the United States.

RIGHT TO REPLACE WITH NEW MATERIAL

The producer would usually negotiate for the right to direct the composer to write or compose musical compositions to augment or replace those musical compositions originally composed by the composer for the motion picture. If agreed, the composer would, as a rule, be required to make any and all changes, modifications, and alterations requested by the producer, including adding scores and musical compositions in addition to those scores and compositions originally planned by the producer or composed by the composer.

EXCLUSIVITY

The producer may require that the composer, during the term of the film producer/composer agreement, perform his or her services exclusively for the producer.

Limitations on Composer's Activities

If the composer enters an exclusivity agreement with the producer, the composer would usually be prohibited from conducting or performing the musical compositions composed or performed under the provisions of the film producer/composer agreement for another producer or on a record for a record company that has not obtained the right to manufacture, record, and distribute the soundtrack of the motion picture, for a period of time equal to

a) an agreed number of years following the release of the soundtrack recording of the motion picture, or

b) an agreed number of years following the recording of the soundtrack album of the motion picture.

DELIVERY OF THE MUSICAL COMPOSITION

The composer's work product, including all original manuscripts, conductor's scores, instrumental parts, vocal segments, and any and all other music work product, would generally be required to be delivered to the producer no later than a fixed and established date. The composer's work would thereafter remain in the possession, and would remain the property, of the producer.

FAILURE TO MAKE TIMELY DELIVERY

If the composer fails to make a timely delivery of the musical composition, the producer could negotiate for the option to terminate the film producer/composer agreement and nullify all obligations due and owing the composer, including, among others, those of compensation and screen credit.

COMPOSER'S BUDGET

The producer would generally require that the composer perform his or her obligations under the terms of the film producer/composer agreement, including creating, producing, engineering, mixing and conducting the musical compositions, within the approved budget.

Dimension of Approved Budget

The producer would typically insist that all musical personnel, including, if required, copyists, arrangers, engineers, mixers, back-up musicians, as well as any and all required musical services, such as all studio, equipment, and instrument rentals, should fall within the approved budget. The composer may emphasize, though, that all musical personnel hired by the producer, in addition to those hired by the composer, are to be paid by the producer and should therefore not be chargeable against the composer's compensation.

In the Event Approved Budget Exceeded

The producer would often stipulate that if the composer exceeds the approved budget in an unreasonable manner, he or she would be solely responsible for the excess. In such a case, the producer may be granted the right to charge all such excess fees to the compensation due and owing the composer, either from the scheduled payments due resulting from the flat-fee compensation or from any royalty payments due and owing the composer.

RIGHTS

The musical composition is generally considered to be a property consisting of a collection of rights, including the rights of copyright, ownership and rights of usage. The film producer/composer agreement typically addresses the rights inherent in the musical composition, discussing which party controls the various rights and how those rights may be commercially exploited.

EMPLOYEE FOR HIRE

The composer may acknowledge that he or she has been employed by the producer as an employee for hire, and has, by accepting that position, relinquished any and all rights he or she may have in the musical composition, including those generally considered to be rights controlled by the composer, such as copyright.

RIGHTS RETAINED BY THE PRODUCER

The producer would usually stipulate that he or she is to be considered the owner of the musical composition as well as the owner and proprietor of any and all unencumbered rights in and to the musical composition throughout the negotiated territory, usually the world. As such, the producer should clarify in clear and unambiguous language the rights he or she is claiming in the musical composition. Those rights may include the rights to

a) the composer's services as rendered during the creation, orchestration, and production of the musical composition.

b) all creative and financial results stemming from the composition.

c) the sound recordings containing the composition, and the results from the commercial exploitation of those sound recordings.

d) any and all mechanical and public performance licenses inherent to, and granted from, the composition. This right is generally subject to the agreement entered into by and between the motion picture distributor and the producer. If the distributor has been granted some or all of the mechanical and performance licenses, the producer may negotiate to retain the synchronization rights in the composition or the adaptation rights stemming from any changes or adaptations made to the original composition.

e) all the music created and all titles, dialogue, characters, action, material, ideas, and any and all other musical, literary, or dramatic material which has been written, composed, prepared, submitted, improvised, suggested, or submitted by the composer regarding the motion picture for which the composer composed, orchestrated, and/or produced the composition.

f) exhibit, record, reproduce, publish, copy, print, sell, license, distribute, televise, broadcast, distribute, and commercially exploit, in any manner or form and over any manner of media, now known or hereafter devised.

g) exploit the composition in synchronization with the motion picture, trailers of the motion picture, as well as in clips and promotional shorts of the motion picture.

h) edit, arrange, rearrange, revise, add to, subtract from, and alter in any manner or form the composition and the composer's work product in any manner without infringing on the composer's rights, including moral rights in the composition and the composer's work.

i) employ an additional composer or writer to edit, add, arrange, revise, or alter in any manner or form the composition, without infringing on any of the composer's rights.

TERRITORY

The territory granted to the producer is typically worldwide, granting him or her control of all the rights granted in the film producer/composer agreement over as wide a distribution and commercially exploitative area as possible. This broad grant of right is intended to allow the producer ample possibilities in which to receive a return on his or her investment. It is a point to be negotiated, but generally it is granted to the producer.

NAME AND LIKENESS

The producer would typically request the right to utilize the composer's name, likeness, photograph, and biographical material in regard to the distribution, advertising and promotion, and commercial exploitation, in general, of the motion picture and of any musical soundtrack resulting from the motion picture containing the composer's musical compositions. While the composer may request permission to approve all such materials prior to their distribution, that approval is rarely withheld if the information presented is accurate.

RIGHTS TO SELL OR DISPOSE OF COMPOSITION

The film producer would usually be granted the unencumbered right to sell, transfer, or license the motion picture, including the composition, or any part of the motion picture or composition, without infringing on any of the rights inherent to the composer. In furtherance of this grant, the producer would typically insist that the provision spell out that his or her rights, as described herein, are not to be limited by any action or claim by the composer, including moral rights.

ASSIGNMENT

The right to assign the screenplay of the final motion picture, the composition, or any aspect of the film producer/composer agreement without hindrance by the composer would customarily be retained by the producer. The composer may attempt to limit the producer's right of assignment by demanding that the assignment be approved by the composer or that the film producer/composer agreement be assigned by the producer only to a third-party producer of at least equal stature, knowledge, and clout in the entertainment industry. Typically, the party with the stronger bargaining position retains the control over the right of assignment.

RIGHT OF PUBLICATION

The composition may be transferred to a publisher for the purpose of its commercial exploitation. The producer would generally reserve the right to designate the publisher retained to exploit and/or administer the musical composition, subject to any arrangements the motion picture distributor has made regarding the selection of a publisher, if such an arrangement has been negotiated in the agreement entered into by and between the distributor and the producer.

PUBLISHING AGREEMENT

Upon entering such a publishing agreement, the producer and the music publisher would usually agree on the method of payment of all fees due and owing the composer as a result of the music publisher's services in commercially exploiting the musical compositions.

- the music publisher may be responsible to pay all fees due and owing the composer, directly to the composer, or
- the producer may agree to pay to the composer his or her fees within an agreed time period after receiving the funds from the publisher.

Types of Exploitation

The parties would usually agree that the musical compositions may be exploited, in addition to soundtrack recordings, by, among others, the following means:

- piano copies and dance arrangements,
- printed copies of the musical arrangements, and
- inclusion in folios, albums, or other publications.

In all such cases, the composer's fees would generally be calculated as a percentage of the retail (or wholesale) selling price of such items, following the deduction of the music publisher's expenses.

Free Items

In most circumstances, the music publisher would not be required to compensate the composer for all units given free of charge as a means of promoting or advertising the musical compositions, and to which the publisher did not receive compensation.

Sums to Be Paid Are Net

All sums due and owing the composer under this provision, are payable after the musical publisher deducts all expenses and costs incurred on the composer's behalf. Those expenses and costs may include, among others, taxes, costs of marketing and promoting the composer's musical compositions, and costs of collection of license fees.

Exceptions to Royalties to Be Paid

The agreement may specify that the musical publisher would generally not be required to pay to the composer any royalties earned as a result of the nondramatic public performances of the musical compositions since those royalties are generally paid to the composer from the applicable performing rights societies, including ASCAP, BMI, or SESAC.

EXPENSES

The producer may agree to pay, or reimburse, the composer for any and all out-of-pocket expenses and disbursements by the composer in the rendering of his or her services under the provisions of the film producer/composer agreement. If he or she so agrees, the producer would usually demand the right to approve all expenses prior to the composer's making such expenditures and may limit the composer's expenses to those deemed necessary by the producer. For example, the producer may require that the composer fly coach class, rather than first class, when traveling in connection with the producer's motion picture.

ROYALTY DISPUTES

In the event an audit conducted by the composer in accordance with the provisions of this clause accurately reveals or discovers that the producer has made an underpayment of royalty compensation due the composer, the composer may insist that the producer pay that amount plus interest, such interest to commence upon the date the error provoking such underpayment occurred. If the discrepancy is found to be based on fraud or purposeful underpayment by the producer, the composer may insist that the producer pay or reimburse the composer for the costs of the accounting audit.

BINDING ROYALTY STATEMENTS

Unless otherwise agreed, all accountings and statements rendered by the producer would be binding upon the composer and would not be subject to objection for any reason unless specific objection is made by the composer by written notice to the producer stating the basis of the objection.

The film producer/composer agreement may contain a sunset provision, stating that if an objection is not made within an agreed period of time subsequent to the composer's receipt of a royalty accounting statement, then the composer would have forfeited his or her right to maintain any action, claim, or proceeding against the producer in any forum or tribunal with respect to any accounting or statement due under this agreement.

EXCLUSIVE RIGHTS

The composer would typically be obliged to warrant and represent to the producer that he or she has the exclusive rights to the music and lyrics which he or she is creating or shall create, and that he or she has the unencumbered authority to grant to the producer the use of such material as agreed upon in this agreement, without infringing on any other person's or entity's rights, including copyright or privacy. By this warranty, the composer is stipulating that he or she is the originator of the compositions, that all compositions are wholly and completely original, and that none of the musical compositions are in the public domain or are the property of any third party or entity.

NO RESTRICTION

The composer would further warrant that he or she is not under any restriction that would prevent or interfere, presently or at any time in the future, with the composer's performing his or her obligations under the provisions of the film producer/composer agreement.

NO THIRD-PARTY AGREEMENTS

The composer would, as a rule, further indicate that he or she will not enter into any third-party agreements which may conflict with the provisions of the film producer/composer agreement, thereby interfering with the composer's obligations under its provisions. By making this statement, the composer is normally warranting and representing that he or she has not granted, and will not grant, any right, title, or interest to any other person or entity effective during the term of this contract which would conflict with, or be in limitation of, any of the rights granted under this agreement.

INDEMNIFICATION

In an effort to shield the producer from any liability or responsibility for a breach or warranty by the composer, he or she would usually require that the composer agree to indemnify, and hold the producer harmless, from any costs, damages, liabilities, expenses, or fees, including legal fees, resulting from a breach of any of the warranties or representations, oral or written, made by the composer and relied upon by the producer, in connection with the film producer/ composer agreement.

ADVANCED WRITTEN NOTICE OF PENDING LAWSUIT

In addition, the parties of this agreement may be required, if they so agree, to give each other prompt written notice of any legal action, claim, or suit instituted regarding the composition. Each party would then be granted the opportunity, at its sole option, to participate in the defense of the alleged claim, utilizing counsel of its own choice, at that party's sole cost and expense.

COPYRIGHT

If the composer was retained by the producer as an employee for hire, the producer, at his or her sole expense, would typically register and maintain, or cause to be registered and maintained, the appropriate copyright(s), trademark(s), and/or service mark(s) for the compositions and lyrics in those territories where the contract is applicable. Under circumstances where the composer has negotiated for the right to own, outright, the copyrights to the compositions, it would usually be the composer's obligation to register and maintain the appropriate copyright(s), trademark(s), and/or service mark(s) for the compositions and lyrics.

TERMINATION

Generally, termination of the film producer/composer agreement would result if it has been discovered that a breach of a material warranty, that is, a warranty which goes to the essence of the contract, has occurred.

Written Notification

Written notification is typically required before the termination clause can become operative. If the agreement calls for the grant of an opportunity to cure the defect or breach, it is common that the party alleged to be in breach would, upon receiving notice of such intent to terminate based on a material breach, have an agreed period of time within which to remedy the breach. If the party alleged to be in breach fails to cure or remedy the alleged breach, then upon the expiration of a predetermined period, the agreement would automatically be terminated.

BANKRUPTCY

If one of the parties is deemed to be unable to carry out its obligations due to bankruptcy or insolvency, then the affected party may be granted the right to terminate the agreement at its election, and without suffering any liability or damage.

FORCE MAJEURE

Those events beyond the control of the producer and composer which cause delay or postponement of certain obligations are usually spelled out in the *force majeure* provision. The events typically considered beyond the control of the parties customarily include but are not limited to the following: acts of God, fire, earthquake, flood, explosion, strike, labor disturbance, civil commotion, acts of government (including acts by its agencies or officers), any order, regulation, ruling, or action of any labor union or association of actors, musicians, directors, writers, or others affecting the composer or producer, its subsidiaries or affiliates or the industry in which it is or they are engaged, or any shortage of or failure or delays in the delivery of materials, supplies, labor, or equipment, or any other cause or causes beyond the control of the parties of this agreement.

Automatic Termination

In instances of *force majeure*, if the performance of the composer's or film producer's obligations under this contract is delayed, hampered, interrupted or interfered with, or otherwise becomes impossible or impracticable, for a certain predetermined time, be it individually or collectively within a given period of time, then providing proper notice is given, termination of the contract may be in order.

Opportunity to Cure

Generally, before the final termination status becomes operative, attempts to cure the event initiating the *force majeure* provision could be undertaken. If such a cure is deemed impossible or impractical, then either party may have the right, upon notice to the other, to terminate this agreement. Any advances given to the composer may be required to be returned to the producer within a prenegotiated amount of time following the termination of the agreement.

Tolling of Obligation If Cured

The agreement may stipulate that should the event placing into motion the *force majeure* provision cease prior to the termination of the agreement, and the obligations of the producer and composer could continue unhindered, then the term of the agreement could be tolled for that period of time and could automatically be extended for a period of time equal to the time that the contract was suspended due to the nonperformance of the parties.

NOTICES

All notices and statements provided for under this agreement would usually be required to be in writing and, together with all payments provided under this contract, be sent by United States mail, postage prepaid, certified or registered mail, return receipt requested, or by verifiable mail (for example, Federal Express, UPS, and DHL) to the addresses listed in the agreement or to any other address that is designated in writing as the preferred address for receipt of all notices.

COPIES OF REQUIRED NOTICE

At times, copies of all notices would be required to be sent to the legal representatives of the parties. The addresses of those representatives should be listed in the agreement as follows:

COMPOSER'S ATTORNEY
Address: ____________________

PRODUCER'S ATTORNEY
Address: ____________________

NO CHANGES, MODIFICATIONS, OR WAIVERS

Both parties would usually agree that no modification, amendment, waiver, termination, or discharge of the film producer/composer agreement would be binding upon either of the parties unless confirmed by a written instrument signed by the parties.

NO WAIVER

The parties may also agree that no waiver by either party of any term or provision of this agreement, or of any default under this contract, would affect that party's rights thereafter to enforce the term or provision in question or to exercise any right or remedy in the event of any other default, whether or not similar.

VOIDABLE PROVISIONS

If any provision of this agreement would be held void, voidable, invalid, or inoperative, the parties would usually agree that no other provision of the agreement would be affected as a result of such action. Accordingly, the remaining provisions of the agreement would remain in full force and effect as though such void, voidable, invalid, or inoperative provision had not been contained in the agreement.

LEGAL RELATIONSHIP OF THE PARTIES

The agreement usually reaffirms the legal positions or relationship between the parties, stipulating that nothing in this agreement could be construed to constitute the creation of a partnership or a joint venture between the parties.

Such an affirmation would usually serve to ensure that neither party to the agreement would be deemed to have the authority or the right to obligate or bind the other in any manner whatsoever nor hold itself out contrary to the terms of this paragraph. In agreeing to this provision, neither party would become liable for any representation, act, or omission of the other contrary to the provisions stipulated in this agreement.

REASONABLE ATTORNEY FEES

In the event that a lawsuit is initiated between the parties, the agreement may provide that the winning side would be entitled to receive as part of the judgment, all reasonable legal fees and costs associated with the lawsuit.

STATE OF JURISDICTION

The parties would generally agree which state would have final jurisdiction in the event of litigation or dispute. Typically, the party with the stronger bargaining position would select the state where he or she resides, has his or her place of business, and/or where the state laws are more favorable.

FUTURE BENEFITS

The film producer/composer agreement typically stipulates that its benefits would inure to the benefit of the producer and composer and to their heirs, representatives, administrators, and executors.

SIGNATURES

The parties to the agreement would usually be required to attest to their understanding and acceptance of all the provisions in the film producer/composer agreement by signing their names, as individuals and/or as agents for their companies, to the agreement.

14

The Synchronization License

Motion Pictures

The right to synchronize the copyright owner's musical compositions with the moving visual images of motion pictures typically requires the granting of a separate license, the synchronization, or "synch," license. It is usually accorded by the owner of the copyrighted composition to the motion picture producer. The license customarily grants the right of that musical composition to be recorded in synchronization with a motion picture and, thereafter, to present that motion picture in theatres, on television, and through home entertainment devices, including video cassettes and laser disks.

PARTIES

The synchronization license agreement would normally include the name of the party who offers (the owner of the copyrighted composition) and of the party who acquires (the producer of the motion picture) the rights to synchronize a particular musical composition with the visual images of a particular motion picture.

CONSIDERATION

The agreement generally stipulates in clear and unambiguous language the compensation the purchaser of the license, the producer, is prepared to pay for the right to license, rent, buy, and commercially exploit in motion pictures the musical composition in question. This clause is of primary interest to the copyright owner, since synchronization rights are a vital source of income generated from the commercial exploitation of the composition. The copyright owner's compensation is usually based on several key elements:

- The history of the copyright owner as a performing artist, as a lyricist, and as a composer for motion pictures.
- The importance of the copyright owner as a popular artist.
- The placement of the composition—whether the composition would be utilized as background music, as a featured vocal and musical performance, and/or over opening or closing credits.
- The length of the composition.
- The importance of the composition to the plot.
- The importance of the composition itself—whether the composition is a recent hit, a standard, a popular "oldie," or an original work.
- The utilization of the composition in other motion pictures.
- The amount of the film budget.
- The caliber of actors performing in the film—stars or contract players.
- The prior track record of the producer.
- The strength and expertise of the film distributor.

The agreement would typically state that for the agreed sum, often a flat fee, the producer has agreed to acquire the synchronization rights detailed in the synchronization license agreement.

Payment Schedule

The synchronization license agreement should define clearly the schedule of payment. The copyright owner's payment may be settled on a one-time basis, usually upon the signing of the "synch" license agreement, or the payment may be divided in accordance with an agreed and fixed schedule. A sample schedule may be as follows:

a) one-third payable on the signing of the synchronization license agreement.

b) one-third payable on the first day of principal photography.

c) one-third payable on the last day of principal photography.

Royalty Payments

Rather than receiving compensation in the form of a flat fee, the producer may agree to pay the owner a royalty, based on the net (or gross) earnings of the motion picture, which would typically include all sales of the soundtrack album as well as box office receipts.

RIGHTS GRANTED

The copyright owner would generally grant to the motion picture producer the following:

a) the right, license, and authority to record the composition, which consists of lyrics and music, for synchronization with the named motion picture,
b) the right to make copies of all such recordings, and
c) the right to exploit the recording in any country and/or territory agreed upon in the synchronization agreement.

SOUNDTRACK

The rights granted to the producer would normally include not just the rights to exploit in general the music as it appears on the film, but the right to license, record, make copies, and distribute the soundtrack itself if the soundtrack is to be marketed as a separate entity. Soundtracks are generally marketed from the musical scores of both musical and nonmusical motion pictures.

LANGUAGE

Since there exists the possibility that the composition may be translated from its original language to a foreign language, the agreement should stipulate the language or languages (English, French, Spanish, Hindi, etc.) granted by the synchronization agreement. If the grant is broad and covers all known languages presently in existence, that too should be spelled out clearly in the agreement.

TERRITORY

The synchronization license agreement normally details the countries, or territories, to which the producer has acquired the ''synch'' license. The grant may limit the territory to a single country, such as the United States, or it may be as expansive as the grant of a worldwide territory.

In general, movies are geared for both domestic and international distribution through a broad-based film release schedule. Therefore, any restrictions imposed on the producer by a limited ''synch'' rights agreement could adversely affect and curb the marketing of the picture, impacting on the movie's popularity, financial returns, and profits. In the final analysis, the producer would usually negotiate for the worldwide rights in the composition or forgo the acquisition of the composition altogether.

COMPOSITION

The core of the synchronization license agreement is the composition itself. After all, it is the license to synchronize the particular composition to the specific motion picture that is being negotiated. In an effort to clarify, as precisely and unambiguously as possible, the composition under discussion, the title (a tentative title, if a definite title has not been determined), owner, writer, and publisher of the composition should be stipulated in the ''synch'' license agreement. Often, a simple chart serves to satisfy the intent for clarity by both parties to the agreement.

Composition	*Owner*	*Writer*	*Publisher*

If several compositions are to be included in the synchronization, the detailed list of the compositions in question may be incorporated in a rider, or exhibit, which should be attached to, and made a part of, the synchronization license agreement.

MOTION PICTURE TITLE

Equally as important as listing the exact name and owner of the composition is incorporating the name of the motion picture in the synchronization license agreement. This provision can be satisfied with a simple chart:

Motion picture, presently titled: ______________________

Producer: ______________________

Director: ______________________

Change of Title

It is not uncommon for a successful motion picture to reproduce itself in sequel, foreign language version, or remake. The agreement should therefore state the possibility of such an event and specify that the grant of the ''synch'' license in the present agreement considers and includes any possible title changes or translations, so long as the content of the motion picture remains substantially the same. The copyright owner may request that all such title changes and translations be added to and made part of the synchronization license agreement as they occur.

LICENSE GRANTED

Normally, if the copyright owner grants to the producer the worldwide rights to the composition, the license granted could include both (a) Performance License—United States, and (b) Performance License—Foreign.

Performance License—United States

By granting a performance license for the United States to the producer, the copyright owner would usually be according the producer, as well as those other parties authorized by the producer, the license and right to perform the composition in synchronization or timed relation with the agreed-upon motion picture and trailers, in the United States as well as its territories and possessions.

In most cases, it is understood that the motion picture would also be exploited in various forms and venues. In anticipation of the varied means of distribution available, the agreement should consider the types of distribution covered.

a) Theatrical distribution to a paying audience. Ordinarily, the synchronization license grants to the producer the right to distribute the motion picture containing the synchronized composition in theatres and other public locations where motion pictures are customarily distributed and exhibited and where the audience is charged an admission fee. The period of this license would generally last for the duration of the copyright, including the original term and any renewals, provided, of course, the owner still retains control of the copyright in the renewal period. The period of this license may be limited, though, if both parties agree to such a provision.

b) Free television. In addition to theatrical distribution rights, the license granted by this agreement would usually include the right to televise the motion picture containing the synchronized composition over television networks or local television stations which have been granted appropriate licenses from the performing rights societies. This grant typically considers network and syndication stations. In the event the local television station or the network has not been granted a license by the appropriate performing rights society, the producer may be required to agree that the grant of license is subject to the provisions of the appropriate performing rights societies.

c) Pay television. Also included in the rights granted the producer is, as a rule, the right to distribute and exhibit the motion picture which contained the synchronized composition by means of pay television, including such forms of pay TV as subscription television, cable system, and closed-circuit television. As with free television, pay television distribution outlets are typically required to have valid and appropriate performing right societies agreements from ASCAP, BMI, and SESAC. If required, the producer or the distributor would secure a clearance from the applicable performing rights society prior to airing the motion picture containing the musical composition which is the subject matter of this synchronization agreement.

Performance License—Foreign

The synchronization license agreement may also stipulate that in the event the composition is to be performed, as a part of the agreed motion picture, in countries and territories outside of the United States, the synchronization license would most likely be subject to clearance by the applicable laws, regulations, customs and codes of the country or territory in question, including the rules and regulations of that country's performing rights societies. Likewise, the synchronization license would probably be subject to the foreign performing rights society's customary fees and conditions of performance.

Typically, the foreign performance license would accord the producer all the rights granted in the national performance license, including motion picture, free television, pay television, and audiovisual devices (including videocassettes).

Synchronization Rights Retained by Copyright Owner for Foreign Territories

If the copyright owner has retained the synchronization rights to all territories outside the United States, the producer may insist on including a provision which would serve to minimize the possibility of confused and repetitive negotiations between the copyright owner, the producer, and the foreign performing rights societies. The agreement may stipulate that the owner would grant the producer the right to negotiate the terms of foreign license for the musical composition, or alternatively, that the owner would license the composition to a recognized foreign performing rights society and would not unreasonably hold back the license.

TRAILERS

A common form of advertisement and promotion for motion pictures, the trailer is defined as a short filmed sample, usually extracted from the completed motion picture, compiled and distributed for the purpose of promoting and marketing the motion picture. It may occur that the owner's composition is to be utilized, in whole or in part, as a component of the trailer.

The synchronization license agreement should grant to the producer the right to utilize the copyrighted composition on the trailer for the specific motion picture to which the synchronization license was granted, for the express purpose of advertising and promoting the motion picture. The trailer may be presented on screen and on television (free and pay), as videotape, laser disks, computer disks or in any and all other means of promotion utilizing trailers, now known or to be devised at any time in the future.

AUDIOVISUAL DEVICES—INCLUDING VIDEOCASSETTES AND COMPUTER SOFTWARE

As methods of distribution increase, the theatrical and television (free and pay) distribution of a motion picture represents only a portion of the commercial exploitation possibilities for a motion picture. Most motion pictures would be distributed in the home entertainment market through various audiovisual means. Videocassettes have captured a sizable position in the market and in most instances have matured into a stable source of revenue. Laser disks, CD-ROM (compact disk-read only memory), and CD-I (compact disk-interactive), to name only a few additional methods of distribution which reproduce the motion picture in its entirety in its original form, are becoming increasingly acceptable outlets for the distribution of a motion picture, and therefore, by association, distribution and licensing of the musical composition.

The producer would usually negotiate for the understanding that the "synch" license agreement would grant the producer the right to sell, lease, license, distribute, and exhibit the motion picture which contains the synchronized composition by means of home video, including videocassettes and videodiscs; by means of computer software; and by all additional audiovisual and computer-based devices to be discovered and utilized at any time in the future for home use by the user. The copyright owner may hold back all, or some, audiovisual rights to the musical composition, intending to negotiate the held-back rights separately. In that case, the copyright owner would normally require that the producer notify him or her of the intention to exercise the rights to exploit the copyrighted composition through the use of audiovisual devices and computer software. It is highly likely, though, that the producer would not enter an agreement with the copyright owner, unless the producer has acquired all audiovisual and computer related rights, within the territory and for the term granted, in the synchronization license agreement. Without such a broad grant, the producer may feel that he or she is limited in the distributing and marketing of the motion picture.

Additional Compensation

While the copyright owner may request royalty payments for each videocassette or computer disk sold or rented, the producer would usually argue that the payment made for the "synch" license should be comprehensive and include all the audiovisual rights. The copyright owner would usually evaluate the royalty due from the producer from the sale of audiovisual devices, including videocassettes and computer software, often basing his or her calculations on the compulsory royalty rate payable for the exploitation of the mechanical royalties paid for musical recordings sold pursuant to the Copyright Law of the United States.

In order to evaluate the additional royalties due from the exploitation of the audiovisual devices, the owner would usually consider the following:

- the number of copies of the audiovisual device sold, rented, or licensed,
- the wholesale and retail price, and the license and rental fee, of the audiovisual device, and
- the type and number of uses of the composition on the audiovisual device as compared to the type and number of uses of other compositions on the audiovisual device.

As a compromise, the producer may agree to pay the copyright owner an additional synchronization fee, a buy-out, paying the copyright owner a fee in advance against the number of audiovisual units sold.

RESTRICTIONS

The copyright owner may negotiate for the right to restrict the use of the composition by the producer in several manners.

Change or Amend the Composition

The copyright owner may restrict the producer's right to change, alter, or amend the original lyrics of the composition or to change, alter, or amend the original music.

Title of Composition

The producer may not be granted the right and authority to use the title of the composition as the title to the motion picture, unless so negotiated by the parties.

Use of Story Line

The copyright owner may restrict the producer's right to utilize the story line, subject matter, and theme of the composition as a basis for a plot or subplot for the present, or for any future, motion picture.

RIGHT TO GRANT

Typically, the copyright owner would be required by the producer to warrant and represent that he or she has the right to grant the synchronization license for the copyrighted composition to the media granted by the agreement.

RESERVATION OF RIGHTS

As a means of clarification, intending to alleviate any possibility of confusion as to the rights granted, the owner may stipulate that all rights not specifically granted to the producer by the synchronization rights agreement would be reserved to the owner, who may grant all other rights as he or she sees fit, in his or her best business judgment.

CUE SHEET

In the case of synchronization with television programs, the producer would generally agree to supply the copyright owner's performing rights society with a cue sheet identifying the music used in the program.

TERMINATION

The parties may agree, and would therefore so stipulate, that if the license fees agreed upon are not paid within an agreed number of days following the occurrence of a stipulated event (the first day of principal photography, for example), then the synchronization license, in its entirety, would be terminated.

However, if a fee is due the copyright owner following the production or release of the motion picture, the above termination provision could naturally not apply. In that case, the most likely remedy would be a financial penalty stipulated by the agreement and, if required, imposed by the courts. It is unlikely for a court to ban or prohibit the exhibition of the motion picture if fees are in fact due since the issue at the bar would most likely not be one of proper copyright clearance but rather a contractual matter regarding payment.

ACCOUNTING

If the parties agreed upon a royalty payment to the copyright owner, the synchronization license agreement would normally require that the producer supply the copyright owner with all pertinent and relevant data necessary to compute royalties payable to the owner, including all box office figures as well as the number and net retail (or wholesale) price of the units sold.

The producer would usually agree to make all royalty payments to the copyright owner according to a regular schedule, which may be quarterly, semiannually, or annually.

Accurate Books

As a matter of course, if the copyright owner is due royalty payments, the synchronization license agreement would probably require that the producer maintain accurate books of account governing all transactions relating to this agreement. The copyright owner would normally request the right, utilizing his or her authorized representative and at his or her sole expense, to audit the books and records of the producer with respect to the subject matter of this agreement.

The producer would generally demand that he or she be given reasonable notice of the copyright owner's intent to initiate such an audit and that the audit be conducted during normal business hours, where the books and records are normally stored.

NO DISABILITY

Both parties would usually warrant that they are under no disability, restriction, or prohibition, whether contractual or otherwise, with respect to the following:

- their rights to execute this agreement,
- their rights to grant the rights listed in this agreement, and
- their rights to perform the obligations stated in this agreement.

NO ADDITIONAL GRANTS

The producer usually insists that the copyright owner warrant that he or she has not granted and will not grant any right, title, or interest in the musical composition to any other person or entity effective during the validity of this contract which may conflict with or be in limitation of any of the rights granted under this contract.

INDEMNIFICATION

As a means of protecting each party from potential expenses, the agreement may contain a provision stipulating that the parties agree to indemnify, defend, protect, save, and hold each other harmless from and against any and all actions, claims, suits, losses, judgments, penalties, liabilities, damages, costs, and expenses (including reasonable attorney's fees) of whatever kind and nature imposed on, incurred, asserted, brought, or made by or against that party arising out of the other party's breach of any of its representations, warranties, or obligations made pursuant to this agreement or through the negligence or intentional acts of its officers, directors, employees, or representatives.

OWNERSHIP OF COPYRIGHT

Customarily, the copyright owner may avail himself or herself of all the benefits and protections provided by the Copyright Act. In the event the producer acquires the right for an existing composition, the producer may require that the copyright owner transfer the copyright in that composition to the producer. The transfer of copyright must be actuated by a signed writing.

EMPLOYEE FOR HIRE

The producer may retain the services of a writer to compose the music and lyrics for a composition to be utilized in a motion picture. In most cases, compositions composed in such a manner are considered "made-for-hire," and the composer, an "employee-for-hire."

Under the Copyright Act, compositions made for hire are compositions that contain certain elements:

- compositions prepared by an employee within the scope of his or her employment,
- compositions specifically commissioned or ordered, and

- compositions which the parties expressly agree, in a written and signed instrument, to be considered works made for hire.

Works made for hire are customarily the property of the employer, in this instance the producer, who owns the composition for the duration of the copyright.

Assignment

The producer would usually insist that the composer not assign his or her obligations under this agreement, if the conditions are those of employer/employee for hire. It is the particular composer's services that the producer intended to acquire, and usually those services are considered unique and irreplaceable.

NOTICE OF COPYRIGHT

A notice of copyright is typically placed on all publicly distributed recordings. The symbol (p) should be prominently displayed on the musical recording, followed by the year the recording was first published and the name of the owner of the copyright. An example of the proper notice copyright is as follows: (p) 19—, XYZ Inc.

The notice on copies of literary, dramatic, and other visually perceptible work is (c), followed by the year the work was first published and the name of the copyright owner, for example, (c) 19__, XYZ Inc.

NOTICES

All notices and statements provided for under this agreement would normally be required to be in writing and, together with all payments provided under this contract, be sent by United States mail, registered or certified mail, return receipt requested, or by other means of verifiable mailing, such as Federal Express or UPS. The notices should be sent to the address stated in the agreement or to such other address as may be designated in writing by the parties.

NO CHANGE

Most agreements contain a provision stipulating that the written agreement contains the entire understanding of the parties and that no modification, amendment, waiver, termination, or discharge of this agreement or any of the provisions included in the agreement would be binding upon either of the parties unless confirmed by a written and signed instrument.

NO WAIVER

Additionally, the parties may stipulate that no waiver by either party of any provision or of any default would affect that party's rights thereafter to enforce that provision or to exercise any right or remedy in the event of any other default, whether or not similar.

VOID PROVISION

If any provision of this agreement would be held to be void, voidable, invalid, or inoperative, the parties may agree that no other provision will be so affected as a result of such action. The remaining provisions would therefore remain in full force and effect as though such void, voidable, invalid, or inoperative provision had not been contained in the agreement.

NO PARTNERSHIP

The parties would usually stipulate that by entering the agreement they have not agreed to the establishment of a partnership or a joint venture between them. By so stipulating, neither party to the contract would normally have the right to obligate or bind the other in any manner whatsoever.

STATE OF JURISDICTION

The parties would usually agree upon the state in which the agreement has been entered, and therefore, the state which would be the final arbiter as to the validity, construction, interpretation, and legal effect of the agreement.

NO PREJUDICE OF THE RIGHTS OF OTHERS

The copyright owner may be required to stipulate that he or she would not take any action during the effectiveness of this agreement that would prejudice any of the rights optioned by the producer.

BREACH OF CONTRACT

Should either party breach, that is fail, refuse, or neglect to comply with any of the agreement's material obligations, then the synchronization agreement could be considered null and void if the parties so agreed.

Insolvency

The copyright owner may insist on including a provision indicating that if the producer becomes financially insecure and files for bankruptcy protection prior to the production of the motion picture, then the copyright owner would be entitled to nullify and void the agreement in its entirety, and the rights to the composition would revert to the copyright owner.

FORCE MAJEURE

The synchronization license agreement is created to ensure the fulfillment of a specific performance, where time may be of the essence. The *force majeure* provision normally considers what would occur if events external to the control of the owner make the performance impossible or impractical. The *force majeure* provision may avoid a breach of the contract and provide for a cure, typically providing for the resumption of the obligation as soon as the event which triggered the clause is declared over.

SIGNATURES

The parties, by placing their signatures on the agreement, signify their understanding of and agreement with its contents.

Television

A synchronization license is normally required to be obtained from the copyright owner of a composition if that composition is to be recorded on a made-for-television movie or for episodic television. The synchronization license agreement—television is somewhat distinct from that agreement specifically geared to the use of a composition in a theatrical motion picture which eventually finds itself in television syndication.

It must be emphasized that while the copyright owner may receive a synchronization fee for the use of his or her composition on free or pay television, the publisher and the songwriter (usually one or both are the copyright owner) may be entitled to receive public performance royalties from one of the public performance societies, ASCAP, BMI, or SESAC, for the performance of the composition over the broadcast medium.

PARTIES

The parties to the synchronization license agreement—television are typically the owner of the copyrighted composition and the producer of the television program. Their names as well as the names and addresses of their corporations should be detailed in the agreement.

CONSIDERATION

The copyright owner generally grants to the producer the right to record the composition specifically named in this agreement for use in a made-for-television movie or on episodic television, in exchange for an agreed sum. In most cases, the payment is a lump sum payable upon the signing of the synchronization license agreement—television, or following an agreed schedule of payments, usually commencing on the signing of the agreement and terminating upon the completion of principal photography.

SYNCHRONIZATION

The composition is typically licensed to be synchronized, or time related, to visual events in the television program to be broadcast over free and/or pay television.

Medium

Free and pay television usually includes network, syndication, cable (premium or subscription), and pay-per-view.

Limitations

The synchronization license agreement—television may limit itself to free television and exclude any other form of exhibition aired over television, including pay television, subscription television, and pay-per-view, though it is likely that the producer would not enter an agreement that so confined his or her ability to distribute and market the produced television program.

The synchronization license agreement—television may also reqire that the free or pay television network have valid performance licenses from ASCAP, BMI and SESAC.

International

Given the growth in the international marketplace, in which made-for-television programming is of interest to foreign markets for television as well as theatrical distribution, the producer may not agree to restrain himself or herself in a manner which would prohibit the exploitation of the television program in overseas markets.

Exclusions

The agreement would usually provide that the synchronization license agreement—television entered by the parties specifically excludes the performance of the program in movie theatres or other venues where an admission fee is to be charged.

COMPOSITION

The copyrighted composition would normally be named specifically in the agreement, in order to diminish the potential for ambiguity or disagreement at a future date. If the composition has been completed and copyrighted, the agreement should contain the copyright number, a lead sheet and recording of the composition. Those items may be added to, and made part of, the agreement, in a rider or exhibit.

PROGRAM

The filmed or videotaped television program should be named with exactness in the agreement. Such clarification is generally required in an effort to facilitate the intentions of the parties, thereby eliminating misunderstandings which could potentially lead to dispute and litigation, if not resolved.

CUE SHEET

The performance rights societies, ASCAP, BMI, and SESAC, usually collect fees resulting from the public performance of the composition and thereafter distribute to the publisher and songwriter (both, or either, of whom may be the copyright owner) their respective shares.

If required, the producer would generally agree to supply the performing rights society representing the publisher and songwriter with a minimum of at least one cue sheet identifying all the music used in a particular television program, on an agreed date, usually on or before the initial telecast of the program.

TERRITORY

As in all contracts, the territory granted the producer should be negotiated between the parties, and can be as broad or as narrow as agreed. In most cases, the territory granted in the synchronization license agreement—television is the world, and the agreement may provide for sublicensing in terms of language or territorial rights.

TERM

The term, or time period within which the agreement remains active and operational, is usually a negotiated element of the synchronization license agreement—television. The parties should consider, when negotiating the term, or extent of the agreement, a time period which would be considered appropriate for the commercial exploitation of the composition through a television program, taking into consideration its initial program date and customary schedule of repeat broadcasts. However, with the syndication market, both domestically and internationally, growing every day, the trend is for the producer to negotiate for a longer termed license.

TERMINATION

Ordinarily, the agreement may terminate upon the expiration of the agreed term, unless the term is extended, upon a written agreement negotiated and signed by the parties. In addition, if either party breaches any of the material conditions of this agreement, the party claiming such breach would generally have the right, if it so elects, to serve upon the party alleged to be in breach of the contract a written notice of its intention to terminate this agreement. The party alleged to be in breach may negotiate for an agreed period within which to remedy the breach.

FORCE MAJEURE

If at any time during the validity of the synchronization license agreement—television, by reason of any act of God, fire, earthquake, flood, explosion, strike, labor disturbance, civil commotion, act of government, its agencies or officers, any order, regulation, ruling, or action of any labor union or association of artists, musicians, composers, or employees affecting either or both parties, its subsidiaries or affiliates, or the industry in which it is or they are engaged, or any shortage of or failure or delays in the delivery of materials, supplies, labor, or equipment, or any other cause or causes beyond the control of the parties of this contract, the performance of either party's obligations under this agreement is delayed, hampered, interrupted or interfered with, or otherwise becomes impossible or impracticable, then either party may have negotiated for the option, upon notice to the other, to terminate this agreement.

Termination, if agreed, would usually not prejudice the party requesting such action. Upon the termination of the license, the right to authorize any further use or distribution of the composition made during the term of the agreement may cease.

PROHIBITIONS

The synchronization license—television may not permit the producer to alter or change the lyrics or the music of the composition, utilize the title of the composition as the title of the program, or use the plot or story of the composition as a plot or subplot on the television program or any sequels, remakes, or additional episodes in a series.

NO SEPARATE SALES OR LICENSE OF COMPOSITIONS

The copyright owner would usually demand that no recordings produced by the producer in accordance with the license granted in this agreement are to be manufactured, sold, licensed, or used in any manner or form independently from its use in the mentioned television program.

DUBBING

There is typically a provision included in the synchronization agreement—television which grants the producer the right to dub the television program into unlimited foreign languages as well as to provide for on-screen subtitling. This provision usually serves to extend the commercial viability of the broadcast, boosting its potential into the various world markets.

PERFORMANCE LICENSE

The owner would generally stipulate that the composition could be performed on the agreed program over free and/or pay television stations or networks so long as the stations or networks are issued the appropriate public performance license. In the event a public performance license has not been issued, the agreement may be subject to the issuance of such public performance license.

ADDITIONAL PROVISIONS

Additional provisions to the synchronization license agreement—television are often similar to the synchronization license agreement—motion pictures, discussed earlier in this chapter.

15

The Foreign License Agreement

The composition owner typically looks to a music publisher to sell, license, and distribute his or her musical compositions through the various means of commercial exploitation available, including the licensing of the composition's mechanical and public performance rights. Most publishers have a mature and developed link to the musical establishment in their local community and throughout the United States. This commercial tie has often been built upon a foundation of years of successful business dealings involving musical compositions that have been licensed and successfully exploited.

While the publisher may control the United States marketplace, he or she would frequently rely upon foreign publishers to exploit the musical compositions in those foreign territories. In many cases, the composition owner, or original owner of the musical composition, would be required to approve, in a signed writing, of the publisher's right to enter the foreign license agreement with a foreign publisher. Most music publishing agreements grant the publisher that right.

PARTIES

The foreign license agreement (sometime called a sublicense agreement) should state the names and addresses of those parties entering the agreement, the publisher of the music composition and the foreign subpublisher, who is often referred to as the licensee. As a means of clarification, the foreign license agreement would typically state that the publisher is actively engaged in the business of music publishing in the United States and that the licensee is engaged in a similar business in the licensed territory.

COMPOSITIONS

The foreign license agreement should address the musical compositions that are to be licensed by the publisher to the licensee. Typically, the musical compositions licensed fall into one of the following categories:

a) The license of a selective group of musical compositions. This option may be addressed by listing the musical compositions' correct or tentative title, their copyright index number, and the name (including pseudonyms, if applicable) of the composition owner. This is typically achieved in an easily readable fashion by laying the facts out in a clearly labeled graph, as follows:

Name of Composition	*Copyright Number*	*Composition Owner*

b) The license of all musical compositions written by the composition owner. The foreign license agreement would usually stipulate that the licensee would be granted the license to all musical compositions presently existing, controlled, or written by the publisher or composition owner.

c) Either of the above options, including any and all musical compositions which would be acquired or written by the composition owner or publisher during the term of the foreign license agreement.

TERRITORY

The territory granted by the publisher to the licensee in the foreign license (sublicense) agreement should be detailed in clear and concise language, relieving the parties or the courts, in the case of dispute, of the need to interpret the intention of the parties. The territory may be granted as follows:

a) for a particular country, such as France or England,

b) for a particular grouping of countries, such as all French-speaking countries, or the European Economic Community (EEC) countries, or

c) for the rest of the world, excluding the United States and its possessions.

TRANSFER OF RIGHTS

The publisher would typically clarify, with clear and unambiguous language, the rights that are being granted to the licensee by the foreign license agreement.

Right to Print

The rights transferred to the licensee would usually include the right to print, publish, license, rent, and sell copies of the licensed musical compositions, as well as to include those copies in albums, folios, and books, in the territory granted by the subpublishing agreement to the licensee.

Right of Public Performance

In addition, the licensee would usually be granted the right to license the public performance rights inherent in the covered musical compositions in the licensed territory. Consistent with the grant of this right would typically be the right to collect any and all royalties earned as a result of the public performances.

Right to Sell Recordings

The licensee would generally be granted the right to collect any and all royalties and other fees earned as a result of the manufacture, sale, and license of all recordings in the licensed territory. Recordings should be defined as all means of recordings, including, among others, long-playing albums, analog and digital audiotapes, CDs, and any and all other means and methods of recordings, now known or to be devised in the future.

Right to Sell Audiovisual Devices

Often included in the foreign license agreement is the grant to the sublicensee of the right to any and all royalties and fees earned from the exploitation in any manner or form of any audiovisual devices, including videocassettes and laser disks.

Right to Synchronize Music to Visual Images

The licensee would often be permitted the right to grant licenses in regard to synchronizing the musical compositions in connection with motion pictures, television films, videotapes, cable films, and in connection with all similar devices now known or to be devised in the future, in the licensed territory, and to collect all royalties and fees earned as a result of such commercial exploitation.

The foreign license agreement should clarify that the publisher typically retains the right to license the synchronization rights in the musical compositions in those territories he or she retains that are not covered by the foreign license agreement.

Often, a stipulation granting the use of these movies in territories outside those articulated in the foreign license agreement is included in the sublicense agreement. This provision considers that, while the actual production or filming of the motion picture may be located within a certain geographic region, the distribution is typically worldwide. If the rights granted are limited to a certain region, clearance problems may result impeding the use of the compositions in the motion picture.

Right to Make Adaptations

Changes in the original musical composition may be required in order to exploit the licensed compositions in the territories granted the licensee. The licensee would usually negotiate for the right to make those necessary changes, including the right to produce new adaptations and arrangements of the original composition. In addition, the licensee often would be granted the right to translate the lyrics of the composition, adding new lyrics in the language commonly used in the licensed territory. The licensee may request permission to change the title and to utilize that new title, in any manner or form, for the purpose of promoting and advertising the composition.

Costs incurred by the licensee in making those modifications are usually his or her sole responsibility. However, effecting changes in the lyrics, or translating them, may require an agreement concerning the ownership of those new lyrics or new compositions, especially if the changes are performed by a third-party songwriter. Under certain conditions, those parties who actually translate or add to existing lyrics may gain the rights to claim copyright ownership of the new works. It is therefore important that this issue be detailed in the agreement. In many instances, the foreign license agreement would stipulate that, notwithstanding the changes made to the original covered musical compositions, those musical compositions, including any and all changes are, and would continue to remain, the property of the publisher and/or the original composition owner.

Right to Sublicense

The foreign license agreement usually grants the licensee the right to sublicense the grant of rights he or she has negotiated from the original publisher, provided that the licensee's sublicensee be a person or business entity regularly involved in the business of music publishing. The original publisher may negotiate to control the right to sublicense by retaining the right to approve all such sublicense arrangements or by insisting that the licensee's sublicensee be an established music publisher in the territory sublicensed.

RIGHTS RESERVED BY THE PUBLISHER

Although the publisher would usually grant to the licensee the bulk of the rights to exploit the licensed compositions in the licensed territory, he or she may reserve some rights for himself or herself.

Copyright

Typically, the publisher reserves for himself or herself all the rights in the copyright of the musical compositions throughout the world, including the licensed territory. All publications of the licensed musical compositions would be required to bear the proper copyright notice, which would appear as follows: Copyright, or (c), 19__, ABCD Inc., while sound recordings would require the copyright notice to read (p) 19__, ABCD Inc.

It will therefore be necessary for the publisher to be certain that the compositions in question are actually registered in a proper manner. Absent such steps, the copyright owner may not be able to obtain any monetary damages from a case of copyright infringement. Typically, under recent regulations, the most the publisher will be entitled to receive, absent proper registration, may be an injunction, or order, directed to the infringing party to cease and desist from the use and exploitation of the musical composition in question, without any monies being awarded to the publisher.

As additional notice to all would-be infringers, the publisher may require that the words "All Rights Reserved" be included on all publications and recordings.

Name of Songwriter

The original songwriter's name is usually required to be printed, visibly and prominently, on every publication and recording of the licensed musical compositions printed or manufactured and recorded in the licensed territory. The licensee would typically be required to warrant and guarantee that all efforts will be made to ensure that the intent of this provision would be fulfilled.

Use of Titles

The use of the titles of the licensed musical compositions may be retained by the publisher as an additional means of commercial exploitation. This provision should clearly exclude the use of the titles on the musical compositions themselves, which certainly are controlled by the licensee in the licensed territory.

Right to Dramatize

It is not uncommon for a musical composition to be the inspiration for a motion picture or television broadcast. The publisher may retain the right to dramatize the musical composition into any and all forms of media, now known or hereafter devised, even in the licensee's licensed territory.

Literary Versions of the Composition

Books and other literary versions of the licensed compositions are an additional means of exploiting the work internationally. The publisher may retain the right to literary publications based on the licensed composition.

NAME AND LIKENESS

In the pursuit of his or her efforts to promote and advertise the musical compositions licensed by the licensee, the licensee would usually be granted the right to utilize, and allow others to utilize, the name, likeness, photograph, and biographical material of the composition owner, composer, and/or publisher of the musical compositions for the purpose of commercially exploiting the compositions.

This grant of rights may be limited to only those promotions and advertising campaigns that are reasonably related to the exploitation of the musical compositions and may not require any additional photographic sessions or sitting by the composer. In the event additional photographic sessions are required, the costs of those sessions are typically borne solely by the licensee.

WARRANTIES AND REPRESENTATIONS

The foreign license agreement, like most agreements, is based on the parties' ability to deliver the goods or services promised.

CONTROL OF COMPOSITIONS

In the foreign license agreement, the publisher would generally be required to warrant, represent, and promise that he or she does, and would continue to, control any and all rights in the musical composition that were granted to the licensee by the foreign license agreement throughout the term of the agreement. The agreement by and between the publisher and the composition owner may be added to the foreign license agreement as an "exhibit" or "rider," if the licensee requires documented proof that the publisher actually does control the rights granted in the foreign license agreement for the duration of the term of the agreement and for the territories granted in the agreement.

NO CLAIMS

The publisher would generally guarantee that there are no claims against, or encumbrances to, the compositions, thereby ensuring the licensee unhampered use of the licensed compositions.

RIGHT TO ENTER AGREEMENT

The publisher would usually be required to warrant and represent that he or she has the right to enter the foreign license agreement without infringing on the rights of any other person or entity, including the composition owner's rights of copyright, publicity, and/or privacy.

ORIGINAL COMPOSITIONS

As an assurance to the licensee of the originality of the composition being licensed, the publisher may be required to guarantee that the licensed musical compositions granted, and to be granted, to the licensee under the provisions of the foreign license agreement are original and would continue to be original. The publisher would also warrant that no segment of any musical composition is, or would be, copied or plagiarized from a third party's composition or literary work.

NO VIOLATION

The publisher would typically state that the compositions do not violate any governmental law or any rights of any person, including rights of privacy or publicity.

SALE OR TRANSFER OF PUBLISHER'S ASSETS

In the normal course of business, the publisher may decide to sell, transfer, or discard the assets in the company controlling the musical compositions, or he or she may negotiate to merge his or her musical publishing company with another company. The licensee would, understandably, require that the terms and provisions of the foreign license agreement be honored and complied with, under any change of ownership in the publisher's company, without any amendments, changes, additions, or deletions to the existing foreign license agreement.

Of course, depending on the bargaining strength of the composition owner, he or she may insist that such a transfer by the publisher be finalized only with the approval of the copyright owner, thus protecting the owner from having the license assigned or transferred to a company which would not be up to the professional standard of the original publisher and therefore may be detrimental to the composition owner's career and earnings.

COMPENSATION

The licensee would customarily agree to pay to the publisher, in the form of a flat fee or as a royalty, compensation earned from the general commercial exploitation of the licensed musical compositions in the licensed territory.

Royalty

Under a royalty agreement, the licensee would usually be required to pay the publisher a royalty of an agreed percentage of the net retail, or selling price (or wholesale price), of the musical compositions that are manufactured and distributed in the form of long-playing albums, audiotapes, CDs, or any and all other forms of recording, now known or to be devised in the future. The compensation due the publisher would usually be based on the sums actually earned and received by the licensee. The licensee may negotiate for the right to deduct from all sums due the publisher any and all returns or free professional copies distributed by the licensee as a means of promotion, advertising, or other forms of commercial marketing.

Limitations on Licensee

In an effort to maximize his or her revenue stream, the publisher may limit the licensee's ability to distribute free copies by demanding the right to approve the distribution of all free copies or by limiting the number of free promotional copies to an agreed number of units per term. While such a stringent means of limitation would rarely be utilized, since both parties realize that under normal music industry distribution standards, placing a restriction on free promotional copies may inhibit those distributing the product from marketing it in its most effective manner. Typically, both parties would be guided by what would be a customary number of promotional copies to be distributed free of charge, under similar circumstances in the recording industry.

Definition of "Net"

In the recording industry, the definition of ''net'' should be clearly and unambiguously stipulated, in an effort to limit future litigations regarding the amount actually earned as a result of a ''net'' deal.

''Net'' may be defined as all sums after taxes, after reasonable and standard expenses incurred in the exploitation of the licensed compositions in the licensed territory, including fees paid to mechanical licensing societies and performing rights societies, are deducted. It must be understood that the publisher and the foreign licensee could agree on a definition of ''net'' among themselves.

Printed Material

The licensee would generally agree to pay to the publisher an agreed percentage, as a royalty, of the net retail selling price for all printed folios, books, or compilations containing the licensed musical compositions actually sold and not returned. Free promotions copies would generally be deducted from the compensation due and owing the publisher, though the number of such free copies may be limited by the agreement between the publisher and the licensee.

Mechanical License

The licensee would usually agree to pay the publisher an agreed royalty equal to a negotiated percentage of the net sum received from the exploitation of the mechanical license. The tabulation of mechanical license fees is usually based on the recording of the licensed musical composition recorded within the borders of the sublicensed territory, and/or recorded in a language different from the original language considered indigenous to the sublicensed territory.

Bonus

As a means of inducing the publisher to enter the foreign license agreement, the licensee and the publisher may agree that the publisher would be entitled to an increase in the agreed royalty in the event the musical composition commercially exploited under the provisions and terms of the foreign license agreement achieves certain performance levels, including the following:

a) the achievement of a top 40 position in a recognized trade publication in the licensed territory, or

b) the sale of an agreed number of units in the sublicensed territory (example: an increase in royalties in the event sales of the recording exceed 250,000 units, an additional increase in the royalty if sales exceed 500,000 units with additional agreed royalty increases for each additional 500,000 units sold).

Performing Rights Societies

Granting performing rights in and to the licensed compositions may be subject to the rights of the U.S. performing rights societies, including ASCAP, BMI, or SESAC. The licensee would usually be required to register the licensed compositions with the performing rights society in the sublicensed territory.

The publisher would generally be bound by the rules and regulations of the performing rights societies in the sublicensed territory and may grant the licensee the right to collect all fees due and owing the publisher with the obligation to pay to the publisher his or her agreed royalty. In the event performance license fees are paid directly to the publisher, the foreign license agreement may stipulate that all those sums would be considered a reduction of any and all royalties due the publisher from the licensee earned from the exploitation of the licensed compositions in the sublicensed territory, under the provisions and terms of the foreign license agreement.

Certain foreign performing rights societies may collect their fees in a manner that differs from the collection methods utilized by performing rights societies in the United States. Foreign performing rights societies may

- log actual live performances and not issue blanket licenses to arenas, clubs, discos, or other venues, and
- collect from compositions performed in motion picture theatres, and collect an annual fee from movie theatres for compositions performed in the theatres. The performing

rights societies usually base their calculations on cue sheets submitted by the motion picture producers.

Advance against Future Royalties

Depending on the strength of the publisher, he or she may negotiate for the receipt of an advance payment against future royalties. The advance is generally defined as a sum paid to the publisher by the licensee, which may be nonrefundable, that is usually intended to be recouped from the royalties due the publisher earned and received from the commercial exploitation, in all manners and forms agreed upon in the sublicensing agreement.

The advance is typically paid in accordance to an agreed schedule. A portion could be paid upon the signing of the foreign license agreement, while an additional portion may be paid on weekly installments, or the full sum may be paid in one lump sum, upon the signing of the foreign license agreement. It should be negotiated in the foreign license agreement the form of currency in which the advance is to be paid, either U.S. dollars or the currency used in the licensed territory in the event that the currency is convertible. The agreement must also stipulate for situations in which foreign exchange is restricted or where the local currency is highly taxed in its conversion to U.S. dollars.

PERFORMANCE PLATEAUS

The licensee's main concern is to exploit the sublicensed compositions within his or her territory. The publisher would often require that the licensee achieve certain performance plateaus in order for an option to extend the term of the foreign license agreement, if so negotiated, to be exercised. Each plateau reached equals earned revenues for the licensee, publisher, and composition owner; therefore, the plateaus are positive goals that benefit all the parties. In addition, the licensee may be required to secure for commercial exploitation an agreed number of cover records within the initial term in order to activate the option clause.

ACCOUNTINGS AND STATEMENTS

The licensee would generally be required to submit to the publisher a statement of all transactions involving the licensed compositions in the licensed territories on fixed and established schedule, along with an accounting of all monies due the publisher as royalties earned and received from the exploitation of the licensed compositions, itemizing in detail the computations of the royalties payable. Depending on the specificity required by the publisher, the itemization may include the mechanical income actually received, the amount and source of performance income, the number of recordings sold as well as the retail selling price of all audiocassettes, long-playing albums, CDs, videocassettes, and other recordings exploiting the licensed compositions.

The schedule of the statements is open to negotiations between the licensee and the publisher, but is usually quarterly, semiannually, or annually, Typically, the publisher would have an agreed period of time within which to contest and challenge the accountings and statements, after which the accountings and statements would be considered to be accurate and exact.

BOOKS AND RECORDS

The books and records contain vital information regarding the number of units sold, the price of the units sold, the amount actually received, and the amount still due and owing the licensee. In most circumstances, the publisher would negotiate for the right to inspect the books and records in connection with the foreign license agreement and would usually consent to the licensee's request that such inspection be done after reasonable written notice, in the place where the books and records are normally kept, and during normal business hours. In addition, it is common that a certified public accountant be specified as the legal representative of the publisher, with the right to inspect the books and records in question.

CURRENCY OF PAYMENT

The agreement should clarify the national currency that will be the currency of record regarding all payments due and owing the publisher, earned and received as a result of the exploitation of the licensed musical compositions by the licensee in the licensed territory. Usually, the publisher would stipulate that he or she be paid in U.S. dollars. In the event the licensee is not in a position to make the required payments in U.S. dollars, the publisher would usually agree that the payments are to be made in the currency of the licensed territory and deposited in the publisher's name and to his or her credit, in a depository, usually a bank account, selected by the publisher.

If, for a reasonable reason, including economic distress and upheaval, the licensee finds it impossible to deposit the payments due the publisher into the bank account stipulated in the agreement by the publisher, then the licensee would generally be granted the right to deposit all sums due and owing under the provisions of the foreign license agreement into a depository selected by the licensee. The licensee would usually be obligated to notify the publisher of the deposit promptly.

In the event that, due to local laws or restrictions, conversion to hard currency is impossible and the exportation of local currency is prohibited, then, if the parties agree the foreign license agreement could stipulate that such a condition would not be deemed a material breach of the agreement. However, depending on the bargaining strength of the parties, the agreement could contain a provision which states that should the subpublisher's inability to pay his or her designated royalties continue for an extended period of time, the publisher would be granted the option voiding the foreign license agreement without penalty or liability.

Laws of the Licensed Territory

If required by the laws of the licensed territory, the licensee would be granted the right to withhold from any and all monies due the publisher all state and local taxes, unless the following conditions are met:

- the publisher agrees to make such payments,
- the publisher notifies the appropriate officials in the sublicensed territory of his or her intention to do so, and
- the publisher's request is approved by the officials of the sublicensed territory.

TERM

The term, or length, of the foreign license agreement should be negotiated among the parties. It may be for a fixed number of years or for an initial term of an agreed number of years, with an option to renew the provisions and obligation of the foreign license agreement upon written notification, and acceptance, among the parties.

DELIVERY OF COMPOSITIONS TO LICENSEE

Upon execution of the foreign license agreement, the publisher would typically be required to deliver to the licensee, usually at the publisher's sole expense, the following material which would be crucial to the licensee in order for him or her to perform his or her services under the foreign license agreement:

a) copies of the sheet music, if published,
b) copies of the lead sheet, if unpublished,
c) completed copyright form, including the copyright index number, and the date of registration,
d) the best quality taped copies of each and every licensed musical composition, if the musical compositions have not been recorded, and
e) copies of the recordings, including long-playing albums, audiotapes, and/or CDs, if the licensed compositions were recorded. The initial release date, the name of the recording artist, the record label, and the record number should be included in the material presented to the licensee.

New Renditions

The composition owner may create a new rendition of the licensed composition during the term of the foreign license agreement. The licensee would generally require that the publisher deliver to him or her copies of the new rendition and, if recorded commercially, copies of the recording including the name of the recording artist, the record label, and the release date.

Delivery of Additional Material during the Term of the Foreign License Agreement

During the term of the foreign license agreement, the publisher may be obligated to deliver to the licensee all musical compositions written and/or composed by the composition owner or composer if the publisher has agreed to license to the licensee all compositions of the composition owner or composer written and/or composed during the term of the foreign license agreement. In that case, the publisher would generally submit to the licensee, upon completion by the author or composer, the following:

a) copies of all tapes, including demonstration tapes, of any and all new musical compositions, and
b) copies of all new compositions, if recorded, including long-playing albums, audiotapes, and/or CDs. The licensee would also require their initial release date, the name of the recording artist, the record label, and the record number.

PAYMENT OF COMPENSATION DUE THE COMPOSITION OWNER

Under the provisions of most agreements, the publisher would be obligated to pay to the composition owner all compensations due him or her, including any and all royalties, advances against future royalties, and expenses. The foreign license agreement would typically specify that the publisher is aware of, and has accepted, those obligations. The provision may also clarify that the licensee would not bear any responsibility for those payments under any circumstances.

INDEMNIFICATION

The publisher would generally agree to indemnify and hold the licensee harmless from any and all claims, damages, liabilities, costs, and fees, including all court and legal fees, incurred by the licensee as a result of any breach of any warranty, representation, or promise made by the publisher, either orally or written, regarding the subject matter of the foreign license agreement.

DEFENDING THE RIGHTS IN THE COMPOSITION

The publisher would usually grant to the licensee the right to defend all rights granted him or her by the terms of the foreign license agreement. Those rights may include a defense of a potential copyright infringement or a trademark infringement of the songwriter's name, likeness, or photograph. In the event the publisher exercises the right to defend the rights inherent in the musical composition, the licensee may negotiate for the right to join the publisher in such lawsuit at his or her sole expense and, if triumphant, to share in the awards.

EUROPEAN ECONOMIC COMMUNITY

With the advent of the European Economic Community, the EEC, the laws and regulations governing intra-European trade may change, radically altering the way the countries do business between themselves. The publisher would typically be required to stipulate that he or she would abide by any and all laws and regulations of the EEC, including those regarding the shipment of printed copies, as well as recorded recordings, of the compositions into a country member of the EEC.

RIGHT TO ASSIGN

The licensee may negotiate for the privilege to assign his or her rights under the provisions of the foreign license agreement if the producer is given the right to approve any assignee of the licensee. The publisher may require that any assignee be of equal stature and reputation in the music publishing industry as the licensee, or may require that the licensee, being a key element in the foreign licensing agreement, remain part of any company that acquires the rights assigned.

BINDING AGREEMENT

The parties to the foreign license agreement would usually stipulate that the agreement and its provisions are to be binding upon the parties to the agreement, as well as upon their heirs, representatives, successors, and executors.

DOCUMENTS

The publisher would customarily be required to make available and to send to the licensee all documents and agreements, in a timely manner, which would be necessary to further the intent of the foreign license agreement.

BREACH

In the event of a breach of any of the provisions or conditions in the foreign license agreement, the parties would usually require that the breaching party be granted written notice of the breach as well as a reasonable period of time within which to cure, or remedy, that breach. If after that period the breach is still not remedied, and if the breach could be considered to be a material, or major, breach, then the breached upon party may have the right to terminate the agreement, remedy the particular breach, or choose to forgo any of the rights and remedies he or she is entitled to without in any way jeopardizing any of his or her other rights and remedies under the foreign license agreement.

NOTICES

All notices would usually be required to be sent from one party to the other by registered or certified mail, return receipt requested, by personal delivery, or by other forms of mail delivery that issue a receipt, such as Federal Express, UPS, or DHL. The notices should be sent to the address specified in the foreign license agreement, and the stipulated addresses should not be changed, except if approved in writing by the parties.

NO CHANGES OR AMENDMENTS

As written, the foreign license agreement would typically represent the entire document between the licensee and the publisher. Both the licensee and the publisher would usually agree, in an effort to protect their negotiated points, that no provision would be changed, altered, or amended except if such change is approved in a writing signed by both parties.

UNENFORCEABILITY

In the event any single provision is deemed unenforceable and void by any court of law, including the governing body of the EEC, and if the parties so agree, that single provision would be considered null and void without affecting the validity, legality, or enforceability of the remaining provisions of the foreign license agreement.

MATERIAL BREACH

A fundamental question to be answered in the event of a breach of any provision of the foreign license agreement is whether that breach is of a material or nonmaterial nature. If it is construed to be a material breach, then the agreement may specify that the whole agreement could be terminated at the election of the breached upon party without the fear of liability. If, on the other hand, the breach is nonmaterial in nature, then it would be considered to be nonsubstantial in nature, and not significant enough to warrant termination of the foreign license agreement. Typically, the breached party is given a period of time within which to cure the breach.

STATE OF JURISDICTION

It is important to elucidate which state, or country, has jurisdiction in the event of a dispute between the publisher and the licensee. Typically, the publisher, if in a stronger bargaining position, would require that the agreement be construed in accordance with the laws of his or her state of incorporation. The proximity of the jurisdiction in the event of dispute, and the more favorable laws, may often be a deciding factor in whether the parties proceed with litigation or are more apt to settle their differences.

NOT A PARTNERSHIP

In an effort to decrease either party's liabilities, the foreign license agreement may stipulate that the publisher and the licensee are not entering a joint venture or partnership, and therefore, in most cases, would not be responsible for the other party's debts, liabilities, or promises.

FORCE MAJEURE

It is important to consider each party's performance in the event situations outside the control of the parties make the performance of either party impossible or impractical. The *force majeure* clause accounts for the unforeseen event that may require delaying or postponing the obligation to perform. The *force majeure* clause may become operational by reason of fire, hurricane, labor disputes, act of public enemy, war, local, state or EEC orders or regulations, or by the occurrence of any other event which is outside the control of the parties.

The provision acts to avoid a breach of contract and may allow for a cure, such as resumption of the party's obligation as soon as the event triggering the *force majeure* clause is deemed over. If so agreed among the parties, the term of the agreement may be extended for a period of time equal to the period of *force majeure*.

SIGNATURES

By their signatures, the parties typically signify their understanding and acceptance of the provisions of the agreement.

16

The Tour Merchandising Agreement

Much of the income derived at live concerts is ancillary, or related to but not earned directly from the actual gate receipts. A popular form of ancillary income is that generated from the sale of licensed merchandise and products. Merchandise may consist of various wearing apparel such as hats, buttons, sweatshirts, and T-shirts. Merchandise may also comprise other memorabilia embodying the name, sound, and/or likeness of the artist as well as the name of the tour, such as mugs, banners, and stickers. Another form of merchandise, tour books or magazines, would typically include photographs of the artist together with products promoting and publicizing the artist and the tour.

The merchandising and licensing rights are typically granted by the artist to a merchandising and licensing company. The contract, usually offered on an exclusive basis, grants the licensee the right to manufacture, distribute, and sell licensed souvenir merchandise at those concerts performed by the artist.

The artist generally is compensated in the form of a one-time fee or on a royalty basis, often accompanied by an advance against future royalties. Because the artist's image and goodwill are tied in to the licensed products being offered to the fans and concertgoers, it is typically in the artist's best interest to consider the quality and reputation of the licensee. When negotiating the compensation due the artist, it is important to review the following key points:

- the average per capita spending at the concert,
- the size of the concert hall(s) reserved for the concerts, and
- the fee each hall will charge the artist to conduct retail sales on the premises, if any.

The tour merchandising agreement, although applicable to all performers, would generally not be available to the newcomer or to an artist who does not have a sizable following and/or a major recording deal. The investment by the licensee is usually substantially high, so he or she would typically launch such a venture with a performer of established repute and following.

The tour merchandising contract is usually negotiated at the same time the actual tour is being planned and organized. The lead time should afford the licensee ample opportunity to produce the licensed product, to create photographs and artwork, and to arrange for proper distribution.

DEFINITION OF TERMS

As in most agreements, it is of prime importance that key words be defined with exactness.

PARTIES

The tour merchandising agreement would typically list the names and addresses of the parties, the artist and the licensee, and the date upon which the agreement becomes valid.

TERRITORY

In discussing territory, it is important for the parties to consider the itinerary of the tour, whether it will be confined to the United States or whether it will include an overseas schedule.

The territory issue becomes of paramount importance when considering the marketing of the licensed product in conjunction with a particular tour. If the tour is international in scope, or even if it will be confined to the United States, the licensee may negotiate for the right to manufacture and distribute the licensed merchandise overseas. In reaching his or her decision, the licensee usually considers the costs inherent in the manufacture and distribution of the licensed goods outside the United States, including the following issues: customs, duties, international airway bills, tariffs, and other regulations affecting international trade. The licensee should also consider the time needed for delivery of the licensed product to the local venues.

In evaluating the territorial grant, the licensee should also give careful study to whether the licensee will market the licensed product utilizing his or her own staff and business connections or whether the licensee will utilize the services of a sublicensee, and if so, in which territories.

Financial Advantages

In deciding the expanse of the grant of territory, the artist would typically ascertain the financial advantages, if any, to negotiating with different licensees in various territories in an effort to obtain a more lucrative fee or royalty as opposed to negotiating with a single licensee.

Overseas Payment

In the event the tour includes overseas venues, and the licensee has acquired the rights to supply the merchandise for the overseas venture, the artist should consider the means and forms of payments for revenues earned outside the United States.

The agreement should address the issues of whether the monies, whether paid as guaranteed fees or royalties would be accrued by the original licensee or by the sublicensee. The agreement should also consider whether the costs incurred by the licensee in the implementation of the sublicensee contract would be considered expenses and, as such, deducted from the compensation due the artist. The artist would, naturally, argue that all expenses should be incurred by the licensee alone. If the licensee does utilize the services of a sublicensee, the agreement should stipulate which party will be responsible to pay the artist his or her compensation, and in which currency.

TERM

The term, or duration, of a typical agreement is usually a simple matter. The obligations of the parties commence on one date and conclude on another. Yet, in the tour management agreement, the definition of the term of the agreement may require more clarity.

Often, on tours, changes of dates and itineraries occur with little or no advance notice, and facing such an event, the licensee risks loss of substantial revenues. Therefore, in order to protect the interests of the licensee, as well as to ensure that potential profits to the artist would not be hampered, the definition of "term" may be referred to as the duration of the actual tour dates rather than fixing exact dates that may be subject to change with little notice and little regard for the licensee's investment in time and money.

RECOUPMENT OF ADVANCE

If the bargaining strength of the licensee bears unequal weight in negotiations, the licensee may demand that he or she be guaranteed full recoupment of the advance paid to the artist, if an advance is actually made, when the revenues generated from the tour do not equal the amount paid the artist as an advance against future royalties.

TOUR

Typically, a "tour" refers to a series of live concert engagements to be performed by the artist in the agreed-upon territory during the term of the tour merchandising agreement. Generally, a tentative tour itinerary is attached to the tour merchandising agreement and is made part of the agreement. It is likely that the licensee looks to this definition of "tour" in order to ensure that his or her investment in the licensed product would be satisfied. Therefore, the definition should include answers to the following questions:

- how do event changes affect the agreement, and
- how do tour date cancellations, as well as additions or modifications to the contracted play dates, affect the agreement?

The definition of "tour" would often include a provision allowing for the tour to be extended by adding one or several live concert engagements by the artist in the territory after, or during, the agreed-upon tour date and schedule. As a rule, this provision would stipulate that if the added live concert engagements are to be considered part of the same tour, the personnel, staging, presentation, merchandise booth, and other elements of the added concert engagement should not vary materially from the live concert engagements originally included in the tour.

No Later Than an Agreed Date

The parties may stipulate that all such added live concert engagements should occur no later than an agreed-upon date and would be performed in specifically stipulated venues, if they are to be considered part of the original tour.

NAME AND LIKENESS

The licensee would usually insist that he or she be granted the right to commercially exploit, during the term of the tour merchandising agreement, the artist's name and likeness on any and all licensed products. Typically, by agreeing to this provision, the artist would be granting to the licensee permission to utilize the artist's name, sound, photographs, caricatures, symbols, emblems, designs, depictions, characterizations, likenesses, and visual representations of the tour and the trademarks, logos, and copyrights, as well as all the other authorized material owned or controlled by the artist. Generally, if he or she retains ample bargaining power and industry clout, the artist would demand creative approval with regard to the use of his or her name and likeness.

PRODUCTS

The licensee would typically demand that the products he or she has licensed, in accord with the tour merchandising agreement, be extensive and be listed in detail. It is obvious, the licensee may argue, that granting him or her the license to a wide and extensive array of products alleviates the need by the artist to award the various licenses to separate and diverse licensees. Accounting would therefore be simplified, and there could be developed a singular selling strategy emanating from a single tour merchandising office, which could result in higher sales. The artist may argue that a single licensee is probably not an expert in the marketing of all the licensed products being offered; therefore, the artist would gain by selecting various licensees as the artist's licensed tour merchandisers, each being an expert in its own field.

List of Licensed Products

Typically, this provision would list, either in the body of the agreement itself, or as an exhibit or rider added to and made part of the agreement, the licensed products approved by the artist to be licensed by the licensee which would typically relate to the artist and/or to the artist's performances, either recorded or live. Products may include T-shirts, jerseys, sweatshirts, programs, posters, pictures, mugs, lunch pails, buttons, lights, and any and all other items bearing the name, likeness, image, or sound of the artist.

CONCERT HALL

The tour merchandising agreement, by definition, affects the grant of limited, or broad, merchandising rights to a licensee for the duration of a live tour, during which the artist performs at particular venues, or concert halls. The phrase "concert hall" would typically include each and every hall, arena, stadium, or theatre in which the artist will perform while on this specific tour.

In order to be more exact, the provision may stipulate the minimum number of seats per venue, if a location is to be considered a concert hall. Since the artist may perform, from time to time, in a nightclub or in a smaller more intimate venue in which seating is limited, the licensee may demand the option not to market the licensed merchandise in a facility with less than the agreed number of seats. The licensee would probably argue that the cost of shipping, setting up, and maintaining the merchandise for the artist's performance in a small room is usually not a cost effective marketing outlet for the licensee. The earnings from the goods sold often would not equal the cost of running the merchandising booth.

ACTUAL COSTS (LICENSEE'S COSTS)

If the artist receives his or her compensation based on net or gross profits, the licensee would usually be required to detail the actual out-of-pocket costs the licensee expects to expend in the production and marketing of the licensed goods. The actual costs usually include those costs incurred in the product's design, artwork, manufacturing, shipping, and registration of trademarks and/or copyrights, if applicable. The licensee's office overhead and interest on bank loans are generally not included in the definition of actual costs paid by the licensee. The artist would usually demand that the licensee's actual costs be verified with invoices, bills, and receipts.

Actual Costs Used by Licensee in Event of Sell-Off

The licensee may also use those documented actual costs as the basis upon which to designate the price at which to market the product in the event of sell-offs. A sell-off usually refers to the sale of licensed goods during an agreed period of time following the expiration of the tour merchandising agreement and/or the tour.

GRANT OF LICENSE

The heart of the tour merchandising agreement, for the licensee, is the actual grant of license from the artist to the licensee. The provision typically grants the following:

a) the legal permission to the licensee to manufacture, market, distribute, and promote, on a sole and exclusive basis, the licensed products, and
b) the grant to the licensee of the right to distribute and sell those products at the venues agreed upon during the term of the agreement.

The grant of license typically serves several purposes. It indicates, with clarity and certainty, that permission has been received by the authorized licensee, and it demonstrates to all other parties that the licensee is the only party authorized to conduct a licensing business with the agreed products during the designated period of time. The grant is a legal tool available to be used again by those who would produce and market products without the authority granted by the artist.

ARTIST'S OBLIGATIONS

The artist would usually agree to certain specific responsibilities and obligations in regard to the grant of the tour merchandising license.

Advance Knowledge of Tour

It is likely that the licensee would demand sufficient advance knowledge of the tour schedule and venues in order to determine manufacturing, shipping, and inventory needs as well as to plan the required personnel needs. Since tour itineraries may change after the licensee is given what was considered a final schedule, it is likely that the artist would stipulate that he or she would, throughout the term of the agreement, give prompt written notice to the licensee of any and all modifications, changes, deletions, and additions with respect to the tour itinerary. The artist could point to this clause if the licensee alleges a breach of the agreement due to the failure of the artist to inform the licensee about last minute changes in the itinerary.

Tour Information

In connection with the tour dates, the artist would probably be required to furnish the licensee with sufficient information about the tour to enable the tour merchandiser adequate time to plan his or her sales and merchandising program. Such data would usually include the approximate length of the artist's performance and intermissions, and if applicable, the scheduling of any acts or other performers playing prior to or after the artist's performance.

No Competing Goods

Depending on whether the other groups appearing in the concert are contractually able to promote their own products, the licensee may require that the artist use his or her reasonable efforts to ensure that no performance group, other than the artist, be permitted to sell licensed products at the tour venues or concert halls during the term of the agreement. In addition, the licensee would probably demand that no competing goods representing the name and likeness of the artist, which may infringe on the rights of the licensee, be sold at any tour venue or concert hall.

No Goods by Sponsors to Be Offered

The licensee may further demand that the artist not grant to any sponsor, nor to any other person or entity, the right to distribute any items of merchandise not granted to the licensee, whether free or otherwise, in and around the concert hall without the express prior written approval of the licensee. The artist would usually be averse to granting such a blanket agreement to the licensee without a substantial monetary settlement in lieu of the loss of potential income the artist could have earned from any additional sales.

CREATIVE CONTROL

The artist, if armed with ample bargaining strength and clout within the entertainment industry, would typically demand absolute creative control over the tour merchandise offered by the licensee, including approval over all artwork as well as the quality of the actual products themselves. If granted such control, the artist would often require that he or she grant written approval over the product, prior to its entering the production cycle. The artist may require that the licensee furnish the artist one sample of each of the licensed products to be created. The artist would usually insist that no products be manufactured or produced prior to the delivery and approval of the actual or prototype product.

Quality Control

The tour merchandising agreement may also contain a provision mandating that certain quality control standards be established and maintained by the licensee. In the event that, during the term of the contract, the quality of the manufactured product falls beneath the established threshold, all manufacturing and distribution of the product would cease until such problem is resolved.

Actual Retail Sales

In order to adequately anticipate certain revenues, the agreement may provide that the licensee furnish the artist with, prior to any actual sale, the anticipated retail selling prices of all the licensed products, and projected profits based on those selling prices, in a business plan. The licensee would probably require that the agreement include the proviso. that unless the artist notify the licensee within an agreed number of days that the artist is against such a pricing schedule, such approval would be considered automatically granted. In most situations, the burden would be on the artist to make a written denial of the proposed pricing schedule rather than requiring the licensee to receive an affirmative approval prior to commencement of the license.

INTERNATIONAL RIGHTS

If the agreement involves the grant to the licensee of international rights as opposed to simply U.S. domestic rights, the tour merchandising agreement may stipulate that the licensee, with the written approval of the artist, prepare and execute documents, as required by the laws and regulations of each territory, demonstrating that the licensee is actually the registered merchandiser of the licensed product. While the costs and expenses of such multinational registrations would be borne by the licensee, it is often imperative that the licensee execute such documents since many countries, including the EEC, have enacted stringent copyright laws. Absent such a registration, the licensee may be fined and penalized, depending on the laws and regulations of the countries in questions, for utilizing a protected service mark, trademark, or copyright in an unlawful and unauthorized manner.

In most instances, the licensee would be advised to utilize the services of local legal counsel in these countries to ensure that such copyright registration requirements are prepared and filed in a proper and timely manner.

NUMBER OF LICENSED PRODUCTS TO BE MANUFACTURED

The agreement may require that the licensee use his or her best efforts to calculate the number of products to actually be produced or manufactured in order to meet the anticipated needs of the tour. A shortage of products not only will result in a loss of potential revenue but may cause damage to the artist's goodwill among the fans and patrons who attend the artist's concert. Conversely, an overabundance of unsold items may increase the likelihood that the surplus would be sold at a markdown price at the end of the tour, possibly lowering the value of the artist's reputation among product licensees.

MANNER OF DISTRIBUTION

The licensee would normally be required to stipulate the manner in which he or she intends to distribute and offer for sale the licensed products. To ensure that the artist does not interfere with the licensee during the course of the licensee's performance, the licensee may insist that the artist agree that, following the artist's approval of the licensee's proposed manner and method of distribution and sale, the artist would refrain from interfering with the licensee while engaged in the actual course of business.

Business Practice

The artist would probably insist that the licensee conduct his or her business in a respectful and tasteful manner. An unacceptible or offensive method of conducting business on the part of the licensee could potentially result in the artist's loss of reputation or goodwill. The artist may require, for example, that the licensee "soft sell" a product as opposed to a "hard sell."

Containing Costs

Since both the artist and the licensee may be entitled to receive a net portion of the proceeds from the sales of the licensed products as compensation, it is to the benefit of all parties that expended costs are kept to a minimum. It is usually the responsibility of the licensee to negotiate with each concert hall (as well as vendors in such premises if they are contractually franchised in such halls and arenas) the payments or fees due the hall.

ADMINISTRATIVE TASKS

The tour merchandising agreement would typically stipulate the administrative tasks the licensee would be obligated to perform.

Inventory of Products

The agreement may provide that the licensee inventory the products prior to the commencement of the tour and thereafter be responsible for the actual shipment of such goods to each concert hall.

Authorized Agents

In addition, the licensee would generally be contractually responsible to obtain the signature of an authorized agent or employee at each tour venue or concert hall. The agent or employee would be required to undertake, and certify, an accounting of the inventory. That is, the agent or employee would typically be responsible to list the products received and sold and then catalogue those remaining goods which would thereafter be shipped to the next hall. In addition, the agent or employee would usually be responsible to supervise the sales force, supervise the accounting at the end of each night of the tour and set aside the sums due and owing the artist, if so negotiated.

The artist may demand the right, at his or her own expense, to conduct, at all reasonable times, a physical inventory of the products being sold and marketed. The artist may also demand the right to have a representative of his or her choosing present during the receiving and shipping process. The artist's presence may serve to ensure that sales reports are accurate.

COSTS

The licensee would frequently be required to pay all costs and expenses in connection with the licensed product, including those costs incurred in the production, manufacturing, packaging, distribution, and marketing of the goods. In addition, the licensee would generally be liable to pay all fees, salaries or shares of profit to sales personnel and concessionaires. If the concert hall provides or requires the use of its own selling staff, then naturally the licensee would not be obligated to duplicate the effort.

When the licensee accounts for his or her receipts, he or she may be required to submit a copy to the tour venue or concert hall as well as to the artist, thereby ensuring that the venue or concert hall would receive its agreed fee or royalty, if so negotiated between the licensee and the venue.

CONFLICT WITH TOUR SPONSOR

The artist may have entered, or may have agreed to enter, a prior contractual understanding with a tour sponsor. A tour sponsor can be defined as a corporate entity that has agreed to pay the artist an agreed sum to associate its name and products with the artist and the tour. If such an understanding has, in fact, been concluded, the sponsor may have been granted the right to promote and distribute items of a similar nature to the products of the licensee.

The licensee may demand that the tour merchandising contract state unequivocally that the licensee would not be obligated or required to incur any cost or expense related to the sponsor's products, nor should the licensee be liable for the sponsor's products with respect to their production, packing, shipping, transportation, distribution, use, sale, and/or commercial exploitation, in any manner or form. In fact, the licensee may negotiate that, since the licensee has acquired the rights as tour merchandiser, the sponsor be prohibited from selling or distributing its products at the venues or concert halls where the tour manufacturer intends to market his or her wares. The artist, in an effort to maintain a relationship with both parties, may agree to a compromise that permits the sponsor's name and logo to be visible on tour banners and programs, yet the sponsor would not be granted the right to sell or distribute its products at those venues or concert halls where the tour merchandiser has acquired his or her license.

SUPPLY OF LICENSED PRODUCTS

The licensee would generally be required to stipulate that during the term of the tour merchandising agreement, he or she would diligently and continuously maintain a supply of products that would satisfy the reasonably anticipated demand of the public.

SUBLICENSE

Citing the desire to service the artist with the very best merchandising licensee for each product licensed and in each territory licensed, the licensee would usually negotiate for the right to sublicense the rights granted under this agreement to a third-party licensee. The artist may demand the right to approve the sublicensee, usually basing his or her decision on a desire to review and approve the sublicensee's prior history as a manufacturer, distributor, and marketing agent of licensed products in its territory. Under most circumstances, while the licensee may agree with the artist's right of approval, the licensee would request that this provision preclude the artist from unreasonably withholding such approval.

Liability of Third-Party Sublicensee

The artist would probably demand that the licensee bear direct liability to the artist in the event of any breach by the sublicensee of his or her responsibilities to the artist.

INABILITY TO PERFORM

The licensee may negotiate for the right to refrain from selling licensed products at those locations at which the licensee determines that he or she would be unable, for any reasonable reason, to render the services stipulated under this contract due to the fault of the artist, the act or acts of the concert hall, or an act constituting *force majeure*.

Typically, the artist would require that the licensee provide as much advance notice as is reasonably possible regarding the cessation of the licensee's services. Furthermore, the artist would typically demand that the licensee agree to a reasonable start date for the recommencement of the licensee's obligations under this agreement.

Artist's Right to Oversee Sales

If the licensee does not sell the licensed products at any of the tour venues or concert hall engagements for any reason, other than the fault of the artist, the artist may negotiate for the right to oversee the sale of the licensed products and to retain all the earned receipts. He or she would probably be required to return to the licensee all verifiable expenses incurred by the licensee as permitted under the provisions of this agreement. If the licensee agreed to the artist's request to oversee the sales of the licensed products at specific locations, the licensee would probably demand that he or she receive a fixed and guaranteed markup, in addition to a return of his or her expenditures, on all products sold by the artist.

LIQUIDATED DAMAGES

In the event of a material breach by the licensee, or if an unreasonably small portion of the licensed products are sold as a result of a failure of the licensee, the artist may be entitled to demand a fee based on the actual loss of potential revenues that would have been due and owing the artist under normal and reasonable market conditions, taking into consideration, the reasonable sale of licensed products at the tour venues and concert halls performed by a performer of the artist's stature.

Guaranteed Audience

The licensee may demand that the artist guarantee to the licensee a minimum audience base, thereby minimizing the risk borne by the licensee. This provision may require that the artist warrant and guarantee that he or she would perform, at a minimum, an agreed number of separate and different tour venues and concert hall engagements, and that the aggregate adjusted seating capacity of the tour venues and concert halls would be no fewer then the agreed-upon number of seats.

The term "adjusted seating capacity" should be defined clearly in the tour merchandising agreement, and may connote the actual authorized seating capacity of each tour venue and concert hall for each performance, less the number of complimentary admissions for each concert. By calculating the number of guaranteed seats filled per performance during the artist's tour, the licensee should be in a position to estimate his or her profit.

TOUR BOOK

A tour book is customarily manufactured in connection with a major artist's tour. If the licensee has been granted the right to manufacture and market the tour book, he or she would usually request that the artist furnish camera-ready photographs, transparencies and/or other artwork, and other material which the licensee would normally require for the production and manufacture of the tour book and posters related to that book. The artist may promise to supply all such artwork, if the licensee agrees to bear all costs incurred in producing the tour book. As an alternative, such production costs may be shared by a tour sponsor if a sponsor has been engaged.

USE OF ARTWORK

The artist would generally agree that, subject to product approval, the artwork may be used, copied, reproduced, and/or exploited by the licensee in any manner in connection with the manufacture of the licensed products. Furthermore, if the artwork is protected by law, the agreement may provide that the licensee must pledge that he or she would comply with all notice requirements, and would ensure the proper placement of all required copyright, trademark, and/or service mark notices on the products.

Artist's Approval

If the artist bears ample industry clout, the licensee would usually agree to submit, for the artist's written approval, all artwork, packaging design, advertising material, and any additional materials to be used in connection with the licensed products. The agreement may stipulate that the artist would be deemed to have granted approval if the artist does not notify the licensee to the contrary. If the artist objects to a particular use of artwork, the licensee may demand that the artist state specific objections to the contested artwork within an agreed number of days after the artist receives the samples, and any artwork submitted to the artist by the licensee would generally be considered approved unless such materials are materially altered by the licensee on the final licensed product.

Purchase of Artwork in Its Final Version

The artist may negotiate for the right, but not the obligation, following the expiration of the tour or the term of the contract, to purchase all rights, title, and interest in and to any and all of the elements comprising the artwork at a mutually agreed upon sum. If such an event transpires, the artist may require that the licensee, at the conclusion of the tour, deliver any and all elements of the artwork, including the screens, to a mutually designated third party and the artwork be held by that party for an agreed period of time, during which period the artist would examine the work and evaluate its purchase. If the artist decides not to purchase the artwork, then the agreement may call for one of two alternatives. Either the artwork would be destroyed by the third party, with a certificate of destruction to be supplied to both the licensee and licensor, or the artwork would be returned to the licensee for storage and use at a later date.

TIME PERIOD WITHIN WHICH TO FINALIZE CREATIVE CONTROL

It is important that both the artist and the licensee work together to create merchandise that not only would sell well but would generate a positive image for the artist. All negotiations regarding which party retains creative control over the licensed product should be consummated, leaving the licensee ample time within which to produce, manufacture, and distribute the licensed products.

ARTIST PURCHASE OF LICENSED PRODUCTS

Since the artist may desire to purchase certain licensed products for his or her own personal use, the agreement may provide that the artist be permitted to acquire from the licensee, provided it is not for resale, an agreed number of licensed product items at an agreed price, usually cost plus a minimal markup. It would probably be negotiated by the licensee that those personal purchases be excluded from any royalty-based calculations.

COPYRIGHT

As the copyright owner of his or her image, name, logo, sound, and likeness, the artist would generally be required to file the appropriate copyright marks for the listed name, likenesses, and sound with the Register of Copyright in Washington, D.C., at his or her sole cost.

Once filed and completed, the artist would typically demand that the following copyright notice appear on all of the licensed products: (c) 19__, Artist

COMPENSATION

The heart of the tour merchandising agreement, from the artist's standpoint, would usually be the compensation he or she earns as a result of granting the rights listed in the agreement.

In consideration of the rights and the licenses granted to the licensee, the artist would typically receive from the licensee either

a) a flat-fee payment, or
b) a royalty computed on the "net" (or gross) receipts earned by the licensee from the sale of all the products.

The terms "net" and "gross" should be clarified clearly and concisely, since a vague definition could spell the difference in substantial income earned by the artist. "Gross," in many cases, could mean all earned income, from any source granted in the agreement, less all sales taxes; local, state, and federal taxes; and all agreed expenses and disbursements. "Net" has been defined elsewhere in this book. It should be clarified that the parties can establish a definition of "net" or "gross" that meets with their specific requirements.

Flat Fee

Under a flat-fee arrangement, the artist would typically receive his or her compensation in a single payment, or the artist may receive his or her compensation in several payments, according to an agreed schedule. The payment schedule may be as follows:

a) the initial payment upon the signing of the tour management agreement,
b) the second payment upon the first day of the tour, and
c) the final payment upon the last day of the tour.

Royalty

If the licensee agrees to pay to the artist a royalty, based on the number of products sold during the tour, as well as all agreed sell-offs following the termination of the tour, the royalty rate will usually depend on the relative strength and bargaining position of the artist, the strength of the licensee as a distributor and marketer, and the payment to be made to the concert halls and tour venues.

The royalty provision may also provide for an escalating threshold element, under which an increase in sales could generate an increase in the royalty percentage.

Advance against Future Royalties

The agreement may stipulate that the licensee would pay the artist an advance payment against future royalties. The agreement should also detail the schedule of payment. A sample schedule may be as follows:

a) the licensee would pay an initial, upfront sum to the artist on the date of execution of the agreement, and
b) the balance would be paid on the first concert date.

The licensee would usually demand that the amount paid to the artist as an advance against future royalties be recoupable by the licensee from any and all royalties due the artist. If the advance is modest, it is likely that the artist would not be obligated to repay the advance. However, in the event a substantial sum is advanced the artist, the licensee may demand that the artist agree to reimburse the licensee the unrecouped balance of the advance within an agreed period of time following the termination of the agreement.

If the licensee believes that the artist will initiate additional tours that may prove more profitable, and based his or her belief on the rising success in the artist's career, the licensee may agree to extend the term of the tour merchandising agreement though one or several additional tours, thereby delaying the payback of the unrecouped advance.

The Amount of the Advance

The precise amount of the advance is generally a hotly negotiated element in the agreement and usually reflects certain known and estimated elements. The licensee and artist would often attempt to determine the total number of attendees and the percentage of those attendees who would purchase the licensed products, thereby estimating the total income to be earned as a result of the tour merchandising agreement. Past records from similar tours may be used as a barometer in the calculation of the number of products purchased, and the sums expected to be spent, by each attendee. In some instances, the artist may guarantee a minimal number of paid admissions, and that number would be considered the watershed figure.

Attendance Less Than Artist's Guarantee

In the event that the calculations and projections were incorrect and the total number of audience did not measure up to guaranteed minimums, the licensee may require that the artist refund to the licensee a pro rata portion of the advance or the unrecouped balance of the advance, whichever is less.

ACCOUNTING

The tour merchandising contract may provide that the licensee render to the artist, nightly at the close of each concert engagement, an informal accounting, in writing, of gross receipts derived from the sale of the licensed merchandise as well as providing all addition, pertinent and relevant data necessary to compute royalties payable to the licensor, including an inventory count, shipping and storage costs, and other marketing expenses. This provision may authorize the artist's representative to be present with the licensee when such accounting occurs, but the licensee may request that the artist not interfere with the licensee's business operations.

Final Accounting

In addition to regular accountings during the term of the tour merchandising agreement, the licensee may be required to furnish to the artist a complete and final accounting of gross receipts derived from the sale of the items within an agreed period of time following the expiration of the tour merchandising agreement.

The accounting report should include detailed information concerning the merchandise sold, categorized by tour venue or concert hall, date, and performance. In addition, a statement of all gross receipts derived from the sale of the licensed products, indicating the number and description of each item sold, the gross sales prices of each such item less applicable taxes, and the calculation of the artist's royalty, would usually also be furnished to the artist.

The artist would, as a rule, request that the final accounting be accompanied by the payment of the balance, if any, of any and all royalties due and owing the artist pursuant to the agreement.

REVIEW OF BOOKS AND RECORDS

The artist would usually insist that the licensee maintain accurate books and records of all accounts governing the transactions relating to the licensed products. The artist, as well as his or her duly authorized representative (usually, a certified public accountant) would typically retain the right, for a specific number of times during a fixed time period following the date that the final accounting is rendered to the artist, to audit the books and records of the licensee with respect to the sale of the licensed products permitted under this tour merchandising agreement.

Reasonable Notice Needed for Such Review

Reasonable notice would generally be required to be given to the licensee in order for the artist's audit to take place. The licensee would probably demand that the audit be conducted at the place where the licensee normally conducts his or her business, during regular business hours, so as not to unreasonably interfere with the licensee's business. Often, the licensee would demand that the audit be conducted at the artist's sole expense.

Inconsistencies

If an audit conducted by the artist, in accordance with the provisions of this agreement, reveals that the licensee has made an underpayment to the artist in terms of the royalties, the agreement may provide that the licensee pay that discrepancy to the artist, in addition to an agreed amount of interest. The artist may demand that, in addition to paying the amount the artist is due under the agreement, the licensee reimburse the artist for the costs of the audit, even if the inconsistency was a matter of a simple oversight, without a finding of fraud or negligence.

Binding Statement

The agreement may provide that all accountings and statements rendered by the licensee would be binding upon the artist and would not be subject to objection by the artist, for any reason, unless specific objection is made by the artist, by written notice to the licensee stating the basis of the objection. This objection would generally be required to be made within an agreed time period following the receipt of the accounting statement, limiting the artist's right to protest to an agreed period.

WARRANTIES AND REPRESENTATIONS

The warranties and representations made by both the artist and the licensee are considered to be of primary importance. They are the legal basis around which the parties enter into the various provisions in this agreement.

Right to Make Grants

Typically, the artist would warrant and represent to the licensee that the artist has the exclusive right and authority to grant the licenses conferred in the contract.

No Disability

Both parties would usually warrant and represent that they are under no disability, restriction, or prohibition, whether contractual or otherwise, to grant or receive the rights enumerated in the agreement or to execute and perform the obligations stated in the tour merchandising agreement.

No Breach of Copyright

The artist usually warrants and represents that none of the grants accorded the licensee pursuant to the terms of this agreement would result in the violation or breach of any statutory or common law or rights of any party, including without limitation, contractual rights, trademarks, copyrights, and rights of publicity and privacy.

No Grant of Rights to Others

In addition, the artist would likely warrant and represent that he or she has not granted, and would not grant, any right, title, or interest granted in this agreement to the licensee, to any other person or entity, during the term of this agreement which would conflict with, or limit, any of the rights granted the licensee. More specifically, the artist would usually warrant and represent that he or she would not enter into any agreement, during the term of this tour merchandising agreement, with any other party with respect to the manufacture, distribution, or sale of those licensed products granted the licensee, for the contracted tour.

Rights Other Than Those Granted

The licensee may be required to underscore that he or she has not secured any additional rights in the licensed products other than those expressly granted within the text of this agreement, and the artist reserves all rights to those licensed rights and products not granted the licensee.

Giveaways

In order to control the exploitation of the licensed products, the artist would typically obligate the licensee to warrant that he or she would not provide the licensed products as give aways, premiums or promotional items without the artist's prior written consent.

No Unauthorized Use

Typically, the licensee would warrant that he or she would not authorize any use, direct or indirect, of the licensed products in any areas outside the agreed tour venues or concert halls during the contracted tour and would not knowingly sell items covered by this contract to persons who intend, or are likely, to resell them in any manner other than as agreed in this agreement.

Validity of Copyright

The artist would most likely demand that the licensee agree not to contest the ownership of any copyright or trademark relating to the licensed products. Furthermore, the licensee should agree not to attack the validity of the license granted the licensee under this agreement.

Misuse

The licensee would usually stipulate that he or she would not harm, misuse, or bring into disrepute the licensed products. The licensee may further assert that he or she would not create any expenses chargeable to the artist without the prior written approval of the artist.

INDEMNIFICATION

The parties to this tour merchandising agreement would typically agree to indemnify, defend, protect, save, and hold each other harmless from and against any and all actions, claims, suits, losses, judgments, penalties, liabilities, damages, costs, and expenses (including reasonable attorney's fees) of whatever kind and nature imposed on, incurred by or against each party arising out of the other party's breach of any of its representations, warranties, or obligations made pursuant to this agreement or through the negligence or intentional acts of its officers, directors, employees, or representatives.

INSURANCE

Since the possibility exists that product liability claims may arise as a result of faulty merchandise being sold or marketed, the artist would usually demand that the licensee obtain and maintain, during the life of the tour merchandising agreement, a products liability insurance policy from a recognized and qualified insurance company. The insurance policy would usually name the artist as an additional insured, against any claims, suits, losses, or damages arising out of the use of the licensed products sold and out of any alleged defect in the products.

Certificate of Insurance

The artist may demand that he or she be provided with a certificate of insurance evidencing the existence of such an insurance policy. The insurance policy should provide that the artist be given reasonable notice by the insurance company in the event the policy is canceled.

SELL-OFF

The sell-off period typically relates to the interval following the expiration of the tour merchandising agreement and details the duties and obligations borne by each party in regard to the licensed merchandise remaining at the end of the tour or concert. Typically, the parties would agree that following the expiration or termination of the agreement, the licensee may, on a nonexclusive basis and in the ordinary course of his or her business, dispose of all remaining licensed products during a fixed and established period of time and at specific retail outlets and markets. Prior to disposing of any licensed products during the sell-off period, the licensee would generally be required to give to the artist a full and complete written inventory of the remaining stock.

The artist may request the option to buy all, or any portion of, the remaining stock, during a reasonable time period following the expiration or termination of the agreement, at the licensee's cost plus an agreed markup. Since there is generally no actual profit made by the licensee when goods are sold to the artist, the artist's payment to the licensee for these leftover products would usually not be deemed gross receipts from which a royalty would be paid the artist.

Recalculation of Royalty

With respect to sales of items made by the licensee during this sell-off period, the artist may request an increase in his or her royalty fees, since the price per licensed product would typically decrease. The licensee would usually counter with a demand to decrease the royalty due and owing the artist, claiming a decrease in per product profits.

INFRINGEMENT

Both the artist and the licensee would typically agree to use their best efforts to protect the other party's rights in and to the licensed products, including without limitation using their best efforts to discover, prevent, and prohibit the illegal sale of items, facsimiles of items, and/or items of similar merchandise by unlicensed third parties.

Prompt Notice of Infringement Claim

Both the artist and the licensee would usually be required to give each other prompt written notice of any action, claim, or suit, and the party so noticed would be granted the opportunity, at its option, to participate in the defense of the alleged claim, through counsel of its own choice and at its sole cost and expense.

TERMINATION

If either party of this contract breaches any of the material terms and conditions of this agreement, the party claiming such breach would generally have the right to serve upon the party alleged to be in breach of the contract a written notice of his or her intention to terminate this tour merchandising agreement. Typically, the tour merchandising agreement would contain a built-in cure element which would enable the breaching party to repair, or mitigate, the breach within a certain amount of time. If the party alleged to be in breach fails to cure or remedy the alleged breach within the agreed time period, then this agreement could automatically be terminated, if so agreed by the parties. The parties may also agree that the termination would be without prejudice to any other rights which either party may otherwise have against the other.

Artist's Right in Case of Breach

In case the breach cannot be mitigated, the agreement may provide that the artist would retain the option of voiding the agreement, obtaining equitable relief, and securing the services of another licensee to fulfill all the obligations of the tour merchandising agreement.

Insolvency

If the licensee becomes insolvent or files a petition in bankruptcy, or if a petition in bankruptcy is filed against the licensee, or if the licensee makes an assignment for the benefit of creditors or makes any arrangement pursuant to any bankruptcy law, or if a receiver is appointed, the licensee may agree to give the artist the option to automatically terminate the agreement, at the artist's sole election.

FORCE MAJEURE

If at any time during the validity of this agreement by reason of any act of God, fire, earthquake, flood, explosion, strike, labor disturbance, civil commotion, act of government, its agencies or officers, any order, regulation, ruling, or action of any labor union or association of artists, musicians, composers, or employees affecting the artist or licensee, its subsidiaries or affiliates or the industry in which it is or they are engaged, or any shortage of or failure or delays in the delivery of materials, supplies, labor, or equipment, or any other cause or causes beyond the control of the parties of this agreement, the performance of the artist's or the licensee's obligations under this agreement is delayed, hampered, interrupted, or interfered with, or otherwise becomes impossible or impracticable, and if such condition exists for an agreed number of consecutive days, then either party may, upon notice to the other, terminate this agreement without liability. The parties should decide whether any advances provided the artist would be returned to the licensee within a reasonable time period following the agreement's termination under the *force majeure* provision.

ASSIGNMENT

The artist would typically demand that the licensee not be granted the right to assign this agreement without the prior written consent of the artist, arguing that he or she entered this agreement with the licensee based on the licensee's unique expertise and experience as tour merchandiser.

NOTICES

All notices and statements provided for under this agreement are typically required to be in writing and, together with all payments provided under this contract, sent by registered or certified mail, return receipt requested, or by verifiable private express mail service, such as Federal Express, DHL, or UPS. A copy of all notices to the licensee should be sent to

LICENSEE
Address: ____________________

A copy of all notices to the artist should be sent to

ARTIST
Address: ____________________

Properly addressed notices delivered or sent as provided under this agreement would usually be deemed given when postmarked if delivered by mail.

NO MODIFICATIONS

In general, the parties would agree that the agreement they are signing sets forth the entire understanding relating to its subject matter. No modification, amendment, waiver, termination, or discharge of this agreement or any of the terms or provisions included in this agreement would be binding upon either of the parties unless confirmed by a written instrument signed by the parties.

WAIVER

Typically, no waiver by either party of any term or provision of this agreement or of any default under this agreement would affect that party's rights thereafter to enforce such term or provision or to exercise any right or remedy in the event of any other default, whether or not similar.

VOID PROVISION

If any provision of this agreement would be considered void, voidable, invalid, inoperative, or unenforceable, then usually the parties may agree that no other provision of this contract would be affected as a result of such action, and accordingly, the remaining provisions of this agreement would remain in full force and effect as though such void, voidable, invalid, inoperative, or unenforceable provision had not been contained in this contract.

NO PARTNERSHIP

Both the licensee and the artist may agree that they have not entered a partnership or a joint venture, that neither party has the right to obligate or bind the other in any manner whatsoever nor hold itself out contrary to the provisions of this agreement.

STATE OF VALID JURISDICTION

The state retaining jurisdiction in the event of lawsuits or other causes of action should be stipulated in this agreement. The most convenient state is usually the one where both maintain their business, which would serve to lessen their expenses in the event of litigation.

SIGNATURES

The parties will typically sign their names to the agreement, indicating their understanding and acceptance of all the included provisions.

17

The Artist Agreement for Commercials, Advertising, and Personal Appearances

Noted personalities and celebrities—movie stars, astronauts, musical artists and even U.S. senators—have been retained to represent a commercial product to the public. It is anticipated by the advertising agency that the well-known and recognizable figures would establish an immediate bond of trust and confidence with the consuming population.

Advertising agencies are keenly aware of the economic benefit of such a trust and would often be willing to pay substantial sums to identifiable musical personalities to be the voice extolling, through the spoken word or song, the benefits of the product. The agreement that details the contractual relationship between the advertising agency and the artist considers the artist's responsibilities, duties, and obligations as well as his or her moral, social, and ethical position within the focused community to which the advertisement is geared.

PARTIES

As in most agreements, the commercial, advertising, and personal appearance agreement should state the names and addresses of the parties, the artist and the advertising agency, and the date upon which the agreement becomes valid.

AGENCY'S CLIENT

The advertising agency, in order to clarify all the parties to the agreement, should state that it represents the client, the owner, maker, producer, and/or manufacturer of the product to be advertised.

FORMS OF MEDIA

The forms of media to be utilized in the agency's advertising campaign should be stipulated in the agreement. Typically, the media include television commercials, cable commercials, radio commercials, print (newspaper and magazine) advertising, and any and all other forms, formats, or manners of media-based advertising, now known or to be devised in the future, employed for the purpose of advertising and promoting the product.

COMPLIANCE

Since the agency would typically be risking its position and status with its client when it bases an advertising campaign on the drawing strength of the artist with the consumer public, the agency would usually insist that the artist agree to comply with all the conditions and provisions of the agreement, as they are detailed. The artist would further be required to stipulate his or her understanding that any failure by the artist to comply with any of the agreement's material provisions could be considered a serious breach of contract and, depending on the violation, a breach which could result in the voiding and termination of the agreement.

TERM

The term, or length, of the agreement should be fixed. The agency would usually negotiate for a term long enough within which to launch, establish, and have its campaign penetrate the marketplace, impacting on its focused consumers. The artist may wish to limit the term, in order to increase his or her chances of being offered additional advertising opportunities by third-party advertising agencies. Generally, the parties would find a compromise which will satisfy both the artist's and the agency's requirements.

Option to Renew

The artist's popularity may be in question, as may the actual selling power of his or her endorsement. Under those circumstances, the agency may not choose to commit itself to an extended contractual relationship with the artist. As a means of satisfying the needs of both parties, the agency and the artist would probably negotiate an initial term, to be followed by one or several options to renew the agreement for specific and fixed periods of time. The option provision would ensure a long-term commitment by the artist to the agency in the event of a successful campaign, while providing all parties with a means of terminating their understanding under amicable relations, if the advertising campaign failed to meet the expectations of the agency and the artist.

Matching Offers

The agency may negotiate for the inclusion of a provision providing that, if the artist solicits offers for endorsements from competing agencies or advertising clients following the termination of the term of this agreement, the agency would be granted the opportunity, within a fixed period of time, to match any such bona fide offer.

Threshold Met

The parties to the commercial, advertising, and live performance agreement may stipulate that if an agreed threshold in sales, as a result of the campaign featuring the artist, would be met, then the option would automatically become activated and effective for an additional term.

No Prejudice

The agency may require that the artist agree not to take any action, during the period prior to the effectiveness of the option, that may prejudice in any way the rights granted the agency. During that period, the artist could be enjoined from negotiating with a third party representing a product similar to the one for which the artist's services have been retained in the commercial, advertising, and live performance agreement.

TERRITORY

The territorial scope of the commercial, advertising, and live performance agreement should be clearly defined, since in the current global marketplace, it is becoming increasingly common for a single product to be marketed internationally. If the territory negotiated is worldwide, the compensation due and owing the artist may be substantially higher than if the territory would be limited to the United States. In addition, some products, are local by nature, and the agency may wish to negotiate an agreement which would be confined to a particular state or section of the United States.

Because of the trend toward satellite transmission of radio and television, the parties may agree that even though the endorsement could be seen or heard in markets other than anticipated, as long as the commercial or endorsement is not actively solicited outside of the planned market, the artist would normally not be entitled to receive additional income.

DUBBING

Questions regarding the dubbing and subtitling of the commercial, endorsement, or advertisement should be negotiated between the parties. It is likely, though, that the agency would demand the right, at its sole discretion, to dub and subtitle all commercial output produced, under the conditions of this agreement, which bear the likeness and/or sound of the artist.

Voice Track

If the artist is not available, or does not wish, to record a voice track for the advertisement or endorsement, the agency would usually retain the right to utilize the services of a substitute voice or narrator.

OBLIGATIONS OF THE ARTIST

Retained for his or her ability to impact favorably on the consumers the agency intends to attract, the target of the advertising drive, the artist would generally be obligated to participate, with a level of professionalism expected of an artist of his or her stature, in a detailed advertising and promotion campaign consisting of responsibilities, obligations, and services that are in compliance with the requirements of the agency, the needs of the client, and are in accordance with a mutually agreeable schedule.

On Camera

The artist may be required to be the on-camera or on-microphone spokesperson and/or endorser of the product on television, cable, satellite transmissions, videocassettes, laser disks, and on any and all other forms, formats, and manners of advertising and commercial, now known or to be invented during the term of this agreement.

Live Spokesperson

In most circumstances, the artist would agree to be the live spokesperson and/or endorser of the product at such locations and on such dates and times as the agency will select. The artist would usually require that he or she be given a reasonable amount of notice prior to all such live appearances, with the stipulation that the live appearances should not conflict with any performances, recording sessions, or other activities of the artist. All expenses incurred as a result of the live performances, including travel, security, living accommodations, and restaurants, would usually be the sole responsibility of the agent.

Photographs

As part of his or her responsibilities under the terms of the agreement, the artist would usually agree to be represented in photographs whose purpose would be to advertise and promote the client's product in any and all print advertising,

advertising displays and posters, and in any and all other publicity and promotional material.

In-house Spokesperson

The agency may negotiate that the artist would, in addition to all other obligations, be the in-house spokesperson and/or endorser of the product and would perform his or her musical talents for the purpose of making internal promotional and advertising pieces, including but not limited to industrial films and sales promotional videos. The artist may also be called upon to perform live for the employees of the client at sales meetings, seminars, or conferences. Reasonable notice would normally be accorded the artist before his or her services would be required.

Typically, the artist would demand that all such in-house appearances not conflict with his or her personal, performance, or recording schedules. Furthermore, the artist would generally be assured that all expenses incurred as a direct result of all such in-house obligations would be the sole responsibility of the agency.

SCHEDULE TO PRODUCE ADVERTISING MATERIAL

In an effort to accommodate the artist's often hectic schedule, which may be planned and fixed months, and even years, in advance, the agency may agree to limit the number of days allotted for each shooting date, photographic and film or video, in the commercial, advertising, and live performance agreement. Both the artist and the agency would normally agree to complete any and all such shootings within an agreed number of days during the term of the agreement. The actual shooting days may be consecutive or nonconsecutive, depending on the artist's and agency's schedules.

The shooting schedule usually considers the various advertising media covered by the commercial, advertising, and live performance agreement, and would frequently require a commitment of a minimum number of days per scheduled shoot, whether it is a television or cable commercial, a photographic session for still shots, a voice recording for radio commercials, or a shooting schedule of in-house industrial or sales marketing films or tapes. All travel days to and from the shoots or sessions may or may not be included in the minimum schedule. The artist would certainly negotiate that all travel days be included since they are days committed to the agency and not elsewhere.

EXPENSES

Shooting schedules or photograph sessions often require that the artist travel a distance from his or her normal residence. The artist would usually insist that it is the obligation and responsibility of the agency to pay any and all expenses directly related to all such shootings or schedules. Those expenses may include airfare, limousine pickup and delivery door to door, hotel accommodations at the location, living expenses, and an additional per diem allowance. The expenses would usually be paid in advance or would be paid to the artist immediately upon submission by the artist to the agency of a detailed statement.

COMPENSATION

The essence of the commercial, advertising, and live performance agreement for the artist is the compensation he or she would be entitled to receive in exchange for the services to be rendered and for the rights granted. The compensation negotiated would often be a flat fee, payable in accordance with an agreed schedule. The payment schedule usually complies with a plan agreed upon among the parties, such as the following:

a) 50 percent upon the signing of the commercial, advertising, and live performance agreement and the remaining 50 percent upon the first day of the scheduled photo session or shooting schedule, or

b) a portion upon the signing of the agreement, and the remaining portion paid on a quarterly basis, during the term of the agreement.

The actual compensation to be paid may vary, depending upon the form, format, or manner of advertising media utilized. The artist and agency may agree upon one price for the making and utilization of all television and cable vision commercials, another price for the making and utilization of the radio commercials, another price for the making and utilization of the still photographs, another price for the making and utilization of live performances, and yet another price for the making and utilization of in-house promotional and marketing films and tapes.

UNIONS

The majority of advertisements and commercials presented over the networks and syndicated television stations, as well as the still photographs advertised in most major magazines and newspapers, would be bound by the regulations of the union and trade guilds and by their policies regarding strict compliance with the union or guild rules. The clients, the owners, makers, manufacturers, or representatives of the advertised and promoted products would also, typically, be aware of the union and trade guild rules and regulations regarding the artist's performances on advertising and promotional material.

In furtherance of the union and trade guild requirements, the agency would usually expect that the artist be, and remain, a member in good standing of the appropriate union or trade guild having lawful jurisdiction over the services to be performed by the artist under the provisions of the advertising, commercial, and live performance agreement. The agency would usually state that he or she would be bound, and would continue to remain bound for the duration of the term of the agreement, by all the rules, regulations, and laws of the appropriate unions and trade guilds.

The agency may be persuaded to be responsible, and pay for, all union pension and welfare contributions on behalf of the artist, as part of the compensatory package offered the artist in exchange for his or her services under the terms of the agreement.

EXCLUSIVITY

As a means of increasing the marketability of the artist's services, the agency may demand that the artist be the exclusive spokesperson and/or endorser for the particular product and not render similar services, or allow his or her name, likeness, voice, photograph, or endorsement to be used in connection with another similar product. The artist would customarily clarify this provision by including a detailed list of those products which would be considered off limits to him or her for the duration of the term. Typically, the products would be those considered similar in nature and theme to the product being endorsed. As an example, an agency representing a soft drink company may demand the artist's exclusivity, barring him or her from endorsing any other soft drink including juices, mineral waters, and alcoholic beverages.

Exclusivity beyond the Term of the Agreement

The period of influence over the consumer, issuing from the artist's product endorsement, may extend beyond the term of the commercial, advertising, and live performance agreement. The agency may wish to capitalize on that extended period, or may intend to alleviate any possibility of confusion in the consumer's mind, by demanding that the artist's period of exclusivity to the client remain in effect for a fixed and established period of time following the termination of the agreement.

SERVICES TO BE PERFORMED BY ARTIST

During the term of the commercial, advertising, and live performance agreement, the artist, after receipt of reasonable notice, would generally be available to render his or her services for video or film shoots or photographic sessions at locations, and on the dates, specified by the agency.

Performance as Scripted

The agency would usually require that the artist perform his or her services as scripted by the agency. The agency has often gone to painstaking and detailed effort to story board the action in an effort to effectively relay the whole message to the public in an effective and proficient manner within the time constraints of the advertisement or commercial. It is common practice that the story board and the script are under the strict and sole supervision and control of the agency.

Reshoots

Inclement weather and reshoots often plague any production, including film or video shoots and photographic sessions. The artist would usually be required to make himself or herself available for any such contingency, with the understanding that he or she will be compensated for each additional production day.

RIGHTS GRANTED

The agency and the artist would typically agree which of the artist's rights have been retained by the agency as a result of the signed agreement.

Rights to the Advertising and Promotional Material

Typically, the artist would agree that all commercials, advertisements, print, film and tape commercials and promotions, as well as any and all other advertising and promotional material produced under the provisions and during the term of the commercial, advertising, and live performance agreement are, and would remain for an agreed period of time, the sole and exclusive property of the client.

Claims of Title or Right

During and following the term of the commercial, advertising, and live performance agreement, the artist would generally be required to agree not to assert any claims of title, interest, or right whatsoever, including rights of privacy, publicity, or moral rights, in or to any of the promotional and advertising material produced under the agreement, as well as in and to any of the material's characters, characterizations, or elements.

Right to Distribute

Typically, the agency and client would be granted the unencumbered right to distribute, reproduce, exhibit, utilize, and commercially exploit in general any and all of the advertised material produced under the provisions, and during the term of, the agreement throughout the agreed territory. This right would usually include the privilege to show the advertising and promotional material at sales meetings and conventions for trade purposes and in connection with marketing, promoting, and advertising the subject product.

Right to Make Commercials

Since the agency usually controls the "look" and "feel" of the advertisements or commercials in question, the agreement would usually provide that the artist would not exercise any control over the length, placement, or composition of the commercial or advertisement. Usually, the agency would retain sole control over the length of the commercial and would have the right, without infringing on any of the rights of the artist, to revise, edit, add, and amend the commercial and to make any number of the commercials and advertisements as the agency or client may deem necessary.

Right of Copyright

As owner of the commercials and advertising produced, the agency and/or the client would typically be granted the copyright of the material, as its owner and author. If the agency utilizes existing copyrighted material belonging to the artist or to a third party, the agency would usually negotiate to secure a license to employ the copyrighted material for its limited purposes.

Right to Use Artist's Name, Likeness, and Voice

The agency would frequently negotiate for the right to use the artist's name, likeness, photograph, voice, and biographical material for commercial trade purposes during the term, and within the territory, granted by the agreement. The artist, in an effort to protect his or her public image, may demand final approval on the actual use of the artist's name, likeness, sound, and photograph on the final advertising or endorsement.

BREACH

By breaching any of the terms and provisions of the agreement, the artist may cause the agency and/or agency's corporate client economic hardship and loss of present and future income. A marketing campaign may have been scheduled, and commercial time may have been purchased on television, cable, and radio stations.

The agency would therefore request the right to terminate the commercial, advertising and live performance agreement, without fault or liability, in the event the artist breaches any of the terms of the agreement. The artist may request that the agency notify him or her of such breach in writing and then be granted a period of time within which to cure, or remedy, the breach prior to the agency's exercising the right of termination. In the case the breach cannot be cured, the agreement would generally provide that the agency would have the option of voiding the agreement, obtaining equitable relief as well as recouping all monies advanced the artist as fees and compensations. Usually, a breach that sets in motion the termination of the agreement would be defined as a failure, refusal, or neglect by the breaching party to comply with any of the contract's material obligations.

ARTIST'S MORALS

A commercial or advertisement that utilizes the services of an artist as a spokesperson or endorser typically relies on that artist's maintaining his or her prominent stature in the community. An action placing the artist in disrepute, whether performed during or prior to the term of the advertising, commercial, and live performance agreement, may cause severe economic distress and loss to the client. Associating a disreputable artist with the client's product would certainly not be what the agency or client had in mind when the artist was retained as the product spokesperson and/or endorser.

The agency may wish therefore, to insulate itself from such a possibility by inserting into the agreement a clause which would serve to assure the agency and its client that the artist would act with respect to reasonable public morals and convention during the term of the agreement. The agency may insist that if the artist commits an act considered offensive by society's definition, which would bring the artist into public disrepute or create a public scandal or which would insult and offend a reasonable community thereby causing injury to the agency or its client, the agency and/or client would have the right to terminate the commercial, advertising, and live performance agreement and initiate any and all additional legal and equitable remedies under federal, state, and local laws and ordinances.

FORCE MAJEURE

As a means of protecting the integrity of the agreement against its termination by means of any activities or actions outside the control of the agency, artist, or client, the parties would usually agree to include the *force majeure* clause. Under the provision of this clause, if any action that cannot be controlled by either party occurs, including war, union strike, hurricane, boycott, riots, delays of commercial carriers or acts of God, and as a direct result of those uncontrollable acts, the agency and client will not be able to produce and/or utilize any of the advertising and promotional material produced under the terms of the agreement, the agency may be granted, if so agreed, the right to extend the term of the agreement for a period of time equal to the delay.

ACCOUNTING

The artist may request the right to inspect the books and records of the client, in an effort to ensure that it is, and would remain, a viable company that is not on the verge of insolvency or bankruptcy, which may, in the consumer's mind, affect the artist's viability and strength as a strong and active performer. Typically, the agency and client would refuse to permit the artist such an intrusion, citing that all payments due the artist are flat fees and do not depend on its sales, earnings, or the attainment of any performance plateaus.

RIGHT TO ENTER AGREEMENT

The agency would usually require that the artist warrant and represent that he or she has the exclusive right and authority to grant the rights which are stipulated in the agreement itself.

NO DISABILITY

Both parties would typically warrant that they are not under any disability, restriction, or prohibition, whether contractual or otherwise, with respect to their rights to execute this agreement, to grant the rights listed in this agreement, and to perform the obligations stated in this agreement.

NO COPYRIGHT VIOLATION

The artist would usually warrant that none of the materials, whether they be, among others, artwork, musical compositions, or creative writings authorized under this agreement, would result in the violation or breach of any statutory or common law or rights of any party, including without limitation, contractual rights, trademarks, copyrights, and rights of publicity.

NO DISREPUTE

To protect its product, the agency may require that the artist warrant that he or she would not harm, misuse, or bring into disrepute the client's product, and that the artist will not create any expenses chargeable to the client without the client's prior written approval.

PAY OR PLAY

If the artist has a strong bargaining position, that is, if he or she is a well-established artist with the potential for various employment opportunities in the advertising and endorsement industry, he or she may negotiate that the agency guarantee the artist his or her fee, regardless of whether the agency actually performs its obligations under the terms of the agreement or retains the services of another talent to take the place of the artist.

INDEMNIFICATION

The agreement may stipulate that the parties would indemnify, defend, protect, save, and hold each other harmless from and against any and all actions, claims, suits, losses, judgments, penalties, liabilities, damages, costs, and expenses (including, without limitation, reasonable attorney's fees and court costs) of whatever kind and nature incurred, asserted, brought, or made by or against each party arising out of the other party's breach of any of its representations, warranties, or obligations made pursuant to this agreement or through the negligence or intentional acts of its officers, directors, employees, or representatives.

In addition, under the provisions of the indemnification clause, the parties of this agreement would typically agree to give each other prompt written notice of any such action, claim, or suit, and the party so noticed would thereafter have the opportunity, at its option, to participate in the defense of the alleged claim, utilizing counsel of its own choice at that party's sole cost and expense.

REGISTRATION OF COPYRIGHT

The commercial, advertising, and live performance agreement would usually stipulate that the agency or its client, at its sole expense, register and maintain or cause to be registered and maintained appropriate copyright(s), trademark(s), and/or service mark(s) for the commercials or advertisements created in those territories where the contract is applicable.

OBLIGATION TO PROTECT COPYRIGHTS

Both the artist and the agency would usually agree to use their best efforts to protect the rights of the client in the client's products, including without limitation using their best efforts to discover, prevent, and prohibit the illegal manufacture or sale of products similar to the client's products by unlicensed third parties.

TERMINATION

If either party of this agreement breaches any of the material terms and conditions of this agreement, the party claiming such breach would usually have the right, if it so elects, to serve upon the party alleged to be in breach of the contract a written notice of its intention to terminate this agreement, and the party alleged to be in breach would thereafter have, if so negotiated, a fixed time period within which to remedy the alleged breach. If the party alleged to be in breach fails to cure or remedy the alleged breach within the agreed time period, the agreement would automatically be terminated. The parties may agree that in such a case, the termination would be considered without prejudice to any other rights which either party may otherwise have against the other.

Effect of Insolvency

If the agency or its client becomes insolvent or files a petition in bankruptcy, or if a petition in bankruptcy is filed against them, or if they make an assignment for the benefit of creditors or make any arrangement pursuant to any bankruptcy law, or if a receiver is appointed, the agreement may be automatically terminated by the artist at his or her election.

Artist's Inability to Perform

In the event the artist is unable to perform his or her services for any reason, be it the fault of the artist or others, the agency may have the right, if it so negotiated, to toll the agreement and to extend the agreement automatically, without any formal statement or notice, for a period of time equal to the time that the agreement was suspended due to the nonperformance of the artist. During any such suspension, the agency would usually require that the artist not render services as an endorser or advertising personality to any third party. To do so, the agency may argue, would constitute a material breach on the artist's part.

ASSIGNMENT

By Artist

Typically, since the artist is hired for his or her unique talents and position in the marketplace, the agency would insist that the artist not assign his or her obligations under this agreement without the prior written consent of the agency.

By Agency

The agency may negotiate for the right to assign this agreement to any wholly owned subsidiary, or to any person, firm, or corporation owning or acquiring a substantial portion of the agency's stock or assets, provided said subsidiary, person, firm, or corporation is a bona fide professional and expert agency, with experience similar to that of the original agency.

Key Person

If a particular copywriter or advertising executive, considered a key person, was instrumental in creating advertisements, commercials, or promotional materials that, in the artist's mind, best captures his or her talents, then the artist may insist that if the agency assigns its rights, the key person be offered the opportunity to be employed with the assignee.

NOTICES

The parties would usually require, as an assurance against subterfuge, that all notices and statements provided for under this contract be in writing and, together with all payments provided under this contract, be sent by United States mail, postage prepaid, or by certified or registered mail, return receipt requested, or by other forms of mail that maintain records and receipts, including Federal Express, UPS, and DHL, to the address set forth in this contract or such other address as may be designated in writing by the parties.

The agreement could list the addresses as follows:

ARTIST
Address: ____________________

ADVERTISING AGENCY
Address: ____________________

Properly addressed notices delivered or sent as provided under this contract would usually be deemed given when postmarked.

ENTIRE UNDERSTANDING

A provision would usually be included to indicate that the agreement, as set forth, contains the entire understanding of the parties relating to the subject matter of this agreement. No modification, amendment, waiver, termination, or discharge of this agreement or any of the terms or provisions included in this contract would be binding upon either of the parties unless confirmed by a written instrument signed by the parties.

NO WAIVER

The agreement would also usually include a provision stating that no waiver by either party of any term or provision of this agreement, or of any default under this agreement, would affect that party's rights thereafter to enforce the term or provision in question or to exercise any right or remedy in the event of any other default, whether or not similar.

VOIDABLE PROVISION

The agreement would usually stipulate that if any provision would be held unenforceable, void, voidable, invalid, or inoperative, no other provision of this agreement shall be affected as a result of such action. Accordingly, the remaining provisions of this agreement would remain in full force and effect as though such unenforceable, void, voidable, invalid, or inoperative provision had not been contained in this agreement.

But the parties may stipulate that, notwithstanding the foregoing, in the event the provision held void, voidable, invalid, or inoperative would impair the artist's right to receive his or her compensation under this agreement or would impair the agency's right to perform its agreed services, then such a provision could be deemed a material provision, and therefore the agreement may be deemed to be terminated without prejudice to either side.

NO PARTNERSHIP

In an effort to limit each party's liabilities, the parties would usually agree to stipulate that nothing in this agreement could be construed to constitute a partnership or a joint venture between them. Under most circumstances; neither party to the agreement would have the right to obligate or bind the other in any manner whatsoever nor hold itself out contrary to the terms of this paragraph, and neither party would therefore become liable for any representation, act, or omission of the other contrary to the provisions stipulated in this agreement.

RECOVERY OF ATTORNEY'S FEES

In the event of any action, suit, or proceeding arising from or based upon this agreement brought by either party against the other, the prevailing party, if so negotiated, would be entitled to recover from the other its reasonable attorney's fees in connection with enforcement of this contract in addition to the costs of such action, suit, or proceeding.

RIGHTS AND REMEDIES CUMULATIVE

The parties would usually agree that all rights and remedies stipulated in this agreement would be cumulative, and none of them shall be in limitation of any other right or remedy.

STATE OF JURISDICTION

The parties would usually agree which state of the union would have jurisdiction in the event of litigation or dispute. By such a stipulation, the parties typically agree that the state maintaining jurisdiction would rule, governing the agreement's validity, construction, and interpretation. The parties may further agree that any lawsuit or proceeding initiated by one party against the other in connection with this contract should be brought in a specified venue. Generally, the party with the stronger bargaining power prevails, and selects the state within which he or she resides, maintains his or her place of business, or where the laws of the state are more favorable to his or her position.

PROPER AUTHORIZATIONS

The artist would typically maintain that he or she has obtained all the necessary authorizations to enter the agreement and to perform all the terms of provisions agreed upon.

DOCUMENTS

The agreement may provide that the artist deliver to the advertising agency all documents required in order for the agency to perform its obligations. Such documents may include copyright registration and third-party powers of attorney.

PREJUDICING RIGHTS OF THE AGENCY

Also provided in this agreement may be a provision stipulating that the artist not take any action during the effectiveness of the agreement which would have the effect of prejudicing the rights optioned by the agency or of harming or diminishing the reputation of the agency.

INSURANCE

The agency and/or client may attempt to secure its investment into the artist as its spokesperson and/or endorser by establishing an insurance policy on the artist's health and ability to perform his or her services under the provisions of the agreement. Typically, if the artist agrees to such a provision, he or she would be required to make himself or herself available for all health examinations, which would be performed upon giving the artist reasonable notice and would not interfere with the artist's performances or recording sessions.

SIGNATURES

By signing the agreement, the agency and the artist customarily stipulate their understanding and acceptance of all the provisions of the agreement.

18

THE LOUNGE ACT AGREEMENT

A steady source of income for musical artists is performance in the many lounges, clubs, and performance rooms that offer the musical entertainment of a live show to their patronage. It is through those live performances that the artist usually perfects and defines his or her act, while establishing a following.

PARTIES

The lounge act agreement would usually detail the names and addresses of the parties to the agreement, the artist and the venue. The name of the entertainment manager or other representative of the venue may also be included. The entertainment manager would normally represent that he or she has the authorized right to enter this agreement with the artist in the name of the venue, and would therefore bind the ownership and management of the venue to the provisions agreed upon in the lounge act agreement.

If the venue is a corporation, the agreement would typically add the name and state of incorporation of the venue, as well as the fact that the corporation is presently, and would continue to remain, in good standing and in compliance with all the laws, rules, and regulations governing corporations in its state of incorporation. If the venue is a partnership or any other form of business entity, the agreement should also state that fact.

REASONS FOR ENTERING AGREEMENT

As a means of clarifying the objective for entering the lounge act agreement and for detailing what each party offers the other, a provision would typically elucidate that the entertainment manager of the venue intends to retain the services of the artist to perform musical acts in the venue or, if the venue consists of several separate lounges, clubs, or rooms, in a particular lounge, club, or room contained within the stated venue. The artist would usually specify that he or she is a musical performer and intends to accept the offer to render his or her unique services at the venue.

DUTIES

As its most basic purpose, the agreement would customarily clarify that the artist is retained by the entertainment manager to perform the artist's musical talents at the prescribed lounge, club, or room. In order to minimize any possibility for dispute or confusion at a later date, the lounge act agreement should detail the number of hours per day and the number of sets, or shows, per hour required of the artist, in order for him or her to fulfill the agreed schedule of performances.

TERM

The term, or length, of the lounge act agreement would usually be negotiated between the parties and stipulated in the agreement. It may be for a single engagement, a weekly engagement, or a commitment for a longer period of time. If the engagement is for an extended period of time, as is the one considered in this study, the entertainment manager would typically assign the artist to a performance schedule that may include five or six days on and one or two days off, though the performance schedule may vary from venue to venue and from season to season. During the holiday season, Christmas or the summer months, for example, the artist and entertainment manager may rearrange the performance schedule to take into account the larger crowds and demands for additional shows.

If the artist is considered the headliner, or the act that has been hired based on his or her reputation in attracting a large and steady clientele, the off days for the artist would typically be the "slow" days for the venue—those days when the attendance level usually drops below average and a substitute act could fill in for the artist without affecting the loyalty of the artist's or the venue's clientele.

COMPENSATION

An artist working for an extended period of time at the venue would generally receive a salary, payable on an agreed schedule, usually weekly or twice a month. Typically, the artist would not be entitled to receive a percentage of the net (or gross) receipts earned and received by the venue for the artist's performances unless such percentage is agreed upon prior to entering the lounge act agreement. If a percentage of the receipts is to be paid to the artist in exchange for his or her services, the entertainment manager would usually insist that the artist's base salary be reduced by an agreed sum.

If the artist has agreed to receive as his or her compensation a percentage of the venue's earned receipts, the artist would usually request that his or her certified representative, typically his or her personal manager, agent or accountant supervise the calculations of the venue's receipts and be granted the right to inspect the books and records of the venue, in regard to the subject matter of this lounge act agreement. The artist may insist on being paid his or her percentage of the venue's receipts following the tabulations of the day's receipts or on another mutually agreeable, schedule.

EXPENSES

If the venue is located beyond an agreed distance from the artist's normal residence, the management of the venue may agree to pay a portion, or all, of the expenses incurred as a result of the artist's entering the lounge act agreement, including meals, drinks, transportation, shipment of the artist's musical equipment, and lodging. If the venue agrees to pay only a portion of those expenses, and the venue advances some of the additional sums to the artist, the venue may be entitled to deduct from the artist's compensation a sum equal to the amount advanced.

AGREEMENT NOT TO COMPETE

Introducing an artist as performer in the venue for the length of the term usually requires an advertising and promotion campaign initiated prior to the commencement of the artist's play date. The advertising campaign may include newspaper and magazine ads, television and radio commercials, and public appearances, all costly ventures. In an effort to maximize its advertising and promotion campaign, without diluting its effect, the entertainment manager of the venue may require that the artist not perform his or her act at any lounge, club, or room, no matter the seating capacity, within a fixed distance from the venue for an agreed amount of time prior to, during, and following the artist's performance commitment to the venue.

If the artist fails to agree to such an agreement not to compete, the entertainment manager of the venue may insist that the artist refrain from advertising or promoting his or her performances or engagements in any other lounge, club, or room, no matter the seating capacity, within a prohibited location and time period without the prior written approval of the entertainment manager or other representative of the venue. As a means of protecting its rights under this provision, the venue may stipulate that it retains the legal capacity to initiate injunctive and any other form of judicial relief, if the artist violates the intent of this provision.

QUESTIONABLE MATERIAL

In an effort to control the questionable, potentially obscene and offensive material which the artist may utilize in his or her act, the artist would typically be required to comply with the customary policy established by the venue regarding all such material. The artist would usually be obligated to submit all his or her performance material for the entertainment manager's written approval prior to the artist's utilizing material which may be considered questionable in his or her act.

ARTIST'S CONDUCT

A lounge, club, or smaller performance room presents a service to its clientele—live musical performances. Its livelihood and continual revenues depend greatly on the performances of the artist as well as on the relationship of the artist to the audience who come to hear his or her performances. Acutely aware of that delicate relationship, the entertainment manager at the venue would ordinarily require that the artist conduct himself or herself in a manner and fashion that would be considered reasonably courteous, respectful, and proper with all the guests, customers, clients, patrons, and invitees of the venue. This provision may also note that even if the guests, customers, clients, patrons, and invitees are openly hostile to the artist, he or she would maintain the agreed level of propriety.

PERFORMANCE SCHEDULE

The entertainment manager would usually establish a performance schedule that would maximize the flow of audience in the lounge, club, or room during the artist's play dates. Lead-in artists or following acts generally rely on a strict adherence to that schedule, as would the restaurant and kitchen staff.

In an effort to control all possible schedule changes, the entertainment manager would usually require that the artist agree to perform his or her services punctually, according to the schedule, at the times and on the dates established by and between the artist and the venue unless the entertainment manager approves of a schedule change. Any deviation, modification, or change from a fixed schedule, without the prior approval of the entertainment manager, may result if so agreed, in a reduction in the compensation due and owing the artist under the terms of the agreement. Such reduction could be based on a pro-rated schedule, with each of the artist's performances given a monetary value, or on a previously established schedule, which could be punitive in nature.

Continual and repeated acts of lateness or delinquency may be, if stipulated in the contract, and often would be considered a material default on the part of the artist, which could result in the termination of the lounge act agreement. The artist would usually attempt to soften the harshness of this clause by requiring that the entertainment manager or other representative of the venue be obligated to give him or her reasonable notice of the venue's intent to terminate the agreement and grant him or her an opportunity to cure, or remedy, the breach.

RIGHTS GRANTED

The lounge act agreement would usually detail the rights granted by the artist to the venue, for the term of the agreement. Those rights would usually be limited to acts or actions directly related to the subject matter of the agreement and for the purposes of trade alone.

Rights to Publicize

The entertainment manager would, as a rule, require that the venue be granted the right to advertise and publicize the appearance of the artist at the venue during, and for an agreed amount of time prior to, the term of the agreement. In addition, the venue would usually retain the right to publicize at any time in the future that the artist did perform at the venue in the past.

Right to Take Candid Photographs

In furtherance of its rights to publicize and advertise the artist's performance at the venue, the entertainment manager would usually demand the right to take photographs of the artist during any of his or her performances in the lounge, club, or room. The artist may request the right to approve the candid photographs prior to their distribution.

Right to Promote Artist

The venue would normally negotiate the right to reproduce, duplicate, print, publish, and distribute in any manner, form, or format, and in any medium, the artist's name, photograph, likeness, voice, and biographical material for the purpose of advertising and promoting the artist's performance at the venue.

Right to Edit Performance

Control over the format of the artist's performance usually lies in the hands of the party with the stronger bargaining position. While the artist may present to the entertainment manager a complete and detailed act, the entertainment manager or other representative of the venue would typically retain the right to add, delete, edit, arrange, rearrange, shorten, and specify the length of the artist's performance in the lounge, club, or room at the venue's sole discretion without infringing on any of the rights of the artist, including rights of privacy, publicity, and copyright.

PHOTOGRAPHS

In an effort to promote the club, lounge, or room, the entertainment manager of the venue may schedule photography sessions of the artist, in contrast to candid shots of the artist, at the venue, intending such photographs to be distributed in the venue's advertising and promotional campaigns. Typically, the artist would be obligated to attend all such sessions, provided he or she receives ample written notice of such an upcoming photography session.

Artist's Press Kits

If available, the artist would usually be obligated to provide the entertainment manager with a complete and approved press kit, photographs (including black and white photos and color transparencies) and a detailed biography. The photographs presented by the artist would typically be used in conjunction with the photographs arranged by the entertainment manager for the purpose of trade, concerning the subject matter of the lounge act agreement.

WARRANTIES AND REPRESENTATIONS

The promises made by the artist to the entertainment manager of the venue are the foundation of the lounge act agreement, and he or she may be required by the entertainment manager to warrant, represent, and guarantee those promises.

Right to Enter Agreement

The artist would customarily warrant that he or she has the unencumbered right to enter the lounge act agreement without infringing on any of the rights of any other third party, whether person or business entity, including the rights of publicity, privacy, and copyright. Furthermore, the artist would usually guarantee that at any time during the term of the lounge act agreement, he or she would not enter into any contract or agreement, oral or written, which could affect the rights granted the performance venue in the agreement.

No Prior Payments

The artist may be required to stipulate that he or she has entered the lounge act agreement without receiving any form of payment, including, but not limited to, monies, gifts, and personal or real property, as an inducement for entering the lounge act agreement, without the express and written approval of the entertainment manager.

Original Material

If the artist writes and performs original material, he or she would usually be required to warrant and represent that all original material to be performed at the venue would be original and owned by the artist and would not infringe on the rights of any other person or third party, including rights of publicity, privacy, and copyright. The entertainment manager may request all pertinent documentation, including notices and assignments or transfers of copyrights, that would corroborate the artist's warranties and representations regarding the originality and ownership of the musical material.

Cover Act

If the lounge, club, or room has retained the services of the artist to perform compositions popularized by other performers, that is, to "cover" the compositions of others, the lounge act agreement would, as a rule, stipulate that condition of employment.

INDEMNIFICATION

The artist would usually be required to indemnify and hold the entertainment manager, representatives of the venue, and the venue harmless and free from any costs, fees, actions, damages, claims, liabilities, and costs incurred as a result of any claim instituted by or against the venue and its representatives resulting from a breach of any of the warranties, representations, promises, or guarantees made by the artist under the provisions of the lounge act agreement. The venue and its representatives would also usually be indemnified by the artist from any musical material or physical acts used by the artist that may cause physical or emotional harm to any customers, guests, clients, or invitees who witnessed and/or heard the artist's performance.

FILMED OR TAPED PERFORMANCES

During the period of time that the artist would be contracted to perform at the venue under the provisions of the lounge act agreement, he or she may have agreed to an exclusive performance provision, limiting and restricting his or her right to perform, whether live, on film or tape, via satellite transmission, on radio, or on or via any other medium, without first obtaining the written approval of the entertainment manager or other representative of the venue. The entertainment manager of the venue may wish to control exclusively the artist's performance schedule during the term of the lounge act agreement, ensuring that any outside activities will not detract from, or affect, the artist's performance at the venue.

ARTIST'S BACK-UP BAND

The artist may be responsible for the financial remunerations of his or her back-up musicians, including

a) paying his or her back-up musicians any and all salaries, expenses, and other reasonable fees,
b) maintaining worker's compensation and unemployment insurance for any and all members of his or her band, and
c) complying with all applicable and appropriate internal revenue service codes regarding the collection and filing of federal income taxes and any and all other requirements, provisions, laws, and regulations, including tax codes, of the federal, state, and local governments.

ARTIST'S MUSICAL EQUIPMENT

The entertainment manager would customarily refuse to accept any responsibility for any losses or damages incurred by the artist for any equipment, property, or belongings leased, rented, or owned by the artist and stored in the venue and utilized by the artist in the performance of his or her services under the terms of the lounge act agreement unless such loss or damage is covered by the venue's insurance policy then in existence.

Insurance

The lounge act agreement may indicate that all insurance required to compensate the artist in the event of any such loss or damage would be the sole responsibility of the artist and should be obtained at the artist's side expense. In the event the artist chooses to obtain such insurance, the artist may require that the management of the venue make the establishment available at reasonable times, during normal working hours and following reasonable notice, to any inspection or examination as required by the artist's appointed insurance carrier.

COLLATERAL USE

The management of the venue would usually insist that the artist not be permitted to make, or permit others to make, any radio, television, cable, motion picture, videotape, computer disk, or any other sound recording of the artist's musical performance in the venue without receiving the prior written permission of the management of the venue.

BREACH

If either party fails to perform its obligations and responsibilities under the terms of the lounge act agreement, the breaching party may have found itself in violation of the intent of the agreement. The party suffering as a result of the breach may then terminate the agreement without liability or loss, if so stipulated in the agreement. The lounge act agreement could also stipulate that the breaching party should be given written notice of the other party's desire to terminate the agreement and a specific amount of time within which to cure or remedy the breach prior to the activation of the termination provision.

FORCE MAJEURE

In an attempt to protect the integrity of the lounge act agreement considering outside forces which may affect the warranties and promises made in good faith by both parties, the parties may agree to a *force majeure* provision which assures the continuance of the terms and provisions of the agreement in the event any act outside the control of the parties prevents, cancels, or delays the artist's performances. Those acts may include floods, fires, hurricanes, labor strikes, war, blackouts, riots, acts of government (federal, state, or local), acts of God, unavoidable delay in delivery of necessary material or equipment, and natural disasters. Under most situations, the term of the lounge act agreement will be extended for a period of time equal to the uncontrollable delay, if such an extension would not result in a conflict with either party's schedule, and all parties will not be penalized for any such delay.

In the event the delay is extensive and the venue no longer desires to retain the services of the artist following the commencement of activities at the venue, the artist may request that he or she be paid his or her pro-rated salary due and owing, based on the date the uncontrollable event activating the *force majeure* clause became operational.

INDEPENDENT CONTRACTOR

Limiting the liabilities of the venue, the entertainment manager would usually require that the lounge act agreement state that the artist's relationship with the venue is that of an independent contractor and that the artist will not be considered to be (a) an employee of the venue, (b) a partner of the venue, or (c) in a joint venture with the venue. Under this relationship, the venue would usually not be legally responsible for, or be bound by, the acts or actions of the artist.

COMMISSION DEDUCTION

In order to clarify any obligations accepted by the venue as its responsibility and commitment, the lounge act agreement may stipulate that the artist and his or her talent agency understand and agree that the venue would guarantee to pay directly to the talent or booking agency, the agency commission earned as a result of securing the position for the artist as a performer in the venue. Often, the entertainment manager of the venue would include a provision in the lounge act agreement verifying the artist's agreement to such a payment schedule, including the amount to be sent to the talent agency as his or her commission, the schedule of payments, and the address where such payments are to be sent. As an additional proof of verification of the artist's and the agent's intentions, the artist/agency agreement may be included and made part of the lounge act agreement, as an exhibit or rider.

SOUND

Cognizant of certain noise restrictions placed on lounges, clubs, and rooms by local authorities, as well as accommodations that must be made to neighbors, the venue would usually retain the right to regulate and control the sound of the artist's performance. The artist may wish to limit the venue's right to one that would be imposed solely to comply with the local ordinances.

ORDINANCES

The artist would usually require that the management of the venue agree to abide by all the ordinances, laws, rules, and regulations as set forth by the local county, city, state, and federal government governing lounges, clubs, or rooms. In furtherance of this provision, the artist would usually insist that all expenses incurred by the artist as a result of the venue's violation of this provision be paid by the venue, including legal and court costs.

NO CHANGE OR MODIFICATION

The parties would usually agree that the lounge act agreement they are signing represents the whole agreement by and between the parties, and may not be amended, changed, or altered except in a writing signed by the parties.

STATE OF JURISDICTION

The lounge act agreement would most often stipulate which state has a controlling authority over the provision of the agreement, in the event of litigation or dispute. Typically, the party with the stronger bargaining position would command the outcome of this negotiation, often selecting the state where that party's business is located.

NOTICES

In an effort to control the flow of documents between the parties, the lounge act agreement may stipulate that all notices sent between the parties are to be sent by registered or certified mail, return receipt requested, or by other forms of express mail delivery, such as Federal Express or UPS.

SPECIAL PROVISIONS

An artist may request special provisions that the entertainment manager supply during the term of the agreement. The requests may range from a particular diet, such as vegetarian or macrobiotic meals, to a specially furnished dressing room, including television sets and recording equipment. These requests and provisions are often personal and should be negotiated prior to the signing of the lounge act agreement rather than being left open for future discussion.

UNENFORCEABILITY

In the event any of the provisions in the lounge act agreement are deemed to be unenforceable or illegal by a court of law, the parties would usually agree that the affected provisions alone would be considered to be unenforceable, null, and void. The remaining provisions of the lounge act agreement would typically not be affected by the ruling and would therefore remain in full effect.

NO CHARGEABLE EXPENSES

The management of the venue would usually insist on including a provision that stipulates that the artist would not create any expenses chargeable to the venue without the prior written approval of the venue, and that the artist would be solely responsible for any damages caused to the venue as a result of the artist's performance, including expenses incurred as a result of the destruction of furniture.

ASSIGNMENT

Since the entertainment manager of the venue has hired the artist for his or her specific and unique talents, the lounge act agreement would usually provide that the artist may not assign this agreement without the prior written consent of the venue.

In the event the owners of the venue own additional clubs, lounges, or rooms, the artist may insist that the management of the venue not be granted the right to assign this agreement to any other club, lounge, or room owned or controlled by the venue owners, without the consent of the artist and without additional compensation.

SIGNATURES

By signing the agreement, the artist and the venue, through its management, signify their understanding and acceptance of all the terms, provisions, and conditions of the lounge act agreement.

19

The License Agreement for Mass Market Distribution of Artist's Recordings

A popular artist may wish to exploit his or her compositions by mass market distribution of his or her recordings. The goal would typically be to reach a broad-based consumer public with reasonably priced albums. The mass market recordings are often manufactured specifically for such wide-scale distribution and frequently are compilations of the artist's earlier recorded works. The recordings are principally marketed utilizing the services and expertise of, among others, fulfillment houses and telemarketing organizations.

In order for an independent record manufacturer, creating such mass market distribution albums, to best exploit in the commercial marketplace the recording, it would often negotiate to capitalize on the artist's popularity by utilizing the artist's personal endorsements and other individualized forms of promotional strategies. It is common for the artist to wait for his or her career to be well established before entering such an agreement with the mass market licensee. Fear of deluging the market place with lower priced albums that may affect the sales of regularly priced recordings is a typical reason for holding off entering a mass market distribution agreement. Trepidations about the effect such a distribution agreement would have on the artist's fans may also dissuade the artist from entering such a license agreement at an early stage in his or her musical career.

The market for mass market distribution is vast, and the economic benefits which the artist may reap from a successful marketing campaign could be immense. An experienced licensee can frequently distribute the recording through the music departments of countrywide chains of retail and general merchandise stores. In addition, the licensee would often distribute the recording utilizing the broad-reaching appeal of television and cable advertisements, home shopping networks, and infomercials. With such a potential for an economic boom to the artist's career, many artists have chosen to enter a mass market distribution agreement with a well-established licensee at different points in their career. The artist's major consideration would, most often, be to balance the promising remunerative rewards of the mass market distribution of his or her recordings against possible career shifts.

Mass market distribution has become, and will most probably continue to be, a standard form of commercial exploitation in the music industry.

PARTIES

The mass market distribution agreement should begin by stating the names and addresses of the parties, the artist and the licensee, including their corporate names and state of incorporation.

PRODUCT TO BE LICENSED

In an effort to clarify with exactness the actual musical compositions granted by the mass market distribution agreement, the artist would usually detail the title, writer(s), and copyright index number of each licensed composition. This clarification should alleviate any ambiguity regarding the musical compositions licensed under the aegis of the mass market distribution agreement.

TERRITORY

The territory granted by the artist to the licensee in the mass market distribution agreement may be as broad as the world or as limited as a particular country. If the territory granted is the United States, the agreement would typically include in the grant all possessions, territories, and protectorates of the United States.

TERM

The term, or length, of the agreement would usually be fixed by the parties for an agreed number of years. The licensee would probably negotiate for a longer term, arguing that it would take an extended period of time to manufacture the recordings and establish a customer base over a diverse marketplace that includes television, cable, radio, and retail establishments.

The artist may agree to a longer term, under the condition that the licensee reach agreed yearly earned revenue and earning goals. Should the licensee fail to meet those goals, the artist may demand that the agreement be terminated without prejudice. By providing for performance levels in the agreement, the artist typically allows himself or herself an escape in the event sales fall below a level considered adequate.

Sell-Off

Following the termination of the mass market distribution agreement, the licensee may find himself or herself with unsold but manufactured recordings of the artist, either as stock inventory or as shipped but unsold goods. The artist would usually allow the licensee a limited period of time following the termination of the agreement within which to sell all remaining recordings containing the licensed compositions.

Master Recordings in Licensee's Possession

The licensee may remain in possession of master recordings, the original recordings from which the recordings of the artist's musical composition were produced and manufactured, following the termination of the mass market distribution agreement. Since the master recording could be considered a valuable asset, the artist would typically insist that, upon his or her request, the licensee either return all master recordings to the artist or destroy them.

Destruction of the Master Recordings

After complying with the artist's request, the licensee would usually be required to submit to the artist verifiable proof indicating the successful completion of the artist's demand to destroy the master recordings.

GRANTS OF RIGHTS TO LICENSEE

The artist's musical compositions are typically a collection of rights which he or she may grant collectively or individually. The artist's decision usually depends on the marketing and distribution strengths of the licensee.

Right to Manufacture and Distribute

The artist would usually grant to the licensee the right to manufacture, produce, promote, advertise, distribute, sell, and commercially exploit any and all musical compositions in the mass market, as the term is understood in the musical retail industry, that are licensed under the terms and provisions of, and in the manner and form as described in, the mass market distribution agreement.

The licensee would usually be granted the right to manufacture the licensed recording in any and all means of recording and reproduction for the purpose of distribution and commercial exploitation, now known or hereafter devised, including albums, audiotapes and CDs.

Additional Retail Outlets

Chain stores, variety stores, retail stores, department stores, and general merchandise stores, to name only a number of retail outlets, would typically be among the venues of distribution granted the licensee under the provisions of the mass market distribution agreement.

However, if telemarketing methods are used, utilizing the services of the audiotext industry to simplify ordering (1–800 or 1–900 numbers), the mass market recording may not be initially available for purchase in stores. Under those instances, the agreement may stipulate that retail chain and discount stores would have access to the mass market recordings only after an agreed period of audio text distribution has expired, allowing for the completion of the television or cable sales campaign.

Special Advertisements

The licensee would typically be granted the right to advertise and promote the licensed musical compositions through the use of special advertisements, including infomercials and ''best of'' compilations, on radio, television, cable, and other forms of media now known or hereafter devised and to fulfill the sales needs through retail operations in the licensed territory or through direct mail packages. The special advertisements may require the grant of the right to utilize the name, likeness, and voice of the artist as well as the right to advertise the titles of the musical compositions contained on the licensed recording.

Name, Likeness, and Biography

In connection with the right to release, distribute, sell, and commercially exploit the licensed recordings of the artist, the licensee may demand the right to utilize the name, likeness, image, sound, and biography of the artist. The artist would typically be obligated to make himself or herself available for a photographic session, which would usually follow reasonable written notice from the licensee. It is likely that the artist would limit the right to advertise and promote the licensed recording solely for the purpose of the mass market trade. The artist may insist that the required photographic session not interfere with a previously scheduled recording session or tour.

Premiums and Gifts

The licensee may also be granted the right to distribute the licensed recording by means of premiums and gifts in conjunction with a third-party business entity, such as offering the licensed recording as a premium in a fast-food restaurant promotion and advertising campaign.

LICENSEE IS EXPERIENCED IN MASS MARKET INDUSTRY

The licensee would usually stipulate that he or she is a specialist in the mass market field, having established relationships with the retail chains, the mail order companies, and/or the broadcast stations. As such, the licensee would insist that he or she understands, and has thoroughly researched the needs of, the mass market. As a maker of the recording, the licensee would have selected from the artist's repertoire, with the advice and approval of the artist if so agreed, the musical compositions best suited to fill the mass market's needs.

TRADEMARK AND LOGO

The licensee may have formed a corporation or business entity with a trademark or logo commonly utilized by the licensee for the release and distribution of musical recordings. The artist would usually be required to grant to the licensee, for the purpose of trade in the mass market, the right to distribute, release, advertise, promote, sell, and commercially exploit the licensed recording under the licensee's trademark, utilizing the licensee's logo.

PUBLIC PERFORMANCE

Aware of the commercial impact of advertising the musical compositions that comprise the licensed recordings, the artist would usually grant to the licensee the right to permit the public performance, such as by means of radio, television, or cable broadcast, segments or samples of the musical compositions contained on the licensed recordings.

If permission is required of the record company which has manufactured, distributed, and exploited the artist's compositions prior to the release of the mass market recording, the artist would usually agree to use his or her best efforts to secure those rights under the most economically favorable condition for the licensee possible.

COMBINED RECORDINGS

The licensee would usually negotiate for the right to combine the artist's musical compositions with those of one, or several, third-party artist(s) on a recording, advertised and promoted as containing the musical compositions from all named artists.

SOCIETIES AND ROYALTIES

Whenever applicable, the licensee would be required to abide by all the requirements and bylaws of the performing rights societies and the regulations of the copyright provisions regarding mechanical royalties.

RIGHT TO ASSIGN

The licensee may negotiate for the right to assign all, or a portion of, the rights granted him or her by the mass market distribution agreement. Considering this right to be too broad a grant, the artist may limit its scope by demanding the right to approve any assignee of the licensee and by requiring that the licensee assign the right only to a mass market distributor of equal or better stature, experience, and expertise in the mass market distribution industry. Such stature may be based on the assignee's prior business history, including

a) the musical compositions and recordings previously manufactured, distributed, sold, released, and commercially exploited by the assignee,

b) the sales earnings and revenues generated by the assignee during prior years of operation, and

c) the assignee's reputation, in general, in the mass market, entertainment, broadcast, and retail communities.

Assignment to Wholly Owned Subsidiary

The artist may also agree to an assignment of this agreement by the licensee to any wholly owned subsidiary, or to any person, firm, or corporation owning or acquiring a substantial portion of the licensee's stock or assets, provided said subsidiary, person, firm, or corporation is a bona fide professional and expert in the mass market distribution industry and the licensee remain responsible for the licensing of the artist's recordings.

ARTIST'S MASTER RECORDING

The licensee would usually require that the artist deliver, within an agreed period of time, a master recording of the musical compositions that are subject to the mass market distribution agreement. The licensee would customarily warrant and represent that the master recording delivered would be used solely as stipulated in the mass market distribution agreement, unless agreed otherwise by the parties, in a signed writing.

The master recording to be delivered to the licensee would usually be of a quality suitable for the commercial production and exploitation of recordings for general use and trade. They should also be of a quality similar to the one utilized by the artist during the general distribution and exploitation of the original recordings of the musical compositions. In this manner, the licensee would attempt to maintain a superior quality level of all the musical compositions that comprise the licensed recording.

In addition, the artist would usually supply the licensee with the actual title of each musical recording as well as the correct names of the writers, composers, and publishers as well as any additional copyright information.

COMPENSATION

The main reason the artist enters the mass market distribution agreement is, most often, the compensation he or she would be entitled to receive from the commercial exploitation of the musical compositions by the licensee. The exact level of compensation due the artist would typically be negotiated in good faith among the parties, with the stronger party commanding a more effective bargaining position. Often, the compensation would be tied in to the artist's history of successful hits, number of records sold over the artist's career, long-term popularity among the consuming public, and recent record sales.

Flat Fee

The artist may agree to receive, as his or her compensation, a flat fee, which could be paid in a single payment or according to an agreed schedule. A sample schedule may be as follows:

a) a portion of the flat fee paid upon the signing of the mass market distribution agreement,
b) a portion upon the release of the recording, and
c) the final portion within a specific time period following the release of the mass market recording.

Royalty

It is probable, though, that the artist would negotiate for the right to receive, as his or her compensation, a royalty based on the number of mass market units sold. The artist would usually be entitled to receive a royalty equal to

a) an agreed amount of money for each album, audiotape, CD, or any other format now known or hereafter devised, sold and not returned, containing the licensed musical compositions, with the understanding that the exact amount may be different for each format, or
b) an amount equal to an agreed net retail (or wholesale) price for each recording sold and not returned, whether in the format of album, audiotape, or CD, or any other format now known or to be devised in the future.

Deduction for Returns

As a rule, the licensee would negotiate for permission to deduct from any and all payments due and owing the artist all returns and credits, tabulated as a result of defective merchandise. In addition, the licensee would usually deduct all promotional and charitable giveaways from the tabulations presented to the artist. Since the artist typically receives his or her compensation based on actual licensed recordings sold and not returned, the artist may wish the place a cap on all such giveaways by requiring that he or she approve, in writing, all giveaways above an agreed amount. If the licensee exceeds the agreed amount of giveaways, the licensee may be obligated to pay to the artist a royalty as detailed in the mass market distribution agreement.

Advance against Future Royalties or Payments

The artist would usually negotiate for an advance against future receipts as an inducement to enter the mass market distribution agreement. The advance would normally become effective upon the signing of the agreement and may be paid according to an agreed schedule, which would often be as follows:

a) a single lump sum payment upon the signing of the mass market distribution agreement, or
b) a portion of the advance due and owing upon the signing of the agreement, and the remainder on the date of the release of the licensed recording, or
c) a portion of the advance payable upon the signing of the agreement, and the remainder to be divided equally among the number of licensed recordings to be released under the provisions of the mass market distribution agreement and payable on each recording's release date.

Mark-Downs

If market conditions, such as a slow or sluggish economy, a recession or a seasonal sale, require the licensee to distribute, sell, or commercially exploit the licensed recording at a marked-down price to the retailer or to the public through a direct mail marketing campaign, then the licensee may negotiate for the right to reduce the royalty rate due and owing the artist from all such marked-down goods by an amount equal to

a) a pro-rated percentage of the original net retail (or wholesale) price, or
b) an agreed reduction in the amount established in the mass market distribution agreement.

PAYMENTS TO UNIONS

The mass market distribution agreement may stipulate that the licensee would be obligated to pay to all pertinent unions or trade guilds, including the AF of M, the required amount to cover all pension, welfare, and other applicable dues.

ARTIST'S PAYMENT OBLIGATIONS

The artist may have entered into separate royalty agreements with third parties that are outside the scope of the mass market distribution agreement, including payments due to the original producer, composer, co-writer, or any other person or entity who may be party to such a payment agreement. Intending to free itself from such an obligation, the licensee would usually state unequivocally and directly that he or she would not be responsible for any such third-party payments nor for any costs or expenses incurred as a result of such third-party agreement. All those third-party payments would therefore be accepted as the sole responsibility of the artist.

Third-Party Indemnification

The licensee may, in addition, require that the artist indemnify, and hold the licensee harmless, from any claims or actions instigated by any third party as a result of any such third-party agreement entered into, by and between the artist and the affected third party.

WARRANTIES AND REPRESENTATIONS

Most agreements and contracts are based upon each party's having the rights granted to the other under the provisions negotiated, agreed and memorialized by their signatures. As such, both would usually warrant and represent that they can deliver the guarantees promised.

ARTIST'S WARRANTIES

The artist would usually stipulate that he or she has all the necessary authorizations and permissions to enter the mass market distribution agreement and is not, and will not become during the term of the agreement, restricted by any liability or prohibition regarding his or her ability to perform its provisions. Typically, the artist would guarantee that he or she would not place himself or herself under any restrictions or liabilities regarding his or her ability and right to grant to the licensee the right to manufacture, sell, distribute, exploit, advertise, and promote the licensed recordings in the agreed territory for the agreed term, as provided in the mass market distribution agreement.

Appropriate Documentation

The licensee would usually insist that the artist warrant that all appropriate permissions as well as transfers and/or grants of rights by any third parties (including producers, songwriters, and record companies) to the artist have been obtained by the artist and are therefore controlled by the artist.

No Infringement

By exercising the rights granted in the mass market distribution agreement, the artist should warrant that the licensee would not infringe an any of the rights of any third party, including all rights of privacy, publicity, and copyright. If required, the artist would agree to submit to the licensee for inspection all relevant agreements, contracts, and documents in connection with the grant of rights by all third parties to the artist.

LICENSEE'S WARRANTIES

The licensee would usually be required to warrant that he or she possesses the full and unencumbered right and authorization to enter the mass market distribution agreement and is not, nor will become during the term of the agreement, under any restriction or liability regarding the exercise of its provisions.

Limited Distribution

Moreover, the licensee would ordinarily assure the artist that the licensee would distribute and exploit the licensed recording only as agreed in the mass market distribution agreement. Therefore, it would typically be agreed by both the licensee and the artist that all rights not granted the licensee specifically in the mass market distribution agreement would remain the property of the artist.

INDEMNIFICATION

Both the artist and the mass market distributor would normally agree to indemnify and hold each other harmless from any liabilities, costs, or fees, including reasonable legal fees, resulting or incurred from any claims, actions, damages, or liabilities initiated by or against the damaged party based on a breach, or alleged breach, of any of the warranties, promises, or guarantees, whether oral or written, made by the breaching party.

FORCE MAJEURE

In an effort to preserve the validity of the mass market distribution agreement in the face of conditions beyond the control of either party, a *force majeure* provision may be included and stipulated by both the artist and the licensee. The *force majeure* clause would usually state that in the event forces beyond the control of either party, including war, labor unrest, natural catastrophe, unavoidable delay in the delivery of required goods, delay or prevent the affected party from performing its obligations under the terms of the agreement, such delay or impossibility of performance would not be considered a default, and the agreement would not be terminated and nullified. The parties may agree to extend the term of the mass market distribution agreement for the period of time equal to any unavoidable delay.

BOOKS AND RECORDS

If the compensation due the artist is royalty based, the maintenance of accurate books and records regarding the subject matter of the mass market distribution agreement by the licensee should be of prime concern to the artist. The artist, in an effort to evaluate the accuracy of those books and records, would usually negotiate for the right to inspect them, following reasonable written notice of his or her intention to do so. It would not be unusual for the licensee to request that the inspection be performed by a licensed certified public accountant, during normal business hours at the location where the books and records are normally held. Moreover, the licensee may demand that the artist be responsible for the expenses incurred as a result of the inspection.

STATEMENTS AND ACCOUNTINGS

Statements regarding the earnings and income received by the licensee as a result of the manufacture, sale, license, distribution, and exploitation in general, in the licensed territory, and payments to the artist of accrued royalties, should be submitted to the artist on an agreed schedule. The schedule of payments may be quarterly or semiannually or may follow any other schedule agreed upon by the parties.

Typically, the artist would be granted an agreed period of time, following his or her receipt of the schedule and payment, to question the licensee's calculations. If the artist would not contest the submitted statement during the agreed period of time, the statement and accounting would usually be considered to be accurate and exact.

Reserves

The mass market licensee would often negotiate the right to maintain an agreed sum, deducted from the royalties due and owing the artist under the terms of the mass market distribution agreement, as a reserve against all licensed recordings shipped and returned unpaid. If approved, the artist would typically require that the reserve be maintained in an established bank, earning interest from the day of deposit until the day of withdrawal. Following an agreed period of time, the reserve, including any and all accumulated interest, would be released and submitted to the artist, accompanied by a statement of account.

Final Accounting

The agreement would usually provide that the licensee furnish the artist a complete and final accounting of gross receipts derived from the sale of the units within a reasonable period of time following the expiration or termination of the mass market distribution agreement. This report should contain detailed data including a statement of all receipts derived from the sale of the units indicating the number of each item sold, the sales price of each such unit less applicable taxes, and a calculation of the artist's royalty.

The agreement may also stipulate that the final accounting be accompanied by the payment of the balance, if any, of any and all royalties payable to the artist pursuant to the provisions of the agreement.

STATE OF JURISDICTION

The parties would usually agree among themselve which state would have jurisdiction in the event of any dispute, disagreement, or litigation in connection with the provisions of the mass market distribution agreement. If both parties reside and have their place of business in the same state, that state is often selected. If the parties reside in different states, the party with the stronger bargaining position would typically negotiate for the state of his or her residence or business as the state governing the interpretation of the provisions of the agreement.

ENTIRE AGREEMENT

The mass market distribution agreement, as drafted, would usually be considered the whole and entire understanding by and between the signatory parties, and could not be amended, altered, or changed except if all parties to the agreement signify their agreement to such changes or amendments in a signed writing.

UNENFORCEABILITY

In the event certain provisions of the mass market distribution agreement are deemed, by a competent court of law, to be unenforceable or illegal, such unenforceability and illegality would usually not affect the remainder of the agreement, which should remain in full force and effect.

NOTICES

By requiring that all notices sent by one party to the other be delivered by registered or certified mail, return receipt requested, or by express mail services, the parties would ensure a record of all correspondence between them, in the event litigation or dispute resolution requires proof of any such mailings.

NO COPYRIGHT INFRINGEMENT

The licensee would usually insist that the artist warrant that the manufacture, sale, license, distribution, and exploitation in general of the compositions authorized under this agreement would not result in the violation or breach of any statutory, common law, or other rights of any third party, including, without limitation, contractual rights, trademarks, copyrights, and rights of publicity and privacy.

NO ADDITIONAL GRANTS

The artist would usually be required to represent that he or she has not granted, and will not grant, any right, title, or interest to any other person or entity effective during the validity of this contract which would conflict with or be in limitation of any of the rights granted under this contract.

NO CHARGEABLE EXPENSES

The artist would typically be required to warrant that he or she would not create any expenses chargeable to the talent without the prior written approval of the licensee.

NO HARM TO ARTIST'S REPUTATION

The artist's name and reputation among his or her fans, is of paramount importance to his or her success in the musical industry. The mass market distributor could damage that reputation by unethical or unqualified distribution efforts. Therefore, the artist would usually require that the licensee stipulate that it will not harm, misuse, or bring into disrepute the artist through any means whatsoever.

TERMINATION

If either party of this agreement breaches any of the material terms and conditions of this agreement, the party claiming such breach may have negotiated for the right to serve upon the party alleged to be in breach of the contract a written notice of its intention to terminate this agreement, and the party alleged to be in breach would thereafter have a period of time, if agreed, within which to remedy said breach. If the party alleged to be in breach fails to cure or remedy the alleged breach within that time period, then the mass market distribution agreement would be automatically terminated.

Insolvency

If the licensee becomes insolvent or files a petition in bankruptcy, or if a petition in bankruptcy is filed against the licensee, or if the licensee makes an assignment for the benefit of creditors or makes any arrangement pursuant to any bankruptcy law, or if a receiver is appointed, the artist may insist that the mass market distribution agreement be automatically terminated.

SIGNATURES

The parties typically signify their understanding and acceptance of the conditions and provisions of the mass market distribution agreement with their signatures.

20

The Tour Sponsorship Agreement

As the cost of producing music concerts, shows, and live performance events increases dramatically year after year, the artist is constantly seeking new avenues in which to offset the price of a tour and to maximize his or her revenues. One such way is tour sponsorship.

Under most tour sponsorship relationships, a major corporation affiliates itself with an artist undertaking an extensive tour. By agreeing to pay a mutually satisfactory sponsorship fee in exchange for the right to sponsor the tour, the corporation could be associated with the artist as the official sponsor of the show, with name and logo and branded product prominently positioned on all banners, tour booklets, performance stages, and on all other locations where the sponsor's name and product could be visibly promoted. If, on the other hand, the sponsor chooses to be one of a group of sponsors, its name, logo, and product would then share positioning with the others. The fee paid by the sponsor to the artist customarily depends on the type of sponsorship offered and accepted. For purposes of this study, we will focus on the artist seeking a solo corporate sponsor for his or her tour.

PARTIES

The sponsorship agreement usually details the names and addresses of the parties to the agreement, the artist and the sponsor.

TERRITORY

In considering the grant of territory, the artist would normally assess the itinerary of the tour, evaluating whether it would be a local, national, or world tour, and would issue the grant accordingly.

Clear Language

The agreement should define the territory granted in clear and concise language, leaving no room for confusion and doubt. The territory may be limited to a single country, such as the United States, a group of countries, such as the EEC countries, or the world.

Single Sponsor vs. Several Sponsors

In addition to the scope of the tour, the artist would ordinarily ascertain whether any goodwill or economic advantages exist by negotiating separate sponsorship agreements for the diverse territories to be covered by the tour. A particular product, for example, may be highly popular in one country but be in disfavor in another.

In considering the economics of a sponsorship agreement, the artist may ascertain that he or she would be in a better position to obtain lucrative sponsorship fees from a series of sponsors, each limited to a single territory, rather than from a single sponsorship fee granted to a sole sponsor accorded a multinational territory. On the other hand, the artist may be in a position to negotiate a larger fee with a single sponsor, asserting that the value of an exclusive sponsor would be greater than that of the collection of sponsors and their accumulated fees. The artist should weigh all sides of the issue prior to making his or her decision.

Product Marketing Concerns

The territory issue also becomes a matter of concern if the sponsor has negotiated for the right to market its product, rather than simply promote its name and trademarked brand during its term as the artist's exclusive tour sponsor. When considering the merchandising and sale of its products on the world tour, the sponsor would normally have researched the feasibility of its marketing strategy, evaluating such concerns as overseas distribution, customs, duties, international airway bills, and tariffs, while thoroughly investigating all regulations affecting international trade.

Worldwide Impact

If the artist's tour is to be worldwide in scope, it is likely that the sponsor would insist upon worldwide sponsorship rights rather than being limited to a single territory. Such an extensive coverage for the sponsor would, as a rule, increase the impact of its marketing and advertising campaign, allowing it to spread its investment over a broader market.

TERM, OR DURATION, OF AGREEMENT

The tour sponsorship agreement would typically be of limited duration and purpose, revolving around the start date and final performance date of the artist tour. As is often the case, tour dates are changed and itineraries juggled with little or no advance notice. The sponsor should, therefore, evaluate all potential tour changes when determining the term of the sponsorship agreement.

In order to protect the interests of the sponsor while ensuring that potential profits for the artist are not lost, the definition of term would often refer, not to the actual dates, but rather to the duration of the tour, including all extensions and modifications. If added performance dates are scheduled, based on the prior sell-out performances of the artist, the sponsor would usually be part of the extension package. In a similar fashion, if dates are deleted, then the sponsor would suffer the loss.

OPTION

The tour sponsorship agreement may include an option granting the sponsor the right to extend its sponsorship for an additional tour. The option may be exercisable by the sponsor upon written notice to the artist, but would typically be granted at the sole election and discretion of the artist. The agreement may stipulate that good faith negotiations should take place by both parties in an attempt to reach a reasonable accord regarding the option.

Clear Language

The agreement should be drafted in clear and concise language, indicating, without any ambiguity whatsoever, that the grant of option, contractually containing provisions similar to those incorporated into the tour sponsorship agreement, would become exercisable only in the event of an extension of the tour or the initiation of a new tour. It should not be considered a promise or commitment by the artist to indeed initiate a new tour or to extend an existing tour. Absent such a clear understanding, the sponsor may be in a position to claim a breach at a later date on the grounds that the artist did not undertake a subsequent tour.

Advance Payment for the Grant of Option

In the event the artist demands and receives an advance against future payments in exchange for granting the option and consequently forgoes the follow-up tour prior to, or during, the life of the option, the tour sponsorship agreement would generally provide for the complete reimbursement of the monies advanced by the sponsor. The agreement may also provide for reimbursement of verifiable expenses incurred by the sponsor in anticipation of the expected tour.

Right of First Refusal

The agreement may grant the sponsor a right of first refusal and/or right of first negotiations. If the sponsor has been granted the right of first refusal, the artist would usually be required to provide written notice to the sponsor of the conditions of any third-party sponsorship offer. Once such written notice is received by the sponsor, then the sponsor would typically have the right to match such an offer within a fixed time period.

Right of First Negotiations

The sponsor may have been granted the right of first negotiations whereby it has bargained for the right to negotiate a subsequent agreement with the artist prior to the artist's undertaking any additional negotiations with any third parties. If the negotiations between the artist and the sponsor prove to be unfruitful, only then would the artist be free to enter negotiations with other potential sponsors. Once those third-party negotiations have been culminated, though, the artist may be obligated, if the parties so agree, to make those identical terms available to the holder of the first refusal, the sponsor, to match or decline such a third-party offer.

TOP-BILLED ARTIST

The sponsor may require that the artist verify that he or she would be the top-billed artist on the tour. Since the sponsor is speculating on the name, recognition, and drawing power of the artist it has chosen to sponsor, it would usually attempt to limit its risk by sponsoring only top-billed artists.

One certain variable to be considered by the sponsor is whether the tour would be called "The Artist's Tour," or whether the tour will be known by the name of another performing group. In addition to the drawing power ascribed to a top-billed artist, a popular act usually has the ability to insist that the concert promoter or concert hall director place the sponsor's banners in prime locations around the concert hall.

SIZE OF THE MARKET

The tour sponsorship agreement would often attempt to define the relative market size and the potential audience in the cities in which the tour would be staged. Some agreements may divide the tour venues into A, B, and C markets, defined according to the potential size of the audience.

In addition, most agreements would consider the capacity of the concert halls in its calculations. While New York City would typically be defined as an A market, the venue played by the artist may be a small club with a capacity of only 250 seats. Performing a B market in a larger arena may attract a larger audience and be of more value to the sponsor. It is apparent that all variables should be considered by the sponsor when it is evaluating the fee to be paid the artist. The sponsor should also consider these variables when it initially considers entering the tour sponsorship agreement in the first place.

BUY-BACK OF AGREEMENT

In certain cases, the sponsor may negotiate the right to sponsor the initial tour, as well as additional tours, till it reasonably believes it has fully recouped the full value of the fee it has paid to the artist. The artist and sponsor may agree that the value would be defined by the number of paid attendees of the tour, or by the number of venues, or a combination of both. If such an open-ended provision would be adopted, then the artist may insist on being granted the right to buy back the agreement, reimbursing the sponsor for its lost value.

TOUR

Generally, a tour is defined as a series of live concert engagements performed by the artist in the agreed territory during the negotiated term. Generally, a tentative tour itinerary is attached to and made part of the agreement. The itinerary is usually found in an exhibit or rider secured to the tour sponsorship agreement.

The definition of "tour" may include, if so decided by the parties, any live concert engagements performed by the artist in the agreed territory occurring after the final engagement, if the additional tour dates are extensions of the original tour. Extensions of the original tour may result from an abundance of sell-out performances and audience demand.

In determining what is an extension of the original tour, the artist may consider one, or a combination, of the following:

a) whether the additional tour dates follow the final date of the original tour by less than a fixed and agreed period of time, and

b) whether the personnel, staging, presentation, and other elements of the live concert vary materially from the live concert engagements performed on the tour prior to the date of the additional play dates.

The artist may wish to limit the extension of the tour by stipulating that in no event would the sponsor extend its sponsorship beyond an established date.

ARTIST'S INTELLECTUAL PROPERTY

Typically, the intellectual property rights owned by the artist include the artist's name, unique sound, costumes, symbols, emblems, designs, depictions, characterizations, likenesses, and visual representations and the trademarks, logos, copyrights, as well as all other authorized material owned or controlled by the artist. Use of all such intellectual property by the sponsor usually requires the approval and permission of the artist prior to its employment by the sponsor.

LICENSED PRODUCTS

At times, the sponsor would be granted the right to merchandise licensed products bearing the image, likeness, photograph, or sound of the artist. The products may include items as diverse as T-shirts, jerseys, sweatshirts, programs, posters, pictures, and buttons. Generally, in order to clarify the licensed products stipulated by the agreement, alleviating any possibility of confusion with a tour merchandiser who may have purchased the rights to manufacture and distribute specific licensed products, the tour sponsorship agreement should include an exhibit or rider which would be attached to and made part of the tour sponsorship agreement. The attachment should list in detail the exact products to be licensed by the sponsor.

CONCERT HALL

The tour sponsor typically is granted the right to present itself—its name, logo, and products—to the audience attending the artist's tour at each and every concert hall, arena, stadium, or theatre in which the artist performs, regardless of the number of seats or the size of the venue or city.

EXCLUSIVITY AND AGREEMENT NOT TO COMPETE

The sponsor may demand that the tour sponsorship agreement stipulate that, for the term of the tour and, in some cases, for an agreed period of time thereafter, the artist refrain from commercially endorsing or providing any services, and refrain from permitting the use of his or her name, likeness, or endorsement, in connection with the advertising, promotion, or sale of any product distributed or sold by another person, firm, or corporation distributing or selling products which are similar or comparable to the products associated with the sponsor of the concert.

The sponsor may also demand that the artist warrant that he or she has not rendered any services, directly or indirectly, in commercials or advertisements, for any person, firm, or corporation which manufactures, distributes, or sells any competitive products within the reasonable past, the parties agreeing upon the definition of the phrase "reasonable."

If the artist has indeed been sponsored by a company of a similar industry, then prior to initiating this sponsorship agreement, the sponsor may institute market studies to ascertain whether such a relationship by the artist with a prior sponsor is still firmly entrenched in the minds of the public, irrespective of whether the past sponsorship is operative or not. Clearly, if the artist was closely associated with a particular product, it would be difficult for a competing sponsor to create a new artist/product association.

CONTROL OF CONCERTS

There exists the possibility of a conflict between the creative and production elements critical to the performance concerns of the tour and the promotional and sponsorship program, for which the sponsor would be paying a valuable consideration. Taking a realistic approach to such a conflict, and being aware that the tour is performance driven, the parties may acknowledge that in most situations the creative and production elements would take precedence over any promotional or other marketing activities of the sponsor so long as these decisions and actions could be considered to be reasonable, made in good faith, and instituted solely for the purpose of enhancing and protecting the opportunities for the audience to appreciate the artist's performance.

In furtherance of this provision, the sponsor would usually agree to comply with any and all reasonable instructions proposed by the artist during the course of the tour which address the enhancement of the performance and improve the quality of the show for the paying audience. While the artist would most likely demand sole and exclusive control over the guidelines that affect the concert performances, the sponsor typically requires a voice in the placement of its corporate presence, including banners, sponsorship products, and its positioning on the tour booklets.

Under most conditions, the artist would agree to exercise his or her best efforts in making whatever arrangements are necessary to facilitate the creative aspects of his or her live performance while fulfilling the spirit and the goals of the agreement with the sponsor.

SPONSOR'S PROMOTIONAL PLAN

The tour sponsorship agreement may stipulate that the sponsor prepare, and make available for the artist's approval, a promotional and marketing plan within a specific period of time in advance of the tour.

ADVANCE CONCERT INFORMATION

The tour sponsorship agreement may stipulate that the artist provide the sponsor, no later than an exact date agreeable to both parties, the following information:

- a full schedule of concert dates and locations for the tour,
- the names, addresses, and phone numbers of each local promoter for each concert,
- the hall capacity at each concert location and, upon request and when reasonably

possible, the status of ticket sales with respect to each concert in advance of the date of the concert, and

- the date tickets for any concert on the tour are scheduled to go on sale to the general public.

CONCERT ADVERTISING AND PROMOTIONAL BILLING REQUIREMENTS

The billing, or placement, of the sponsor's name and logo is certainly one of the most important elements of the contract in the eyes of the sponsor, since it customarily enters the tour sponsorship agreement with the goal of maximizing its name and trademarked brands by its association with the artist.

The agreement would usually stipulate that, subject to local restrictions, the artist would ensure that all of the concert tickets, posters, flyers, radio advertisements, television advertisements, and print advertisements prominently include the name of the sponsor, in a manner to be mutually agreed upon by both artist and sponsor.

Wording

The exact wording may be as follows: "SPONSOR PRESENTS ARTIST," or "A SPONSOR EVENT, PRESENTING ARTIST."

In most situations, the final wording and the positioning of the sponsor's logo are decided to the mutual satisfaction of the artist and the sponsor.

Sizing

In an effort to ensure satisfactory placement, the sponsor may demand that, when mentioned in conjunction with a local concert promoter, the sponsor's name be prominently billed. The sponsor may demand, as an example, that its name appear in size and type at least 50 percent larger that that of the local promoter. Typically, the artist's name would be placed more prominently than that of the sponsor, on all advertising, tickets, and promotions.

To ensure the satisfactory fulfillment of the billing requirements agreed upon in the tour sponsorship agreement, the artist may be required to include the billing requirements of the sponsor in all agreements entered into, by and between the artist and the various concert promoters promoting the tour.

CONCERT ADVERTISING SCHEDULE

The value earned by the sponsor typically extends beyond its name placement on banners and tour booklets. Local television, radio, and print advertising increases its association with the tour and the artist, to local audiences. It is therefore likely that the sponsor would insist on a guaranteed amount of broadcast and print advertising in each market. For example, the advertising ratio may be 2 or 3 to 1 (for every $1.00 the sponsor pays as a sponsor fee, the artist would guarantee to spend $2.00 or $3.00 in retail advertising, whether the expenditure is in direct dollar cost or by means of barter) or any other advertising ratio agreeable to both parties.

Copy of Completed Advertising Schedule

If the parties agree to a guaranteed advertising and promotion ratio, the artist could be required to provide to the sponsor, within an agreed time period prior to the commencement of the tour, a true and accurate copy of the advertising schedule, exactly as it was provided to the artist, along with whatever additional information is available to the artist with respect to the advertising agenda of the tour. The artist may also be required to present the identity of radio stations, television stations, and newspapers carrying advertisements in support of the concert tour, the number of commercial spots, the number of advertising newspaper prints, as well as a copy of the audio and/or video commercials produced and aired by the local media.

Number of Tickets Sold

In addition to the above, the artist would usually be obligated to provide to the sponsor the actual number of tickets sold per concert, as soon as that information becomes available.

Withholding Information

To withhold any of the information required by the sponsor may be deemed a material breach of this agreement, since failure to provide such information may serve to frustrate the sponsor's purposes and its ability to ascertain the success of the sponsorship. Consequently, the artist would typically ensure the performance of the requirements of this provision by causing the requirements of this provision to be included in the artist's agreement with the various concert promoters.

NO INTENT TO INTRUDE ON PRIVACY MATTERS

In an attempt to protect the privacy of the artist, the sponsor would usually acknowledge that it has no interest in discovering the amounts earned or expended by the artist or any person, firm, or company associated with the tour. As such, the artist may be entitled to withhold any information from the sponsor which he or she reasonably considers unnecessary to accomplish the goals and purposes of the sponsor or which would infringe on any of the privacy rights of the performers, concert promoters, or any other affiliated entity.

In requesting information on the artist's advertising and promotional strategies, the sponsor is generally solely interested in ascertaining the quantity and quality of the advertising and promotional activities in support of the tour so that it can evaluate the success, or failure, of its sponsorship program,

SPONSORSHIP ACTIVITIES

Although subject to negotiation considering the actual needs of both the sponsor and the artist, the sponsor may be entitled to specific commercial ventures, all of which should be agreed upon prior to signing the tour sponsorship agreement.

Sponsor/Media Tie-In

The sponsor would typically demand the right to identify itself as the sole sponsor of the tour and promote its association with the artist within the context of any and all local, regional, or national advertising campaigns.

Sweepstakes/Contest

The sponsor would often negotiate for the right to conduct, or cause to be conducted, a local sweepstakes or other form of promotional contest, which would serve to tie in with the artist's tour engagements. Those sweepstakes and contests often feature the artist as a principal in the advertising and promotional materials. In the event that such a sweepstakes or contest is effected, the artist may authorize the use by the sponsor of a selection of compositions from the artist's recent release and, in conjunction with the artist's recording label, may authorize promotional giveaways of the artist's recordings in addition to free concert tickets and after-concert backstage passes. As a rule, promotional items would be furnished to the sponsor free of charge or at cost. It should be clarified that ticket giveaways are ordinarily exclusive of any other ticket provisions of the tour sponsorship agreement.

The sponsor would usually be required to warrant that all local, regional, and/or national sweepstakes would comply with all applicable laws, local as well as state and federal. Furthermore, the artist would typically agree to use his or her best efforts to cause his or her record label and concert promoters to comply with the sweepstakes/contest provision by offering their recordings and tickets without charge or at cost.

Media Support

The sponsor would normally negotiate for the right to create and tag all on-air television and radio promotional and advertising spots with its exclusive sponsorship identification. In furtherance of that grant, the artist may be required to permit the sponsor royalty-free use of brief segments of recent album releases in all radio and television advertisements, unless the artist and his or her publishing and/or recording affiliate do not own the rights to the recordings and are, therefore, not in a position to make such an offer. In that case, the artist would generally be required to use his or her best efforts to obtain the royalty-free use of his or her recordings from the rightful owners of the requested compositions.

Furthermore, the artist may permit the sponsor royalty-free use of segments of video presentations (including the compositions contained within the video) of the artist's recent recording release for use in television commercial advertising and promotion unless the artist or his or her publishing and/or recording affiliate does not own such synchronization rights to the desired songs and its video rights. In that case, the artist may be obligated to use his or her best efforts to obtain the royalty-free use of the video recordings and compositions from their rightful owners.

Name and Likeness

Both the artist and the sponsor would usually agree and acknowledge that the sponsor would be granted the right to produce and present one or several television commercials advertising its products nationally, regionally, and/or locally utilizing the artist's name and likeness as well as the video performance featuring the artist. In addition, the artist may agree to supply his or her services, if required by the sponsor, to participate in a promotional advertisement for the purpose of announcing the sponsor's sponsorship of the tour, for use on cable or television or as promotional videos distributed directly to retailers and the sponsor's employees. Those promotional videos are usually not intended for commercial broadcast.

The artist may also be required, if specified in the agreement, to create promotional video advertisement spots for the purpose of promoting the sponsorship of his or her local concert performances on local broadcast and cable networks. Because this service could be deemed an endorsement of the sponsor's product, the artist may demand a substantial bonus payment in order to comply with the sponsor's demands. The sponsor would usually argue that the act of appearing in an in-house promotion or on a commercial advertising is not an endorsement but is, rather, part and parcel of the artist's obligation to the sponsor under the intent and spirit of the agreement. Therefore, the sponsor may claim that the artist should not be entitled to any additional payments for his or her participation is such promotion and advertising spots.

Radio Commercials

The artist would, in most cases, comply with the sponsor's request to provide his or her services to participate in the production of standard radio commercials.

ARTIST'S MUSIC VIDEO

Music videos have become a dominant form of promotion in the music industry, being a highly visible means of marketing the artist and any product utilized by the artist in the video. Aware of the enduring visual impact of the videos, the sponsor may negotiate the use of its product on the artist's music videos. If agreed, the artist would be asked to display, often subject to the approval of his or her record company, the sponsor's product in a manner mutually agreeable to the artist, the artistic director of the music video, and the sponsor.

Additional Video Footage

In the event the sponsor requests the taping of additional video footage in an effort to accommodate its marketing plans and promotional requirements, such as the sponsor's intent to utilize the music videos as television commercials, in-store displays, or interoffice promotions, the costs for the creation of such additional taped footage would, as a rule, be the sole responsibility of the sponsor. The artist, though, would usually be required to ensure that all directors, producers, members of the crew, and support staff work collectively with the sponsor's representatives and advertising agencies to create such additional footage.

Joint Production of Videos

Under circumstances in which the artist and sponsor agree, from the outset, to create music videos that realize their mutual requirements, the artist may arrange for the sponsor's creative personnel to be involved in the planning of the video from the earliest stages of preproduction. Such joint efforts tend to maximize the potential of accomplishing the goals put forward by the sponsor while satisfying the creative needs of the artist.

The artist would usually grant to the sponsor, and use his or her best efforts to ensure that his or her record company grants similar permission, the unlimited right to utilize approved portions of the mutually conceived music video in any manner deemed desirable by the sponsor, royalty-free and without claim of any sort, for television commercials, in-store displays, interoffice promotions, or in any other manner agreed to by both parties.

Inability to Air Music Video

While it may be the artist's intention to utilize the sponsor's product in his or her music video, in the event such usage could result in the video presentation being barred from airing on any commercial, cable, or other broadcast service for any reason whatsoever, the artist would usually demand the right not to utilize the sponsor's product under such prohibitive circumstances.

ARTIST'S PRESS CONFERENCE

Since a major purpose of sponsoring the artist's tour is the positive benefit gained by such a collaboration, the sponsor would most likely desire its sponsorship and association with the artist to generate as much publicity as possible.

To further that objective, the sponsor would ordinarily demand that the artist appear and participate in one or several press conferences for the purpose of announcing and publicizing the upcoming tour. Typically, the press conference would be held prior to the commencement of the tour, at a time and location satisfactory to both parties. The sponsor would usually insist that the press conferences occur at such time and place as to allow it reasonable time to utilize the results in its marketing, promotion, and sponsorship programs. Generally, the sponsor would bear the costs of all special travel, lodging, and per diem requirements of the press conference.

ARTIST'S PHOTO SESSION

To accommodate the specifications of the print medium, the artist would typically guarantee to make himself or herself available for photo sessions. The artist and sponsor would usually agree on the number of photo sessions required as well as on the placement of the sponsor's name, logo, and product within the photograph.

The artist would probably demand creative approval on the final photo prints, usually agreeing to use reasonable judgment as the basis for approval. The sponsor may agree to the artist's request if the artist's strength within the musical industry and among the musical fans warrants such creative control.

Timing of the Photo Session

While the time and place for the photo sessions would usually be mutually determined by the sponsor and the artist, the timing would probably be geared to allow the sponsor ample opportunity to exploit the material for use in its marketing and promotion activities, specifically relating to the tour. Typically, the artist would insist that the sponsor be responsible for paying all expenses, including any special travel, lodging, and per diem expenses, relating to the photo sessions.

USE OF SPONSOR'S PRODUCTS

Intending to be associated, on a daily basis, with the artist, the sponsor would probably demand that the artist use his or her best efforts to employ the sponsor's products, when reasonable and possible, in the following situations:

- while performing in each concert of the tour,
- while performing the music video being created by and for the artist's record company in support of the artist's album,
- while participating in all press conferences, and
- while attending all photo sessions.

Moreover, in an effort to further enhance the sponsor's association with the tour and the artist, the artist may be requested to instruct and cause its road crew to utilize the sponsor's products, and to dress in T-shirts, sweatshirts, and jackets bearing the names of the sponsor and the artist. The cost of providing the required attire would usually be borne completely by the sponsor.

SPONSOR'S MERCHANDISE

The artist would typically agree to the placement of the sponsor's name and logo on agreed tour merchandise, such as T-shirts, sweatshirts, posters, and tour program books. If agreed, the sponsor's name and logo would be displayed prominently on all products, yet would not overshadow the name, image, and logo of the artist.

In addition, should the tour include a souvenir book, the sponsor would most probably negotiate for the right to advertise and promote its name, logo, and branded product on one or several of its pages, at no charge. All advertising costs, including photography, printing, layout and text, the sponsor may argue, should be provided by the artist.

Manufacture of Special Items

During the term of this agreement, the sponsor would probably demand the right to manufacture, or cause to be manufactured, whatever sponsor-related tour merchandise would be required by the sponsor, for the duration of the tour. As such, the sponsor should negotiate for the right, subject to the creative approval of the artist, to create special items which have been agreed upon by both the artist and the sponsor, and may include banners, T-shirts, sweatshirts, and specialty items.

If the artist granted rights to sell licensed products to a tour merchandiser other than the sponsor, the tour sponsorship agreement may stipulate and mandate that the sponsor not offer for sale these promotional items. The purpose of the sponsor's manufactured tour goods would be in that case to make the public aware of its association with the artist rather than to sell merchandise.

SIGNAGE

Often, the decision to allow the placement of flags, banners, placards, and other signs promoting the name, logo, and branded trademarked products of the sponsor would be outside the realm of the negotiating parties. Typically, the venue has established policies regarding what may or may not be displayed, especially if the concert hall has preexisting contracts with other advertisers. In addition, all local police and fire codes must be respected.

Therefore, the artist would usually guarantee that, subject to local commitments and restrictions at each concert location, the signage containing the sponsor's name and logo would be prominently displayed at each concert. The actual location of the signs, within the confines of each concert hall, should be mutually agreed upon in advance, considering the needs of the sponsor and the commitments of the local venue. In addition, the artist and the sponsor would generally agree to use their respective best efforts to place the specific signs onstage in a manner that the displayed signage would not interfere with the aesthetics of the artist's performance, with the stage speakers, lighting effects, and the artist's decor, nor would, in any way, interfere with the sight lines of the audience.

In order to ensure that there would be adequate promotional space for the sponsor under any circumstances, the parties may stipulate that a banner, of mutually agreeable size, design, and wording, be placed at tour merchandise concession stands or at similar locations where the sponsor's signage would receive maximum attention from concert attendees.

CONCERT TICKETS

The availability of a limited number of free tickets for promotion as well as for the use of the sponsor's corporate needs is usually an established policy in all sponsorship agreements. The artist and the sponsor would usually comply with the following conditions:

- the availability to the sponsor of an agreed number of prime location tickets in addition to a selection of general location tickets,
- the availability of a limited number of additional tickets upon request and upon the submission of a valid justification,
- the furnishing of a limited number of additional tickets to be made available for promotional and advertising campaigns, and
- permission for ticket holders, guests of the sponsor, to attend backstage events.

The artist would usually agree to use his or her best efforts to ensure that the sponsor receives all its tickets a reasonable number of weeks prior to each concert date. The sponsor may negotiate for the option to purchase an additional number of tickets for each concert of the tour, at wholesale or market prices.

BACKSTAGE HOSPITALITY

Intending to generate corporate excitement, the sponsor may request that the artist make himself or herself available in certain key markets to attending after-performance parties and to make the backstage available to the sponsor's guests prior to and after the performance. Typically, the sponsor would insist that the artist greet the sponsor's guests, sign autographs, and pose for pictures.

The artist would usually agree to attend such promotional events, providing they are limited to certain key locations and venues. The tour sponsorship agreement should detail those key cities. As a security precaution, the sponsor would usually provide the artist's management a list of persons attending the backstage party or hospitality suite.

RECORD COMPANY ACTIVITIES

The artist generally plans his or her tour around a release date for a new recording. He or she may include in the scheduled concerts many songs contained on the new releases. It is therefore important for the artist, sponsor, and record company to work together to best promote their special interests in harmony with the interests of the others.

To further the needs of the sponsor in this regard, the artist would usually guarantee to use his or her best efforts to cause the artist's record company to agree to, and perhaps even to provide, the following:

- point-of-sale merchandising materials to be utilized at retail outlets at which the sponsor's products are sold, if applicable. Those materials may include audiotapes, compact disks, graphic materials, music videos, and singles.
- coordination with the sponsor in regard to providing promotional activities, items, and distributor/dealer support in connection with the tour. Those support items and activities may include in-store posters, point-of-sale items, product giveaways, and promotional contests.
- a reasonable number of the artist's prerecorded CDs and tapes when the recordings may be required by the sponsor for promotional purposes and product giveaways. Such prerecorded materials may be supplied to the sponsor at no cost or at wholesale cost. In most cases, the sponsor would be responsible for all costs of shipping and taxes.
- The record company's best effort to identify the sponsor, as the sponsor of the tour, on all posters, advertising, point-of-sale activities, and promotional activities in language and wording substantially similar to "SPONSOR PRESENTS ARTIST." In consideration of this action, the record company may demand that the sponsor use its best efforts to merchandise the album graphics, the artist's recording catalogue, and the record company identification in all the sponsor's promotional activity in a manner deemed desirable to both the record company and the sponsor.
- a reasonable quantity of approved artwork, photographs, and album graphics required by the sponsor to manufacture promotional materials required in accordance with the terms of this contract.
- cooperation in regard to the creation and production of the artist's music videos in which the sponsor's presence will be included. The record company may also grant, license, and make any appropriate arrangements required to permit the sponsor to exploit

the video for advertising, in-store merchandising, and sponsorship purposes at no charge to the sponsor.

- the license and permission, at no cost to the sponsor, to utilize the prerecorded music of the artist for the purpose of television and radio commercials as well as in-store merchandising videos, utilizing the name, likeness, and performance of the artist and the tour dates and venues.

THE AGENT

As the sponsorship of performance tours becomes more prevalent and costly, agencies specializing in the sponsorship market have been established to satisfy the needs and requirements of both the sponsor and the artist.

Typically, the agent would introduce the sponsor to the artist, assist in negotiating the sponsorship fees and, in general, be the liaison between the sponsor and the artist, the artist's record company, the promoters, the venue managers, and any other person, firm, or corporation whose cooperation is essential to the success of the sponsorship program. For his or her services, the agent would usually be entitled to receive, as his or her compensation, a percentage of the sponsorship fee negotiated. The parties may agree that all information required under the terms of the tour sponsorship agreement be made available to the agent for review and for his or her records.

SPONSOR'S REPRESENTATIVE

The sponsor may be granted the right to appoint a representative to accompany the artist throughout the tour. The representative's basic function would be to ensure that the interests of the sponsor are considered. Consequently, the artist, by accepting the sponsor's representative, would usually agree to accord the representative the necessary cooperation needed to accomplish his or her assignment. The representative, then, would usually travel with the artist, would be present at all meetings with, among others, the promoters, marketing personnel, advertising personnel, and tour venue coordinators, and would be treated as a full-time member of the artist's touring entourage. The tour sponsorship agreement would usually provide that the sponsor would be solely responsible for the salary, expenses, and touring costs of its representative, and would reimburse the artist promptly in the event the artist incurs an expense on behalf of the representative.

CONSIDERATION

The artist is, understandably, interested in the consideration earned in exchange for the service rendered. In most circumstances, the sponsor would agree to pay to the artist an agreed flat fee as full and complete payment for all the rights granted in the tour sponsorship agreement. The parties may agree that the fee would be paid over a period of time and according to a particular schedule. The schedule may be as follows:

- the first payment would be made by the sponsor to the artist upon execution of this agreement,
- the second payment would be made by the sponsor to the artist upon the commencement of the tour, and
- the third and final payment would be made by the sponsor within an agreed number of days following the complete performance of all the provisions and conditions undertaken by the artist as fashioned in the tour sponsorship agreement.

BREACH AND MORALS

A large part of the sponsor's desire to be associated with the artist is built on two factors: association with the artist and accessibility to the sponsor's customer base. An embarrassing episode by the artist may damage the sponsor's image in the marketplace. It is therefore likely that the sponsor would demand the right to sever the contractual relationship with the artist without incurring any liability, upon the occurrence of certain unacceptable and unreasonable events.

Most sponsors would require that the artist act and perform in a moral and suitable manner when off, as well as on, the stage. The provision may stipulate that if the artist is charged with the commission of any act which is considered offensive and involves moral turpitude under federal, state, or local laws, or should the artist commit any act which would reasonably and objectively bring the sponsor or its products into disrepute, contempt, scandal, or ridicule, at any time during the tour, or if the artist failed to perform his or her duties and liabilities required for reason of depravity or illegality, then the sponsor may be entitled to the following actions:

- to terminate this agreement after giving the artist a reasonable number of days' notice within which to cure the alleged such offense, act, or failure to perform. If the artist fails to cure the breach or offense within the time period, then the sponsor would be deemed to be no longer responsible for any fees or payments due under this agreement.
- the receipt of a refund of a pro rata portion of the sponsorship fee.

CANCELLATION OF THE TOUR

If the artist misses a specific number of performances, the sponsor would argue that it be entitled to terminate the tour sponsorship agreement immediately, without liability and without any further responsibility for the payment of any fees or payments required under this contract. If sponsorship fees were already advanced, then a pro rata refund may be negotiated.

POWER TO GRANT RIGHTS

Each party to the tour sponsorship agreement would usually represent and warrant that it has the power and authority to enter, to grant the rights, and to perform the duties and obligations described in the agreement.

NO ENCUMBRANCE

Furthermore, both parties would typically warrant that they will not take any action which might prevent the exercise of, or which may encumber, the rights granted.

PERMITS AND LICENSES

The artist, by entering the tour sponsorship agreement, would usually acknowledge and agree that he or she would be fully responsible for, and acquire, or cause local concert promoters to acquire at their sole cost and expense, all licenses, permits, authorizations, and insurance which may be required under federal, state, or local law or regulations in order to legally conduct each concert of the tour and the activities contemplated under this agreement, including but not limited to licenses from performing rights organizations and any payments or royalties required to be made.

The sponsor would typically agree to be responsible for any royalties due and owing any performing rights organization as a result of the sponsor's television and radio commercials and in-store presentations if any would be required by a performing rights, or other, agency or society.

INDEMNITY

In all likelihood, the sponsor would require that the artist agree to indemnify, defend, and hold the sponsor, its officers, directors, agents, representatives, shareholders, and employees harmless from and against any and all claims, suits, expenses, damages, or other liabilities, including reasonable attorney's fees and court costs, arising out of the breach by the artist of any of the representations or warranties made by the artist in this agreement and any personal injury or property damages arising out of or in connection with an individual's attendance at a concert featuring the performance of the artist.

INSURANCE

The sponsor would probably insist that the artist obtain liability insurance and name the sponsor as a secondary insured party. If the artist does procure the insurance, he or she would usually agree to maintain, at his or her sole expense, commencing at an agreed date prior to the commencement of the tour, general and public liability insurance naming the sponsor as an additional insured party from a qualified insurance carrier acceptable to the sponsor in an agreed amount, for personal injury and property damage. The sponsor would usually require that the insurance policy run for the duration of the term of the tour sponsorship agreement, and that it be given immediate notice of any intention by the insurance company, the artist, or the venue to cancel such insurance policy. Prior to the commencement of the tour, the artist would usually be required to provide the sponsor with a copy of the insurance policy.

NOTICES

Notices by either party to the other are usually sent by registered or certified mail, return receipt requested, or by an independent mailing service with a verifiable proof of mailing (such as Federal Express or UPS). All statements and notices under this agreement should be given as follows:

SPONSOR
Address: ______________________

ARTIST
Address: ______________________

FUTURE OPPORTUNITIES

Because of the time and effort used in cementing this relationship, the sponsor may negotiate for the opportunity to extend this relationship beyond the particular tour. The sponsor may be granted a first right of refusal to become either the primary or sole sponsor for any radio, network television, free or pay television, or pay-per-view special production featuring the performance of the artist when such production is created, developed, produced, piloted, and aired during the tour. Usually, the sponsor would be accorded an agreed period of time from written receipt of all relevant details and financial information regarding the special production in which to enter into good faith negotiations to accomplish such a sponsorship.

STATE OF JURISDICTION

The parties must agree on which state will have final jurisdiction in the event of a dispute or litigation among the parties. Typically, the party with the stronger bargaining power selects as the governing state the one where it has established its corporate presence and residence. Both parties would usually acknowledge that the courts of the agreed state would have final and authoritative jurisdiction over any and all claims, controversies, disputes, and disagreements arising out of this agreement.

FORCE MAJEURE

Neither party would customarily be liable for any failure of, or delay in, the performance of their respective obligations under this agreement to the extent such failure or delay is due to circumstances beyond its reasonable control, including without limitation, acts of God, or acts of a public enemy, fires, floods, wars, civil disturbances, sabotage, accidents, insurrections, blockades, embargoes, storms, explosions, labor disputes, and/or acts of any governmental body. Both parties would usually be obliged to use their best efforts to minimize the duration and consequences of any failure of, or delay in, performance resulting from the *force majeure*.

ENTIRE AGREEMENT

The artist and the sponsor would typically acknowledge that the tour sponsorship agreement, as written, represents their complete agreement and understanding. All prior or contemporaneous agreements of the parties, whether oral or written, would typically be deemed merged into the present agreement. The parties would usually also recognize that the agreement is not to be modified, changed, or amended except by an instrument in writing, duly executed by both parties.

FAILURE TO ENFORCE ANY RIGHTS

The failure of either party to enforce any of its rights under this agreement would generally not be considered a continuing waiver. Therefore, that party would be granted the prerogative, within an agreed time period, to enforce any and all of its rights.

SIGNATURES

The parties, by signing the agreement, usually agree to bind themselves, their successors, and their representatives to the provisions agreed upon in the agreement.

21

COPYRIGHT

The ownership of a musical composition is usually held in the hands of its copyright owner. The most common application forms filed by musical artists, writers, and composers are form PA, Performing Arts, and form SR, Sound Recording (see appendixes A through E for sample forms).

FORM PA

As described under the Copyright Act of the United States, form PA is typically used in the copyright registration of published or unpublished performing arts compositions which ''are prepared for the purpose of being performed directly in front of an audience or indirectly by means of any device or process.'' The compositions which require the filing of form PA include musical compositions as well as the accompanying lyrics, dramatic works, and any accompanying music, choreographic works, and motion pictures and audiovisual works.

FORM SR

Form SR, as detailed in the Copyright Law, should be filed in the registration of a sound recording. A ''sound recording'' is defined in the the Copyright Act as the ''fusion of a series of sounds'' which are separate and distinct from the underlying musical or dramatic work. Form SR is used when the copyright claim is limited to the sound recording.

Along with the completed forms, the applicant should submit to the Register of Copyrights at the Copyright Office copies or phonorecords of the musical composition work to be copyrighted. The copies are defined by the copyright registration form as sheet music or other ''objects from which a work can be read or visually perceived directly or with the aid of a machine or device, such as manuscripts, books, sheet music, film or video tape.'' Phonorecords are defined as ''objects embodying fixations of sound, such as tapes and phonograph disks, commonly known as phonograph records.''

The Copyright Law provides that each copy of each published musical composition must contain a copyright notice that follows the required format. The copyright notice must include the following: the copyright symbol (c), or the word ''copyright,'' or the abbreviation ''copr.''; the year the copyrighted work was first published; and the name of the copyright owner, as follows: (c) 19—, ABCD Inc. Phonorecords carry a (p) notice, followed by the year the copyrighted work was first published and the name of the copyright owner, as follows: (p) 19__, ABCD Inc.

Copyright owners typically add the words ''All Right Reserved'' as part of the copyright notice included on all material to secure additional copyright protections in those countries abiding by the various international treaties, including the Buenos Aires Convention.

APPENDIXES

Appendix A

Circular 56a

Copyright Registration of Musical Compositions and Sound Recordings

This circular explains the difference, for copyright purposes, between **MUSICAL COMPOSITIONS** and **SOUND RECORDINGS**.

A **Musical Composition** consists of music, including any accompanying words, and is normally registered in Class PA. The author of a musical composition is generally the composer, and the lyricist, if any. A musical composition may be in the form of a notated copy (for example, sheet music) **or** in the form of a phonorecord (for example, cassette tape, LP, or CD). Sending a musical composition in the form of a phonorecord does **not** necessarily mean that there is a claim to copyright in the sound recording. See examples 1 and 2 on the chart.

A **Sound Recording** results from the fixation of a series of musical, spoken, or other sounds, and is always registered in Class SR. The author of a sound recording is the performer(s) whose performance is fixed, or the record producer who processes the sounds and fixes them in the final recording, or both.

USE THE CHART TO HELP CHOOSE THE APPROPRIATE FORM FOR COPYRIGHT REGISTRATION

How the work was created; what is being registered:	Form to use:	How to describe the authorship in space 2, "Nature of Authorship":*	What should be deposited:	
			Published in the United States**	Unpublished
1. Composer/author creates a song, wishes to claim copyright in the song	PA	Music and Words	2 complete copies of the "best edition" if published in a notated copy: 1 phonorecord of the "best edition" if published only on a phonorecord (disk, tape, cassette,etc.)	1 complete copy (lead sheet, etc.) or phonorecord (disk, tape, cassette, etc.)

Copyright in a sound recording is not the same as, or a substitute for, copyright in the underlying musical composition. See example 3 on the chart.

REGISTRATION OF A MUSICAL COMPOSITION AND A SOUND RECORDING WITH A SINGLE APPLICATION

Although they are separate works, a musical composition and a sound recording may be registered together on a single application providing ownership of the copyrights in both is exactly the same. See example 4 on the chart. To register a single claim in both works, complete Form SR; give information about the author(s) of both the musical composition and the sound recording.

> **NOTE: Phonorecords (tapes, cassette tapes, cartridges, disks) are not sound recordings.**
>
> **Phonorecords are physical objects in which various kinds of works can be fixed—the works themselves may be musical compositions, literary works, dramatic works, or sound recordings. Before registering a claim to copyright, you must analyze your work to determine which classification of work it is.**

2. Composer/author creates musical composition, wishes to claim copyright in the musical composition	PA	Music	2 complete copies of the "best edition" if published in a notated copy; 1 phonorecord of the "best edition" if published only on a phonorecord (disk, tape, cassette, etc.)	1 complete copy (lead sheet, etc.) or phonorecord (usually disk, tape, cassette, etc.)
3. Performer(s) (for example, vocalist and band) perform and record musical work; wish to claim copyright in the recorded performance only	SR	Performance and Sound Recording	2 complete phonorecords of "best edition"	1 complete phonorecord
4. Composer/author/performer creates music and performs it, recording the performance; wishes to claim copyright both in the music and the recording	SR	Music and Performance OR Music, Words, Performance	2 complete phonorecords of "best edition"	1 complete phonorecord

NOTE: To make a single registration, copyright ownership in the recorded work and in the sound recording must be the same.

* DO NOT LEAVE SPACE 2 BLANK. DO NOT USE "entire work" to describe "Nature of Authorship."

**For foreign publications, 1 copy or phonorecord of the first published edition.

Filling Out Application Form SR

Detach and read these instructions before completing this form. Make sure all applicable spaces have been filled in before you return this form.

BASIC INFORMATION

When to Use This Form: Use Form SR for copyright registration of published or unpublished sound recordings. It should be used where the copyright claim is limited to the sound recording itself, and it may also be used where the same copyright claimant is seeking simultaneous registration of the underlying musical, dramatic, or literary work embodied in the phonorecord.

With one exception, "sound recordings" are works that result from the fixation of a series of musical, spoken, or other sounds. The exception is for the audio portions of audiovisual works, such as a motion picture soundtrack or an audio cassette accompanying a filmstrip; these are considered a part of the audiovisual work as a whole.

Deposit to Accompany Application: An application for copyright registration of a sound recording must be accompanied by a deposit consisting of phonorecords representing the entire work for which registration is to be made.

Unpublished Work: Deposit one complete phonorecord.

Published Work: Deposit two complete phonorecords of the best edition, together with "any printed or other visually perceptible material" published with the phonorecords.

Work First Published Outside the United States: Deposit one complete phonorecord of the first foreign edition.

Contribution to a Collective Work: Deposit one complete phonorecord of the best edition of the collective work.

The Copyright Notice: For sound recordings first published on or after March 1, 1989, the law provides that a copyright notice in a specified form "may be placed on all publicly distributed phonorecords of the sound recording." Use of the copyright notice is the responsibility of the copyright owner and does not require advance permission from the Copyright Office. The required form of the notice for phonorecords of sound recordings consists of three elements: (1) the symbol "℗" (the Letter "P" in a circle); (2) the year of first publication of the sound recording; and (3) the name of the owner of copyright. For example: "℗ 1989 XYZ Record Co." The notice is to be "placed on the surface of the phonorecord, or on the label or container, in such manner and location as to give reasonable notice of the claim of copyright." Works first published prior to March 1, 1989, **must** carry the notice or risk loss of copyright protection.

For information about notice requirements for works published before March 1, 1989, or other copyright information, write: Information Section, LM-401, Copyright Office, Library of Congress, Washington, D.C. 20559.

PRIVACY ACT ADVISORY STATEMENT Required by the Privacy Act of 1974 (P.L. 93-579)
The authority for requesting this information is title 17, U.S.C., secs. 409 and 410. Furnishing the requested information is voluntary. But if the information is not furnished, it may be necessary to delay or refuse registration and you may not be entitled to certain relief, remedies, and benefits provided in chapters 4 and 5 of title 17, U.S.C.

The principal uses of the requested information are the establishment and maintenance of a public record and the examination of the application for compliance with legal requirements.

Other routine uses include public inspection and copying, preparation of public indexes, preparation of public catalogs of copyright registrations, and preparation of search reports upon request.

NOTE: No other advisory statement will be given in connection with this application. Please keep this statement and refer to it if we communicate with you regarding this application.

LINE-BY-LINE INSTRUCTIONS

1 SPACE 1: Title

Title of This Work: Every work submitted for copyright registration must be given a title to identify that particular work. If the phonorecords or any accompanying printed material bear a title (or an identifying phrase that could serve as a title), transcribe that wording completely and exactly on the application. Indexing of the registration and future identification of the work may depend on the information you give here.

Nature of Material Recorded: Indicate the general type or character of the works or other material embodied in the recording. The box marked "Literary" should be checked for nondramatic spoken material of all sorts, including narration, interviews, panel discussions, and training material. If the material recorded is not musical, dramatic, or literary in nature, check "Other" and briefly describe the type of sounds fixed in the recording. For example: "Sound Effects"; "Bird Calls"; "Crowd Noises."

Previous or Alternative Titles: Complete this space if there are any additional titles for the work under which someone searching for the registration might be likely to look, or under which a document pertaining to the work might be recorded.

2 SPACE 2: Author(s)

General Instructions: After reading these instructions, decide who are the "authors" of this work for copyright purposes. Then, unless the work is a "collective work," give the requested information about every "author" who contributed any appreciable amount of copyrightable matter to this version of the work. If you need further space, request additional Continuation Sheets. In the case of a collective work, such as a collection of previously published or registered sound recordings, give information about the author of the collective work as a whole. If you are submitting this Form SR to cover the recorded musical, dramatic, or literary work as well as the sound recording itself, it is important for space 2 to include full information about the various authors of all of the material covered by the copyright claim, making clear the nature of each author's contribution.

Name of Author: The fullest form of the author's name should be given. Unless the work was "made for hire," the individual who actually created the work is its "author." In the case of a work made for hire, the statute provides that "the employer or other person for whom the work was prepared is considered the author."

What is a "Work Made for Hire"? A "work made for hire" is defined as: (1) "a work prepared by an employee within the scope of his or her employment"; or (2) "a work specially ordered or commissioned for use as a contribution to a collective work, as a part of a motion picture or other audiovisual work, as a translation, as a supplementary work, as a compilation, as an instructional text, as a test, as answer material for a test, or as an atlas, if the parties expressly agree in a written instrument signed by them that the work shall be considered a work made for hire." If you have checked "Yes" to indicate that the work was "made for hire," you must give the full legal name of the employer (or other person for whom the work was prepared). You may also include the name of the employee along with the name of the employer (for example: "Elster Record Co., employer for hire of John Ferguson").

"Anonymous" or "Pseudonymous" Work: An author's contribution to a work is "anonymous" if that author is not identified on the copies or phonorecords of the work. An author's contribution to a work is "pseudonymous" if that author is identified on the copies or phonorecords under a fictitious name. If the work is "anonymous" you may: (1) leave the line blank; or (2) state "anonymous" on the line; or (3) reveal the author's identity. If the work is "pseudonymous" you may: (1) leave the line blank; or (2) give the pseudonym and identify it as such (for example: "Huntley Haverstock, pseudonym"); or (3) reveal the author's name, making clear which is the real name and which is the pseudonym (for example: "Judith Barton, whose pseudonym is Madeline Elster"). However, the citizenship or domicile of the author **must** be given in all cases.

Dates of Birth and Death: If the author is dead, the statute requires that the year of death be included in the application unless the work is anonymous or pseudonymous. The author's birth date is optional, but is useful as a form of identification. Leave this space blank if the author's contribution was a "work made for hire."

Author's Nationality or Domicile: Give the country of which the author is a citizen, or the country in which the author is domiciled. Nationality or domicile **must** be given in all cases.

Nature of Authorship: Give a brief general statement of the nature of this particular author's contribution to the work. If you are submitting this Form SR to cover both the sound recording and the underlying musical, dramatic, or literary work, make sure that the precise nature of each author's contribution is reflected here. Examples where the authorship pertains to the recording: "Sound Recording"; "Performance and Recording"; "Compilation and Remixing of Sounds." Examples where the authorship pertains to both the recording and the underlying work: "Words, Music, Performance, Recording"; "Arrangement of Music and Recording"; "Compilation of Poems and Reading."

3 SPACE 3: Creation and Publication

General Instructions: Do not confuse "creation" with "publication." Every application for copyright registration must state "the year in which creation of the work was completed." Give the date and nation of first publication only if the work has been published.

Creation: Under the statute, a work is "created" when it is fixed in a copy or phonorecord for the first time. Where a work has been prepared over a period of time, the part of the work existing in fixed form on a particular date constitutes the created work on that date. The date you give here should be the year in which the author completed the particular version for which registration is now being sought, even if other versions exist or if further changes or additions are planned.

Publication: The statute defines "publication" as "the distribution of copies or phonorecords of a work to the public by sale or other transfer of ownership, or by rental, lease, or lending"; a work is also "published" if there has been an "offering to distribute copies or phonorecords to a group of persons for purposes of further distribution, public performance, or public display." Give the full date (month, day, year) when, and the country where, publication first occurred. If first publication took place simultaneously in the United States and other countries, it is sufficient to state "U.S.A."

4 SPACE 4: Claimant(s)

Name(s) and Address(es) of Copyright Claimant(s): Give the name(s) and address(es) of the copyright claimant(s) in this work even if the claimant is the same as the author. Copyright in a work belongs initially to the author of the work (including, in the case of a work made for hire, the employer or other person for whom the work was prepared). The copyright claimant is either the author of the work or a person or organization to whom the copyright initially belonging to the author has been transferred.

Transfer: The statute provides that, if the copyright claimant is not the author, the application for registration must contain "a brief statement of how the claimant obtained ownership of the copyright." If any copyright claimant named in space 4 is not an author named in space 2, give a brief, general statement summarizing the means by which that claimant obtained ownership of the copyright. Examples: "By written contract"; "Transfer of all rights by author"; "Assignment"; "By will." Do not attach transfer documents or other attachments or riders.

Changed Version: If the work has been changed, and you are now seeking registration to cover the additions or revisions, check the last box in space 5, give the earlier registration number and date, and complete both parts of space 6 in accordance with the instructions below.

Previous Registration Number and Date: If more than one previous registration has been made for the work, give the number and date of the latest registration.

6 SPACE 6: Derivative Work or Compilation

General Instructions: Complete space 6 if this work is a "changed version," "compilation," or "derivative work," and if it incorporates one or more earlier works that have already been published or registered for copyright, or that have fallen into the public domain, or sound recordings that were fixed before February 15, 1972. A "compilation" is defined as "a work formed by the collection and assembling of preexisting materials or of data that are selected, coordinated, or arranged in such a way that the resulting work as a whole constitutes an original work of authorship." A "derivative work" is "a work based on one or more preexisting works." Examples of derivative works include recordings reissued with substantial editorial revisions or abridgments of the recorded sounds, and recordings republished with new recorded material, or "any other form in which a work may be recast, transformed, or adapted." Derivative works also include works "consisting of editorial revisions, annotations, or other modifications" if these changes, as a whole, represent an original work of authorship.

Preexisting Material (space 6a): Complete this space **and** space 6b for derivative works. In this space identify the preexisting work that has been recast, transformed, or adapted. For example, the preexisting material might be: "1970 recording by Sperryville Symphony of Bach Double Concerto." Do not complete this space for compilations.

Material Added to This Work (space 6b): Give a brief, general statement of the **additional** new material covered by the copyright claim for which registration is sought. In the case of a derivative work, identify this new material. Examples: "Recorded performances on bands 1 and 3"; "Remixed sounds from original multitrack sound sources"; "New words, arrangement, and additional sounds." If the work is a compilation, give a brief, general statement describing both the material that has been compiled **and** the compilation itself. Example: "Compilation of 1938 Recordings by various swing bands."

5 SPACE 5: Previous Registration

General Instructions: The questions in space 5 are intended to find out whether an earlier registration has been made for this work and, if so, whether there is any basis for a new registration. As a rule, only one basic copyright registration can be made for the same version of a particular work.

Same Version: If this version is substantially the same as the work covered by a previous registration, a second registration is not generally possible unless: (1) the work has been registered in unpublished form and a second registration is now being sought to cover this first published edition; or (2) someone other than the author is identified as copyright claimant in the earlier registration, and the author is now seeking registration in his or her own name. If either of these two exceptions apply, check the appropriate box and give the earlier registration number and date. Otherwise, do not submit Form SR; instead, write the Copyright Office for information about supplementary registration or recordation of transfers of copyright ownership.

7,8,9 SPACE 7, 8, 9: Fee, Correspondence, Certification, Return Address

Deposit Account: If you maintain a Deposit Account in the Copyright Office, identify it in space 7. Otherwise leave the space blank and send the fee of $10 with your application and deposit.

Correspondence (space 7): This space should contain the name, address, area code, and telephone number of the person to be consulted if correspondence about this application becomes necessary.

Certification (space 8): The application cannot be accepted unless it bears the date and the **handwritten signature** of the author or other copyright claimant, or of the owner of exclusive right(s), or of the duly authorized agent of the author, claimant, or owner of exclusive right(s).

Address for Return of Certificate (space 9): The address box must be completed legibly since the certificate will be returned in a window envelope.

MORE INFORMATION

"Works": "Works" are the basic subject matter of copyright; they are what authors create and copyright protects. The statute draws a sharp distinction between the "work" and "any material object in which the work is embodied."

"Copies" and "Phonorecords": These are the two types of material objects in which "works" are embodied. In general, **"copies"** are objects from which a work can be read or visually perceived, directly or with the aid of a machine or device, such as manuscripts, books, sheet music, film, and videotape. **"Phonorecords"** are objects embodying fixations of sounds, such as audio tapes and phonograph disks. For example, a song (the "work") can be reproduced in sheet music ("copies") or phonograph disks ("phonorecords"), or both.

"Sound Recordings": These are "works," not "copies" or "phonorecords." "Sound recordings" are "works that result from the fixation of a series of musical, spoken, or other sounds, but not including the sounds accompanying a motion picture or other audiovisual work." Example: When a record company issues a new release, the release will typically involve two distinct "works": the "musical work" that has been recorded, and the "sound recording" as a separate work in itself. The material objects that the record company sends out are "phonorecords": physical reproductions of both the "musical work" and the "sound recording."

Should You File More Than One Application?

If your work consists of a recorded musical, dramatic, or literary work, and both that "work," and the sound recording as a separate "work," are eligible for registration, the application form you should file depends on the following:

File Only Form SR if: The copyright claimant is the same for both the musical, dramatic, or literary work and for the sound recording, and you are seeking a single registration to cover both of these "works."

File Only Form PA (or Form TX) if: You are seeking to register only the musical, dramatic, or literary work, not the sound recording. Form PA is appropriate for works of the performing arts; Form TX is for nondramatic literary works.

Separate Applications Should Be Filed on Form PA (or Form TX) and on Form SR if: (1) The copyright claimant for the musical, dramatic, or literary work is different from the copyright claimant for the sound recording; or (2) You prefer to have separate registrations for the musical, dramatic, or literary work and for the sound recording.

FORM SR
UNITED STATES COPYRIGHT OFFICE

REGISTRATION NUMBER

SR SRU

EFFECTIVE DATE OF REGISTRATION

Month Day Year

DO NOT WRITE ABOVE THIS LINE. IF YOU NEED MORE SPACE, USE A SEPARATE CONTINUATION SHEET.

1

TITLE OF THIS WORK ▼

PREVIOUS OR ALTERNATIVE TITLES ▼

NATURE OF MATERIAL RECORDED ▼ See instructions

☐ Musical ☐ Musical-Dramatic
☐ Dramatic ☐ Literary
☐ Other ________

2 a

NAME OF AUTHOR ▼

DATES OF BIRTH AND DEATH
Year Born ▼ Year Died ▼

Was this contribution to the work a "work made for hire"?
☐ Yes
☐ No

AUTHOR'S NATIONALITY OR DOMICILE
Name of Country
OR { Citizen of ▶ ________
Domiciled in ▶ ________

WAS THIS AUTHOR'S CONTRIBUTION TO THE WORK
Anonymous? ☐ Yes ☐ No
Pseudonymous? ☐ Yes ☐ No

If the answer to either of these questions is "Yes," see detailed instructions

NATURE OF AUTHORSHIP Briefly describe nature of the material created by this author in which copyright is claimed. ▼

NOTE

Under the law, the "author" of a "work made for hire" is generally the employer, not the employee (see instructions). For any part of this work that was "made for hire" check "Yes" in the space provided, give the employer (or other person for whom the work was prepared) as "Author" of that part, and leave the space for dates of birth and death blank.

b **NAME OF AUTHOR** ▼

DATES OF BIRTH AND DEATH
Year Born ▼ Year Died ▼

Was this contribution to the work a "work made for hire"?
☐ Yes
☐ No

AUTHOR'S NATIONALITY OR DOMICILE
Name of country
OR { Citizen of ▶ ______
Domiciled in ▶ ______

WAS THIS AUTHOR'S CONTRIBUTION TO THE WORK
Anonymous? ☐ Yes ☐ No
Pseudonymous? ☐ Yes ☐ No
If the answer to either of these questions is "Yes," see detailed instructions.

NATURE OF AUTHORSHIP Briefly describe nature of the material created by this author in which copyright is claimed. ▼

c **NAME OF AUTHOR** ▼

DATES OF BIRTH AND DEATH
Year Born ▼ Year Died ▼

Was this contribution to the work a "work made for hire"?
☐ Yes
☐ No

AUTHOR'S NATIONALITY OR DOMICILE
Name of Country
OR { Citizen of ▶ ______
Domiciled in ▶ ______

WAS THIS AUTHOR'S CONTRIBUTION TO THE WORK
Anonymous? ☐ Yes ☐ No
Pseudonymous? ☐ Yes ☐ No
If the answer to either of these questions is "Yes," see detailed instructions.

NATURE OF AUTHORSHIP Briefly describe nature of the material created by this author in which copyright is claimed. ▼

3

a **YEAR IN WHICH CREATION OF THIS WORK WAS COMPLETED** **This information must be given in all cases.**
______ ◀ Year

b **DATE AND NATION OF FIRST PUBLICATION OF THIS PARTICULAR WORK** **Complete this information ONLY if this work has been published.**
Month ▶ ______ Day ▶ ______ Year ▶ ______
______ ◀ Nation

4

See instructions before completing this space.

COPYRIGHT CLAIMANT(S) Name and address must be given even if the claimant is the same as the author given in space 2.▼

TRANSFER If the claimant(s) named here in space 4 are different from the author(s) named in space 2, give a brief statement of how the claimant(s) obtained ownership of the copyright.▼

DO NOT WRITE HERE OFFICE USE ONLY

APPLICATION RECEIVED

ONE DEPOSIT RECEIVED

TWO DEPOSITS RECEIVED

REMITTANCE NUMBER AND DATE

MORE ON BACK ▶
- Complete all applicable spaces (numbers 5-9) on the reverse side of this page
- See detailed instructions.
- Sign the form at line 8

DO NOT WRITE HERE

Page 1 of ______ pages

EXAMINED BY

FORM SR

CHECKED BY

☐ CORRESPONDENCE Yes

☐ DEPOSIT ACCOUNT FUNDS USED

FOR COPYRIGHT OFFICE USE ONLY

DO NOT WRITE ABOVE THIS LINE. IF YOU NEED MORE SPACE, USE A SEPARATE CONTINUATION SHEET.

PREVIOUS REGISTRATION Has registration for this work, or for an earlier version of this work, already been made in the Copyright Office? **5**

☐ **Yes** ☐ **No** If your answer is "Yes," why is another registration being sought? (Check appropriate box) ▼

☐ This is the first published edition of a work previously registered in unpublished form.

☐ This is the first application submitted by this author as copyright claimant.

☐ This is a changed version of the work, as shown by space 6 on this application.

If your answer is "Yes," give: **Previous Registration Number ▼** **Year of Registration ▼**

DERIVATIVE WORK OR COMPILATION Complete both space 6a & 6b for a derivative work; complete only 6b for a compilation. **6**

a. Preexisting Material Identify any preexisting work or works that this work is based on or incorporates. ▼

See instructions before completing this space.

b. Material Added to This Work Give a brief, general statement of the material that has been added to this work and in which copyright is claimed. ▼

DEPOSIT ACCOUNT If the registration fee is to be charged to a Deposit Account established in the Copyright Office, give name and number of Account. **7**

Name ▼ **Account Number ▼**

CORRESPONDENCE Give name and address to which correspondence about this application should be sent. Name/Address/Apt/City/State/Zip ▼

Area Code & Telephone Number ▶

Be sure to give your daytime phone ◀ number.

CERTIFICATION* I, the undersigned, hereby certify that I am the

Check one ▼

☐ author

☐ other copyright claimant

☐ owner of exclusive right(s)

☐ authorized agent of ____________________

Name of author or other copyright claimant, or owner of exclusive right(s) ▲

of the work identified in this application and that the statements made by me in this application are correct to the best of my knowledge.

8

Typed or printed name and date ▼ If this application gives a date of publication in space 3, do not sign and submit it before that date.

date ▶

Handwritten signature (X) ▼

MAIL CERTIFICATE TO

Certificate will be mailed in window envelope

Name ▼

Number/Street/Apartment Number ▼

City/State/ZIP ▼

YOU MUST:

- Complete all necessary spaces
- Sign your application in space 8

SEND ALL 3 ELEMENTS IN THE SAME PACKAGE:

1. Application form
2. Non-refundable $10 filing fee in check or money order payable to *Register of Copyrights*
3. Deposit material

MAIL TO:

Register of Copyrights
Library of Congress
Washington, D.C. 20559

9

* 17 U.S.C. § 506(e): Any person who knowingly makes a false representation of a material fact in the application for copyright registration provided for by section 409, or in any written statement filed in connection with the application, shall be fined not more than $2,500.

June 1990—25,000

U.S. GOVERNMENT PRINTING OFFICE: 1990—262-308 16

Filling Out Application Form PA

Detach and read these instructions before completing this form. Make sure all applicable spaces have been filled in before you return this form.

BASIC INFORMATION

When to Use This Form: Use Form PA for registration of published or unpublished works of the performing arts. This class includes works prepared for the purpose of being "performed" directly before an audience or indirectly "by means of any device or process." Works of the performing arts include: (1) musical works, including any accompanying words; (2) dramatic works, including any accompanying music; (3) pantomimes and choreographic works; and (4) motion pictures and other audiovisual works.

Deposit to Accompany Application: An application for copyright registration must be accompanied by a deposit consisting of copies or phonorecords representing the entire work for which registration is to be made. The following are the general deposit requirements as set forth in the statute:

Unpublished Work: Deposit one complete copy (or phonorecord).

Published Work: Deposit two complete copies or one phonorecord of the best edition.

Work First Published Outside the United States: Deposit one complete copy (or phonorecord) of the first foreign edition.

Contribution to a Collective Work: Deposit one complete copy (or phonorecord) of the best edition of the collective work.

Motion Pictures: Deposit *both* of the following: (1) a separate written description of the contents of the motion picture; and (2) for a published work, one complete copy of the best edition of the motion picture; or, for an unpublished work, one complete copy of the motion picture or identifying material. Identifying material may be either an audiorecording of the entire soundtrack or one frame enlargement or similar visual print from each 10-minute segment.

The Copyright Notice: For works first published on or after March 1, 1989, the law provides that a copyright notice in a specified form "may be placed on all publicly distributed copies from which the work can be visually perceived." Use of the copyright notice is the responsibility of the copyright owner and does not require advance permission from the Copyright Office. The required form of the notice for copies generally consists of three elements: (1) the symbol "©", or the word "Copyright," or the abbreviation "Copr."; (2) the year of first publication; and (3) the name of the owner of copyright. For example: "© 1989 Jane Cole." The notice is to be affixed to the copies "in such manner and location as to give reasonable notice of the claim of copyright." Works first published prior to March 1, 1989, **must** carry the notice or risk loss of copyright protection.

For information about notice requirements for works published before March 1, 1989, or other copyright information, write: Information Section, LM-401, Copyright Office, Library of Congress, Washington, D.C. 20559.

PRIVACY ACT ADVISORY STATEMENT Required by the Privacy Act of 1974 (P.L. 93-579)

The authority for requesting this information is title 17, U.S.C., secs. 409 and 410. Furnishing the requested information is voluntary. But if the information is not furnished, it may be necessary to delay or refuse registration and you may not be entitled to certain relief, remedies, and benefits provided in chapters 4 and 5 of title 17, U.S.C.

The principal uses of the requested information are the establishment and maintenance of a public record and the examination of the application for compliance with legal requirements.

Other routine uses include public inspection and copying, preparation of public indexes, preparation of public catalogs of copyright registrations, and preparation of search reports upon request.

NOTE: No other advisory statement will be given in connection with this application. Please keep this statement and refer to it if we communicate with you regarding this application.

LINE-BY-LINE INSTRUCTIONS

1 SPACE 1: Title

Title of This Work: Every work submitted for copyright registration must be given a title to identify that particular work. If the copies or phonorecords of the work bear a title (or an identifying phrase that could serve as a title), transcribe that wording *completely* and *exactly* on the application. Indexing of the registration and future identification of the work will depend on the information you give here. If the work you are registering is an entire "collective work" (such as a collection of plays or songs), give the overall title of the collection. If you are registering one or more individual contributions to a collective work, give the title of each contribution, followed by the title of the collection. Example: "'A Song for Elinda' in *Old and New Ballads for Old and New People*."

Previous or Alternative Titles: Complete this space if there are any additional titles for the work under which someone searching for the registration might be likely to look, or under which a document pertaining to the work might be recorded.

Nature of This Work: Briefly describe the general nature or character of the work being registered for copyright. Examples: "Music"; "Song Lyrics"; "Words and Music"; "Drama"; "Musical Play"; "Choreography"; "Pantomime"; "Motion Picture"; "Audiovisual Work."

2 SPACE 2: Author(s)

General Instructions: After reading these instructions, decide who are the "authors" of this work for copyright purposes. Then, unless the work is a "collective work," give the requested information about every "author" who contributed any appreciable amount of copyrightable matter to this version of the work. If you need further space, request additional Continuation Sheets. In the case of a collective work, such as a songbook or a collection of plays, give information about the author of the collective work as a whole.

Name of Author: The fullest form of the author's name should be given. Unless the work was "made for hire," the individual who actually created the work is its "author." In the case of a work made for hire, the statute provides that "the employer or other person for whom the work was prepared is considered the author."

What is a "Work Made for Hire"? A "work made for hire" is defined as: (1) "a work prepared by an employee within the scope of his or her employment"; or (2) "a work specially ordered or commissioned for use as a contribution to a collective work, as a part of a motion picture or other audiovisual work, as a translation, as a supplementary work, as a compilation, as an instructional text, as a test, as answer material for a test, or as an atlas, if the parties expressly agree in a written instrument signed by them that the work shall be considered a work made for hire." If you have checked "Yes" to indicate that the work was "made for hire," you must give the full legal name of the employer (or other person for whom the work was prepared). You may also include the name of the employee along with the name of the employer (for example: "Elster Music Co., employer for hire of John Ferguson").

"Anonymous" or "Pseudonymous" Work: An author's contribution to a work is "anonymous" if that author is not identified on the copies or phonorecords of the work. An author's contribution to a work is "pseudonymous" if that author is identified on the copies or phonorecords under a fictitious name. If the work is "anonymous" you may: (1) leave the line blank; or (2) state "anonymous" on the line; or (3) reveal the author's identity. If the work is "pseudonymous" you may: (1) leave the line blank; or (2) give the pseudonym and identify it as such (for example: "Huntley Haverstock, pseudonym"); or (3) reveal the author's name, making clear which is the real name and which is the pseudonym (for example: "Judith Barton, whose pseudonym is Madeline Elster"). However, the citizenship or domicile of the author **must** be given in all cases.

Dates of Birth and Death: If the author is dead, the statute requires that the year of death be included in the application unless the work is anonymous or pseudonymous. The author's birth date is optional, but is useful as a form of identification. Leave this space blank if the author's contribution was a "work made for hire."

Author's Nationality or Domicile: Give the country of which the author is a citizen, or the country in which the author is domiciled. Nationality or domicile **must** be given in all cases.

Nature of Authorship: Give a brief general statement of the nature of this particular author's contribution to the work. Examples: "Words"; "Co-Author of Music"; "Words and Music"; "Arrangement"; "Co-Author of Book and Lyrics"; "Dramatization"; "Screen Play"; "Compilation and English Translation"; "Editorial Revisions."

3 SPACE 3: Creation and Publication

General Instructions: Do not confuse "creation" with "publication." Every application for copyright registration must state "the year in which creation of the work was completed." Give the date and nation of first publication only if the work has been published.

Creation: Under the statute, a work is "created" when it is fixed in a copy or phonorecord for the first time. Where a work has been prepared over a period of time, the part of the work existing in fixed form on a particular date constitutes the created work on that date. The date you give here should be the year in which the author completed the particular version for which registration is now being sought, even if other versions exist or if further changes or additions are planned.

Publication: The statute defines "publication" as "the distribution of copies or phonorecords of a work to the public by sale or other transfer of ownership, or by rental, lease, or lending"; a work is also "published" if there has been an "offering to distribute copies or phonorecords to a group of persons for purposes of further distribution, public performance, or public display." Give the full date (month, day, year) when, and the country where, publication first occurred. If first publication took place simultaneously in the United States and other countries, it is sufficient to state "U.S.A."

4 SPACE 4: Claimant(s)

Name(s) and Address(es) of Copyright Claimant(s): Give the name(s) and address(es) of the copyright claimant(s) in this work even if the claimant is the same as the author. Copyright in a work belongs initially to the author of the work (including, in the case of a work made for hire, the employer or other person for whom the work was prepared). The copyright claimant is either the author of the work or a person or organization to whom the copyright initially belonging to the author has been transferred.

Transfer: The statute provides that, if the copyright claimant is not the author, the application for registration must contain "a brief statement of how the claimant obtained ownership of the copyright." If any copyright claimant named in space 4 is not an author named in space 2, give a brief statement explaining how the claimant(s) obtained ownership of the copyright. Examples: "By written contract"; "Transfer of all rights by author"; "Assignment"; "By will." Do not attach transfer documents or other attachments or riders.

earlier registration number and date. Otherwise, do not submit Form PA; instead, write the Copyright Office for information about supplementary registration or recordation of transfers of copyright ownership.

Changed Version: If the work has been changed, and you are now seeking registration to cover the additions or revisions, check the last box in space 5, give the earlier registration number and date, and complete both parts of space 6 in accordance with the instructions below.

Previous Registration Number and Date: If more than one previous registration has been made for the work, give the number and date of the latest registration.

6 SPACE 6: Derivative Work or Compilation

General Instructions: Complete space 6 if this work is a "changed version," "compilation," or "derivative work," and if it incorporates one or more earlier works that have already been published or registered for copyright, or that have fallen into the public domain. A "compilation" is defined as "a work formed by the collection and assembling of preexisting materials or of data that are selected, coordinated, or arranged in such a way that the resulting work as a whole constitutes an original work of authorship." A "derivative work" is "a work based on one or more preexisting works." Examples of derivative works include musical arrangements, dramatizations, translations, abridgments, condensations, motion picture versions,or "any other form in which a work may be recast, transformed, or adapted." Derivative works also include works "consisting of editorial revisions, annotations, or other modifications" if these changes, as a whole, represent an original work of authorship.

Preexisting Material (space 6a): Complete this space **and** space 6b for derivative works. In this space identify the preexisting work that has been recast, transformed, or adapted. For example, the preexisting material might be: "French version of Hugo's 'Le Roi s'amuse'." Do not complete this space for compilations.

Material Added to This Work (space 6b): Give a brief, general statement of the **additional** new material covered by the copyright claim for which registration is sought. In the case of a derivative work, identify this new material. Examples: "Arrangement for piano and orchestra"; "Dramatization for television"; "New film version"; "Revisions throughout; Act III completely new." If the work is a compilation, give a brief, general statement describing both the material that has been compiled **and** the compilation itself. Example: "Compilation of 19th Century Military Songs."

5 SPACE 5: Previous Registration

General Instructions: The questions in space 5 are intended to find out whether an earlier registration has been made for this work and, if so, whether there is any basis for a new registration. As a general rule, only one basic copyright registration can be made for the same version of a particular work.

Same Version: If this version is substantially the same as the work covered by a previous registration, a second registration is not generally possible unless: (1) the work has been registered in unpublished form and a second registration is now being sought to cover this first published edition; or (2) someone other than the author is identified as copyright claimant in the earlier registration, and the author is now seeking registration in his or her own name. If either of these two exceptions apply, check the appropriate box and give the

7,8,9 SPACE 7, 8, 9: Fee, Correspondence, Certification, Return Address

Deposit Account: If you maintain a Deposit Account in the Copyright Office, identify it in space 7. Otherwise leave the space blank and send the fee of $20 with your application and deposit.

Correspondence (space 7): This space should contain the name, address, area code, and telephone number of the person to be consulted if correspondence about this application becomes necessary.

Certification (space 8): The application cannot be accepted unless it bears the date and the **handwritten signature** of the author or other copyright claimant, or of the owner of exclusive right(s), or of the duly authorized agent of the author, claimant, or owner of exclusive right(s).

Address for Return of Certificate (space 9): The address box must be completed legibly since the certificate will be returned in a window envelope.

MORE INFORMATION

How To Register a Recorded Work: If the musical or dramatic work that you are registering has been recorded (as a tape, disk, or cassette), you may choose either copyright application Form PA or Form SR, Performing Arts or Sound Recordings, depending on the purpose of the registration.

Form PA should be used to register the underlying musical composition or dramatic work. Form SR has been developed specifically to register a "sound recording" as defined by the Copyright Act—a work resulting from the "fixation of a series of sounds," separate and distinct from the underlying musical or dramatic work. Form SR should be used when the copyright claim is limited to the sound recording itself. (In one instance, Form SR may also be used to file for a copyright registration for both kinds of works—see (4) below.) Therefore:

(1) File Form PA if you are seeking to register the musical or dramatic work, not the "sound recording," even though what you deposit for copyright purposes may be in the form of a phonorecord.

(2) File Form PA if you are seeking to register the audio portion of an audiovisual work, such as a motion picture soundtrack; these are considered integral parts of the audiovisual work.

(3) File Form SR if you are seeking to register the "sound recording" itself, that is, the work that results from the fixation of a series of musical, spoken, or other sounds, but not the underlying musical or dramatic work.

(4) File Form SR if you are the copyright claimant for both the underlying musical or dramatic work and the sound recording, *and* you prefer to register both on the same form.

(5) File both forms PA and SR if the copyright claimant for the underlying work and sound recording differ, or you prefer to have separate registration for them.

"Copies" and "Phonorecords": To register for copyright, you are required to deposit "copies" or "phonorecords." These are defined as follows:

Musical compositions may be embodied (fixed) in "copies," objects from which a work can be read or visually perceived, directly or with the aid of a machine or device, such as manuscripts, books, sheet music, film, and videotape. They may also be fixed in "phonorecords," objects embodying fixations of sounds, such as tapes and phonograph disks, commonly known as phonograph records. For example, a song (the work to be registered) can be reproduced in sheet music ("copies") or phonograph records ("phonorecords"), or both.

FORM PA
UNITED STATES COPYRIGHT OFFICE

REGISTRATION NUMBER

PA PAU

EFFECTIVE DATE OF REGISTRATION

Month Day Year

DO NOT WRITE ABOVE THIS LINE. IF YOU NEED MORE SPACE, USE A SEPARATE CONTINUATION SHEET.

1

TITLE OF THIS WORK ▼

PREVIOUS OR ALTERNATIVE TITLES ▼

NATURE OF THIS WORK ▼ See instructions

2

a **NAME OF AUTHOR ▼**

DATES OF BIRTH AND DEATH
Year Born ▼ Year Died ▼

Was this contribution to the work a "work made for hire"?
☐ Yes
☐ No

AUTHOR'S NATIONALITY OR DOMICILE
Name of Country
OR { Citizen of ▶ ______
Domiciled in ▶ ______

WAS THIS AUTHOR'S CONTRIBUTION TO THE WORK
Anonymous? ☐ Yes ☐ No
Pseudonymous? ☐ Yes ☐ No
If the answer to either of these questions is "Yes," see detailed instructions.

NOTE

Under the law, the "author" of a "work made for hire" is generally the employer, not the employee (see instructions). For any part of this work that was "made for hire" check "Yes" in the space provided, give the employer (or other person for whom the work was prepared) as "Author" of that part, and leave the space for dates of birth and death blank.

NATURE OF AUTHORSHIP Briefly describe nature of the material created by this author in which copyright is claimed. ▼

b

NAME OF AUTHOR ▼

DATES OF BIRTH AND DEATH
Year Born ▼ Year Died ▼

Was this contribution to the work a "work made for hire"?
☐ Yes
☐ No

AUTHOR'S NATIONALITY OR DOMICILE
Name of country
OR { Citizen of ▶ ____
Domiciled in ▶ ____

WAS THIS AUTHOR'S CONTRIBUTION TO THE WORK
Anonymous? ☐ Yes ☐ No
Pseudonymous? ☐ Yes ☐ No
If the answer to either of these questions is "Yes," see detailed instructions.

NATURE OF AUTHORSHIP Briefly describe nature of the material created by this author in which copyright is claimed. ▼

c

NAME OF AUTHOR ▼

DATES OF BIRTH AND DEATH
Year Born ▼ Year Died ▼

Was this contribution to the work a "work made for hire"?
☐ Yes
☐ No

AUTHOR'S NATIONALITY OR DOMICILE
Name of Country
OR { Citizen of ▶ ____
Domiciled in ▶ ____

WAS THIS AUTHOR'S CONTRIBUTION TO THE WORK
Anonymous? ☐ Yes ☐ No
Pseudonymous? ☐ Yes ☐ No
If the answer to either of these questions is "Yes," see detailed instructions.

NATURE OF AUTHORSHIP Briefly describe nature of the material created by this author in which copyright is claimed. ▼

3

a **YEAR IN WHICH CREATION OF THIS WORK WAS COMPLETED** **This information must be given in all cases.**
____ ◀ Year

b **DATE AND NATION OF FIRST PUBLICATION OF THIS PARTICULAR WORK**
Complete this information ONLY if this work has been published.
Month ▶ ____ Day ▶ ____ Year ▶ ____
____ ◀ Nation

4

See instructions before completing this space

COPYRIGHT CLAIMANT(S) Name and address must be given even if the claimant is the same as the author given in space 2.▼

TRANSFER If the claimant(s) named here in space 4 are different from the author(s) named in space 2, give a brief statement of how the claimant(s) obtained ownership of the copyright.▼

DO NOT WRITE HERE OFFICE USE ONLY

APPLICATION RECEIVED

ONE DEPOSIT RECEIVED

TWO DEPOSITS RECEIVED

REMITTANCE NUMBER AND DATE

MORE ON BACK ▶
- Complete all applicable spaces (numbers 5-9) on the reverse side of this page.
- See detailed instructions.
- Sign the form at line 8.

DO NOT WRITE HERE

Page 1 of ____ pages

FORM PA

EXAMINED BY

CHECKED BY

☐ CORRESPONDENCE
Yes

FOR COPYRIGHT OFFICE USE ONLY

DO NOT WRITE ABOVE THIS LINE. IF YOU NEED MORE SPACE, USE A SEPARATE CONTINUATION SHEET.

5

PREVIOUS REGISTRATION Has registration for this work, or for an earlier version of this work, already been made in the Copyright Office?

☐ **Yes** ☐ **No** If your answer is "Yes," why is another registration being sought? (Check appropriate box) ▼

a. ☐ This is the first published edition of a work previously registered in unpublished form.

b. ☐ This is the first application submitted by this author as copyright claimant.

c. ☐ This is a changed version of the work, as shown by space 6 on this application.

If your answer is "Yes," give: **Previous Registration Number** ▼ **Year of Registration** ▼

6

DERIVATIVE WORK OR COMPILATION Complete both space 6a & 6b for a derivative work; complete only 6b for a compilation.

a. Preexisting Material Identify any preexisting work or works that this work is based on or incorporates. ▼

See instructions before completing this space.

b. Material Added to This Work Give a brief, general statement of the material that has been added to this work and in which copyright is claimed. ▼

7

DEPOSIT ACCOUNT If the registration fee is to be charged to a Deposit Account established in the Copyright Office, give name and number of Account.

Name ▼ **Account Number** ▼

CORRESPONDENCE Give name and address to which correspondence about this application should be sent. Name/Address/Apt/City/State/Zip ▼

Area Code & Telephone Number ▶

Be sure to give your daytime phone ◀ number.

8

CERTIFICATION* I, the undersigned, hereby certify that I am the

Check only one ▼

☐ author

☐ other copyright claimant

☐ owner of exclusive right(s)

☐ authorized agent of ______

Name of author or other copyright claimant, or owner of exclusive right(s) ▲

of the work identified in this application and that the statements made by me in this application are correct to the best of my knowledge.

Typed or printed name and date ▼ If this application gives a date of publication in space 3, do not sign and submit it before that date.

date ▶

Handwritten signature (X) ▼

9

MAIL CERTIFI-CATE TO

Certificate will be mailed in window envelope

Name ▼

Number/Street/Apartment Number ▼

City/State/ZIP ▼

YOU MUST
- Complete all necessary spaces
- Sign your application in space 8

SEND ALL 3 ELEMENTS IN THE SAME PACKAGE

1. Application form
2. Nonrefundable $20 filing fee in check or money order payable to *Register of Copyrights*
3. Deposit material

MAIL TO

Register of Copyrights
Library of Congress
Washington, D.C. 20559

* 17 U.S.C. § 506(e): Any person who knowingly makes a false representation of a material fact in the application for copyright registration provided for by section 409, or in any written statement filed in connection with the application, shall be fined not more than $2,500.

▲ February 1991—200,000

☆U.S. GOVERNMENT PRINTING OFFICE: 1991- 282-170/20,011

Appendix F: Record Companies

Los Angeles

A & M Records
1416 North La Brea Avenue
Hollywood, CA 90028
Tel: (213) 469-2411
Fax: (213) 856-2600

ATC/East West Records
9229 Sunset Blvd.
Los Angeles, CA 90069
Tel: (310) 205-7420
Fax: (310) 285-9834

Atlantic & Associated Labels
9229 Sunset Blvd.
Los Angeles, CA 90069
Tel: (310) 205-7450
Fax: (310) 205-7475

Capital Records
1750 North Vine Street
Hollywood, CA 90028
Tel: (213) 462-6252
Fax: (213) 467-6550

Charisma Records
9247 Alden Dr.
Beverly Hills, CA 90210
Tel: (310) 275-9071
Fax: (310) 275-9148

Columbia Records
Sony Music Entertainment
1801 Century Park East
Los Angeles, CA 90067
Tel: (310) 556-4700
Fax: (310) 552-1350

Curb Records
3907 West Alameda Avenue
Burbank, CA 91505
Tel: (818) 843-2872
Fax: (818) 843-4659

Def American Records
3500 West Olive Avenue

Burbank, CA 91505
Tel: (818) 973-4545
Fax: (818) 973-4571

Elektra Entertainment
345 North Maple Drive
Beverly Hills, CA 90210
Tel: (310) 288-3800
Fax: (310) 274-9491

EMI Records Group North America
8730 Sunset Blvd.
Los Angeles, CA 90060
Tel: (310) 659-1700
Fax: (310) 659-9008

Geffen Records
9130 Sunset Blvd.
Los Angeles, CA 90069
Tel: (310) 278-9010
Fax: (310) 271-4358

Giant Records
8900 Wilshire Blvd.
Beverly Hills, CA 90211
Tel: (310) 289-5500
Fax: (310) 289-5501

Hollywood Records
500 South Buena Vista Street
Burbank, CA 91521
Tel: (818) 560-5670
Fax: (818) 841-5140

Impact Records
6255 Sunset Blvd.
Hollywood, CA 90028
Tel: (213) 962-5511
Fax: (213) 957-2311

I.R.S. Records
3939 Lankersheim Blvd.
Studio City, CA 91604
Tel: (818) 508-3130
Fax: (818) 373-7173

MCA Records
70 Universal City Plaza
Universal City, CA 91608

Tel: (818) 777-4000
Fax: (818) 760-1104

Mercury Records
11150 Santa Monica Blvd.
Los Angeles, CA 90025
Tel: (310) 996-7200
Fax: (310) 477-7622

Motown Records
6255 West Sunset Blvd.
Los Angeles, CA 90028
Tel: (213) 468-3500
Fax: (213) 856-0341

Polygram Label Group
11150 Santa Monica Blvd.
Los Angeles, CA 90025
Tel: (310) 996-7200
Fax: (310) 477-7622

RCA Records
6363 Sunset Blvd.
Hollywood, CA 90028
Tel: (213) 468-4000
Fax: (213) 468-4040

Reprise Records
3300 Warner Blvd.
Burbank, CA 91510
Tel: (818) 953-3750
Fax: (818) 953-3211

Rhino Records
2225 Colorado Avenue
Santa Monica, CA 90404
Tel: (310) 828-1980
Fax: (310) 453-5529

Virgin Records
338 North Foothill Rd.
Beverly Hills, CA 90210
Tel: (310) 278-1181
Fax: (310) 278-6231

Warner Bros. Records
3300 Warner Blvd.
Burbank, CA 91510
Tel: (818) 846-9090
Fax: (818) 846-8474

Windham Hill Productions
3500 West Olive Avenue
Burbank, CA 91505
Tel: (818) 972-4242
Fax: (818) 972-4247

Zoo Entertainment
6363 Sunset Blvd.
Los Angeles, CA 90028
Tel: (213) 468-4200
Fax: (213) 468-4207

New York City

A & M Records
595 Madison Avenue
New York, NY 10022
Tel: (212) 826-0477
Fax: (212) 838-8786

Arista Records
6 West 57 Street
New York, NY 10019
Tel: (212) 489-7400
Fax: (212) 333-2534

Atco/East West Records
75 Rockefeller Plaza
New York, NY 10019
Tel: (212) 275-2500
Fax: (212) 956-2270

Atlantic & Associated Labels
75 Rockefeller Plaza
New York, NY 10019
Tel: (212) 275-2995
Fax: (212) 956-7332

Blue Note Records
810 Seventh Avenue
New York, NY 10019
Tel: (212) 603-8700
Fax: (212) 603-4143

Capital Records
810 Seventh Avenue
New York, NY 10019
Tel: (212) 603-8700
Fax: (212) 603-8787

Charisma Records
1790 Broadway
New York, NY 10019
Tel: (212) 586-7700
Fax: (212) 765-0989

Columbia Records
Sony Music Entertainment
P.O. Box 4450
New York, NY 10101
Tel: (212) 445-4321
Fax; (212) 445-3285

Elektra Entertainment
75 Rockefeller Plaza
New York, NY 10019
Tel: (212) 275-4000
Fax: (212) 974-9314

EMI Records Group North America
1290 Avenue of the Americas
New York, NY 10104
Tel: (212) 492-1200
Fax: (212) 245-4115

Epic Records
P.O. Box 4450
New York, NY 10101
Tel: (212) 445-4321
Fax: (212) 445-3285

Geffen Records
75 Rockefeller Plaza
New York, NY 10019
Tel: (212) 484-7170
Fax: (212) 484-8930

Giant Records
75 Rockefeller Plaza
New York, NY 10019
Tel: (212) 275-4664
Fax: (212) 275-4670

GRP Records
555 West 57 Street
New York, NY 10019
Tel: (212) 245-7033
Fax: (212) 757-0713

Hollywood Records
500 Park Avenue

New York, NY 10022
Tel: (212) 735-5458

I.R.S. Records
594 Broadway
New York, NY 10012
Tel: (212) 334-2170
Fax: (212) 334-2178

Island Records
400 Lafayette Street
New York, NY 10003
Tel: (212) 995-7800
Fax: (212) 477-5918

Jive/Silvertone Records
137-139 West 25 Street
New York, NY 10001
Tel: (212) 727-0016
Fax: (212) 645-3783

MCA Records
1755 Broadway
New York, NY 10019
Tel: (212) 841-8000
Fax: (212) 644-3906

Mercury Records
825 Eighth Avenue
New York, NY 10019
Tel: (212) 333-8000
Fax: (212) 333-8249

Polygram Label Group
825 Eighth Avenue
New York, NY 10019
Tel: (212) 603-3900
Fax: (212) 333-8142

Profile Records
740 Broadway
New York, NY 10003
Tel: (212) 529-2600
Fax: (212) 420-8216

RCA Records
1133 Avenue of the Americas
New York, NY 10036
Tel: (212) 930-4000
Fax: (212) 930-4468

Sire Records
75 Rockefeller Plaza
New York, NY 10019
Tel: (212) 275-4560
Fax: (212) 581-6416

Sony Classical
1285 Avenue of the Americas
New York, NY 10019
Tel: (212) 445-4763
Fax: (212) 445-4093

Virgin Records
30 West 21 Street
New York, NY 10010
Tel: (212) 206-5200
Fax: (212) 462-9248

Warner Bros. Records
75 Rockefeller Plaza
New York, NY 10019
Tel: (212) 275-4500
Fax: (212) 275-4595

Zoo Entertainment
1133 Avenue of the Americas
New York, NY 10038
Tel: (212) 930-4750
Fax: (212) 930-4719

Nashville

Arista Nashville
One Music Circle North
Nashville, TN 37203
Tel: (615) 780-9100
Fax: (615) 780-9191

Asylum Records
1906 Acklen Avenue
Nashville, TN 37212
Tel: (615) 292-7990
Fax: (615) 292-8219

Atlantic Nashville
1025 16th Avenue South
Nashville, TN 37212
Tel: (615) 327-9394
Fax: (615) 329-2008

BNA Entertainment
One Music Square North
Nashville, TN 37203
Tel: (615) 780-4400
Fax: (615) 780-4464

Curb Records Nashville
47 Music Square East
Nashville, TN 37203
Tel: (615) 321-5080
Fax: (615) 327-3003

Giant Records
45 Music Square West
Nashville, TN 37203
Tel: (615) 256-3110
Fax: (615) 256-4011

Liberty Records
3322 West End Avenue
Nashville, TN 37203
Tel: (615) 269-2000
Fax: (615) 269-2059

MCA Records Nashville
1514 South Street
Nashville, TN 37212
Tel: (615) 244-8944
Fax: (615) 244-4428

Mercury Nashville
901 18th Avenue South
Nashville, TN 37212
Tel: (615) 320-0110
Fax: (615) 327-4856

RCA Nashville
One Music Square West
Nashville, TN 37203
Tel: (615) 664-1200
Fax: (615) 664-1237

Sony Music Nashville
34 Music Square East
Nashville, TN 37203
Tel: (615) 742-4321
Fax: (615) 244-2549

Warner Bros. Nashville
1815 Division Street

Nashville, TN 37203
Tel: (615) 320-7525
Fax: (615) 329-1739

Warner/Alliance Records
24 Music Square East
Nashville, TN 37203
Tel: (615) 242-4780
Fax: (615) 248-3565

Appendix G: Performing Rights Societies

American Society of Composers, Authors and Publishers (ASCAP)

1 Lincoln Plaza
New York, NY 10023

6430 Sunset Blvd.
Hollywood, CA 90028

2 Music Square West
Nashville, TN 37203

Broadcast Music, Inc. (BMI)

320 West 57 Street
New York, NY 10019

8730 Sunset Blvd.
West Hollywood, CA 90069

10 Music Square East
Nashville, TN 37203

The Society of European Stage Authors and Composers (SESAC)

156 West 567 Street
New York, NY 10019

55 Music Square East
Nashville, TN 37203

Bibliography

Baskerville, David. *Music Business Handbook and Career Guide*. Los Angeles: Sherwood Company, 1985.

Berk, Lee Elliot. *Legal Protection for the Creative Musician*. Boston: Berklee Press, 1970.

Biederman, Donald E., Edward P. Pierson, Martin E. Silfen, Jeanne A. Glasser, and Robert C. Berry. *Law and Business of the Entertainment Industries*. 2d ed. New York: Praeger, 1991.

Billboard's International Buyer's Guide. New York: BPI Communications.

Black, Henry Campbell. *Black's Law Dictionary*. Chicago: West Co., 1990.

Brahem, John. *The Craft and Business of Songwriting*. Cincinnati, OH: Writer's Digest Books, 1988.

Chickering, Robert B., and Susan Hartman. *How to Negotiate a Copyright and Protect Your Creative Work*. New York: Charles Scribner's Sons, 1987.

Connelly, Will. *The Musician's Guide to Independent Record Production*. Chicago: Contemporary Books, 1981.

Corbin, Arthur L. *Corbin's Text on Contracts*. St. Paul, MN: West Publishing Co., 1952.

Csida, Joseph. *The Music/Record Career Handbook*. New York: Billboard Publications, 1980.

Dann, Allan, and John Underwood. *How to Succeed in the Music Business*. London: Wise Publications, 1978.

Davis, Clive. *Inside the Record Business*. New York: Ballantine Books, 1975.

Domler, Egon, and Robert F. Cushman. *Entertainers and Their Professional Advisors*. Homewood, IL: Dow Jones-Irwin, 1987.

Engel, Lehman. *Getting Started in the Theatre*. New York: Macmillan Press, 1973.

Farber, Donald C., ed. *Entertainment Industry Contracts*. New York: Matthew Bender & Co., Inc., 1987.

Fremlin, Robert. *Entertainment Law*. New York: Clark Boardman Co.,

Hurst, Walter E. *Copyright*. Los Angeles: Seven Arts Press, 1977.

Johnston, Donald F. *Copyright Handbook*. New York: R. R. Bowker Company, 1982.

Klavens, Kent J. *Protecting Your Song and Yourself*. Cincinnati, OH: Writer's Digest Books, 1988.

Koonz, Harold, and Cyril O'Donnell. *Essentials of Management*. New York: McGraw, 1986.

Liggett, Mark, and Cathy Liggett. *The Complete Handbook of Songwriting*. New York: Plume Books, 1985.

Lindey, Alexander. *Lindey on Entertainment, Publishing and the Arts*. New York: Clark Boardman Co., 1990.

Martin, George. *Making Music*. New York: William Morrow and Co., 1985.

Meyer, Michael, and John David Viera, eds. *Entertainment, Publishing and the Arts*. New York: Clark Boardman Co., 1941.

Milgrim, Roger M. *Milgrim on Licensing*. New York: Matthew Bender & Co., Inc., 1990.

Miller, Ellen J. *Video: A Guide for Lawyers*. New York: Laws-Arts, 1982.

Monaco, Robert, and James Riordan. *The Platinum Rainbow: How to Succeed in the Music Business without Selling Your Soul*. Chicago: Contemporary Books, 1988.

Muller, Peter. *Show Business Law: Motion Pictures, Television, Video*. Westport, CT: Quorum Books, 1991.

Musical Directory: International Directory of the Performing Arts. New York: Musical America Publications, 1993.

Nelson, Lester, ed. *The Digest of Intellectual Property Laws of the World*. Oceana Publications, 1990.

Netzer, Dick. *The Subsidized Muse: Public Support for the Arts in the United States*. New York: Cambridge University Press. 1978.

New York Law School Law Review. *The Complete Guide to the New Copyright Law*. Dayton, OH: Lorenz Press, Inc., 1977.

Nimmer, Melville B. *Nimmer on Copyrights*. Albany, NY: M. Bender, 1982.

Nimmer, Melville B., and Paul E. Geller. *International Copyright Law and Practice*. New York: Matthew Bender & Co., Inc., 1988.

Orenstein, Harold and David Guinn. *Entertainment Law Business*. Stoneham, MA: Butterworth, 1989.

Papolos, Janice. *The Performing Artist's Handbook*. Cincinnati, OH: Writer's Digest Books, 1984.

Passman, Donald S. *All You Need to Know about the Music Business*. New York: Prentice-Hall Press, 1991.

Poe, Randy. *A Songwriter's Guide to Music Publishing*. Cincinnati, OH: Writer's Digest Books, 1990.

Practicing Law Institute. *Counseling Clients in the Entertainment Industry*. New York: Practicing Law Institute, 1992.

Rachlin, Harvey. *The Encyclopedia of the Music Business*. New York: Harper and Row, 1981.

Rapaport, Diane Sward. *How to Make and Sell Your Own Records*. Jerome, AZ: Headlands Press, 1988.

Rappaport, Victor D. *Making It in Music*. Englewood Cliffs, NJ: Prentice Hall, Inc., 1979.

Reed, Gregory J. *The Business of Entertainment and Its Secrets*. Detroit: New National Publishing Company.

Riordan, James. *Making It in the New Music Business*. Cincinnati, OH: Writer's Digest Books, 1991.

Roberts, Neal, David Matheson, and Harry Goldgut. *Music Industry: Contract Negotiations and the Law*. Toronto, Canada: York University Press, 1980.

Selz, Thomas D., Melvin Simensky, and Patricia Acton. *Entertainment Law: Legal Concepts and Business Practice*. 2d ed. Colorado Springs, CO: Shepard's/McGraw-Hill, 1992.

Shemel, Sindey, and William Krasilovsky. *This Business of Music*. New York: Billboard Publications, 1985.

Siegel, Alan H. *Breakin' in to the Music Business*. Port Chester, NY: Cherry Lane, 1986.

Siegel, Howard, ed. *Entertainment Law*. New York: New York State Bar Association, 1989.

Songwriter's Market. Cincinnati, OH: Writer's Digest Books, 1979.

Strong, William S. *The Copyright Book*. Cambridge, MA: MIT Press, 1990.

Taubman, Joseph. *Performing Arts Management and Law*. New York: Law-Arts, 1972.

Thorne, Robert, and John D. Viera, eds. *Entertainment, Publishing and Arts Handbook*. New York: Clark Boardman.

UCLA Extension. *The Recording Contracts—1980*. Los Angeles: UCLA Extension, 1980.

U.S.C. Title 17. The 1976 Copyright Act of the United States.

Uscher, Nancy. *Your Own Way in Music*. New York: St. Martin's Press, 1990.

Volunteer Lawyers for the Arts. *To Be or Not to Be: An Artist's Guide to Not-for-Profit Incorporations*. New York: Volunteer Lawyers for the Arts, 1982.

Wadham, Wayne. *Sound Advice: The Musician's Guide to the Recording Industry*. New York: Schirmer Books, 1990.

Weinstein, David A. *How to Protect Your Creative Work*. New York: John Wiley and Sons, 1987.

Weissman, Dick. *The Music Business: Career Opportunities and Self-Defense*. New York: Crown Publishers, 1979.

INDEX

AAA, 24
A&R, 79
Accounting, 11, 23, 43–45, 60–62, 72, 73, 91, 122–23, 141–42, 159–60, 174, 186–87, 208, 226–27, 248–49, 294
Actor, 201
Administer (right to), 68
Administration, 55; administration agreement, 67–77; administration fees, 36
Administrator, 37, 115, 199
Advance: against future earnings, 23; against future receipts, 174; against royalties, 34, 39, 92, 109, 182, 226, 247–48; payment, 155–56, 158; recoupment of, 235
Advertise (right to), 85, 106
Advertising, 20, 161, 287, 305, 308; agency, 257–72; campaign, 299; fees, 58; schedule, 305–6
AF of M, 19, 22, 23, 24, 26, 96, 183, 291
AFTRA, 19, 183
American Arbitration Association. *See* AAA
American Federation of Musicians. *See* AF of M
American Federation of Television and Radio Artists. *See* AFTRA
American Society of Composers, Authors and Performers. *See* ASCAP
Antitrust laws, 143
Artist and repertoire. *See* A&R
Artist approval, 151, 152, 245
Artist/producer, 102–16
ASCAP, 31, 56, 72, 74, 127, 194, 204, 212, 214, 225
Assign (right to), 114–15, 230, 289
Assignment, 25–26, 39–40, 55, 64, 69, 98, 124, 136, 144, 165, 178, 192, 210, 254, 269, 283
Attorney, 3; attorney fees, 59, 64, 71, 75, 101, 113, 162, 199, 271
Attorney-in-fact, 6–7, 51, 126, 133
Audiotapes, 53, 78, 80, 86–87, 109, 110, 185, 219, 223, 229, 286, 290
Audiovisual works, 319

Back-up band, 280
Bankruptcy, 14, 49, 76, 99, 114, 144, 176, 196–97, 211
"Best of" album, 81
Big band, 20
Blanket license, 127, 130
Booking agent, 3, 4, 10, 11–26, 281; third party agent, 21
BMI, 31, 56, 72, 74, 127, 194, 204, 212, 214, 225

Breach, 230, 253–54, 265–66, 280–81, 315; of contract, 147
Broadcast Music, Inc. *See* BMI
Buenos Aires Convention, 320

Cable, 95, 127, 213, 280, 285
CD (compact disc), 53, 56, 78, 80, 84, 86–87, 105, 109, 110, 185, 219, 223, 227, 229, 286, 290
CD-ROM, 7, 56, 109, 205
Choreographic work, 319
Clearance sheet, 129
Club, 130, 274, 277, 279; club owner, 16
Compilation: printed, 224; record, 91
Composite book, 32
Compulsory license. *See* Mechanical license
Concert hall, 233, 237, 244, 301, 303
Concert tickets, 312
Conduct, artist's, 266
Co-publishing, 53–66
Copyright, 13, 25, 27, 28, 41, 45, 47, 53, 54–56, 60, 63, 64, 65, 67, 69, 74, 84, 94, 103, 107, 113, 127, 129, 130, 132, 138, 139, 142, 144, 150, 161, 163, 175–76, 190, 196, 205; assignment of, 107, 214, 220–21, 222, 237, 240, 246, 250, 265, 267, 268, 278, 295–96, 319–20; copyright notice, 68, 221, 246, 320; copyright registration number, 138, 218
Copyright Act, 27, 137, 139, 140, 141, 209
Copyright Royalty Tribunal, 137
Cover act, 279
Cover lines, 108
Creative control, 239–40, 246
Credits, 107–8, 186, 187–88
CRT. *See* Copyright Royalty Tribunal
Cue sheet, 207, 214
Cumulative remedies, 167
Cure, 197
Currency, 227–28

Dance: cut, 81; recording, 103
Demo. *See* Demonstration tape
Demonstration tape, 42, 43, 58, 102
Discotheques, 127, 129
Dramatic performance, 131
Dramatic works, 319
Dramatize (right to), 221
Droit moral. *See* Moral rights
Dubbing, 216, 259–60

Employee for hire, 191, 209–10
Endorsement, 153, 259
Entertainment industry, 7
Estate: parties, 115; songwriter's, 37

Fiduciary relationship, 154
Film composer, 180–99
Film producer, 180–99, 200–12
First negotiation (right of), 301
First refusal (right of), 301
Fixed term of years, 171
Fixed term with option, 171–72
Folio, 170, 173, 193, 224
Form PA, 319
Form SR, 319–20
Force majeure, 14, 25, 51–52, 66, 76, 115, 125, 135, 144, 176, 197, 212, 244, 254, 281, 293
Foreign license, 217–32
Free copies, 174, 193

Goodwill, 167, 241
Gospel, 78
Grand rights, 128
Gross: earnings, 70; income, 21, 22, 58; receipts, 36, 163, 247; retail price, 173; revenues, 7–9, 157

Harry Fox Agency, 33, 56, 137
Heavy metal, 20
Home shopping, 284
Hotels, 19, 127, 130

Indemnification, 14, 41, 72, 75, 113, 124, 143, 162, 175, 177, 195, 209, 229, 252, 268, 279, 292, 293
Independent contractor, 281
Infomercials, 284
Infringement, 48–49, 59–60, 132, 163–64, 229–30, 253, 292–93
Insolvency. *See* Bankruptcy

International: rights, 240; sales, 156–57; television, 213
Insurance, 13, 162–63, 252, 272, 280, 316–17
Inventory, 242

Joint venture, 12, 25, 50, 65, 77, 101, 114, 125, 135, 211
Juke boxes, 53
Jurisdiction, 12, 25, 66, 77, 99, 114, 125, 136, 178, 199, 232, 255–56, 271

Key person, 70, 158, 269–70

Language, 202
Laser disks, 205, 219, 260
Lead-in artists, 276
Lead sheet, 45, 58, 228
Library of Congress, 45
Licensing agreement, 148–68
Licensed products, 148–68, 233, 236–37, 241, 243, 246, 251, 303
Liquidated damages, 244
Long playing album. *See* Record
Lounge act, 273–83
Lyrics, 38, 105, 106, 202, 207, 215, 319

Manufacture (right to), 106, 286
Mark down, 291
Market value, 28
Master recording, 80, 83, 84, 85, 91, 97, 103, 104, 106, 108, 118, 120, 121, 122, 188, 286, 289
Master tape, 82
Mass market distribution, 284–97
Material breach, 99, 164, 231
Mechanical license, 58, 137–45, 169, 191, 224–25
Mechanical: fees, 70; reproduction, 56, 68; rights, 32, 183–84; royalties, 53, 93, 137, 288
Media, 258, 306, 307–8
Merchandise, sponsor's, 311
Merchandising, 7, 89–90, 109; tour, 233–56
Moral rights, 189, 191, 264
Motion picture, 56–57, 68, 131, 180, 181, 184, 189, 200, 203, 204, 205, 219, 280, 319
Motion picture producer. *See* Film producer
Music video, 3, 4, 78, 81, 83, 109, 309
Musical comedies, 131
MTV, 83

NAPC, 1–2
National Council of Personal Managers. *See* NAPC
Net, 194, 224; earnings, 70–71; income, 58; receipts, 36, 247; retail price, 173
Nightclubs, 127, 129
Nondramatic public performance rights, 127
Notice, 46–47, 66, 76, 100, 112, 125, 135, 145, 166, 198, 210, 231, 255, 270
Notice of copyright, 107, 175–76, 210. *See also* Copyright

Orchestral arrangement, 57
Orchestrator, 181
Opera, 131

Partnership, 25, 39, 50, 65, 77, 101, 114, 125, 135, 211, 232, 273
Pay or play, 267–68
Performance: level, 225; plateau, 226
Performance license, 203–5, 216
Performing rights societies, 31, 56, 74, 127–36, 194, 225–26
Personal manager, 1–15, 17
Per-program license, 127, 130
Piano copy, 32, 193
Plays, 131
Posters, 149
Power of attorney, 18, 74
Premiums, 152, 251, 284
Press conference, 310
Press kits, 278
Print rights, 169–79
Producer. *See* Film producer; Records, producers
Promoter, 16
Promotion, 17–18, 153
Promotional records, 90

Public performance, 67, 72, 85, 169, 191, 212, 219, 288
Publicity, 20, 93
Publicize (right to), 106, 277
Publisher, 27–52, 53–66, 67, 128, 129, 134, 169, 193, 203, 217–32

Quality, 153; control, 149, 240

Radio, 127, 129, 130, 259, 280, 285, 308, 317
Rap, 20, 78
Records, 81, 84, 95, 103, 105; clubs, 89, 109; companies, 3, 42, 78–101, 103–4, 106, 110, 117, 119, 120, 137, 140, 185, 313–14; producers, 16, 97–98, 102–16, 117–26
Recording, 102, 105, 139, 140, 185, 284; agreement, 78–101, 117, 118; artist, 121; costs, 92–93, 110–11; studio, 105, 119
Register of Copyrights, 54, 246, 319
Reserve, 35, 87, 294
Reshoot, 264
Retail, 287
Reversion, 65
Road manager, 3, 10
Royalty, 33, 36, 39, 41, 61, 67, 71, 72, 86, 87–88, 89, 109, 110, 111, 117, 120, 122, 132, 133, 154, 155, 156, 163, 183, 185, 194–95, 201, 223–24, 235, 247, 253, 290, 308

Satellite transmission, 85, 95, 259, 260
Scrap, 90
Sell-off, 163, 238, 252–53, 286
SESAC, 31, 56, 72, 74, 127, 194, 204, 212, 214, 225
Session tapes, 103
Sheet music, 67, 170, 173, 228, 319
Side letter, 117–26
Signage, 311–12
Signing bonus, 92
Single, 81
Society of European Stage Authors and Composers. *See* SESAC
Song books, 173
Songwriter/publisher agreement, 27–52
Soundtrack, 180, 181, 185, 186, 189
Sponsor, 239, 242–43, 298–318
Sublicense, 153, 217, 218, 220, 243; agreement, 153
Sublicensee, 235, 243
Subpublishing, 218
Sunset provision, 62, 160
Sweepstakes, 307
Synchronization, 53, 68, 180, 191
Synchronization rights, 32; synchronization license, 67; motion pictures, 200–212; television, 212–16

Talent agency. *See* Booking agent
Tariffs, 299
Television, 56, 68, 85, 95, 127, 129, 130, 138, 204, 212, 219, 259, 285, 317; producer, 27, 212–16
Termination, 49, 75, 99, 113, 124, 144, 164, 176, 177, 207, 215, 253, 296
Territory, 17, 29, 54, 68, 79, 128, 154, 170, 192, 202, 218, 234, 259, 298–99
Test pressing, 106
Tour, 234, 235–36, 238, 239, 242–43, 298, 300, 308; book, 245; booklet, 304; venue, 244, 302
Tour merchandising, 233–56
Tour sponsorship, 298–318
Trademark, 13, 47, 63, 74, 113, 142, 237, 240, 288; brand, 299
Trailer, 205
Translation, 29, 57

Unenforceability, 178
United States Copyright Office, 28

VH–1, 83
Video, 308, 309; tapes, 78, 280; cassettes, 200, 205, 219, 227, 260
Virtual reality, 7
Voice: recording, 261; track, 260

About the Author

PETER MULLER is an attorney at law with extensive experience in the entertainment business. He is the former President of ACA Joe and is presently an adjunct professor of entertainment law at New York University. Among his earlier publications is *Show Business Law* (Quorum Books, 1990).